OUR "REGULAR" READERS RAVE!

"I want to sit down and be counted! *Uncle John's Bathroom Readers* have just bowled me over. You guys are really on a roll. And now that you've got a website! It almost makes one consider getting a tanktop computer (rim shot). Tank you for providing endless hours of quality reading material for the porcelain library."

"The *Bathroom Readers* are my number one (and number two) source of facts to amaze my friends."

"I love you guys!! I've been an avid reader since your first book in 1988. I actually built a book shelf in my bathroom just to hold your books!!"

"I think they're GREAT! I've bought all the books, and have thoroughly enjoyed each one. I can hardly have a conversation with someone that I am not reminded of a relevant article that provides meat for discussion. Keep up the good work!"

"I am unable to relax on the "throne" without a copy of Uncle John's good book within reach. To me, the book is more essential than toilet paper. I have finally found a way to get inner peace at last!! Thanks, Uncle John!!!!"

"Just think if all the political meeting places around the world were equipped with *Bathroom Readers*, BRI could use it's influence and wisdom to promote peace and prosperity for all! Doable? I think so!"

Uncle John's GREAT BIG BATHROOM READER®

The Bathroom Readers' Institute

Bathroom Readers' Press
Ashland, Oregon

UNCLE JOHN'S
GREAT BIG BATHROOM READER®

For information, write The Bathroom Readers' Institute,
P.O. Box 1117, Ashland, OR 97520.
www.bathroomreader.com

Cover design by Michael Brunsfeld

BRI Technician on back cover: Larry Kelp

Uncle John's Great Big Bathroom Reader®
by The Bathroom Readers' Institute

Library of Congress Catalog Card Number: 98-074781

ISBN: 1-879682-69-9

Printed in the United States of America
First Printing 1998
Second Printing 1999
Third Printing 1999

12 11 10 9 8 7 6 5 4

☆ ☆ ☆

☆ ☆ ☆

THANK YOU!

The Bathroom Readers' Institute sincerely thank the people whose advice and assistance made this book possible.

John Javna
John Dollison
Jeff Altemus
Adam Silver
Jennifer & Sage
Michael Brunsfeld
Julie Roeming
Lonnie Kirk
Paul Stanley
Bennie Slomski
Paul Hadella
Chris Rose-Merkle
Lenna Lebovich
Ben Brand
Erik Linden
Jessica Vineyard
Dee Smith
Antares Multimedia
Jeff Cheek
Jay Newman
Jennifer Wahpahpa
Bill Varble
Nancy Chew
Bass Pike
Shawn Davis
Bob Weibel
Andy Nilsson
Andrea Freewater
William Davis
Gordon Javna
Rich Stim
Tom Boerman
Bo Adan
Gary Pool
Harry Bartz
Richard Moeschl
Jonah Bornstein
Karen Carnival
Rachael Markowitz
Leeann Drabenstott
Moira Gleason
Mustard Press
Thomas Crapper
Marley & Catie Pratt
Jesse & Sophie, *B.R.I.T.*
Hi to Emily and Molly!

According to BRI-member Billy Russo: "Native Americans made glue by mixing buffalo brains and tree sap."

CONTENTS

NOTE

Because the B.R.I. understands your reading needs, we've divided the contents by length as well as subject.

Short—a quick read

Medium—1 to 3 pages

Long—for those extended visits, when something a little more involved is required.

***Extended**—for a leg-numbing experience.

☆ ☆ ☆

* * *

GOLDEN OLDIE
(From our *5th Bathroom Reader*)

BIRTHDAY CELEBRATIONS. The first people known to celebrate birthdays were the ancient Egyptians—starting around 3000 B.C. But only the queen and male members of the royal family were honored. No one even bothered recording anyone else's birthdates.

• The ancient Greeks expanded the concept a little: they celebrated the birthdays of all adult males...and kept on celebrating, even after a man had died. Women's and children's birthdays were considered too unimportant to observe.

• The Greeks also introduced the birthday cake (which they got from the Persians) and birthday candles (which may have been used to honor Artemis, goddess of the moon, because they symbolized moonlight).

• It wasn't until the Middle Ages that German peasants became the first to celebrate the birthdays of everyone in the family. Children's birthday celebrations were especially important. Called *kinderfestes*, they were the forerunner to our toddler birthday parties.

INTRODUCTION

Well, we've just finished writing the rest of the book... which means it's time to write the introduction.

In a few weeks, this *Bathroom Reader* will start rolling into homes all over North America—thanks to an incredibly dedicated BRI staff, our distributors, and the printers who accommodate our insane schedules. (Thanks, Julie.)

You'd think that with a whole year to work on this edition, we'd be taking it easy by now. But no, Uncle John does everything (and we mean *everything*) at the last minute.

So once again, we've spent a sleepless week trying to get this book out before the end of the year.

You may wonder why, after 11 crazy seasons, we're still writing the books. Well, first and foremost, it's because we love the work. Researching and writing *Bathroom Readers* is an adventure—like digging through a treasure chest of information, and then sharing the wealth.

But there's another compelling reason: you. The enthusiastic response that our books have generated from loyal readers over the years makes it all worthwhile. We know you're going to enjoy our work, and make it a part of your lives—often in unexpected ways. Take this letter, for example:

> **Dear Gentleperson:**
> I just received a copy of *Uncle John's 8th Bathroom Reader*, and I feel compelled to express my whole-hearted thankfulness. Because of your series, I survived a harrowing pediatric rotation during my training for my Family Medicine specialty.
>
> Unbeknownst to most lay people, family medicine residents are often looked down upon by other specialists and specialty trainers, so you [can] imagine what I was up against, being the *only* family medicine resident amongst the rest of the pediatric residents. To make matters worse, one of our pediatrician trainers would ruthlessly question us regarding our hospital cases, asking us terribly difficult questions, not merely for educational purposes, but to humiliate us before our peers,

superiors, and inferiors. Even if we gave the correct answer, he would then grill us to quote the exact source of our answer, including journal, article and author....

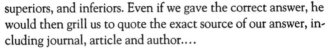

Among the patients I was assigned to, was one—this trainer smugly told me—that four pediatric residents couldn't help, because they couldn't get his fluids balanced (fluids in should equal fluids out). Could I, a *family practice resident*, do what four other pediatric residents couldn't do?

I looked at the situation and told him, "He's about two quarts dry from what I can tell."

"Oh? And why is that so?"

"You're suctioning out his saliva. The average daily production of saliva is approximately two quarts."

"Two quarts? And where did you read this?"

By this time, I was very irritated by his pompous and insulting attitude, and I guess I was spoiling for a fight. Making very direct eye contact, I gave him the following snarky answer: "*Uncle John's Bathroom Reader*, Volume I, bottom of page 85. And you can look that up yourself."

I made the appropriate changes [with the patient], and the next day, everything was right on the nose!! Perfect balance!

The good news is that this pediatrician never questioned me again and never asked for the source of an answer.

Thank you very much, Bathroom Readers' Institute. Not only did you allow me to pass my rotation with the least amount of resident abuse, you also saved my sanity.

—*Ann H., Ohio*

While we don't recommend using a *Bathroom Reader* as a medical textbook (or any kind of textbook, for that matter), we really enjoy knowing that our work is more than just a way to pass the...uh ... time. And frankly, we're already working on the next edition.

Until then, thanks for your support, and remember:

Go with the flow

YOU'RE MY INSPIRATION

It's fascinating to find out the inspiration behind cultural milestones like these.

CLINT EASTWOOD. "Developed his distinctive manner of speech by studying the breathy whisper of Marilyn Monroe."

THE WWI GERMAN ARMY. Kaiser Wilhelm, the leader of Germany, was so impressed with the efficiency of Buffalo Bill's Wild West Show when it toured Europe in the early 1900s, that he modeled his army on it.

THE CHEVROLET INSIGNIA. Billy Durant, founder of General Motors, liked the wallpaper pattern in a Paris hotel so much that he ripped off a piece and brought it back to Detroit to copy as the symbol for his new Chevrolet car.

THE QUEENS in a deck of cards were originally depictions of Queen Elizabeth, wife of Henry VII of England.

LUCY. Perhaps the most famous human fossil ever discovered. The bones were dug up in Ethiopia in 1975—at the time, the oldest human remains in the world (3.2 million years old). They were named after the song playing on a tape recorder at the time—"Lucy in the Sky with Diamonds."

ROMEO and JULIET. Were real lovers in Verona, Italy in the early 1300s—and they really did die for each other. The story was passed from writer to writer until Shakespeare found it, apparently in a 1562 poem by Arthur Brooke, called *Romeo and Juliet, containing a rare example of loves constancie...*

FAT ALBERT. The slow-witted, good-natured cartoon character was modeled after Bill Cosby's dyslexic brother, Russell.

Ugh! If you're average, you'll swallow three spiders this year.

COURT TRANSQUIPS

We're back, with one of our regular features. Do court transcripts make good bathroom reading? Check out these quotes. They're things people actually said in court, recorded word for word.

Q: "Well, sir, judging from your answer on how you reacted to the emergency call, it sounds like you are a man of intelligence and good judgement."
A: "Thank you, and if I weren't under oath I'd return the compliment."

Q: "And you're saying because she's dead she's no longer alive; is that what you're saying?"
A: "Is there a dispute there?"

Q: "What did he say?"
A: "About that? All the way back he—I've never been called so many names."
Q: "You're not married, I take it.

Q: "You say that the stairs went down to the basement?"
A: "Yes."
Q: "And these stairs, did they go up also?"

Q: "What is the meaning of sperm being present?"
A: "It indicates intercourse."
Q: "Male sperm?"
A: "That is the only kind I know."

Q: "You said he threatened to kill you."
A: "Yes. And he threatened to sue me."
Q: "Oh, worse yet."

Q: "And lastly, Gary, all your responses must be oral. O.K.?"
A: "Oral."
Q: "How old are you?"
A: "Oral."

Q: "Please state the location of your right foot immediately prior to impact."
A: "Immediately before the impact, my right foot was located at the immediate end of my right leg."

Q: "Doctor, how many autopsies have you performed on dead people?"
A: "All my autopsies have been on dead people."

Q: "Now, Mrs. Marsh, your complaint alleges that you have had problems with concentration since the accident. Does that condition continue today?"
A: "No, not really. I take a stool softener now."

The "Ye" in "Ye Olde Taverne," is pronounced "the," not "yee."

GOOD LUCK!

You're familiar with these lucky customs.
Here's where they come from.

LUCKY STAR. Centuries ago, people believed that every time a person was born, a new star appeared in the sky. The star was tied to the person's life: it would stay in the sky until the person died, and it rose or fell as the individual's fortunes rose and fell (that's where the expression "rising star" comes from). The Hebrew phrase *mazel tov*, which means "good luck," also translates as "good constellation," or "may the stars be good to you."

LUCKY CHARM. "Charm" comes from the Latin word *carmen*, which means "song" or "incantation." People once believed that certain words or phrases had magical powers when recited—something which survives today in words like "abracadabra" and "open sesame." In time, anything that brought luck, not just "magic words," became known as charms.

STARTING OUT ON THE RIGHT FOOT. A term from the ancient Romans, who believed that entering a building with the left foot was bad luck. They took the belief to extremes, even stationing guards or "footmen" at the entrances of buildings to make sure every visitor "started out on the right foot."

THIRD TIME'S A CHARM. Philip Waterman writes in *The Story of Superstition*, "Of all the numbers in the infinite scale, none has been more universally revered than three." The Greek philosopher Pythagoras thought the number three was the "perfect number," and many cultures have used triangles to ward off evil spirits. The reason it's bad luck to walk under a ladder (aside from the obvious ones) is that you're "breaking" the triangle that the ladder makes with the ground.

LUCKY SEVEN. Seven is the sum of three and four, the triangle and the square, which ancient Greeks considered the two "perfect figures." The lunar cycle, which is 28 days, is divided into four seven-

In its ancient form, the carrot was purple, not orange.

day quarters: New Moon, First Quarter, Full Moon, and Third Quarter. It may also come from the game of craps, where rolling a seven wins the roll.

LUCKY HUNCHES. Believe it or not, this is from the days when rubbing a hunchback's hump was considered good luck. The ancient Egyptians worshipped a hunchbacked god named Bes, and the ancient Romans hired hunchbacks as servants because they thought it brought the household good luck.

* * * *

AMAZING LUCK

"In December 1948, Navy Lieutenant Jimmy Carter was on night duty on the bridge of his submarine, the USS *Pomfret*, which was riding on the surface, recharging its batteries. Suddenly, an enormous wave crashed over Carter's head and across the sub. Unable to keep his hold on the railing, Carter found himself swimming inside the wave with no sense of what was up or down. Had the current been broadside, he would have been lost. By pure chance, the wave set Carter down on the submarine's gun turret thirty feet from the bridge. He felt he was watched over by Providence, and said, 'I don't have any fear at all of death.'"

—*Oh Say Can You See,* by John and Claire Whitcomb

"In March 1997, the Sunday *Oklahoman* profiled Oklahoma City homemaker Mary Clamser, 44, whose deterioration with multiple sclerosis had been abruptly halted in 1994 when lightning struck her house while she was grasping metal objects with each hand and wearing her metal leg brace....

"Suddenly, she began walking easily, and though doctors told her the condition was probably only temporary, she still walks easily today. As if that weren't enough good luck, Clamser, in order to fly to California for a TV interview in April 1995, was forced to cancel a local appointment she had made at the Oklahoma City federal building for 9 a.m. on April 19."

—News of the Weird

Only female mosquitoes bite; they need the blood to nourish their eggs.

OOPS!

Everyone's amused by tales of outrageous blunders—probably because it's comforting to know that someone's screwing up even worse than we are. So go ahead and feel superior for a few minutes.

WANT FRIES WITH THAT?

"The building of a new staff canteen in 1977 gave the U.S. Department of Agriculture the opportunity to commemorate a famous nineteenth-century Colorado pioneer.

"Amidst a blaze of enthusiastic publicity, the Agriculture Secretary, Robert Bergland, opened The Alfred Packer Memorial Dining Facility, with the words: 'Alfred Packer exemplifies the spirit and care that this agriculture department cafeteria will provide.'

"Several months later the cafeteria was renamed when it was discovered that Packer had been convicted of murdering and eating five prospectors in 1874."

—*The Book of Heroic Failures*

NEXT TIME, ORDER OUT

"Astronomers using the radio telescope at Parkes Observatory in Australia thought they had important evidence of alien life when they picked up a distinctive radio signal at 2.3 to 2.4 gigahertz every evening about dinnertime. They later discovered that the signal was coming from the microwave oven downstairs."

—*Strange Days #2*

VICTOR VICTORIA

"An unidentified, 31-year-old man was sentenced to 20 lashes in Tehran [Iran] in October after a prank backfired.

"He had bet his father about $30 that he could dress in robe and veils and ride unnoticed in the women's section of a segregated municipal bus, but he was detected because he failed to wear women's shoes underneath the robe. A court ruled the prank obscene."

—Universal Press Syndicate

JUST SAY NO

"Police in England pounced on an elderly man when they raided a pub looking for a drug dealer. The suspect explained that his bag of white powder was actually the ashes of his late wife, Alice, which he carried everywhere."

—***Fortean Times***

THE KINDER, GENTLER IRS

"As a public service to taxpayers, the Internal Revenue Service provides a free tax information service by phone. All you have to do is call the 800 number listed in your local directory, and you can get your tax questions answered.

"But in Portland, Oregon, taxpayers got a different type of service. When the phone was answered, callers heard a sultry voice breathing, 'Hi, sexy.' The embarrassed IRS later explained that the Portland phone directory had misprinted the number. Instead of the IRS, callers were reaching Phone Phantasies."

—***The 176 Stupidest Things Ever Done***

HOLY MATRIMONY!

"A 22-year-old Los Angeles man advertised in a magazine as a lonely Romeo looking for a girl with whom to share a holiday tour of South America. The joyful Juliet who answered his plea turned out to be his widowed mother."

—***The World's Greatest Mistakes***

COOL CUSTOMER

"Robert Redford was making a movie in New Mexico...[and a] lady who encountered him in an ice cream parlor on Canyon Street between takes was determined to stay cool....She pretended to ignore the presence of the movie star....But after leaving the shop, she realized she did not have the ice cream cone she'd bought and paid for. She returned to the shop....to ask for her ice cream cone. Overhearing, Robert Redford said, 'Madame, you'll probably find it where you put it—in your purse.'"

—**Paul Harvey's *For What It's Worth***

THE STORY OF ECHO AND NARCISSUS

This ancient Greek myth tells how the echo was created...and explains why the word "narcissistic" means "self-involved." It's from a BRI favorite, Myths and Legends of the Ages.

In ancient times, the fields and forests were peopled by lovely enchanted creatures called nymphs. Their homes were the trees and flowers and streams. Their food was fairy food.

Echo was one of these charming creatures. She was lovely to look at as she flitted about the forests. She might have been a perfect delight to her companions—except for one thing. Echo talked too much! Not only that, but she insisted on having the last word in every conversation.

This annoying habit finally so angered Juno, the queen of the gods, that she decided to punish Echo.

"This shall be your punishment," Juno said. "You shall no longer be able to talk—with this exception: you have always insisted on having the last word; so, Echo, you will never be able to say anything *but* the last word!"

Now in the forest where the nymphs dwelt, a handsome young man named Narcissus used to go hunting. So handsome was he, even the lovely nymphs fell in love with him at first sight. But Narcissus was terribly vain. He felt that no one was good enough to deserve his love.

One day, Echo caught sight of Narcissus and straightaway fell in love with him. She yearned to tell him of her love; but because of Juno's punishment, she was powerless to speak. Echo followed Narcissus adoringly wherever he went. But now, in her affliction, Echo became very shy.

One day, while out hunting, Narcissus became separated from his companions. Hearing a sound in the woods nearby, he called out, "Who's there?"

It was Echo. But all she could answer was the last word

the title have ever been No. 1: *Summer in the City* and *Theme From a Summer Place.*

"There!"

Narcissus called again. "Come!" he said.

"Come!" replied Echo.

Still seeing no one, Narcissus cried, "Why do you shun me?"

"Shun me!" came back the reply.

"Let us join each other," called Narcissus.

Then Echo, full of love, stepped out from between the trees.

"Each other!" she said, giving Narcissus both of her hands.

But Narcissus drew back in his pride. "Go away," he said. "How dare you be so forward! I would rather die than that you should have me."

"Have me," wept Echo.

But in his cold pride Narcissus left her.

Echo was heartbroken. From then on, she pined away. Echo grew thinner and thinner. Finally, nothing was left of her—but her voice.

Echo still lives among the rocks and caves of the mountains where she answers anyone who calls. But she answers with only the last word.

But cruel Narcissus did not escape punishment He continued his vain self-love until such a day when he spurned another nymph who sought his affection. The hurt creature in her anguish entreated the goddess of Love:

"Oh, goddess," she prayed, "make this hard-hearted young man know what it is to love someone who does not return his love. Let him feel the pain I now suffer."

The nymph's prayer was heard. In the middle of the forest, there was a clear fountain. Here Narcissus wandered one day, and bending over to drink, he caught sight of his own reflection in the water. He thought he saw a beautiful water nymph. Gazing in admiration, Narcissus fell in love with himself!

He stretched out his arms to clasp the beautiful being he saw in the water. The creature stretched out its arms, too. Narcissus plunged his arms into the water to embrace his beloved. Instantly, the water shivered into a thousand ripples and the creature disappeared.

A few moments later his beloved reappeared. Now Narcissus brought his lips near to the

Women look at other women more than they look at men.

water to take a kiss. Again the image fled!

He begged his adored one to stay.

"Why do you shun me?" he begged. "If I may not touch you, at least let me look at you."

Narcissus would not leave the pool. Now he knew the pain of loving in vain. Gradually, he grew pale and faded away. As he pined in hopeless love, he lost his beauty. The nymph Echo hovered near him and sorrowed for him. And when he murmured, "Alas, alas!" she answered, "Alas!"

Finally, he died in grief. The nymphs prepared to bury him. But when they came for him, he was nowhere to be found. In his stead, bending over the pool, they found a beautiful flower.

And to this day, this lovely flower grows near the water and is called narcissus.

* * * *

ASK THE EXPERTS

Q: *Why do we use only 10 percent of our brains?*

A: We don't. "The 10 percent myth dates back to the nineteenth century, when experiments showed that stimulation of small areas of the brain could have dramatic results. Touch a tiny part of brain tissue and you might be able to induce the patient to extend a limb. There was an easy, if unscientific, extrapolation: If a small percentage of the brain could do so much, then obviously most of the brain was unused.

"In reality, most of the brain mass *is* used for thinking. Any small-brained creature can extend limbs or see what's across the room, but it takes a big brain to handle the wiring necessary for a profound and abstract thought, such as, 'I stink, therefore I am.'

"Today it is possible to watch brain activity through positron-emission tomograms, or PET scans, which show electrical firing among billions of brain cells. Not every cell is involved in every thought or nerve impulse, but there is no evidence that any gray matter is superfluous. The brain has no unused parts, no equivalent of the appendix." (From *Why Things Are, Vol II: The Big Picture*, by Joel Achenbach)

The District of Columbia has one lawyer for every 19 residents.

"ALWAYS SPIT AFTER A FISHERMAN"

Want people from other countries to think you're polite? Of course you do. So here are a few BRI tips about what's considered good manners around the world.

In Japan: Wear a surgical mask in public if you have a cold.

In Switzerland: Buy wine for your table if you drop your bread in the fondue.

In Italy: Don't allow a woman to pour wine.

In Samoa: Spill a few drops of kava, the national beverage, before drinking.

In Belgium and Luxembourg: Avoid sending a gift of chrysanthemums. They are a reminder of death.

In Sweden: Wait until you're outside your guest's house before putting your coat on.

In Jordan: Leave small portions of food on your plate. Also, refuse seconds at least twice before accepting.

In Greece: Cheerfully participate in folk dancing if invited.

In Fiji: Fold your arms behind you when conversing.

In Portugal: Signal you enjoyed a meal by kissing your index finger and then pinching your earlobe.

In China: Decline a gift a few times before accepting. Use both hands to give or receive one.

In Iran: Shake hands with children. (It shows respect for their parents.)

In Spain: Say "buen provecho" to anyone beginning a meal.

In Finland: If you pass the salt at the dinner table, don't put it in anyone's hand—put the salt shaker down and let them pick it up.

In Norway: When a fisherman walks by, spit after him. It's a way of wishing him good luck.

In Korea: Allow others to pass between you and the person you are conversing with. Don't make anyone walk behind you.

The blue whale's tongue weighs as much as an adult elephant.

MODERN MYTHOLOGY

These characters are as famous in our culture as Pegasus or Hercules were in Greek myths. Where did they come from?

SMOKEY THE BEAR. In 1942, at the peak of World War II, U.S. officials realized that forest fires could jeopardize national security. They began a poster campaign about fire prevention. In 1944, the posters featured Disney's Bambi. But in 1945, the Forest Service introduced its own character—Smokey the Bear (named after "Smokey Joe" Martin, assistant fire chief in New York City from 1919 to 1930). The campaign was successful, but really took off in 1950, when an orphaned bear cub was rescued from a fire in New Mexico and was nursed back to health by a forest ranger's family. They named him Smokey and sent him to the National Zoological Park in Washington, D.C.…where he became a popular attraction as a living icon. He got so much mail that the postal service gave him his own zip code.

UNCLE BEN. From 1943 to 1945, Texan Gordon Harwell sold a special "converted" rice—made by special process, so it would last longer than usual—to the U.S. government. After World War II, Harwell and his business partner decided to sell it to the general public. But what would they call it? They were in a Chicago restaurant one night when Harwell remembered a black farmer in the Houston area who'd been famous for the high quality of his rice. He was known simply as Uncle Ben. Since Ben was long dead, Harwell asked Frank Brown, maître d' of the restaurant, to pose for the now-famous portrait on every box of Uncle Ben's Converted Rice.

CHIQUITA BANANA. During World War II, almost no bananas made it to U.S. shores—the United Fruit Company's fleet of ships had been comandeered to move war supplies. After the war, the company wondered how to reintroduce the fruit to the American public. Their solution: a radio ad campaign featuring a singing banana. ("I'm Chiquita Banana and I'm here to say / Bananas have to ripen in a certain way…") Their calypso-style jingle became so popular that it was even released as a record…and hit #1 on the pop music charts!

People clamored to know what Chiquita looked like. So the company hired cartoonist Dik Browne (later, creator of "Hagar the Horrible") to create her. He gave her a familiar Latin look by "borrowing" movie star Carmen Miranda's fruit-salad hat and sexy dress. Chiquita became so famous dancing on TV commercials that in 1990, United Fruit changed its name to Chiquita Brands.

LEO, THE MGM LION. In 1915 Howard Dietz, a young adman who had just graduated from Columbia University, was ordered by his boss to create a trademark for the Goldwyn Movie Company. He was stumped...until he remembered that his alma mater's insignia was a lion. "If it's good enough for Columbia, it's good enough for Goldwyn," he said...and Leo began roaring at the beginning of each Goldwyn film. A few years, later Goldwyn merged with the Metro and Mayer film companies, forming Metro-Goldwyn-Mayer. Leo became their logo, too. Today, he is Hollywood's most durable star—featured in films for over 80 years.

JUAN VALDEZ. "This is the tale of Juan Valdez / Stubborn man, as the story says / Lives way up on a mountaintop / Growing the finest coffee crop." In the early 1960s, about 25% of all coffee sold in America came from Columbia, but consumers didn't know it. So Columbian coffee-growers hired an ad agency to make Americans aware of their product. The agency hired New York singer José Duval and sent him to Columbia with a film crew. Clothed in traditional garb—a "mulera" (shawl), a straw sombrero, white pants and shirt—José was filmed picking coffee beans and leading a bean-laden burro down mountain trails. It was a huge success—people in New York greeted Duval with "Hi, Juan" wherever he went. Today, a stylized picture of Juan Valdez is part of the Columbian coffee logo.

JACK, (the Cracker Jack boy) and BINGO (his dog). The sailor boy was added to Cracker Jack packages during World War I as a salute to "our fighting boys." But he was modeled after the company founder's young grandson, Robert, who often wore a sailor suit. The dog was named Bingo after the children's song ("B-I-N-G-O, and Bingo was his name-O"). Sad footnote: As the first "sailor boy" packages rolled off the presses, Robert got pneumonia and died. So the logo can also be seen on his tombstone in Chicago.

FAMOUS FOR 15 MINUTES

Here it is again—our feature based on Andy Warhol's prophetic comment that "in the future, everyone will be famous for 15 minutes." Here's how a few people have been using up their allotted quarter hour.

THE STAR: Alan Hale, a backyard astronomer in New Mexico.

THE HEADLINE: *Hale, Hearty Fellow, Finds Comet but No Job.*

WHAT HAPPENED: Late in the evening of July 22, 1995, Hale set up his telescope and was observing star clusters when he noticed a fuzzy blur that didn't appear in any astronomical charts. It turned out to be a comet, the brightest one to pass near the earth in more than 20 years. The same night another amateur astronomer, Thomas Bopp, made a sighting in Arizona. The comet was named Hale-Bopp in their honor.

AFTERMATH: Hale and Bopp appeared on TV talk shows, and made personal appearances all over the country. For a time they were the most famous astronomers in America. But Hale, who had a Ph.D. in astronomy when he discovered the comet, was unemployed—the only job he could find in his field was a temporary one in a space museum two hours away. Even after the discovery, he remained unemployed. He made news again when he posted a letter on the Internet in 1998, saying that because of lack of jobs, he couldn't encourage kids to be scientists when they grew up.

THE STAR: Jessie Lee Foveaux, a 98-year-old great-great grandmother living in Manhattan, Kansas.

THE HEADLINE: *Great-Great-Granny Lays Golden Egg.*

WHAT HAPPENED: In 1979, Foveaux signed up for a senior-citizen writing class and began compiling her memoirs as a Christmas present for her family. In 1997, the *Wall St. Journal* ran a front-page story on the class...and featured Jessie's work. The article ignited a bonfire of interest in her life story. The next day her phone rang off the hook as publishers fought to buy the manuscript. Foveaux chose Warner Books, which paid her $1 million for the rights.

It's lonely at the top: Only one-third of Americans say they'd want their boss's job.

AFTERMATH: *Any Given Day: The Life and Times of Jessie Lee Brown Foveaux*, hit bookstore shelves a few months later, spurring articles in *People* and other magazines and an appearance on the *Rosie O'Donnell* show. "I never thought anyone would read it but my own," Foveaux says. "If I had, I probably wouldn't have told as much." Book sales were disappointing, but Foveaux became rich off the book. She was able to leave more than just a manuscript to her family.

THE STAR: Kato Kaelin, moocher ordinaire—O.J.'s house guest on the night Simpson's wife and her companion were murdered.

THE HEADLINE: *Trial of the Century Makes O.J.'s Sidekick House Guest of the Century.*

WHAT HAPPENED: His eyewitness account was central to the O.J. murder trial—he was the last person to see Simpson before the murders, and he heard a thump outside his guest-house wall near where the bloody glove was found. His testimony helped exonerate Simpson at the criminal trial, but helped convict him in the civil trial. Kato later admitted that he, too, thought Simpson was guilty.

AFTERMATH: Kaelin's aging surfer-boy persona helped make him one of the most recognizable celebrities to come out of the trials. He appeared in photo spreads for GQ and *Playgirl* magazine, endorsed hair products and cigarettes, and even wrote an article for *P.O.V.* magazine on "How to Score a Free Pad."

An aspiring actor before the trials, he was now a *famous* aspiring actor. He got bit parts in a handful of movies, but not much more. For a while he was also a talk show host at KLSX radio in Los Angeles. Topics included "Don't you hate waiting," and other equally stimulating fare. That fizzled too, and not just because listeners were bored. "He quit," a spokesperson for the station reports. "He found out it was hard work."

THE STAR: Divine Brown, a Hollywood, California hooker.

THE HEADLINE: *Hugh's Hooker a Huge Hit.*

WHAT HAPPENED: In June 1995, a police officer observed a white BMW parked off a side street on LA's seedy Sunset Strip, a boulevard notorious for streetwalkers. He checked it out...and observed a prostitute performing a sex act on actor Hugh Grant. Both suspects were arrested. Grant was fined $1,800 for the incident; Brown was fined $1,350 and spent 180 days in jail. Overnight she went from down-and-out streetwalker to celebrity.

AFTERMATH: In the months that followed she made more than $500,000 from interviews, appearances, and TV commercials in England, Brazil, and the U.S. She spent the money on designer clothes, an expensive apartment, two Rolls-Royces, a Mercedes, a stretch limo, and other goodies. "I'm blessed by God," Brown told a reporter in 1996. "I ruined his life, but he made mine."

Grant rebuilt his career and even his relationship with girlfriend Elizabeth Hurley. Brown burned through her money in about a year. She was evicted from her home, her cars were repossessed, her kids were sent back to public schools. By June 1996, she was working in a strip joint for $75 a night. In 1997, she attempted suicide. "She tasted the good life and knows she can't have it anymore," her publicist told reporters. "No wonder she's depressed."

THE STAR: William "Refrigerator" Perry, defensive lineman for the Chicago Bears.

THE HEADLINE: *Rotund Refrigerator Romps in End Zone.*

WHAT HAPPENED: Perry was a 1st-round draft pick for the Bears in 1985. When he reported to training camp at 330 pounds—too fat even by football standards—the Bears benched him.

He might have stayed there if the Bears hadn't lost the 1984 NFC title game to the SF 49ers. With the score 23-0, the 49ers used a 271-pound guard in the backfield. Bears coach Mike Ditka took it as a personal insult....So the next time he faced the 49ers, he had Perry, the team's fattest player, carry the ball on two plays.

People loved it. A week later, Ditka did it again...and Perry scored a touchdown. For some reason, it became national news.

AFTERMATH: By midseason, Perry was making appearances on *David Letterman* and the *Tonight Show*. By the time the Bears won the Superbowl he was a media superstar, making a tidy sum on product endorsements. Perry's fame lasted until the next season, when Ditka realized Perry had a life-threatening weight problem, and put him on a diet. He retired from pro football in 1994, then signed on with the World League of American Football, a league that plays American football in Europe.

Smallest mammal on Earth: The bumblebee bat. It weighs less than a penny.

FAMILIAR PHRASES

Here are still more origins of everyday phrases.

GET SOMEONE'S GOAT

Meaning: Annoy someone; make them lose their temper.

Origin: "This very American phrase came from the practice of putting a goat inside a skittish racehorse's stall because it supposedly had a calming influence. A gambler might persuade a stableboy to remove the goat shortly before the race, thereby upsetting the horse and reducing its chance of winning (and improving the gambler's odds)." (From *It's Raining Cats and Dogs*, by Christine Ammer)

THE HIGH MUCKY MUCK or HIGH MUCK-A-MUCK

Meaning: A person in charge who acts like a big shot.

Origin: "The dictionaries usually give the spelling high-muck-a-muck, and that's a bit closer to the original Chinook version *hiu muckamuck*, which means 'plenty of food.' In the Alaska of a century or more ago, a person with plenty to eat was a pretty important fellow—and that's what the expression means. A high-muck-a-muck is usually not only a person of authority but one who likes to be sure that everyone knows how important he is." (From the *Morris Dictionary of Word and Phrase Origins*, by William and Mary Morris)

HERE'S MUD IN YOUR EYE

Meaning: A toast wishing good luck.

Origin: "The expression is not a toast to another; it is a toast to yourself—because it means, 'I hope I beat you.' The allusion is to a horse race. If the track is at all muddy, the rider of the losing horse is very likely to get mud in his eye from the horse that is winning." (From *Why Do We Say...?*, by Nigel Rees)

Second most popular place to eat breakfast in the U.S.: The car.

LEGENDARY BETS

Some of history's most famous bets may never have happened at all. Here are a few you may have heard of. Did they really happen?

PEARL JAM

The Wager: According to Roman historian Pliny the Elder, Cleopatra once bet her lover Marc Antony that she could spend the equivalent of over $3 million in "one evening's entertainment." He didn't believe it.

The Winner: *Cleopatra.* Here's how she supposedly did it:

> There were dancers garbed in specially-made costumes of gold and rare feathers; there were jugglers and performing elephants; there were a thousand maid-servants attending to the couple's every need; and there was a seemingly endless banquet of indescribable splendor. At the end of the evening, Cleopatra proposed to toast her lover with a vessel of vinegar. But first she dropped her exquisite pearl earrings, each worth a small kingdom, into the cup and watched them dissolve. Then she raised the sour cocktail of untold value to her lips and drank it down.

Truth or Legend? It's possible, but not likely. Pearls are "largely carbonate, and will dissolve in a mild acidic solution such as vinegar." But it would take at least a few hours, and the vinegar would have to be so strong you could hardly drink it. However, if Cleo crushed the pearls first, they would have dissolved immediately.

THE SECRET WORD IS...

The Wager: In 1780, James Daly, manager of a theater in Dublin, Ireland, bet that he could coin a word that would become the talk of the town overnight—even though it had no meaning. Daly's boast seemed so preposterous that everyone within earshot took him up on it.

Daly immediately paid an army of children to run around town and write a single word in chalk on walls, streets, billboards, etc.

The Winner: *Daly.* The next morning, Dubliners were asking what this strange word meant...and why it was written everywhere they looked. People speculated that it was "indecent," but no one knew for sure. The word was *quiz*. According to the *Morris Dictionary of Word and Phrase Origins:*

> At first it became synonymous with 'practical joke'—for that was what Daly had played on the citizenry. Gradually it came to mean making fun of a person by verbal bantering. In time, it came to mean what 'quiz' means today—a question asked of a person in order to learn the extent of his knowledge.

Truth or Legend? No one knows. The tale has never been authenticated, and as far as most lexicographers are concerned, the definitive origin of the word *quiz* is still unknown.

THE FIRST MOVIE?

The Wager: In 1872, Leland Stanford, former governor of California, railroad tycoon, and dabbler in horses, bet newspaperman Frederick MacCrellish that for a fraction of a second, a trotter has all four feet off the ground simultaneously. The bet was for anywhere from nothing to $50,000 (depending on who tells the story). To settle the question, Stanford hired English photographer Eadward J. Muybridge to photograph one of his prime racers, Occidental, in motion. There was one problem: photographic technology in 1872 was still too primitive to capture the desired image. The bet was left unsettled and all parties moved on.

The Winner: *Stanford.* Five years later, Stanford was still burning to know whether he was right. This time, using the latest technology, Muybridge was able to take a picture that showed all four of Occidental's feet off the ground at once. Fascinated with the results of the new photographic technology, Stanford told Muybridge to spare no expense and buy state-of-the-art photographic equipment for another test. In 1878, with the new equipment in hand, Muybridge set up a battery of 24 cameras alongside Stanford's private track, and by precisely timing the exposures, successfully captured every position in a horse's stride. This approach to rapid-motion photography paved the way for development of the movie camera.

Truth or Legend? The story about the photo is true, but it probably didn't happen as part of a bet for two reasons. Stanford wasn't a betting man, and, in 1872, MacCrellish was using the *Alta Californian* to lambast Stanford for unsavory business practices—hardly conducive to a "friendly wager."

Poll results: 50% of all Oreo-eaters say they pull them apart before eating them.

STRANGE TOURIST ATTRACTIONS

Next time you're traveling across America, set aside some time to visit these unusual atractions. From the hilarious book, Roadside America.

THE CEMENT OX

Location: Three Forks, Montana

Background: The ox, nicknamed "New Faithful," is one of two 12-foot tall cement oxen statutes that stand outside the Prairie Schooner Restaurant, and appears to be pulling the restaurant—which is shaped like an enormous covered wagon.

Be Sure to See...the cashier gleefully asking customers, "Have you seen old faithful?" and then adding, "Well, take a look at *new* faithful!" She pushes a secret button, and the cement ox starts peeing.

THE HAIR MUSEUM

Location: Independence, Missouri

Background: This museum is all that remains of an art form developed by cosmetology schools in the 19th century to keep hair clippings from going to waste.

Be Sure to See...the museum's collection of 75 items made entirely from hair, including hair wreaths, hair bookmarks, and a hair diary that belonged to a convict. You can even get a discount haircut, performed by "fully licensed" cosmetology students.

THE HOEGH PET CASKET CO.

Location: Gladstone, Michigan

Background: Hoegh makes seven different sizes of coffins for pets, including boxes tiny enough for birds and large enough for Great Danes.

Be Sure to See...the "model" pet cemetery and demonstration. Note the brass sign over the crematorium that reads, "If Christ had a dog, he would have followed Him to the cross."

Squirrels lose at least half the nuts they hide—they forget where they put them.

NATIONAL MUSEUM OF HEALTH AND MEDICINE

Location: Bethesda, Maryland

Background: The museum is actually quite respectable and has been around for more than a century, but the definition of what is "respectable" has changed a lot over the years. Some of the older items on display are pretty disgusting.

Be Sure to See...the amputated leg of Major General Daniel E. Sickles, who lost the leg during the Civil War when it was hit by a 12-lb. cannonball—which is also on display. "For many years," the sign reads, "Sickles visited the museum on the anniversary of its amputation." Also: the computer terminal that lets you play doctor to a mortally wounded Abraham Lincoln. "Congratuations! You've scored an 84 out of a possible 100. The nation applauds your effort as a doctor and as a responsible member of society. Unfortunately, the president is dead."

THE WORLD'S SECOND-LARGEST BALL OF TWINE

Location: Cawker City, Kansas.

Background: When Frank Stoeber learned of the existence of the World's Largest Ball of Twine (12 feet in circumference, 21,140 lbs. of twine) in Darwin, Minnesota, he set out to roll an even bigger one...but died when his ball was still one foot too small in circumference. The city fathers put it on display anyway.

Be Sure to See... Stoeber's ball of twine, displayed outside in a gazebo. Note the aroma: a musty smell, kind of like damp, rotting...twine.

THE HOLE 'N' THE ROCK

Location: Moab, Utah

Background: In 1940, a man named Albert Christensen took some dynamite and started blasting holes in a rock. He kept blasting until 1952, when he had enough holes—14 in all—to build a house, a cafe, and a gift shop. The Hole 'N' the Rock attracts 40,000 visitors a year.

Be Sure to See...the bathroom, which has an entire cavern to itself. Christensen named it "a toilet in a tomb."

Fart Fact: The average human body has about 100 milliliters of bowel gas at one time.

THE MUSEUM OF QUESTIONABLE MEDICAL DEVICES

Location: In a strip mall in Minneapolis, Minnesota

Background: Operated by Bob McCoy, the museum was founded to encourage interest in science and medicine.

Be Sure to See...the Prostate Warmer, which plugs into a light socket and "stimulates the abdominal brain," and the Nemectron Machine, which "normalizes" breasts through the application of metal rings of various sizes.

THE CORAL CASTLE

Location: Homestead, Florida

Background: Edward Leedskalnin was a young man when his 16-year-old fiance, Agnes Scuffs, ended their engagement. Leedskalnin spent the next 20 years carving a massive memorial castle to Agnes out of coral, using tools he made from junked auto parts. By the time he died in 1951, Leedskalnin (who weighed approximately 100 lbs.) had quarried, carved and positioned more than 1,100 tons of coral rock for the castle. Some of the blocks weighed more than 25 tons—but because Leedskalnin worked alone, in secret, and usually at night, nobody knows how he managed to position the blocks in place. He never explained, other than to say, "I know how the pyramids were built."

Be Sure to See...a coral sundial that tells time, a throne for Agnes that rocks, and a heart-shaped table that made it into *Ripley's Believe it or Not* as the world's biggest valentine.

Note: Leedskalnin's ex-fiance Agnes Scuffs was still alive in 1992. She had never visited the castle.

* * * *

BONUS DESTINATION: O'Donnell, Texas, hometown of Dan Blocker, who played Hoss on TV's *Bonanza*.

Be Sure to See... The Dan Blocker Memorial Head. When Blocker made it big, the town fathers had a likeness of his head, carved in granite, installed on a stand in the town square.

IF YOU LIKE "IKE"

Here are a few thoughts from former president Dwight D. Eisenhower.

"There is one thing about being a president—nobody can tell you when to sit down."

"Farming looks mighty easy when your plough is a pencil and you're a thousand miles from the cornfield."

"You do not lead by hitting people over the head—that's assault, not leadership."

"When people speak to you about a preventive war, you tell them to go and fight it."

(On Vietnam): "We are going to have peace even if we have to fight for it."

"Politics should be the part-time profession of every citizen."

"Things have never been more like the way they are today in history."

"Do not needlessly endanger your lives...until I give you the signal."

"The middle of the road is all of the usable surface. The extremes, right and left, are in the gutters."

"There are no easy matters that come to you as president. If they are easy, they are settled at a lower level."

"Every gun that is made, every warship launched, every rocket fired, signifies, in the final sense, a theft from those who hunger and are not fed, those who are cold and are not clothed."

"An intellectual is a man who takes more words than necessary to tell more than he knows."

"There is no amount of military force that can possibly give you real security. You wouldn't have that amount in the first place, unless you felt there was a similar amount that could threaten you, somewhere else in the world."

IT'S JUST SERENDIPITY...

The word "serendipity" means "making happy and unexpected discoveries by accident." It was coined by the English writer Horace Walpole, who took it from the title of an old fairy tale, The 3 Princes of Serendip. *The heroes in the story are always "making discoveries they are not in quest of." For example, it's just serendipity...*

THAT BUBBLE GUM IS PINK

Background: In the 1920s, the Fleer Company of Philadelphia wanted to develop a bubble gum that didn't stick to people's faces. A 23-year-old employee, Walter Diemer, took the challenge. He started experimenting with different mixtures, and in a year, he had the answer. In 1928, the first workable batch of bubble gum was mixed up in the company mixing machines. "The machines started groaning, the mix started popping, and then I realized I'd forgotten to put any coloring in the gum," Diemer recalled.

Serendipity: The next day, he made a second batch. This time he remembered to color it. But the only color he could find was pink. "Pink was all I had at hand," he says. "And that's the reason ever since, all over the world, that bubble gum has been predominantly pink."

...THAT WE PLAY *BASKETBALL* INSTEAD OF *BOXBALL*

Background: When James Naismith invented his game in 1891, he decided to put a horizontal "goal" high over players' heads. He figured that would be safer—there would be no violent pushing and shoving as people tried to block the goal...and shots would be lobbed, not rocketed, at it.

Serendipity: As one historian writes: "The goal was supposed to be a box. Naismith asked the janitor for a couple of suitable boxes, and the janitor said he didn't have any...but he did have a couple of round peach baskets in the storeroom. So it was baskets that were tacked to the walls of the gym." A week later one of the players suggested, "Why not call it basketball?" The inventor answered: "We have a basket and a ball...that would be a good name for it."

...and as a result, their nestlings sometimes drown during rainstorms.

...THAT MEL GIBSON GOT HIS BIG BREAK

Background: According to *The Good Luck Book*, "When director George Miller was looking for someone to play the male lead for his 1979 post-apocalyptic road movie *Mad Max*, he was specifically looking for someone who looked weary, beaten-up, and scarred.

Serendipity: "One of the many 'wannabes' who answered the cattle call for the part was a then-unknown Australian actor named Mel Gibson. It just so happened that the night before his scheduled screen test, Gibson was attacked and badly beaten up by three drunks. When he showed up for the audition the next morning looking like a prize fighter on a losing streak, Miller gave him the part. It launched Gibson's career as an international movie star in such films as *The Year of Living Dangerously*, *Lethal Weapon*, and the 1995 Oscar-winning *Braveheart*."

...THAT YELLOW PAGES ARE YELLOW

Background: The phone was invented in 1876, and the first Bell business directory came out in 1878. As we wrote in our *Ultimate Bathroom Reader*, it was printed on white paper. So were subsequent editions all over the country.

Serendipity: In 1881, the Wyoming Telephone and Telegraph Company hired a printer in Cheyenne to print its first business directory. He didn't have enough white paper to finish the job and didn't want to lose the company's business. So he used the stock he had on hand—yellow paper. Other companies around the country adopted it, too...not realizing it was an accident.

...THAT HOLLYWOOD STARS PUT THEIR PRINTS IN CEMENT AT GRAUMAN'S CHINESE THEATER

Background: In the early days of Hollywood, Sid Grauman's movie theater, fashioned after a Chinese pagoda, was the biggest and fanciest of its kind.

Serendipity: One day in 1927, movie star Norma Shearer accidentally stepped in wet cement as she walked in the courtyard of the theater. Rather than fill the prints in, Graumann got other stars to put their hand- and footprints in the cement. That turned it into one of Hollywood's biggest tourist attractions.

FOUNDING FATHERS

Some people have achieved immortality because their names became identified with products. You already know the names—now here are the people.

JAMES DRUMMOND DOLE. In 1899, his cousin, the governor of Hawaii, helped him get some land to pursue his dream of growing pineapples for export. He revolutionized the fruit industry by packing the highly perishable pineapple in cans, shoving pieces through a small slit in the top and sealing it with a bead of solder.

FRANK GERBER. In 1928, his seven-month-old grandaughter, Sally, became seriously ill. The girl's physician suggested she might benefit from a diet of strained fruits and vegetables, and he put his tomato-canning factory to work on it. When Sally recovered, mothers in the area began requesting samples of the food. He started marketing the product, and within six months, Gerber Strained Peas, Prunes, Carrots, and Spinach were available across the U.S.

CHARLES PILLSBURY. Bought his first flour mill in St. Anthony Falls, Minnesota in 1865, at a time when the state imported most of its flour. Minnesota flour was hard and brittle, and considered inferior to the imported flour. Charles installed a purifier that enabled him to produce flour which made more and better bread per barrel than the softer imported winter wheat. Ten years later, his plant was turning out 10,000 barrels of flour a day.

JOHN LANDIS MASON. In 1858, he worked with glass blowers to produce an alternative to home-canning with tin. His solution: a threaded glass container with a screw-top lid. It preserved flavor better, enabled housewives to see the contents at a glance, and was easy to clean and reuse. Over a hundred billion Mason jars have been made since then.

LEON LEONWOOD (L.L.) BEAN. Sewed leather uppers to rubber overshoe bottoms in 1912 to keep his feet dry on deer-hunting trips. He sold a few pairs to friends and neighbors and as the word spread, orders for his boots came pouring in. He turned it into an outdoor clothing business.

7-11 sells 10,000 pots of coffee an hour, every day of the year.

WORDS OF WISDOM

Jon Winokur compiled these pearls of wisdom in his book Friendly Advice.

"Wise men don't need advice. Fools don't take it."
—Benjamin Franklin

"Always obey your superiors. If you have any."
—Mark Twain

"Life is a sh— sandwich. But if you've got enough bread, you can't taste the sh—."
—Jonathan Winters

"Rise early. Work late. Strike oil."
—J. Paul Getty

"To succeed in the world it is not enough to be stupid, you must also be well-mannered."
—Voltaire

"Never take top billing. You'll last longer that way."
—Bing Crosby

"It is better to be beautiful than to be good, but it is better to be good than to be ugly."
—Oscar Wilde

"It is fatal to look hungry. It makes people want to kick you."
—George Orwell

"If you see a snake, just kill it—don't appoint a committee on snakes."
—H. Ross Perot

"It's not whether you win or lose, it's how you play the game."
—Grantland Rice

"Grantland Rice can go to hell as far as I'm concerned."
—Gene Autry

"I always advise people never to give advice."
—P.G. Wodehouse

"Honesty is the best policy, and spinach is the best vegetable."
—Popeye the Sailor

"To succeed with the opposite sex, tell her you're impotent. She can't wait to disprove it."
—Cary Grant

The two jobs where people expect "friendly" breath: Dentists and salespeople.

HEADLINES

These are 100% honest-to-goodness headlines.
Can you figure out what they were trying to say?

Textron Inc. makes offer to screw company stockholders

SQUAD HELPS DOG BITE VICTIM

Man Minus Ear
Waives Hearing

IRAQI HEAD SEEKS ARMS

MAN SHOT, STABBED; DEATH BY NATURAL CAUSES RULED

Police begin campaign to run down jaywalkers

Once-sagging cloth diaper saved by full dumps

BILLS OVERWHELM CHARGERS

32 Ignorant Enough to Serve on North Jury

UTAH GIRL DOES WELL IN DOG SHOWS

Local High School Dropouts Cut In Half

TYPHOON RIPS THROUGH CEMETERY; HUNDREDS DEAD

Pastor Aghast At First Lady Sex Position

Padres Hit On Penguins

Death Causes Loneliness, Feelings of Isolation

SKI AREAS CLOSE DUE TO SNOW

Child's Stool Great For Use In Garden

FIRE OFFICIALS
GRILLED OVER
KEROSENE HEATERS

Woman Improving After Fatal Crash

STUD TIRES OUT

Death in the Ring: Most boxers Are Not the Same Afterward

FFA proposes name change to FFA

REAGAN WINS ON BUDGET, BUT MOORE LIES AHEAD

Man Struck By Lightning Faces Battery Charges

British Union Finds Dwarfs in Short Supply

MAN FOUND DEAD IN CEMETERY

Legislators Tax Brains to Cut Deficit

The world's most expensive spice: Spanish saffron. It can cost more than $2,000 per pound.

PAGE 42

Here's a page we've never tried before. It was sent to us by BRI member Tim Harrower.

Elvis Presley died at **42**.

The angle at which light reflects off water to create a rainbow is **42** degrees.

The city of Jerusalem covers an area of **42** square miles.

The Torah (the holy book of Judaism) is broken into columns, each of which always has exactly **42** lines.

Fox Mulder (*The X-Files*) lives in apartment number **42**.

There are **42** decks on the Enterprise NCC1701-D (the *Next Generation* ship).

Bill Clinton is the **42**nd U. S. president.

A Wonderbra consists of **42** individual parts.

There are **42** Oreo cookies in a 1-pound package.

"The beast was given a mouth uttering proud boasts and blasphemies, and it was given authority to act for **42** months."
—***Revelation 13:5***

In *Romeo and Juliet*, Juliet sleeps for **42** hours.

The right arm of the Statue of Liberty is **42** feet long.

Jimi Hendrix and Jerry Garcia were born in 19**42**.

The number of dots on a pair of dice: **42**.

Dogs have a total of **42** teeth over their lifetimes.

In *The Catcher in the Rye*, Holden Caufield lies and says that he is **42**.

The world-record jump by a kangaroo is **42** feet.

The natural vibration frequency of white mouse DNA: **42**.

The natural vibration frequency of human DNA: **42**.

There were **42** generations from Abraham to Jesus Christ.

And most important:
According to Douglas Adams' *The Hitchhiker's Guide to the Galaxy*, "the meaning of life, the universe, and everything" is the number **42**.

HITS OF THE 1970s: A QUIZ

Now it's time to find out how much you know about a few of the hits of the '70s. (Answers on page 457.)

1. "You Don't Bring Me Flowers," a duet by Barbra Streisand and Neil Diamond, was a #1 song in 1976. How did this unlikely pair get together?

a) They each recorded the song separately, and a disc jockey spliced the two recordings together.

b) They ran into each other at a recording session and—as a joke—decided to record the sappiest song they knew.

c) It was the dying request of Diamond's mother that he record a song with Streisand—her favorite singer.

2. Led Zeppelin's "Stairway to Heaven" was the most-requested FM song of the decade...but some Christian fundamentalists cite it as an example of devil-worship in rock. Robert Plant, the group's singer, composed the lyrics. He says...

a) Even *he* doesn't know what they mean.

b) It's strange that fundamentalists would criticize it, because he's a born-again Christian.

c) He purposely put "satanic" messages on the record to shock his critics. "If they're idiotic enough to play it backwards, they deserve it," he said.

3. Cheap Trick's "I Want You to Want Me" sold a million copies in 1979. It was an incredible turnaround for the group. Their third album had just flopped, and Epic Records had pretty much given up on them. So how did they become stars?

a) An L.A. deejay became their champion, urging listeners to write to Epic and release "I Want You to Want Me" as a single.

b) The group was asked to tour as an opening act for the Rolling Stones, which sparked new interest in their album.

A cow has four stomachs.

c) Somehow, a quickie album that they made exclusively for the Japanese market wound up receiving air time on U.S. FM radio.

4. The #1 song of 1975 was "Love Will Keep Us Together," by The Captain and Tennille who were, according to news reports, blissfully married. But few of the fans who heard the song knew it was really about...

a) Two men.

b) Two pets—a dog and a chipmunk.

c) A mother and child.

5. Melanie had a huge hit in 1971 with "I've Got a Brand New Key." She had an innocent voice, but the lyric "I've got a brand new pair of roller skates, you've got a brand new key" sounded like sex to most people. The truth would have disappointed them—the song was really inspired by...

a) A new pair of roller skates she got for her birthday.

b) A McDonald's hamburger.

c) A sporting goods store near her house.

6. The Bee Gees were the hottest group of the late '70s, and the record that started their meteoric comeback—before *Saturday Night Fever* was released—was "Jive Talkin'," a #1 hit in 1975. The song actually started out as...

a) "Jive Walkin'"—inspired by the British comedy troupe Monty Python and their "Department of Silly Walks."

b) "Drive Talkin'"—inspired by a rickety wooden bridge.

c) "Hive Stalkin'"—inspired by their hobby of keeping bees.

7. One of the biggest-selling records of the '70s was Terry Jacks's "Seasons in the Sun." He didn't plan to release it as a single, but...

a) His paper-boy heard his demo tape and really liked it...then brought his friends to Jacks's house to hear it.

b) The Beach Boys heard his demo tape and talked about recording it themselves. Jacks figured if they liked it, it must be good.

c) He'd recently broken up with his wife, Susan Jacks (of the Poppy Family), and needed a quick $10,000 to pay his divorce lawyer.

A bloody wound on your body starts to clot in less than 10 seconds.

WELCOME TO WASHINGTON!

Politicians aren't getting much respect these days—but then, it sounds like they don't think they deserve much, either.

"If hypocrisy were gold, the Capitol would be Fort Knox."

—Senator John McCain

"It is perfectly American to be wrong."

—Newt Gingrich

"My choice early in life was either to be a piano player in a whorehouse or a politician. And to tell the truth, there's hardly any difference."

—Harry S. Truman

"My God! What is there in this place (Washington D.C.) that a man should ever want to get into it?"

—President James Garfield

"I think the American public wants a solemn ass as president and I think I'll go along with them."

—President Calvin Coolidge

"Political promises go in one year and out the other."

—Anonymous

"The single most exciting thing you encounter in government is competence, because it's so rare."

—Senator Daniel Patrick Moynihan

"You can lead a man to Congress, but you can't make him think."

—Milton Berle

"If...everybody in this town connected with politics had to leave town because of [chasing women] and drinking, you'd have no government."

—Senator Barry Goldwater

"If you don't want to work for a living, this is as good a job as any."

—Congressman John F. Kennedy in 1946

"There they are—See No Evil, Hear No Evil, and Evil."

—Bob Dole, on a gathering of ex-presidents Gerald Ford, Jimmy Carter, and Richard Nixon

The three foods Americans say they hate the most: #1 tofu; #2 liver; #3 yogurt.

LET ME WRITE SIGN—I SPEAK ENGLISH GOOD

When signs in a foreign country are written in English, any combination of words is possible. Here are some real-life examples.

"Guests are prohibited from walking around in the lobby in large groups in the nude."

—Havana hotel

"If this is your first visit to the USSR, you are welcome to it."

— Moscow hotel

"It is forbidden to enter a woman even if a foreigner is dressed as a man."

—Seville cathedral

"Visitors two to a bed and half an hour only."

—Barcelona hospital

"All customers promptly executed."

—Tokyo barbershop

"We highly recommend the hotel tart."

—Torremolinos hotel

"I slaughter myself twice daily."

—Israel butcher shop

"Because of the impropriety of entertaining persons of the opposite sex in the bedroom, it is requested that the lobby be used for this purpose."

—Colon restaurant

"All vegetables in this establishment have been washed in water especially passed by the management."

—Sri Lanka restaurant

"Gentlemen's throats cut with nice sharp razors."

—Zanzibar barbershop

"Very smart! Almost pansy!"

—Budapest shop

"Swimming is forbidden in the absence of the savior."

—French swimming pool

"Dresses for street walking."

—Paris dress shop

"Go away."

—Barcelona travel agency

Victorians believed if you put a silver coin under your pillow on

MADE IN FRANCE

This started out as a "Random Origins" page...until we noticed that everything on the page was invented by French people. Ooh La-La!

DRY CLEANING

In 1825, the maid of a Frenchman named Jean-Baptiste Jolly knocked over a camphene (distilled turpentine) lamp on a table, spilling the camphene all over the table cloth. The harder she rubbed the tablecloth to get up the camphene, the cleaner and brighter it became. Jolly, who made a living dying fabrics, added fabric cleaning to his business. By the mid-1850s there were thousands of *dry* cleaners (the process used no water) all over France.

NON-STICK FRYING PANS

Teflon or polytetrafluorethylene (PTFE) was discovered by the Du Pont company in 1938. Teflon *pans* were invented in the mid-1950s by an engineer named Mark Gregoire, who got the idea from something his wife said to him as he was leaving to go fishing. Gregoire used PTFE to keep his fishing line from sticking, and his wife complained that there was nothing like PTFE to keep her pots and pans from sticking. He founded the Tefal company to make Teflon coated pans in 1955. Today, more than 75% of U.S. kitchens contain at least one non-stick pan.

STETHOSCOPES

In 1816, a French pathologist named René Théophile Hyacinthe Laënnec happened to walk through the courtyard of the Louvre as some kids hunched over two ends of some long pieces of wood. When the kids at one end tapped the wood with a small pin, the kids at the other end could hear it as it travelled through the wood. Laënned wondered if the same principle could be used to study diseases of the heart. That afternoon he rolled up a piece of paper into a narrow tube and placed it on the chest of a man suffering from heart disease. He called it a "stethoscope," from *stethos*, the Greek word for "chest."

Valentine's Day eve, your true love would propose to you by the end of the year.

FLY ME TO THE MOON

Want to go to the moon? During the late 1960s, in one of the more unusual business promotions in airline history, Pan American World Airways began taking reservations for a commercial moon flight scheduled to depart in the year 2000. Of course, it never happened. In fact, today, there's no moon flight...and no Pan Am. This selection is from our book Uncle John's Indispensable Guide to the Year 2000.

BRIGHT IDEA

On December 21, 1968, the crew of Apollo 8—Frank Borman, James Lovell Jr., and Williams Anders—lifted off from Cape Kennedy. Their flight was covered extensively on TV, and the world was captivated by the spectacular images of space they beamed back.

During one of Apollo 8's transmission blackouts, two executives at Pan Am (then one of America's premier airlines) decided on a whim to call ABC-TV. They announced that the airline was now accepting reservations for flights to the moon—which would begin by the year 2000.

SURPRISE SUCCESS

The next day, the *New York Times* reported that Pan Am had been deluged by inquiries. What began as a practical joke quickly turned into a publicity bonanza. Pan Am established the "First Moon Flights Club" and began sending out reservation confirmations.

Unbelievably, when Pan Am began running TV and radio ads with the tag line "Who ever heard of an airline with a waiting list for the moon?", TWA announced they would accept reservations, too.

DETAILS, DETAILS

In 1969, one Pan Am official estimated the cost of a round-trip ticket to the moon—based on six cents a mile—at $28,000. "It will be the longest and most expensive commercial airline flight in history," reported the *New York Times*. "But the first flight to the moon will also be the most in demand."

Membership cards for the First Moon Flights Club were issued to residents of every state and citizens of more than 90 countries. "The amazing thing you find," one official told the *Times*, "is that most of these people are very serious about the whole idea."

ENOUGH, ALREADY

By 1971, more than 30,000 people (including future president Ronald Reagan) had signed up. That's when Pan Am decided to suspend reservations.

Membership cards are a collector's item today, and Pan Am is just a memory. In the 1980s, the company declared bankruptcy. Then in 1997, entrepreneurs bought the name and began operating a *new* airline as Pan Am; in 1998, they declared bankruptcy, too. A few months later, the name was transferred again...to a railroad. They have no moon flights planned.

* * * *

PREDICTIONS FOR 2000

Commuting: "However the [businessman of 2000] travels...he will not be obliged to handle the controls by himself. He may well be able to doze or read, while, from a distant point, his car or plane will be held on its course by short-wave impulses."

—Arthur Train, Jr.,
***The Story of Everyday Things* (1941)**

Home Life: "In the year 2000, we will live in pre-fabricated houses light enough for two men to assemble....[We'll] cook in our television sets and relax in chairs that emit a private sound-light-color spectacular."

—*New York Times*,
January 7, 1968

Food: "The businessman in 1999 [will only need] a soup-pill or a concentrated meat-pill for his noonday lunch....Ice-cream pills [will be] very popular."

—Arthur Bird,
***Looking Forward* (1903)**

THE WORLD'S TALLEST BUILDINGS, PART I

Last winter, Uncle John was reading a book on architecture (you know where he was). He was looking at a picture of the Empire State Building, and it suddenly occurred to him that everyone knows the building—but hardly anyone knows its history. His Bathroom Reader *antennae went up—it sounded like a perfect subject for this edition. And here it is—an expanded version that includes other skyscrapers as well.*

HOW HIGH CAN YOU GO?

Question: What was the invention that made tall buildings feasible? *Answer:* The elevator.

In 1850, few buildings were taller than 4 stories tall. This was partly because construction materials and techniques weren't suitable for tall buildings yet. But even if they had been, there was no reason to bother going any higher—no one would have wanted to walk up that many flights of stairs.

The closest thing anyone had to an elevator was a hoist. This was simply a platform connected to ropes and a pulley that could be used to move heavy objects from one floor of a building to another. Guide rails running from floor to ceiling kept the hoist from swinging back and forth, but it was still very dangerous—if the rope broke, there was nothing to stop it from plummeting to the ground, killing anyone riding in it...or standing nearby. Accidents were common.

MR. OTIS REQUESTS

In 1852, the hoist at the Bedstead Manufacturing Company in Yonkers, New York, broke and the superintendent assigned a master mechanic named Elisha Graves Otis to fix it. Otis had seen many brutal mishaps with hoists....So he decided to add a safety feature to the one he was building.

He took a spring from an old wagon and connected it to the top of the platform where the rope was tied. When the the rope was pulled taut, the spring was compressed. But if the rope broke, the spring released and shoved two hooks into the guide rails, holding it in place and preventing it from falling.

Otis' contraption was simple, and was intended primarily to carry freight. But it was actually the first "safety" elevator—the first one that could reliably carry human passengers.

STARTING OVER

Not long after, the Bedstead Manufacturing Company went out of business and Otis lost his job. He decided to head west to join the California Gold Rush...but before he could leave, another furniture company hired him to build two new "safety hoisters;" two men had recently been killed using an old one.

The company paid Otis with cash, a gun and a carriage which convinced him to stay. On September 20, 1853, he opened a business in Yonkers selling "Patented Life and Labor Saving Hoisting Machinery."

Seeing is Believing

Unfortunately, Otis couldn't sell even one more elevator. So he decided to demonstrate his contraption personally. He entered it in an exhibition on "progress in industry and arts" at the Crystal Palace in New York City. When a substantial crowd had gathered, Otis climbed into his hoist, went up about 30 feet, and as onlookers gasped in horror, had his assistant cut the rope with a knife. The rope snapped, the hoist lurched briefly...and then stopped in place. "All safe, gentlemen, all safe," Otis called down to the crowd.

Public demonstrations like this generated some sales, but business remained slow for the first few years: Otis sold 27 hoists in 1856, all of them designed to carry freight. In 1857, in an attempt to expand his business, he designed his first passenger elevator, a steam-powered model capable of lifting 1,000 pounds 40 feet per minute.

UNSUNG HERO

Otis died from diphtheria in 1861 at age 49. He left a business that employed fewer than a dozen people and was only worth about $5,000. The first true skyscraper was still many years off, so it's likely Otis never fully realized the impact his invention would have on mankind.

Surveys say: If you watch at least 2 prime-time comedies a week, you probably drive a foreign car.

UPS AND DOWNS

Otis's sons, Charles and Norton, took over the business following his death. In 1868, they patented a speedier and more elaborate steam elevator. But since there were no electric controls, the elevators required a lot of manpower: Someone had to ride inside the car to operate it (via a rope connected to the steam engine in the basement), and elevator "starters" had to be posted on every floor. Their job was to yell into the elevator shaft to the elevator operator whenever someone needed a lift.

The shouting system was crude, but it worked. The only problem was that it meant buildings could only be as high as the elevator starters could shout. Also, since the elevator was powered by a steam engine that burned coal, the elevator shaft eventually filled with steam and thick smoke, limiting the amount of time people could stand to spend riding in it. This also served to restrict the height of buildings. Elevators, which made tall buildings feasible, were starting to become an obstacle to further growth.

Picking up the Pace

That changed when the first high-speed hydraulic elevator was introduced in the early 1870s. It could travel an amazing 700 feet per minute—which created new problems: Otis's original safety mechanism stopped a falling elevator instantly by grabbing the guide rails that held the elevator in place. It worked fine when the elevator was only travelling 40 feet per minute. But at 700 feet per minute a sudden, jarring stop could be as bad for the passengers as letting the car plunge to the ground. The Otis brothers fixed this in 1878 when they patented a braking system that slowed the elevator gradually. In 1890, they perfected the first electric elevator...and the skyscraper era was underway.

OTIS FACTS

Today, the Otis Elevator Company is the largest elevator company on earth, with 66,000 employees in 1,700 different offices. It has built elevators for the White House, Eiffel Tower, Vatican, and even the space shuttle launch pad.

Part II of the World's Tallest Buildings is on page 138.

By any other name: Apples are part of the rose family.

FAMOUS HOLLYWOOD PUBLICITY STUNTS

Publicity is the mother's milk of Hollywood, and over the years, it has been refined to an art by a handful of practitioners. Here are three publicity stunts that built Hollywood legends.

"I VANT TO BE ALONE."

Background: When Greta Garbo came to Hollywood from Sweden in the 1920s, she didn't realize how conservative America was. In her first newspaper interview, she mentioned casually that she was living with director Mauritz Stiller. Today that's no big deal, but in the '20s, it was a shocking revelation.

Publicity Stunt: When MGM head Louis B. Mayer heard about the interview, he was furious. He banned Garbo from ever speaking to the press again. That suited Garbo fine—she was shy anyway. But how to explain it to the press? Someone in the MGM publicity department came up with the famous quote: 'I vant to be alone.'"

THE SEARCH FOR SCARLETT

Background: Producer David O. Selznick wanted the perfect actress to play Scarlett O'Hara in the film adaptation of *Gone with the Wind*, so he launched a nationwide talent search that lasted (coincidentally) for the two years it took to prepare for filming. Joan Crawford, Bette Davis, and Tallulah Bankhead all wanted the part. So did Katharine Hepburn, who told Selznick, "the part was practically written for me." "I can't imagine Rhett Butler chasing you for ten years," Selznick replied.

"George Cuckor, the intended director, was sent scurrying southward to scout locations, but also, supposedly, to check out high school plays for ingenues," explains a film historian. "To keep the game of who-will-play-her alive, every female willing to try out was tested." Newspapers and radio stations kept the country updated on the progress of the search.

According to legend, just when the search seemed hopeless, Selznick's brother escorted a young British actress named Vivian Leigh onto the set. They signed her on the spot.

Publicity Stunt: Selznick had Leigh in mind for the part from the very beginning. But there were two problems: Leigh was a foreigner, which might not go over well with Southern audiences, and she was in the middle of a scandalous affair with actor Laurence Olivier (both were married to other people at the time). M. Hirsch Goldberg writes in *The Book of Lies:*

> A scenario was devised in which Vivian Leigh would be discovered at the last minute after an extensive search for the right Scarlett had not been successful. In this way the foreign-born aspect would be diffused, especially since Scarlett, the character, and Vivien, the actress shared the same Irish-French background. And with Olivier and Leigh agreeing not to move for a divorce at the time, the scandal would be abated in the flurry of good news that the Scarlett part had finally been settled.

WONG KEYE, PIANO TUNER

Background: When Barbra Streisand announced that she wouldn't give any interviews to promote *On a Clear Day You Can See Forever*, publicity man Steve Yeager was stuck—if the star wouldn't cooperate, he'd have to find another publicity angle.

Publicity Stunt: Yeager called AP gossip columnist Jim Bacon and "suggested we do a story on one Wong Keye, a mythical tone-deaf Chinese piano tuner who was tuning all the pianos on the Streisand movie." Bacon agreed. According to Bacon, in his book *Made in Hollywood:* "The story was written with appropiate tongue-in-cheek. It told how Wong Keye had started out in life as a fortune-cookie stuffer in a Chinatown bakery, then sold exotic fish for awhile until he found his niche tuning pianos. Since then he had been in great demand because he was such a superb piano tuner.

What Happened: It worked—the story ran all over the country, and was picked up by the London *Daily Mirror*, which even ran a photo (an actor hired to dress up in Chinese costume). Bacon even got calls from piano owners asking how they could get in touch with Keye. "But the funniest repercussion of all," Bacon writes, "came when Streisand—who had refused to give interviews in the first place—complained to the producer because the piano tuner in the movie was getting more publicity than the star."

"Seersucker" comes from a Persian word—shir-o-shakar—that means "milk and sugar."

THE BIRTH OF POST-ITS

Post-It Notes now seem like a logical and obvious product. In fact, you're probably so used to seeing Post-Its around your house or office that sometimes it's hard to imagine there was a time when they didn't exist. Actually, they began as a mistake, and almost didn't even make it into the market. Here's Jack Mingo's story of how they were invented.

STICKIES

In 1964, a 3-M chemist named Spencer Silver was experimenting with a new adhesive. Out of curiosity, he added too much of a "reactant" chemical...and got a totally unexpected result: a milky white liquid that turned crystal-clear under pressure. He characterized it as "tacky" but not "aggressively adhesive."

He also found that it was "narcissistic"—i.e., it tended to stick to itself more than anything else. If you put it on one surface and stuck a piece of paper on it, either all or none of the adhesive would come off when you peeled off the paper.

STICKY SITUATION

Silver was intrigued with the stuff, but couldn't get his superiors at 3-M excited. So he wandered the hallways of the company giving demonstrations and presentations. He nearly had to beg 3-M to patent it.

Silver was sure there was a use for his adhesive—he just didn't know what it was. "Sometimes I was so angry because this new thing was so obviously unique," he says. "I'd tell myself, 'Why can't you think of a product? It's your job!'"

EUREKA

Finally, in 1974, someone came up with a problem to match Silver's solution.

Every Sunday, Arthur Fry, another 3-M chemist, directed the choir in his church. He always marked songs in the hymnal with little scraps of paper. But one Sunday, while signaling the choir to stand, he fumbled his hymnal and all the bookmarks fell to the floor. As he frantically tried to find his place, he thought, "If only there was a way to get them to stick to the page." That's when he remembered seeing Silver's "now-it-sticks, now-it-doesn't" demonstration years earlier....And while the choir sang, he started thinking of situations where semi-sticky paper might be helpful.

The next morning, he rushed to work and tracked down some of Silver's adhesive. He found there were still problems to work out—like how to make sure the adhesive didn't come off on the document—and he worked with company chemists to solve them. He even created a machine in his basement that would make manufacturing easier by applying the adhesive in a continuous roll. When he was done, he found that the machine was bigger than his basement doorway...and it couldn't be disassembled without ruining it. So he knocked out a part of his basement wall.

NOT YET

Fry and his team began producing prototype Post-Its. As a form of informal marketing research, they distributed the sticky notes to offices around the building. They were a hit. "Once you start using them," one enthusiastic co-worker told him, "you can't stop."

Despite in-house success, the 3-M marketing department didn't believe Post-Its would sell. They kept asking: "Why would anybody buy this 'glorified scratch paper' for a dollar a package?" Their lack of enthusiasm showed up in test-marketing. It failed miserably.

STUCK ON YOU

Fry's boss couldn't believe that they wouldn't succeed if marketed properly. After all, they were using thousands of them at 3-M. The company decided to try a one-shot test-market blitz in Boise, Idaho. Their sales reps blanketed Boise with free samples and order forms. The result: a 90% reorder response from the companies that received samples—more than twice the 40% the company considered a success.

Post-Its went into full national distribution in 1980 and caught on across America. They've since become an international hit as well.

"The Post-It was a product that met an unperceived need," says Fry. "If you had asked somebody what they needed, they might have said a better paper clip. But give them a Post-It Note, and they immediately know what to do with it."

"Too bad 90% of the politicians give the other 10% a bad reputation."— Henry Kissinger

Q&A: ASK THE EXPERTS

Everyone's got a question or two they'd like answered. Here are a few of those questions, with answers from some of the nation's top trivia experts.

MAKE A WISH

Q: *How do trick birthday candles (which keep relighting after being blown out) work?*

A: "The wicks are treated with magnesium crystals. The crystals retain enough heat to reilluminate the wick after the candles are blown out. Because the magnesium-treated wicks retain heat so well, experts recommend extinguishing the candles permanently by dipping them in water." (From *Why Do Dogs Have Wet Noses?*, by David Feldman)

FOILED AGAIN

Q: *Does it matter which side of the aluminum foil is used?*

A: "The dull and shiny sides of the foil have no special meaning; they are simply a result of the way that the foil is made. In the final rolling step of the manufacturing process, two layers of aluminum foil are passed through the rolling mill at the same time. The side that comes in contact with the mill's highly polished steel rolls becomes shiny. The other side, which does not come in contact with the heavy metal rolls, comes out dull.

"Shiny or dull, it does not matter." (From *Why Does Popcorn Pop?*, by Don Voorhees)

UMM...WHAT WAS THAT?

Q: *Is it true that elephants never forget?*

A: Believe it or not, yes. "We know this because of an experiment many years ago by a professor in Germany. He taught an elephant to choose between two wooden boxes, one marked with a square, the other with a circle. The box with a square had food in it, the other didn't.

"It took 330 tries before the elephant figured out that 'square' meant 'food.' Once it got the idea, though, things went a lot quicker. Soon the professor could put any two markings on the boxes. The elephant would experiment a few times, figure out which sign meant 'food,' then pick the right box from there on out.

"The professor came back a year later and tested the elephant again using the old markings—circles, squares, and so on. Amazingly enough, the elephant *still remembered* which markings were the signs for food.

"That's why elephants are so popular in circuses. It may take them a while to learn the act, but once they've got it, they've got it for good." (From *Know It All!*, by Ed Zotti)

TEE-HEE

Q: *Why don't we laugh when we tickle ourselves?*

A: "The laughter which results from being tickled by someone else is not the same as laughter that comes from being amused. When someone tickles us, the laugh is a reflex action [that] is really a cry of distress, essentially begging the person to stop stimulating our sensitive skin. When we tickle ourselves, we're not at the mercy of someone else. If the feeling becomes too intense, we stop. Therefore, no distress signal is needed." (From *A Book of Curiosities*, by Roberta Kramer)

OIL'S WELL

Q: *What's the world's tallest man-made structure?*

A: "It is not the Sears Tower, which is 110 stories and 1,454 feet high. A Shell Oil company offshore oil rig in the Gulf of Mexico is more than twice as tall as Chicago's Sears Tower. Altogether, it rises 3,280 feet from seabed to flare top. Thirty-five 'stories' are above water level. Installed in 1994, it is the world's deepest oil platform. The $1.2 billion rig is called the Auger Tension Leg Platform, or Auger TLP for short. It's the first tension leg platform that combines both oil and gas drilling and production in U.S. waters. Designed to withstand 72-foot-high waves in 100-year hurricanes, it can sway up to 235 feet off center without damage. It was built to survive a 1,000-year storm." (From *Blue Genes and Polyester Plants*, by Sharon Bertsch McGrayne)

THE TOP 10 HITS OF THE YEAR, 1956–1959

In our last Bathroom Reader, *we included lists of the annual Top 10 TV shows. That prompted requests for a similar list of the Top 10 songs of each year. So here's the first of our series of lists, compiled from a number of sources with help from New York's #1 oldies deejay, Bob Shannon of WCBS-FM.*

1956

(1) Heartbreak Hotel —*Elvis Presley*
(2) Don't Be Cruel —*Elvis Presley*
(3) My Prayer —*The Platters*
(4) Lisbon Antigua —*Nelson Riddle*
(5) Hound Dog —*Elvis Presley*
(6) The Wayward Wind —*Gogi Grant*
(7) Poor People of Paris —*Lee Baxter*
(8) Que Sera, Sera —*Doris Day*
(9) Memories Are Made Of This —*Dean Martin*
(10) Rock And Roll Waltz —*Kay Starr*

1957

(1) All Shook Up —*Elvis Presley*
(2) Little Darlin' —*The Diamonds*
(3) Young Love —*Tab Hunter*
(4) Love Letters In The Sand —*Pat Boone*
(5) So Rare —*Jimmy Dorsey*
(6) Don't Forbid Me —*Pat Boone*
(7) Singin' The Blues —*Guy Mitchell*
(8) Young Love —*Sonny James*
(9) Too Much —*Elvis Presley*
(10) Round And Round —*Perry Como*

1958

(1) Volare (Nel Blu Dipinto Di Blu) —*Domenico Modugno*
(2) All I Have To Do Is Dream —*The Everly Brothers*
(3) Don't —*Elvis Presley*
(4) Witch Doctor —*David Seville*
(5) Patricia —*Perez Prado*
(6) Tequila —*The Champs*
(7) Catch A Falling Star —*Perry Como*
(8) Sail Along Silvery Moon —*Billy Vaughn*
(9) It's All In The Game —*Tommy Edwards*
(10) Return To Me —*Dean Martin*

1959

(1) Mack The Knife —*Bobby Darin*
(2) The Battle Of New Orleans —*Johnny Horton*
(3) Personality —*Lloyd Price*
(4) Venus —*Frankie Avalon*
(5) Lonely Boy —*Paul Anka*
(6) Dream Lover —*Bobby Darin*
(7) The Three Bells —*The Browns*
(8) Come Softly To Me —*The Fleetwoods*
(9) Kansas City —*Wilbert Harrison*
(10) Mr. Blue —*The Fleetwoods*

A cow spends eighteen hours of every day chewing.

THE HISTORY OF ASPIRIN

Today we take aspirin so much for granted that it's hard to believe that when it was first discovered, it was considered one of the most miraculous drugs ever invented. It turns out that the history of aspirin also makes a good story.

PAIN KILLER

In the late 1890s, Felix Hoffman, a chemist with Germany's Friedrich Bayer (pronounced "By-er") & Company, started looking for a new treatment to help relieve his father's painful rheumatism.

Drugs to treat the pain and inflammation of rheumatism had been around for 2,000 years. In 200 B.C., Hippocrates, the father of medicine, observed that chewing on the bark of the white willow tree soothed aches and pains. In 1823, chemists had finally succeeded in isolating the bark's active ingredient. It was salicylic acid.

TOUGH STUFF

The problem was, salicylic acid wasn't safe. In its pure form, it was so powerful that it did damage at the same time it was doing good. Unless you mixed it with water, it would burn your mouth and throat. And even *with* water, it was so hard on the stomach lining that people who took it became violently ill, complaining that their stomachs felt like they were "crawling with ants."

Salicylic acid had given Hoffman's father multiple ulcers. He had literally burned holes in his stomach trying to relieve his rheumatism pain, and was desperate for something milder. So Hoffman read through all the scientific literature he could find. He discovered that every scientist who had tried to neutralize the acidic properties of salicylic acid had failed...except one. In 1853, a French chemist named Charles Frederic Gerhart had improved the acid by adding sodium and acetyl chloride—creating a new compound called *acetylsalicylic acid*. However, the substance was so unstable and difficult to make that Gerhart had abandoned it.

No Pain, No Gain

Hoffman decided to make his own batch of Gerhart's acetylsalicylic acid. Working on it in his spare time, he managed to produce a purer, more stable form than anyone had ever been able to make. He tested the powder on himself successfully. Then he gave some to his father. It eased the elder Hoffman's pain, with virtually no side effects.

The Bayer Facts

Hoffman reported his findings to his superiors at Bayer. His immediate supervisor was Heinrich Dreser, the inventor of heroin. (At the time, it was thought to be a non-addictive substitute for morphine. Heroin was a brand name, selected to describe the drug's *heroic* painkilling properties.) Dreser studied Hoffman's acid, found that it worked, and in 1899 Bayer began selling their patented acetylsalicylic acid powder to physicians under the brand name *aspirin*. The name was derived from the Latin term for the "queen of the meadow" plant, *Spiraea ulmaria*, which was an important source of salicylic acid. A year later, they introduced aspirin pills.

IN THE BEGINNING

Within ten years of its introduction, aspirin became the most-commonly prescribed patent medicine in the world for two reasons: (1) it actually worked, and (2) unlike heroin, morphine, and other powerful drugs of the time, it had few side effects. There was nothing on the market like it, and when it proved effective at reducing fever during the influenza epidemics at the start of the twentieth century, its reputation as a miracle drug spread around the world.

"This was a period of time when a person only had a life expectancy of 44 years because there were no medications available," says Bayer spokesman Dr. Steven Weisman. "Aspirin very quickly become the most important drug available." It seemed to be able to solve any problem, large or small—gargling aspirin dissolved in water eased sore throats, and rubbing aspirin against a baby's gums even helped sooth teething pain.

UPS AND DOWNS

Aspirin was initially a prescription-only medication, but it became available over the counter in 1915. Sales exploded, and demand for the new drug grew at a faster rate than ever. Since Bayer owned the patent on aspirin—and there were no other drugs like it—the company didn't have to worry about competition; it had the worldwide market to itself.

But the forces of history would soon get in the way.

HEADACHE MATERIAL

In 1916, Bayer used its aspirin profits to build a massive new factory in upstate New York. They immediately started manufacturing the drug for the American market and sold $6 million worth in the first year.

Then they ran into problems. World War I made Germany America's enemy, and in 1918 the U.S. Government seized Bayer's American assets under the Trading With the Enemy Act. They auctioned the factory off to the Sterling Products Company of West Virginia. (The two Bayers would not reunite again until 1995, when the German Bayer bought Sterling's over-the-counter drug business for $1 billion.) Sterling continued marketing aspirin under the Bayer brand name, which by now had been Americanized to "Bay-er."

The original American patent for aspirin expired in 1917, and the "Aspirin" trademark was lost in 1921. Anyone who wanted to make and sell aspirin was now legally free to do so. By the 1930s there were more than a thousand brands of pure aspirin on the market; there were also hundreds of products (Anacin, for example) that combined aspirin with caffeine or other drugs. A bottle of aspirin in the medicine cabinet was as common in American households as salt and pepper were on the kitchen table.

Ready for more? "Aspirin: the Miracle Drug" is on page 254.

Historical note: In 1763, an English clergyman named Edward Stone administered tea, water, and beer laced with powdered willow bark to more than fifty people suffering from fever. They all got better, proving that willow bark reduced fever, too.

STRAIGHT FROM MICK'S LIPS

Mick Jagger is like the Energizer Bunny—still going...and going... and going. He's had over 30 years to come up with enough comments to make at least one interesting page of quotes.

"People have this obsession: They want you to be like you were in 1969. They want you to, because otherwise their youth goes with you."

"I'd rather be dead than singing 'Satisfaction' when I'm forty-five."

"You get to the point where you have to change everything —change your looks, change your money, change your sex, change your women—because of the business."

"Of course we're doing this for the money....We've always done it for the money."

"Sometimes an orgasm is better than being onstage. Sometimes being onstage is better than an orgasm."

"People ask me, 'Why do you wear makeup? Why don't you just come off the street?' The whole idea is you don't come off the street. You put on different clothes, you do your hair and you acquire this personality that has to go out and perform. When you get off the stage, that mask is dropped."

"Fame is like ice cream. It's only bad if you eat too much."

"The best rock 'n' roll music encapsulates a certain high energy—an angriness—whether on record or onstage. That is, rock 'n' roll is only rock 'n' roll if it's not safe."

"When I'm 33, I'll quit. That's the time when a man has to do something else. I can't say what it will definitely be. It's still in the back of my head—but it won't be in show business. I don't want to be a rock star all my life. I couldn't bear to end up as an Elvis Presley and sing in Las Vegas with all those housewives and old ladies coming in with their handbags. It's really sick." (1972)

women off are: barbecued meat, cherries, and men's cologne.

WORDS OF WISDOM

More points to ponder while poised upon the pot.

"The two biggest sellers in any bookstore are the cookbooks and the diet books. The cookbooks tell you how to prepare the food, and the diet books tell you how not to eat any of it."

—Andy Rooney

"I never believed in Santa Claus because I knew no white dude would come into my neighborhood after dark."

—Dick Gregory

"If you have a job without aggravations, you don't have a job."

—Malcolm Forbes

"The way to make money is to buy when blood is running in the streets."

—John D. Rockefeller

"Glory is fleeting, but obscurity is forever."

—Napoleon

"The length of a film should be directly related to the endurance of the human bladder."

—Alfred Hitchcock

"My grandmother is over eighty and she still doesn't need glasses. Drinks right out of the bottle."

—Henny Youngman

"Happiness is having a large, loving, caring, close-knit family in another city."

—George Burns

"Children today are tyrants. They contradict their parents, gobble their food, and tyrannize their teachers."

—Socrates (470-399 B.C.)

"Just because your voice reaches halfway around the world doesn't mean you are wiser than when it reached only to the end of the bar."

—Edward R. Murrow

"Few things are harder to put up with than a good example."

—Mark Twain

"Wise men talk because they have something to say; fools talk because they have to say something."

—Plato

The Wright brothers built their first airplane for less than $1,000.

STRANGE LAWSUITS

These days, it seems that people will sue each other over practically anything. Here are a few real-life examples of unusual legal battles.

THE PLAINTIFF: Mortimer Hetsberger, a 22-year-old bank robber.

THE DEFENDANT: Laura Gonzalez, a teller at the Fleet Bank in Atlantic City, New Jersey.

THE LAWSUIT: In July 1998, Hetsberger handed Gonzalez a note at her teller window. It said: "I want the money now." According to Gonzalez, he also told her "Now, or I'll shoot." She handed him $4,000. He was captured the same day. When he heard that Gonzalez had accused him of threatening her, he filed a $1.5 million lawsuit for slander, explaining that he'd never even spoken to her.

VERDICT: No ruling yet.

THE PLAINTIFF: A 25-year-old mortuary driver.

THE DEFENDANT: A California Highway Patrol officer.

THE LAWSUIT: The driver was stopped in Orange County and given a ticket for driving in a carpool lane with no passengers. He protested that he had four passengers—the frozen corpses he was transporting. He went to court to overturn the ticket.

VERDICT: He had to pay the fine.

THE PLAINTIFF: Kevin McGuinness.

THE DEFENDANT: The University of New Mexico.

THE LAWSUIT: When McGuinness flunked out of the University of New Mexico Medical School, he sued for reinstatement under the Americans with Disabilities Act. What's his disability? He gets very anxious when he takes exams, and doesn't do well on them.

VERDICT: Unknown.

Medically speaking, the correct order of intelligence is: Moron, imbecile, idiot.

THE PLAINTIFF: David Earl Dempsey, a 27-year-old inmate at the Pima County, Arizona jail.

THE DEFENDANT: Pima County and state prison officials.

THE LAWSUIT: In February 1998, Dempsey tied a sheet around his neck and jumped out the jailhouse window, trying to commit suicide. The sheet broke, and he plummeted to the concrete below. He sued for negligence.

VERDICT: Case dismissed. While waiting for the trial, Dempsey tried suicide again. This time he succeeded.

THE PLAINTIFF: Carol Ann Bennett.

THE DEFENDANT: Warren Woodrow Bennett, her husband.

THE LAWSUIT: When Ms. Bennett moved out of their condo, she left her breast implants behind. She sued to get them back.

THE VERDICT: Implants returned.

THE PLAINTIFF: Sheila Tormino.

THE DEFENDANT: Montclaire Bowl, in Edwardsville, Illinois.

THE LAWSUIT: While she was bowling, Torino got a piece of popcorn caught in her shoe, and during her approach, she slipped and fell. She sued for $50,000, claiming the alley was negligent for not putting up warnings about popcorn on the floor.

THE VERDICT: Unknown.

THE PLAINTIFF: Eric Edmunds.

THE DEFENDANT: Humana Hospital Bayside, in Virginia Beach.

THE LAWSUIT: In 1987, Edmunds went into the hospital to get his stomach stapled, making it smaller. According to reports, "within 48 hours of the surgery, he snuck out of his room and raided the hospital refrigerator and ate so much he burst his staples." Edmunds sued the hospital for $250,000 for "failure to keep its refrigerator locked."

VERDICT: Unknown.

A government study has determined that pigs can become alcoholics.

I DREAM OF JEANNIE

It wasn't a huge hit in the 1960s, when it first aired...but 30-plus years later, I Dream of Jeannie *is still airing in reruns all over the world. How did the beautiful female in harem pants wind up living, unmarried, with her "master" in suburbia? Here's the story.*

HOW IT STARTED

Before Sidney Sheldon was one of America's bestselling schlock authors, he applied his talents to screenplays and television scripts.

He arrived in Hollywood in 1939, when he was 22. By 1947, he'd won an Oscar for best original screenplay, for *The Bachelor and the Bobby Soxer*, starring Cary Grant and Shirley Temple. In 1962, he gave up film work to write and create *The Patty Duke Show* for Screen Gems. The one-joke sitcom about identical cousins was an immediate hit—the #18 show for the 1963–64 season. So Screen Gems asked him for another sitcom and all but guaranteed they'd air anything he created.

Sheldon worked fast. It took him two days to come up with a whole new show. As he told Richard Barnes in *Diary of a Genie*, it was a Saturday, and he was planning to fly from New York to L.A. the next day to meet with studio execs. "I decided to bring them an outline of [the] show that I wanted to do....On Saturday I started dictating the outline of *I Dream of Jeannie*." It started out as a few ideas, but "as I started dictating, it began to get fuller and fuller....[So] I decided to turn it into an entire script."

He handwrote most of the script the next day on the plane heading west and presented it at the meeting. Screen Gems bought it as the pilot for *Jeannie*. "The moral of the story," Sheldon says, "is that when you get an idea, write it down immediately." The show aired for five years, from 1965 to 1970.

INSIDE FACTS

The inspiration for *Jeannie* was the 1964 Universal motion picture, *The Brass Bottle*. The familiar plot: A portly ancient genie (Burl Ives) appears from a lamp to serve his master (Tony Randall). Though he's filled with good intentions, the genie keeps getting Randall into trouble. Sheldon said: "I thought that it would be fun to make the genie a beautiful young girl who says, 'What can I do for you, Master?'"

Sheldon got one other thing from the film—his star. Barbara Eden played Randall's girlfriend. Sheldon thought she'd be perfect for what he described as "the all-American fantasy," and never even considered anyone else for the part.

THE GREAT NAVEL WAR

Although Sheldon and the network censors had no objection to Barbara Eden's sexy costume or the fact that the unmarried Jeannie was living with a man for whom she would do *anything*, they refused to let her show her navel on network TV.

The solution: She put a flesh-colored cloth plug in it during filming. The joke on the set was that genies weren't born with navels.

When George Schlatter, producer of TV's *Laugh-In* wanted to debut Eden's navel on his program, Sheldon and NBC censors stopped him. It wasn't until the reunion movies that Jeannie ever appeared on TV with a belly button.

THE NASA CONNECTION

The astronauts in *Jeannie* were often bumbling idiots, but NASA was happy to cooperate fully with the show. All they really cared about was eliminating anything that smacked of militarism. They wanted to guarantee that the show would "project the image of the space program as a peaceful, scientific exploration of space."

BOTTLED UP

The recognizable "Jeannie bottle" used in the series was originally made from a 1964 Jim Beam liquor decanter that had been given to producer Sidney Sheldon for Christmas. It was painted by the show's prop department. In October, 1995, a bottle used on the series was auctioned off for $10,000.

FLOP TREATMENT

Screen Gems didn't think *Jeannie* was going to be a hit, so they decided to save money and shoot the first season in black and white. It was one of NBC's last black-and-white shows ever.

So far, every U.S. president with a beard has been a Republican.

BATHROOM ORIGINS

We've all heard of these products before. Here's where they come from.

EX-LAX

In 1906 Max Kiss (that's his real name), a Hungarian-born pharmacist living in the U.S., came up with an over-the-counter version of a new prescription laxative called *phenolphthalein*. Kiss called his new chocolate tablets Bo-Bos, but one afternoon he happened to read in the local Hungarian language newspaper about a deadlock in Hungary's parliament. The Hungarian words for "parliamentary deadlock" are sometimes shortened to "ex-lax" in print. Kiss thought it sounded like "excellent laxative."

PAY TOILETS

So few people owned indoor toilets in Terre Haute, Indiana in 1910, that when the Pennsylvania Railroad installed some at the train station, they became one of the town's major attractions. Some locals came to use the facilities, others, merely to marvel. But the restrooms were so jammed with admirers that when the trains pulled into the station, passengers literally had no place to go. So the railroad installed coin-operated locks, and gave the stationmaster a key to let ticket holders in for free.

WASH 'N DRY MOIST TOWELETTES

Ross Williams served in the Navy during World War II, and one of the things he hated most about life onboard a ship was that during water shortages he could not wash up before going to bed at night. Unfortunately for him, it wasn't until 1953 that he finally figured out a solution to the problem: paper towels soaked in liquid soap and sealed in tinfoil. According to Colgate-Palmolive, makers of Wash 'n Dry, one towelette provides as much cleaning power as a quart of water.

THE JIG IS UP

Everything has a history—even jigsaw puzzles. They started as a toy for rich kids...became a hobby for wealthy adults...and then, when mass production made it possible, became a pastime for the rest of us.

THE FIRST JIGSAW PUZZLE

Jigsaw puzzles were one of Western Europe's first educational toys. In 1762, a London mapmaker/printer named John Spilsbury glued a few of his maps onto thin wood panels. Then, using a small hand-saw, he cut them up along the borders of each country. He called them "dissected maps," and sold them to well-to-do parents "for the edification of the young." It was the beginning of an industry.

Spilsbury's timing was excellent—the first children's books had been published only a year earlier, and there was a blossoming interest in new ways to educate the young. By 1800 twenty different London publishers were cranking puzzles out. Most featured historical subjects and moral lessons—and Bible stories. Religious puzzles were an especially popular diversion on Sundays, when ordinary "secular" play was not permitted.

REAL JIGSAW PUZZLES

Until the late 19th century, jigsaw puzzles were made one at a time, gluing expensive prints to fine mahogany or cedar. Each piece was cut out with a hand saw, and each puzzle had no more than 50 pieces. Only the border pieces interlocked; anything more complicated would have cost too much money—and there was a limit to what even wealthy parents were willing to pay. Early jigsaw puzzles cost the equivalent of a week's wages for a common laborer.

Then, in 1876, the power scroll saw, also known as the *jigsaw,* was exhibited at the Philadelphia Centennial Exposition. It was inexpensive (some foot-powered treadle saws sold for as little as $3), and was capable of making incredibly intricate cuts. It immediately revolutionized furniture design. By the 1890s it had an impact on puzzles, too: craftsmen began making completely interlocking puzzles with smaller pieces...which could challenge adults as well as children.

PUZZLE-MANIA

The new puzzles were a hit in high-society circles. Their popularity grew until, in 1908, a jigsaw puzzle craze swept America. No one was left out; if you couldn't afford to buy puzzles, there were puzzle lending libraries, and even puzzle *rental* companies. Sales were so strong that Parker Brothers gave up manufacturing games for a year to focus exclusively on puzzles (It was during the 1908 craze that the company pioneered the idea of cutting the pieces into shapes that people could recognize—stars, ducks, dogs, flowers, snowflakes, etc.).

THE GOLDEN AGE OF PUZZLES

When the craze died down, jigsaw puzzles had become a part of American life. By the 1920s, they were so cheap that just about anyone could afford them...manufacturers were using softer woods, which were easier to saw, and fancy engraving had been replaced by black and white lithographs that kids could paint with stencils and watercolors. By 1930, wood and jigsaws had given way to cardboard and die-cutting, so it was possible to buy a beautiful puzzle for as little as 10¢.

As America got deeper into the Great Depression, these inexpensive puzzles became increasingly attractive family entertainment. The result: people went on another puzzle-buying binge. For about six months in the early 1930s, the U.S. could not get enough puzzles. At the peak of the fad, Americans were purchasing 6 million puzzles *a week*. Things got so frantic that newsstands began offering a service called "puzzle-a-week," with new puzzles hitting the shelves every Wednesday. In less than a year, manufacturers sold more than $100 million worth of jigsaw puzzles (in 1930s money!).

STAND-UP GUY

Puzzles remained more or less unchanged after the 1930s. The artwork improved and special "luxury" puzzle makers sprang up to handcraft custom puzzles for movie stars and captains of industry, but they were really just more of the same thing. By the 1980s, puzzles had become a stale staple of the toy industry.

Then in 1989, a Canadian broadcasting executive named Paul Gallant decided to start a toy company. But he wasn't sure what kind of toys he wanted to make. "I started thinking about puzzles, and how they hadn't changed much since the 1700s," he told the *New York Times* in 1997, "and wondered why no one had ever made a three-dimensional puzzle." He experimented with ordinary cardboard puzzle pieces, but they fell over when he tried to stand them up. So he made some out of the same kind of polyethylene foam that is used to insulate airliner cockpits. The pieces were sturdy enough to build miniature walls.

Gallant made a 3-D puzzle resembling a Victorian mansion and took it to the F.A.O. Schwartz toy store in Manhattan, where he showed it to the store's toy and game buyer. "I took the puzzle and I threw it in the air," Gallant says. It didn't break. "I said, 'No glue, no pins, no nothing, it just stays like this interlocking.' And I pushed the wall off and I separated the pieces and showed him this was really a puzzle. And he said, 'Wow, where did you get that?'" F.A.O. Schwartz bought 74 puzzles that afternoon in 1991; Gallant's company now sells more than $100 million worth of 3-D puzzles—shaped like skyscrapers, castles, the Eiffel Tower, the Titanic, and even *Star Wars* spaceships—every year, making it another of the biggest puzzle fads in history.

PUZZLING INNOVATIONS

Has it been a while since you've bought a puzzle? Here are some new products you might find on your next trip to the toy store:

- **Mono-colored Puzzles.** No pretty pictures, just puzzle pieces, hundreds of them, all painted the same color so that there are no clues as to where they belong in the puzzle.
- **Multiple-border Puzzles.** Pieces with straight edges that appear to be border pieces, but actually are inner pieces.
- **Impossibles.** 750-piece borderless puzzles with too many pieces. No taking the easy way out by connecting outer edges first, because edge pieces look like inner pieces. To make it even more puzzling: five extra pieces that don't fit anywhere in the puzzle.
- **Triazzles.** All of the pieces are triangle shaped with similar designs, but with only one correct solution.
- **The World's Most Difficult Jigsaw Puzzles.** Double-sided puzzles with 529 pieces. The same artwork is on both sides, rotated 90 degrees with respect to each other.

First female boxing match in the U.S.: March 16, 1876. The winner got a silver butter dish.

THE GROUCHO WARS

One of Uncle John's favorite Marx Brothers scenes is from Duck Soup. *Groucho is Rufus T. Firefly, head of a country called Freedonia...which is close to war with its neighbor, Sylvania. At the 11th hour, a conference is arranged with the Sylvanian ambassador to make an effort to avert the conflict. Groucho is amenable...until he works himself up into such a state that when the Sylvanian ambassador enters, Groucho slugs him. And, of course, there's war. We bring this up because as preposterous as it seems, that kind of thing has happened more than once in the real world. We call these occurrences the Groucho Wars.*

DIPLOMACY...GROUCHO-STYLE

Here's Groucho's Duck Soup *soliloquy about war and peace.*

Mrs. Teasdale (Margaret Dumont): "I've taken the liberty of asking the ambassador to come over here, because we both felt that a friendly conference would settle everything peacefully. He'll be here in a moment."

Rufus T. Firefly (Groucho): "Mrs Teasdale, you did a noble deed. I'd be unworthy of the high trust that you've placed in me if I didn't do everything in my power to keep our beloved Freedonia at peace with the world. I'd be only too happy to meet Ambassador Trentino and offer him, on behalf of my country, the right hand of good fellowship. And I feel sure that he will *accept* this gesture in the spirit in which it is offered....

"But what if he doesn't? A fine thing *that* would be. I hold out my hand, and he refuses to accept it. (*Sarcastically*) *That'll* add a lot to my prestige, won't it? Me, the head of a country, snubbed by a foreign ambassador. Who does he think he is, that he can come here and make a sap out of me in front of all my people? Think of it...I hold out my hand, and that hyena refuses to accept it. WHY THE CHEAP, FOUR-FLUSHING SWINE—HE'LL NEVER GET AWAY WITH IT, I TELL YOU—HE'LL NEVER GET AWAY WITH IT! (*The ambassador enters*) So! You refuse to shake hands with me, eh?" (*Groucho slaps him in the face*)

Ambassador: "...There's no turning back now. This means WAR!"

Per capita, what U.S. city has the greatest number of psychiatrists? Washington, D.C.

THE REAL GROUCHO WARS

These are not *out of a movie script. People really died in them.*

Napoleonic Wars (1865)

Between: Pararguay and its neighbors—Argentina, Brazil, Uraguay

What Started It: Francisco Solano Lopez, president of Paraguay believed he was Napoleon. To prove it, he declared war simultaneously on all three countries.

Outcome: Paraguay was decimated. Nearly half its population was killed in five years of battle.

War Of The Oaken Bucket (1325)

Between: The independent Italian states of Modena and Bologna

What Started It: Modena soldiers invaded the state of Bologna to steal a bucket. They succeeded, but hundreds of Bologna citizens were killed in the process. Bologna declared war to avenge the deaths...and to get the bucket back.

Outcome: They fought for 12 years, but Bologna never did get the bucket. To this day it's still in Modena, stored in the bell tower of a 14-century cathedral.

War of the Whiskers (1152)

Between: England and France

What Started It: King Louis VII of France had a beard when he was married, but shaved it off when he got home from the Crusades. According to *The Book of Lists*, his wife, Duchess Eleanor, thought he looked ugly without it and insisted he grow it back. He refused—so Eleanor divorced him to marry King Henry II of England. Louis wouldn't relinquish control of Eleanor's ancestral lands, so Henry declared war to get them back.

Outcome: This conflict lasted longer than any of the the people who started it—301 years.

War of the Stray Dog (1925)

Between: Greece and Bulgaria

What Started It: A Greek soldier's dog ran across the Bulgarian border. When he followed it across the border, a Bulgarian border guard shot him. Greece declared war and invaded Bulgaria.

An average chicken-plucking machine can pluck a whole chicken in 14 seconds.

Outcome: The League of Nations called an emergency session to deal with the crisis, and convinced the two nations to end it quickly.

The War of Jenkins' Ear (1739)

Between: Spain and Britain

What Started It: The British ship *Rebecca*, under the command of Robert Jenkins, was sailing off the coast of Cuba when it was boarded by the Spanish coast guard. After looting the ship, the coast guard commander cut off Jenkins' ear—which Jenkins saved and carried around with him, preserved in a jar. Seven years later the British Parliament invited British Jenkins to the House of Commons to tell his story and show off the mummified ear. It became the rallying point of a war with Spain.

Outcome: The Spanish were defeated.

The Soccer War (1969)

Between: El Salvador and Honduras

What Started It: The neighboring countries were facing each other in a World Cup soccer match on June 27, 1969. Late in the game, a referee gave El Salvador a penalty kick. They scored from the penalty spot and won, 3-2. When news of the ref's call spread, riots broke out in both capital cities. Fans went on the rampage, looting and beating up opposition supporters. On July 3, war was declared.

Outcome: 2000 people were killed and the Central American Common Market—on which both countries depended—collapsed. The result: serious food shortages and starvation. To add insult to injury, El Salvador lost the next round and was eliminated from World Cup competition.

The Cricket War (1896)

Between: Britain and Zanzibar

What Started It: According to one source, "a British ship stationed near Zanzibar entered the harbor in plain sight of Khalid Ben Bargash, the Sultan of Zanzibar. The crew wanted to watch a cricket match on shore." The Sultan, incensed that they hadn't asked his permission, declared war on Britain.

Outcome: The shortest war in history. The Brits sank the sultan's only ship, an old steamer, and destroyed his palace, in 37 minutes.

A well-known jail was once located on Clink Street, in London. That's why jails are called "clinks."

THEY WENT THAT-A-WAY

Malcolm Forbes wrote a fascinating book about the deaths of famous people. Here are a few of the stories he found.

JOHN JACOB ASTOR IV

Claim to Fame: Heir to an enormous fur-trading and real estate fortune. He was one of the wealthiest men in the U.S. in the early 1900s.

How He Died: On the Titanic.

Postmortem: One measure of Astor's social stature was the way he learned the *Titanic* was doomed—the captain warned him privately *before* he sounded the general alarm. According to the accounts of several *Titanic* survivors, Astor and his wife waited until the last lifeboat was loading, then Madeline climbed aboard. When it appeared there would be enough room for him, Astor climbed in and joined her. But just as the boat was about to be lowered into the water, some women appeared on deck. Astor gave up his seat, telling his wife, "the ladies have to go first." He then lit a cigarette and said to his wife, "Good-bye dearie. I'll see you later."

Astor's body was found floating in the ocean 10 days later, his pockets filled with more than $2,500 in cash.

GEORGE WASHINGTON

Claim to Fame: First President of the United States.

How He Died: Bled to death by doctors who were treating him for a cold.

Postmortem: On December 12, 1799, Washington, 67, went horseback riding for five hours in a snowstorm. When he returned home he ate dinner without changing his clothes and went to bed. Not surprisingly, he woke up feeling hoarse and complaining of a sore throat. But he refused to take any medicine. "You know I never take anything for a cold," he told an assistant. "Let it go as it came."

Washington felt even worse the next day. He allowed the estate supervisor at Mount Vernon (a skilled veterinarian, he was the best person on hand for the job) to bleed him. In those days people thought the best way to treat an illness was by removing the "dirty" blood that supposedly contained whatever was making the patient sick. In reality, it only weakened the patient, making it harder to fight off the original illness.

That didn't work, so three doctors were called. First, they dehydrated Washington by administering laxatives and emetics (chemicals that induce vomiting). Then they bled the former president three more times. In all, the veterinarian and the doctors drained 32 ounces of Washington's blood, weakening him severely. He died a few hours later while taking his own pulse.

BABE RUTH

Claim to Fame: One of the greatest baseball players who ever lived.

How He Died: Cancer of the nose and throat.

Postmortem: When Ruth fell ill in 1946, "his condition became a matter of nationwide concern, exceeding that usually accorded to the country's most important public officials, industrialists and princes of the church," wrote the *New York Times*. By the time of his last ceremonial trip to Yankee Stadium on June 13, 1948, Ruth was so weak that he had to use a baseball bat for a cane.

The Bambino knew he was sick, but no one ever told him what he was suffering from. One afternoon he paused while entering New York's Memorial Hospital and said to his nurse, "Hey, isn't this a hospital for *cancer?*" "Cancer and *allied diseases*," his quick-thinking nurse replied, apparently leaving Ruth none the wiser.

As Ruth got closer to death, Hollywood quickly threw together *The Babe Ruth Story*, a low-budget movie about his life, starring William Bendix (who was so inept an athlete that he had to be coached on how to hold a baseball bat). The Babe managed to live long enough to see it...but apparently, he didn't approve. In the last public gesture of his life, he walked out in the middle of the film. Ruth never left the hospital again, and died on Aug. 16, 1948.

"Death is Nature's expert advice to get plenty of Life."

—Johann von Goethe

Dream on: The odds of the average golfer making a hole-in-one are 33,676-to-1.

LIFE IMITATES ART

When Wag the Dog *came out in 1997, Uncle John was reminded of a few other examples of films that seemed to predict a real-life event. Is it just coincidence...or are people in Hollywood psychic?*

ON THE SCREEN: *The China Syndrome*, a 1979 film about a near-meltdown at a nuclear power plant. The "China syndrome" refers to the potential of nuclear materials to melt "all the way to China" when a reactor goes bad. The film spurred debate between anti- and pro-nuke forces. One pro-nuke executive for Southern California Edison told reporters, "[The movie] has no scientific credibility, and is in fact ridiculous."

IN REAL LIFE: *The China Syndrome* opened on March 16, 1979. Twelve days later, the nuclear plant on Three Mile Island near Harrisburg, Pennsylvania, reported a partial core meltdown. The incident was so similar to the movie's plot that its executive producer feared "someone had seen the picture and sabotaged the plant." Costar Jack Lemmon said incredulously: "Every goddamned thing we had in there came true."

ON THE SCREEN: *The Godfather*, the 1972 film adaptation of Mario Puzo's novel about the Mafia. The Oscar-winner featured Marlon Brando as the crime boss known as "the Godfather."

IN REAL LIFE: People assumed "Godfather" was a word the mob really used. Actually, according to Puzo, "The term 'godfather' was one I invented...nobody ever used the term 'godfather' in reference to criminals, not even the Mafia." Nonetheless, it immediately began showing up in news stories, and is reportedly now even used in the crime world.

ON THE SCREEN: *Wag the Dog*, a political satire starring Dustin Hoffman and Robert De Niro, about political spin doctoring and an administration that "orchestrates a war with Albania to divert attention from a president caught with his pants down."

IN REAL LIFE: Released in late 1997, the film seemed eerily prophetic when the Clinton-Lewinsky scandal broke in January 1998—only a few weeks later. Soon after the scandal hit the headlines, the

U.S. was threatening air strikes against Iraqi leader Saddam Hussein for breaking a United Nations treaty. "It's surreal," said Hoffman. "It's the first time I've ever felt so clearly that the actual news is like a movie."

ON THE SCREEN: *Back to the Future Part II*. Marty McFly's (Michael J. Fox) nemesis, Biff Tannen, brings a copy of *Gray's Sports Almanac* back from the future to his younger self and tells him to use the book to bet on sporting events. Biff, skeptical, looks through it and comes across an unlikely entry. "Florida's going to win the world series in 1997," he reads. "Yeah, right." At the time there wasn't even a major league baseball team in Florida.
IN REAL LIFE: By 1997, Florida *did* have a baseball team—the Florida Marlins. And amazingly, they did win the World Series in 1997.

ON THE SCREEN: *The Chase*, an action film spoof starring Charlie Sheen as a wrongly convicted guy whose pursuit by cop cars is captured live on TV. It was released in March 1994.
IN REAL LIFE: A couple of months later, the world watched as O.J. Simpson sped along the freeway with police cars and news helicopters close behind. About 75 million people tuned in to the live chase. The film's writer/director, Adam Rifkin, told reporters: "People called and said it was just like my movie. I told them, 'No, no, my movie is just like *this*.' It's a perfect case of art imitating life imitating art."

ON THE SCREEN: *2001: A Space Odyssey*, a 1968 science-fiction film written by Arthur C. Clarke. In one scene, HAL, the talking computer, informs NASA of a malfunction with, "Houston, we've got a problem."
IN REAL LIFE: Just before the explosion that ended the Apollo 13 mission, as the crew played *2001*'s theme song (*Thus Spake Zarathustra)*, Captain Jack Swigert radioed to Mission Control, "Houston, we've got a problem." Later, NASA Administrator Tom Paine sent Clarke a copy of a report, and noted under Swigert's words: "Just as you always said it would be, Arthur." Clarke writes: "I still get a very strange feeling when I contemplate this whole series of events—almost, indeed, as if I share a certain responsibility."

Most unusual perspiration: Hippopotamuses exude red sweat when hot, excited, or in pain.

LOST NAMES

When something's named after someone, we automatically assume it's an honor, and they're proud of it. But not always. Here are three examples of people who felt they'd lost their names...and wanted them back.

OLDSMOBILE

Named After: Ransom Eli Olds

How He Got It: In 1897, Olds formed a car company called the Olds MotorWorks in Lansing, Michigan. He didn't have enough money to go into production, so he gave Samuel L. Smith 95% of the Olds stock in exchange for working capital. In 1899, their factory burned down; the only thing left was one little buggy with a one-cylinder engine and a curved dashboard, called the "Oldsmobile." They concentrated all efforts on this model. It took off and became the first car in the world to be mass-produced.

How He Lost It: In the early 1900s, the "Merry Oldsmobile" was America's best-selling car. But Smith wanted to drop it to start producing a larger, heavier family car. When Olds angrily left the company to form the R.E. Olds Co., Smith sued for infringement, and won—Olds was never again allowed to use his own name in business. (He changed his company name to REO.)

SEATTLE, WASHINGTON

Named After: Chief Sealth

How He Got It: In the 1850s, Chief Sealth, a Suquamish Indian, was friendly to white settlers (who called him Seattle)—at least at first. The chief and his tribe traded flour and sugar to the whites for metal, cloth, guns and tobacco. To make trading easier, Seatlh encouraged Dr. David Maynard to open a store at the little settlement of Duwanmps. Maynard, in turn, suggested changing the name of the town to Seattle in honor of the friendly Indian chief.

How He Lost It: From Sealth's point of view this wasn't a compliment—it was an attack. It violated a tribal custom that forbade naming a place after a person who was still alive because it would offend his guardian spirit. When the townspeople refused to change the name, Sealth asked the residents for gifts to repay him for problems that using his name would cause him in the next life. They refused that, too.

Ultimately, the Suquamish tribe was exiled from their homeland and driven onto the Port Madison Indian Reservation. Tourists can visit Chief Sealth's grave today on Bainbridge Island where the inscription on his tombstone, *I.H.S.*—Latin for "in this spirit"—was interpreted by his Indian kinsmen to stand for "I have suffered."

FAMOUS AMOS COOKIES

Named After: Wally Amos

How He Got It: Amos was a talent agent at the William Morris Agency who used home-baked chocolate chip cookies as a calling card (he found it put producers and executives at ease and in a good mood for negotiations). After awhile, some of his famous clients began encouraging him to sell the cookies. They even invested in the Famous Amos Cookie Company, which he started in 1975—making him one of the pioneers of the gourmet cookie trend. Sales at Famous Amos hit $12 million by 1982.

How He Lost It: His cookies were a success, but he was no manager, and his company started losing money. Amos had to bring in new money; from 1985 to 1988 he went through four different co-owners. Each time a change was made, Amos gave up more of his share of the pie. By the time the Shanby Group bought it in 1988, Amos had nothing left; he even signed away his trademark rights. In 1992, when he started a new company called "Wally Amos Presents: Chip and Cookie," the Famous Amos Corp. sued him for infringement and libel.

After an acrimonious dispute, Wally Amos agreed not to use his own name or a caricature of himself on his cookies and not to badmouth the company that owns his name. Wally Amos then moved to Hawaii and started another cookie company called the "Uncle Noname Cookie Co."

* * *

"Names are not always what they seem. The common Welsh name Bzjxxllwcp is pronounced Jackson."

Julia Ward Howe sold her "Battle Hymn of the Republic" to the *Atlantic Monthly* for $4.

THE POPCORN CHRONICLES

Whenever people at the BRI crave junk food, we pop a bunch of popcorn. As we were munching away the other day, Uncle John asked if anyone knew why popcorn popped, or where it came from. That sent us scrambling for a few answers. Here's what we found.

BACKGROUND

There are five strains of corn on the family tree: sweet, dent, flint, pod, and popcorn. The first four are essential to world nutrition; 23% of all arable land in the world is used to grow corn. Their country cousin, popcorn, is grown on less than half of 1% of those acres. It's less productive—the kernels and ears are smaller—but it's the only one that pops.

What makes it pop? The popcorn kernel has a hard shell. When it dries, microscopic droplets of water are sealed inside. If a kernel is heated above 212°F, the water inside boils and turns to steam, creating internal pressure. When the pressure reaches about 135-165 pounds per square inch, the kernel explodes, or pops. It literally turns inside out as the soft white interior bursts out.

EARLY HISTORY

• Popcorn is native to the Americas. Corn cobs dating back to 5,600 B.C. have been found in excavations in a bat cave in New Mexico.

• Native Americans believed that a tiny demon lived in each kernel. When the demon's house was heated, the demon became so angry that it exploded. (Another version: the demon *escaped* in the explosion).

• Popcorn was introduced to European settlers at the first Thanskgiving in 1621. Chief Massasoit's brother, Quadequinea, arrived with a deerskin sack of popcorn. It was part of the feast, but the next morning some was leftover—so the Pilgrims ate it with milk and sugar for breakfast. They had no way of knowing they had just eaten the first puffed breakfast cereal.

• Settlers learned about popcorn from each other and from local Native American tribes. For 250 years, it remained a homegrown treat—not a national phenomenon. Farmers planted a few rows of popcorn for their children or to share with their neighbors. At first, they called it *popped corn*, *parching corn*, or *rice corn*. Finally, around 1820, it became *popcorn*.

THE POPCORN BOOM

It wasn't until the 1880s that popcorn moved from the family kitchen to the public market. In 1885, C. Cretors and Company of Chicago patented a popcorn machine. Soon street vendors were selling bags of popcorn all over the country.

In 1893, Chicago celebrated its 100th birthday with a world's fair, the Columbian Exposition. The firm of F.W. Rueckheim and Brother opened several booths at the fair, selling a new treat made of caramelized popcorn and peanuts. When the fair closed, Rueckheim decided to package and sell it on the national market. He called it Cracker Jack—contemporary slang for something first rate. "Before long," says food historian John Mariani, "Cracker Jack was a staple at baseball games throughout America."

Over the next 20 years, a number of other innovations kept popcorn interesting for vendors and consumers. For example:

• In 1914, an Iowa farmer developed a new strain of popcorn that left only about 2% of the kernels unpopped (until then, as much as 30% of the kernels were duds). The more efficient popcorn made it possible for vendors to keep selling bags at 1-5¢ each—and still turn a profit.

• In 1918, a company named Butter-Kist added a new twist—and a lot more calories. Their popcorn machines squirted melted butter on the popcorn after it was popped.

But the two innovations that really established popcorn in American culture were the movies...and the microwave.

AT THE MOVIES

Today, popcorn is synonymous with moviegoing. But for a while, theater owners resisted the idea.

In the early 1920s, during the reign of silent films, street vendors would park their popcorn machines outside theaters, and movie patrons would buy a bag or two before entering. At first, owners objected because they had to clean up the mess. Some even refused to let customers bring popcorn into their theaters. But disgruntled movie buffs simply walked to another theater with less rigid standards.

The lesson wasn't lost on an enterprising popcorn entrepreneur in Chicago. He developed a commercial popper, and convinced several theater owners that they could make a profit by installing it in their lobbies. The profits would more than pay for the cost of cleaning up the mess.

Saving Hollywood

He was right, of course. In fact, some historians credit popcorn with *saving* the movie industry during the Great Depression. Money was so tight that theaters had to resort to gimmicks to attract customers—like "dish nights" (free dishes) and "ladies nights" (girlfriends or wives got in free), etc. This cut into profits so deeply that without the extra revenue from popcorn stands, many theaters would have closed.

To a lesser degree, the same conditions prevail today. About $3 of every $4 the customer pays for a movie ticket goes to the distributor (although there's a sliding scale; if the movie is popular enough to have an extended run, the percentage to the distributor is reduced). Often, the difference between a profit or loss for the theater is the sales of food. Popcorn accounts for 35% of all sales at the "refreshment" stand.

THE POPCORN HERO

Popcorn was still a long way from being an international agribusiness in 1941 when a 34-year-old, Purdue-educated agronomist named Orville Redenbacher decided to make popcorn his life's work. His axiom was: "Learn one thing, but know it better than anyone else."

The self-proclaimed "King of Popcorn" began a series of crossbreeding experiments to increase fluffiness. Up to that time, the popped grain was 15 to 20 times the size of the uncooked kernel. Redenbacher's new strains of popcorn doubled that. They had a volume of 40 times the original kernel.

For the next three decades, Redenbacher continued his pursuit of the perfect popcorn kernel. At least five new strains were developed and tested. Finally, in 1960, he announced his ultimate discovery—a new strain he labelled Gourmet Popcorn.

Redenbacher tried to sell it to large food companies, but no one was interested. Finally, he decided to market it himself. He planned to call it *Redbow*, a combination of his and his partner's (Bowman) names. But a consulting firm insisted that he use his own name and photo instead.

Orville Redenbacher Gourmet Popcorn was first sold at the Marshall Fields Department Store in Chicago. Five years later, it was the leading brand in the U.S.—and popcorn had been reborn as a sophisticated snack.

Redenbacher was so closely identified with popcorn that, when his company was sold to the giant Hunt-Weston conglomerate, they kept his name on the package.

MEANWHILE...

From 1980 to 1990, two consumer products combined to double America's popcorn consumption: the microwave oven and the VCR. People were starting to watch movies at home. When Pillsbury invented microwave popcorn in 1982, it was suddenly simple to make popcorn part of the experience.

A year later, Redenbacher developed the first "shelf-stable" microwave popcorn. "Pillsbury came out with the first microwave popcorn," he explained, "but it had to be refrigerated to preserve the fat and everything that's in there to pop it with. 'Shelf-stable' meant we could put it on the shelf for a minimum of seven months [without spoiling]." This shifted popcorn consumption back to where it all started—the home. Today about 90% of retail popcorn sales are microwave popcorn.

POPCORN TRIVIA

- Americans today eat 17.3 billion quarts of popcorn a year. The average American eats about 68 quarts.
- About 70% of all popcorn is prepared and eaten in the home. Most of the remaining 30% is sold at the movies, sports events, etc.
- A popped kernel will form either a "snowflake" shape (popped big

and shaped like an unruly cloud) or "mushroom" shape (popped into a ball).

• Newly harvested popcorn is better than old corn—the water content is higher, which means more of the kernels will pop. One way to preserve moisture content: keep popcorn in the refrigerator, in an airtight container.

Nutrition

• According to *The Almanac of Food*, four cups of air-popped, plain popcorn have only 92 calories, with 1 gram of fat. If oil is used, the calorie and fat content more than doubles.

• Nutritional content: 71% starch and other carbohydrates, 10.5% protein, 3% fat, a sprinkling of vitamins and minerals, and up to 14% water.

Popcorn Weirdness

• Orlando, Florida created the world's largest box of popcorn on December 17, 1988. A square box, measuring 25 feet on each side, was built at Jones High School. Thousands of citizens showed up, with popcorn and poppers. When the signal was given, the poppers were turned on. Volunteers dumped the popcorn into the box. When the day ended, the box was filled to an average depth of 6.06 feet, and ended up in the *Guinness Book of World Records*.

• Marion, Ohio is the Popcorn Capital of the U. S. Every year, a quarter of a million visitors show up for their three-day Popcorn Festival. There are the usual beauty pageants, popcorn sculptures, popcorn foods, and guided tours of the popcorn museum, which features displays of antique corn poppers dating back to 1892.

And...

• The Aztecs threw ears of popcorn into the fire, then collected the popped grains. Or, if time permitted, they heated stones in the fire, then spread a layer of popcorn on the flat surface.

• Corn is the most hybridized of any major plant in the world. It can grow in more places than any other plant—from the polar regions to the hottest rain forest.

• More popcorn is eaten in the fall than any other time of year.

Yikes! The Pentagon spends $8,612 per second; about $271.6 billion a year.

FOR YOUR READING PLEASURE...

Recently, we stumbled on Bizarre Books, *a collection of weird-but-true book titles, compiled by Russell Ash and Brian Lake. Hard to believe, but these titles were chosen and published in all seriousness. How would you like to spend your time reading...*

Why People Move, edited by Jorge Balan (1981)

Oh Angry Sea (a-ab-ba, hu-luh-ha): the History of a Sumerian Congregational Lament, by Raphael Kutscher (1975)

Animals as Criminals, by J. Brand (1896)

A Pictorial Book of Tongue Coating, Anonymous (1981)

The Dentist in Art, by Jens Jorgen Pindborg and L. Marvitz (1961)

How to Get Fat, by Edward Smith (1865)

A Frog's Blimp, by Shinta Cho (1981)

The Fangs of Suet Pudding, by Adams Farr (1944)

How to Cook Husbands, by Elizabeth Stong Worthington (1899)

Cold Meat and How to Disguise It, by Ms. M.E. Rattray (1904)

How to Boil Water in a Paper Bag, Anonymous (1891)

Sex Life of the Foot and Shoe, by William Rossi (1977)

How to Be Happy Though Married, by E. J. Hardy (1885)

Let's Make Some Undies, by Marion Hall (1954)

Be Bold With Bananas, by Australian Banana Growers Council

One Hundred and Forty-one Ways of Spelling Birmingham, by William Hamper (1880)

Children Are Wet Cement, by Ann Orlund (1981)

Scouts in Bondage, by Geoffrey Prout (1930)

Do Snakes Have Legs? by Bert Cunningham (1934)

Let Me Hold It Till I Die, by H. Lovegrove (1864)

Life and Laughter 'midst the Cannibals, by Clifford Whiteley Collison (1926)

Unmentionable Cuisine, by Calvin W. Schwabe (1979)

Nasal Maintenance: Nursing Your Nose Through Troubled Times, by William Alan Stuart (1983)

Old Age: Its Cause and Prevention, by Sanford Bennett (1912)

According to astronautical footnotes, the moon smells a little like exploded firecrackers.

LUCKY FINDS

Ever find something valuable? It's a great feeling. Here's a look at some people who found some valuable stuff and got to keep it! You should be so lucky...

HOLY GRAIL

The Find: A first edition copy of a book called *Tamerlane.*

Where it was Found: In a New Hampshire antique shop.

The Story: In the winter of 1988, an antique dealer named Robert Webber paid $500 for a large collection of musty old books at another dealer's estate auction.

One of the books was titled *Tamerlane and Other Poems*, and was dated 1827. "It was an awful looking thing," Webber recalled. The slim brown book had a ring stain from a drinking glass. Its edges were faded and the printing was poor. Even if the book had been new, it wouldn't have looked pretty. "By a Bostonian" was all it said about the author.

Webber put a price tag of $18 on it. "My wife wanted to keep it and read it," he said. "But I said, 'What do you want that dirty old thing for?'" It sat there for a few days in his antique bar, with a pile of pamphlets on fertilizer and farm machinery. A man came into the store, saw the book and the $18 price tag, and offered $15 for it. Sold.

The customer was either really cheap or just slow to realize what he'd bought. *Tamerlane* is nicknamed "the black tulip" by book collectors because it is the rarest and most valuable book in American literature. "A Bostonian" was Edgar Allen Poe and *Tamerlane* was his first book of poetry, a self-published failure. Eventually, the man who bought the book (his identity is secret) notified Sotheby's of his find; they picked it up in an armored truck and later auctioned it for $198,000.

WAGGA WAGGA TREASURE

The Find: An etching of a river scene.

Where It was Found: On a pig breeding trophy at Charles Stuart University in Southeastern Australia.

The Story: In the 1950s, the Wagga Wagga Agricultural College created the Brighton Trophy to be awarded to the "five highest-producing sows of one sire." Someone in town donated the etching to serve as the centerpiece of the trophy.

When the college was taken over by Charles Stuart University in 1989, administrators put the trophy on top of a filing cabinet and forgot about it. It sat there, gathering dust, for almost a decade. Then someone decided to include it in a local exhibit of Wagga Wagga memorabilia. When the show was over, they sent it directly to Charles Stuart University. The university's art curator happened to walk past it...and recognized it as an original work of the French impressionist Auguste Renoir. Estimated value: $25,000.

MISSING LINK

The Find: A flat, jagged rock about the size of a quarter.

Where It Was Found: On a camping trip, in Rio Puerco, New Mexico.

The Story: In 1995, the Shiffler family was returning from a camping trip when they decided to stop and explore the desert. With a toy shovel in his hand, David, the three-year-old son, began digging for dinosaur eggs. He had just seen *The Land Before Time*, a cartoon about dinosaurs, and according to his father, "everything he picked up that day was a dinosaur egg." One rock attracted him more than any other. He insisted they take it home.

The Shifflers put the rock on a shelf in the garage. It was just a jagged fragment of some kind, but David insisted it was a dinosaur egg, and his father decided to humor him. He took it to scientists at the New Mexico Museum of Natural History and Science and asked them to look at it.

To his shock, they told him it *is* a dinosaur egg (a fragment of one)—and not just any dinosaur egg, either. It is believed that a meat-eating dinosaur laid it 150 million years ago—which makes it 80 million years older than any other egg like it ever found in North America. David Shiffler's egg may force scientists to revise many of their theories about dinosaurs in the Jurassic period. David's reaction: "I knew it was an egg," he announced.

MYTH AMERICA

Here are a few more patriotic stories we all learned when we were young...all of which are 100% baloney. The information is from Bill Bryson's book, Made in America.

THE MYTH: Representatives from the 13 colonies met in Philadelphia in 1787 and drafted the U.S. Constitution.

THE TRUTH: Rhode Island and Vermont didn't send delegates, and Maryland almost didn't, because officials there had a hard time finding anyone who wanted to go. The first five people who were asked refused, and the state was still looking for people to send when the convention opened for business. New Hampshire was willing to send two delegates, but it refused to pay their expenses, and went for weeks without any representation at the convention. "Many delegates attended only fitfully, and six never came at all," Bryson writes. "Altogether only about thirty of the sixty-one elected delegates attended from start to finish."

THE MYTH: The framers of the U.S. Constitution saw it for the great document that it was.

THE TRUTH: A lot of the delegates at the Constitutional Convention hated it. So many compromises had to be made in order secure agreement that many participants viewed it, as Alexander Hamilton put it, "a weak and worthless fabric." Fifteen delegates refused to sign it, and even the Constitution's biggest supporters saw it as little more than a stopgap measure—after a few years passed, new delegates could meet at another convention and try to pass something better.

THE MYTH: The founding fathers believed in democracy.

THE TRUTH: "The Founding Fathers, that is, the men who framed the Constitution, disagreed about many things," writes Paul Boller in *Not So!*, "but on one point they were in complete agreement: that democracy meant mob rule and if unchecked, it would pose a grave threat to life, liberty and property....There was nothing

The term "karaoke" means "empty orchestra" in Japanese.

unusual in the Founding Fathers' distrust of democracy; it was conventional wisdom in the 18th century. Even well into the 19th century, in the United States as well as Western Europe, the word 'democracy' had an unsavory connotation, especially among conservatives."

THE MYTH: The United States came very close to making German the official language of the country.

THE TRUTH: For some reason, history books occasionally report that German missed being designated our language by *one vote* at the Continental Congress. The reason they give: Colonists wanted to put as much distance between themselves and England as possible. Actually, dumping English was never considered—in fact, it's an absurd notion. By 1790, 90% of the white population of the U.S. was of English descent. "The only known occasion on which German was ever an issue was in 1795," Bryson writes, "when the House of Representatives briefly considered a proposal to publish federal laws in German as well as in English as a convenience to recent immigrants, and the proposal was defeated."

THE MYTH: Samuel Morse invented the telegraph in 1844.

BACKGROUND: That was the version that Morse liked to tell.

THE TRUTH: Morse did invent Morse Code, but the telegraph itself was invented in 1831 by a Princeton University professor named Joseph Henry, who never bothered to patent it. Morse's telegraph was based largely on Henry's design. Morse "not only stole lavishly from Henry's original papers," Bryson writes, "but when stuck would call on the eminent scientist for guidance. For years, Henry encouraged and assisted his efforts. Yet later, when Morse had grown immensely famous and rich, he refused to acknowledge even the slightest degree of debt to his mentor."

THE MYTH: The first message sent by Morse Code was, "What hath God wrought?"

THE TRUTH: Morse's first message was, "Everything worked well." It wasn't until a later public demonstration that the message, "What hath God wrought?" was sent. Morse didn't even choose the words: the daughter of the Commissioner of Patents did that.

Typical life span of a cow: 30 years.

FAMILIAR PHRASES

Here are more origins of everyday phrases.

KIT AND CABOODLE

Meaning: All of something; the whole thing.

Origin: "The Dutch word *boedel* means 'effects'—what a person owns. Robbers, especially housebreakers, adopted the term—calling whatever they stole 'boodle.' They carried their burglar's tools in a 'kit.' If they were able to enter a house, gather up everything valuable, and make a clean escape, they said they had gotten away with 'kit and boodle.' In time, the phrase was shortened to 'caboodle'—the 'ca' standing for the 'kit.' The 'kit' was reintroduced into the phrase—probably for emphasis." (From *Why Do We Say It*, by Webb Garrison)

GUINEA PIG

Meaning: The subject of an experiment; the first person to try something untested.

Origin: "This small South American rodent first came to Europe in the 17th century and was either misnamed 'guinea' (Guinea being in West Africa) for Guiana (in South America) or it was named for the Guineamen, slave traders who took blacks from Guinea to the West Indies and then conveyed a variety of goods from the Indies and North America to Britain.

"In the 19th century 'guinea pig' became British slang for a person of standing who allowed his name to be put on a company's roster of directors for a fee paid in guineas, but who was not active in the company." In the 20th century, guinea pigs "came to be widely used in scientific and medical experiments—leading to the transfer of the name to the subject of any kind of experiment." (From *It's Raining Cats and Dogs*, by Christine Ammer)

(TO GIVE—OR GET) THE THIRD DEGREE

Meaning: An intense and sometimes brutal grilling to get information from someone.

Origin: "The term 'third degree' has no connection with criminality or brutal treatment....It refers to the third and final stage of proficiency demanded of one who seeks to become a master Mason...

Before the candidate is fully qualified for the third degree he must undergo a very elaborate and severe test of ability. It is from this examination that 'third degree' became applied to the treatment of prisoners by the police, and it was through the fact that the police sometimes did employ brutality in efforts to extort confession or information that our present expression obtained its common modern meaning." (From *Heavens to Betsy!*, by Charles Earle Funk)

A SPINSTER

Meaning: An older, unmarried woman.

Origin: "Until spinning was mechanized in the late eighteenth century, turning wool or flax into yarn or thread was almost always 'woman's work.' A spinster was a woman spinner—often a professional; in the seventeenth century, it came to mean an unmarried woman—presumably because, having neither husband nor children, she could devote herself full-time to her spinning." (From *The Book of Lost Metaphors*)

TO BLACKMAIL SOMEONE

Meaning: To extort money from someone.

Origin: "Blackmail has nothing whatever to do with the post office. Black is used in the figurative sense of 'evil' or 'wicked.' Mail is a Scots word meaning 'rent' or 'tribute.' The term 'blackmail' originated in Scotland, where Highland chiefs at one time extorted tribute from Lowlanders and Englishmen on the Scottish border in return for protection from being plundered." (From *Word Mysteries & Histories*, by the Editors of the American Heritage Dictionaries)

THE GRAVEYARD SHIFT

Meaning: A night shift for workers.

Origin: It wasn't coined by morticians, but by shipbuilders. "The name originated during World War I, when for the first time shipbuilders and munitions workers found it necessary to work 'round the clock in order to produce enough for the war effort. It is still used today for any shift covering the midnight and early morning hours." (From *Fighting Words*, by Christine Ammer)

COURT TRANSQUIPS

Here's more real-life courtroom dialogue.

Q: "Do you remember what shoes you were wearing?"
A: "You mean the day I fell down?"
Q: "Yes."
A: "The same shoes I'm wearing."
Q: "What do you call those shoes? Are they flats...or how would you describe them?"
A: "I'd describe them as 'these shoes.'"

Q: "Please review this document. Do you know what a fax is?"
A: "Yeah, I do, man. It's when you tell the truth, man, tell it like it is. That is what the facts is."

Q: "What is the relationship?"
A: "She's my aunt."
Q: "Who's brother or sister to whom here?"
A: My mother is his brother—is her—my mother is—what is it? By marriage, I guess you would say. My mother is her brother—is his brother by marriage, so she's just an aunt."

A: "You know, I don't know, but I mean, you know—you don't know but you know. You know what I'm saying?"
Q: "Do I? No. Do I know? No."

Q: "You assumed narcotics in reaching your opinions."
A: "Yes."
Q: "You didn't assume a Frito or a Chee-to or a banana. You assumed narcotics."
A: "It was a narcotics raid. It wasn't a Frito raid, counselor."

Q: "So you remember who the doctor was who performed that?"
A: "Yes. Very easy name to remember, Mee."
Q: "Martin?" (The witness's name.)
A: "No, Mee."
Q: "You?"
A: "That was his name."
Q: "Me?"
A: "Mee."
Q: "M-e?"
A: "M-e-e. That was his name, Dr. Mee."

Q: "Mr. Jones, do you believe in alien forces?"
A: "You mean other than my wife?"

Q: "Were you acquainted with the decedent?"
A: "Yes, sir."
Q: "Before or after he died?"

Q: "Did he ever kill you before?"
A: "Pardon me?"

***Time* magazine's "Man of the Year" in 1938 was Adolf Hitler.**

BRAND NAMES

We all know these names—many are a part of our everyday lives. But where did they come from?

SEALY MATTRESS. In 1881, an inventor from Sealy, Texas developed a cotton-filled mattress. Word spread around the Southwest, and people began asking for the "mattress from Sealy." Eventually it became known simply as the "Sealy mattress."

SAMSONITE LUGGAGE. Named after Samson, the biblical strong man, to symbolize "strength and durability."

DORITOS. Rough translation from Spanish: "little bit of gold."

SANYO. Means "three oceans" in Japanese. Toshio Iue, who founded the company in 1947, planned to sell worldwide—across the Atlantic, Pacific, and Indian Oceans.

HUSH PUPPIES. At a dinner in 1957, Jim Muir, sales manager for Wolverine World Wide, Inc., was served tiny fried balls of corn dough known in the South as "hush puppies." When he wondered about the name, his host explained that local farmers used the food to quiet barking dogs. Muir decided it was a perfect name for a new pigskin shoe his company was developing. The reason: the shoe "could soothe a customer's aching feet, a.k.a. their 'barking dogs.'"

AMANA. In 1854, a German religious sect moved to Iowa and founded the Amana Colonies. Nearly a century later (1932) George Foerstner, a member of the group, started a business making freezers. It was run by the Amana community under their own brand name until 1943, when they sold it to back Foerstner. He kept the name.

MINOLTA. A loose acronym for **M**achinery and **IN**struments **O**ptica**L** by Kazuo **TA**shima (founder of the Japanese-German Camera Company). The first Minolta-brand camera was introduced in 1932.

Demographers say New Jersey has the lowest suicide rate of any state...but they don't say why.

CHEESE GEOGRAPHY

This started out as a "How did the cheeses get their names?" page. Then we found out that most of the cheeses we're interested in are named for the places they were first made. So here's what we wound up with, for you cheeseheads.

BRIE. In 1815, following the Napoleonic Wars, diplomats at the Congress of Vienna were served Brie; they enjoyed it so much they pronounced it the King of Cheeses. Birthplace: a northeastern region of France known as (surprise) Brie.

PARMESAN. A hard, well-aged cheese named after the Italian city of Parma (where it is called *parmigiano*).

COLBY. A granular cheese first made in Colby, Wisconsin at the end of the 19th century.

CAMEMBERT. Originated in the village of Camembert in France's Normandy region. To test the ripeness of Camembert, touch your eye with one finger and the cheese with another. If they feel the same, the cheese is ripe.

LIMBURGER. Created by Trappist monks in the Belgian town of Limburg.

CHEDDAR. The world's most popular cheese. Gets its name from the village of Cheddar in Somerset, England, where it was first produced in the 16th century.

GOUDA. A compressed sphere of cheese named for the Dutch town of Gouda.

SWISS. In Switzerland, where it originated, they call it emmenthaler. "Swiss" is the generic term for imitations. The holes, by the way, come from pockets of natural carbon dioxide gases expanding in the cheese as it ages.

MONTEREY JACK. Created in Monterey, California by David Jacks, in the 1890s.

TILLAMOOK. American Cheddar made in Tillamook County, Oregon.

C3PO is the first character to speak in *Star Wars*.

THE ORIGIN OF THE WHITE HOUSE

The White Houseis more than just a building—it's an important national symbol—as well one of the most recognizable buildings on Earth. How much do you know about its history? Here's an introduction.

BOOM TOWN

When the founding fathers began making plans for the nation's capital city in 1789, they couldn't agree on a location. The northerners wanted a northern city to serve as the capital; the southerners wanted a southern city. Finally, they compromised: Instead of establishing the capital in an existing city, they'd create a new one from scratch. And they'd build it somewhere in the *middle* of the country, not too far north and not too far south.

On July 12, 1790, President Washington signed an Act of Congress declaring that on "the first Monday in December 1800," the federal government would move to a new Federal District "not exceeding ten miles square...on the river Potomac." Philadelphia would serve as a temporary capital until then.

LOCATION, LOCATION, LOCATION

But the act didn't say exactly *where* on the Potomac the new city should be. A lot more arguing took place before Secretary of State Thomas Jefferson and Secretary of the Treasury Alexander Hamilton finally agreed on a ten-mile by ten-mile area of farmland and swamps, a mile east of Georgetown, Maryland, and just over the Potomac from Arlington, Virginia.

Maryland and Virginia donated the land, and George Washington hired engineer Pierre L'Enfant, a friend of Jefferson, to lay out the new city. Washington also appointed three federal district commissioners to oversee the work that was done in the new capital. One of their first decisions: they named the new city "Washington." (Although, for the rest of his life, George Washington insisted on calling the city the "Federal District.")

AD HOC

Since the idea of a president was so new—most European countries were still ruled by royalty—nobody really knew what a president's house should look like. So in 1792, Thomas Jefferson took out a newspaper ad offering $500 to the architect who came up with the best design for a president's house, with George Washington making the final decision. Newspaper contests were an unusual way to solicit architectural designs even in the 1790s, but Jefferson figured it was the only way to guarantee that the architect would be chosen based on the merits of his design and not on favoritism or connections. Jefferson probably came to regret the newspaper contest idea, because he entered his own plans in the contest under the pseudonym "Mr. AZ" and lost.

TEMPORARY HOUSING

George Washington admired the work of architect James Hoban, an Irish immigrant who had designed the State Capitol of South Carolina. Washington encouraged Hoban to enter the contest...and then decided in his favor.

Hoban's design called for a three-story mansion and, as asked, included plans for wings that could be added on later when the time came. (They were never built.) He set the dimensions of the presidential palace at 170 feet long, 85 feet deep, and three stories high. Washington thought Hoban's building was beautiful, but he also complained that it was too small. He suggested increasing its size by about 20%. Since that would have cost a fortune, the suggestion was politely ignored.

HOUSE PAYMENTS

Hoban estimated that the president's house would cost about $400,000 to build. But no one knew how to pay for it. George Washington thought he could raise the funds through the sale of building lots in the Federal District. But building an entire city from the ground up, in the middle of farmlands and swamps, for a republic barely ten years old, seemed such an impossible undertaking that many people doubted whether the city would ever really be built. In fact, the new city was the laughing stock of New York and Philadelphia; the state of Pennsylvania had even begun building its own permanent federal buildings in the expectation that Washington, D.C. would eventually be abandoned.

In the face of such skepticism, the few District of Columbia lots that sold at all, sold at much lower prices than anticipated.

So the planners had to cut corners. The third floor of the president's house was eliminated, as were the North and South Porticoes (the large, columned overhangs that were planned for the front and rear of the building). The marble fireplaces that had been ordered were cancelled and replaced with simpler ones made of wood. The "presidential palace" was becoming less palatial.

Part II of the "Origin of the White House" is on page 159.

* * *

FRUSTRATIONS OF THE RICH & FAMOUS

"When his car broke down on a busy New York road, William Shatner (of "Star Trek" fame) stuck out his thumb and tried to hitch a ride. But no one stopped.

"'Eventually, I tried to play the celebrity card,' the actor said. 'I made this pickup truck slow down by jumping out and shouting, "*Hi, it's me, Captain Kirk!*"'

"The woman driving said, 'Yeah?' then stuck up her middle finger and went 'Well, beam *THIS* up!'

"As she sped off down the road, Shatner decided to walk."

—The Edge, Portland Oregonian

"Treasury Secretary Michael Blumenthal found himself in an embarrassing situation in Beethoven's, an expensive San Francisco restaurant in 1979. Blumenthal was confronted with a sizable dinner bill, an expired Visa card, and a waiter who wanted proof of signature to back up an out-of-town check. Blumenthal thought for a minute, and solved his predicament the only way he could: He produced a dollar bill and pointed to his own signature, W. M. Blumenthal, in the bottom right-hand corner. The signatures matched, and Blumenthal's personal check was accepted."

—*Strange Facts and Useless Information*, by Scot Morris

If your bed is typical, there are 6 million dust mites living there.

NOT FOR EXPORT

It's not easy selling things in the global economy—a lot of product names lose something in translation. These products are real...but you probably aren't going to find them at your Wal-Mart any time soon:

Strange Taste—a popular Chinese candy.

Zit!—a German "gourmet chocolate and fruit confection."

Pschit—a French soft drink, and *Mucos*, a soda sold in the Philippines.

Ass Glue—a Chinese patent medicine that is marketed as a "blood nourishing paste."

Koff—a Finnish beer sold briefly in the United States.

Shitto—a spicy pepper sauce from Ghana.

Super Piss—a Finnish solvent that unfreezes car locks.

Little Hussy—a writing tablet for little girls, sold in Taiwan.

AND FROM JAPAN...

Japanese cars displayed at a 1997 Tokyo auto show:

- Subaru Gravel Express
- Mazda Bongo Friendee
- Nissan Big Thumb Harmonized Truck
- Suzuki Every Joy Pop Turbo
- Mazda Scrum
- Mitsubishi Delica Space Gear Cruising Active
- Mazda Proceed Marvie
- Daihatsu Town Cube
- Isuzu Giga 20 Light Dump

Kowpis—a "popular fermented milk drink."

Homo Sausage—beef jerky.

Ease Your Bosoms—coffee marketed as an antidote to stress.

Pokari Sweat—a sports drink.

Green Piles—lawn fertilizer.

Hand Maid Queen Aids—Band-Aid shaped chocolates.

IRONIC, ISN'T IT?

There's nothing like a good dose of irony to put the problems of day-to-day life in proper perspective.

IRONIC DEATHS

• "Evan Wheeler, a veteran actress, was playing a death scene in a Baltimore production of *The Drunkard* in November, 1986, when she dropped to the stage and, to tremendous applause, died." (*Hodgepodge II*)

• "The wife of Claudius I tried to poison her husband with poisonous mushrooms in 54 A.D. Claudius' doctor tried to make him throw up by tickling his throat with a feather. Claudius choked on the feather and died." (*Oops*)

• In 1955, actor James Dean made an ad warning teens about driving too fast. ("The life you save may be mine," he said.) Shortly after, he died when his Porsche Spider, going 86 mph, hit another car.

• In 1871, attorney Clement Vallandigham was demonstrating to a jury that the man his client was accused of shooting could have accidentally done it himself. Vallandigham took out a gun, held it as it was held at the scene of the crime, and pulled the trigger. The gun was loaded; he proved his point.

MUSICAL IRONY

• The man who wrote "Home Sweet Home," John Howard Payne, "never had a permanent residence." (*The Book of Lists*)

• "The man who wrote 'Dixie,' Dan D. Emmett, was a Northerner. He was born in Ohio and wrote the song in a New York boarding house." (*The Book of Lists*)

• Joni Mitchell, who wrote "Woodstock," wasn't at the Woodstock music festival. She watched it on TV.

• The couple who wrote "Take Me Home Country Roads" had never been to West Virginia. They had only seen pictures of it on postcards a friend sent.

• The men who wrote "Take Me Out to the Ballgame," Albert von

In 1659, it was illegal to celebrate Christmas in Massachusetts.

Tilzer and Jack Norworth, had never been to a baseball game.

• "The music that played as President Bush stepped to the podium at the 1992 Republican convention in Houston—following his wife's speech on family values—was taken from the gay musical *La Cage Aux Folles*." (*Forbes*)

BITTER IRONY

• The inmates at the prison in Concord, New Hampshire, spend their days making the state's license plates, which bear the motto LIVE FREE OR DIE.

• "The memorial statue erected in Vienna to the memory of composer Franz Schubert cost more than the luckless genius earned from his work during his lifetime." (*Oops*)

• "In 1853 John Coffee built the jail in Dundalk, Ireland. He went bankrupt on the project and became the first inmate of his own jail." (*Not a Good Word About Anybody*)

• "I. N. Terrill, a member of the legislature, wrote the criminal law statutes for Oklahoma...and was the first person convicted under the law for murder." (*Ripley's Believe It or Not*)

• "Fernande Olivier lived with Picasso for seven years when she was young and poor. She was not impressed with his paintings, which included many portraits of her that she thought unflattering. In 1912 she moved out and took with her a little heart-shaped mirror as her only memento of the years with her Spanish painter. She never saw Picasso again, and died in poverty in 1966. A few years after her death, a cubist painting of her by Picasso sold for $790,000." (*Not a Good Word About Anybody*)

PRESIDENTIAL IRONY

• "Ronald Reagan was rejected for the leading role in the 1964 movie *The Best Man* because "he doesn't look presidential." (*Not a Good Word About Anybody*)

• The man known as the Father of Our Country, George Washington, may well have been sterile....He fathered no children, and according to experts, suffered from a variety of debilitating diseases, including smallpox, rotten teeth, consumption, amoebic dysentery, pleurisy, malaria, and a genetic impairment called Kleinfelter's syndrome, "which could well have rendered him sterile."

The first TV commercial: a Bulova watch ticking onscreen for exactly 60 seconds.

"MAKE MY DAY..."

Feelin' lucky, punk? Are ya? Then, go ahead... read this stuff from Clint Eastwood.

"In the complications of society as we know it today, sometimes a person who can cut through the bureaucracy and red tape is a hero."

"I don't like the idea of anybody getting killed, but especially me. I'm against war, all war."

"They say marriages are made in Heaven. So are thunder and lightning."

"I see my films as first aid to the modern male psyche. Most jobs today can be held by women. Many men have become defensive and enjoy being taken to another time, another period, where masculinity was important to survival."

"Women are superior to men. You see a lot of smart men with dumb women, but you don't see a lot of smart women with dumb guys. A lot of guys will go out with a bimbo, but women who are smart don't do that."

"The self-sufficient human being has become a mythological character in our day and age."

"I'm interested in the fact that the less secure a man is, the more likely he is 'to have extreme prejudice.' "

"There's nothing wrong with glamorizing the gun. I don't think that hurts anybody. I'm for gun legislation myself."

"It's not the bloodletting that people come to see in the movies. It's vengeance. Getting even is important to the public. They go to work every day for some guy who's rude and they can't stand, and they just have to take it. Then they go see me on the screen and I kick the s—t out of him."

"If I just wanted to go out and make some dough I could gun 'em down as good as I ever did. But I'd rather not do movies where there are 800 guys in the theater and one chick who was coerced into going by her brother."

Guinness world record: Minnie the cat killed 12,480 rats between 1927 and 1933.

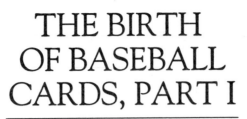

THE BIRTH OF BASEBALL CARDS, PART I

People in the U.S. have been collecting baseball cards for over 100 years. Bubblegum hadn't even been invented yet when Old Judge cigarettes gave birth to this American institution.

BACKGROUND

Baseball cards have grown from a kid's hobby to a $2 billion-a-year industry. Their history goes back to the early days of baseball.

The Duke of Tobacco. Until the 1880s, when "Buck" Duke took over the Duke Tobacco Company (later The American Tobacco Co.) from his father, most tobacco was sold loose, in tins; people would roll their own cigarettes. In 1885, Buck bought the rights to a machine that put out 200 ready-made cigarettes at a time. Now he was able to concentrate on selling cigarettes instead of tobacco. What he needed was more customers. So he began a huge ad campaign. Soon Duke had 40% of the cigarette market.

To cut costs, Duke replaced tobacco tins with paper cigarette packs. As Pete Williams recounts in *Card Sharks*:

> When he discovered that many of the packs were crushed in shipping, Duke came up with the idea of placing a cardboard insert to stiffen the pack. Not only would they prevent damage, but the "cards" would serve as advertising pieces and premiums to boost sales...He included cards of actors and actresses...[and] his idea inspired competitors to place baseball cards in their products.

The first cards were sold with Old Judge Cigarettes in 1886. They were 1-1/2" X 2-1/2"—much smaller than today—and pictured stoic-looking players wearing neckties with their uniforms. Eventually they started using "action" shots, which were actually staged photographs of players reaching for, or swinging at, balls on a string. Instead of the statistics and trivia found on the back of today's cards, these early cards had advertising.

WHY BASEBALL?

Baseball cards had three advantages for tobacco companies:
1) They capitalized on the growing popularity of the sport, which was just coming into its own; 2) The connection with sports heroes helped combat the notion that store-bought cigarettes were effeminate; and 3) They were collectible. Pete Williams notes:

> With the cards came card collecting, which presented a challenge since the cards came one to a pack. Collecting became something of a family affair, as young boys would obtain the cards from their fathers and urge them to buy more tobacco products. Non-tobacco users who wished to collect had to pick up the tobacco habit—as the companies hoped—or find a user willing to part with the cards.

THE PRECIOUS SET

Duke Tobacco got out of the baseball card business in 1890, when it combined with other tobacco companies to form American Tobacco. With a virtual monopoly on cigarettes, there was no need for promotions.

But from 1909 to 1911, anti-trust laws were used to break American Tobacco up, so the company went back to using baseball cards as a promotion. They came out with a 524-card set called the "T206"—which has turned into the most valuable baseball card series in history. According to *Card Sharks*, here's why:

> Shortly after production began, shortstop Honus Wagner of the Pittsburgh Pirates (now a Hall of Famer) objected to the use of his photo and threatened legal action if his card was not removed from the set. American Tobacco complied, but not before a quantity of Wagners had been printed and shipped with tobacco.

For a long time, baseball historians believed Wagner objected because he disapproved of cigarette-smoking. Then they found out he'd once endorsed a brand of cigars...and realized he just didn't want them using his likeness without paying for it.

Today, the few Wagner cards that slipped out have become the Holy Grail of baseball card collecting.

In 1997, one was sold at auction for $641,000!

There's more. For part II of the baseball card story, turn to page 368.

TALL IN THE SADDLE: WESTERN FILM QUOTES

Peggy Thompson and Saeko Usukawa have put together a collection of great lines from Westerns called Tall in the Saddle. *Some samples:*

Young Eddie: "He don't look so tough to me."
Cowboy: "If he ain't so tough, there's been an awful lot of sudden natural deaths in his vicinity."

—*The Gunfighter* (1950)

"I always say the law was meant to be interpreted in a lenient manner. And that's what I try to do. Sometimes I lean to one side of it, sometimes I lean to the other."

—Paul Newman, *Hud* (1963)

"Sonny, I can see we ain't going to have you 'round long enough to get tired of your company."

—Richard Widmark, *The Law and Jake Wade* (1958)

Cowboy: "For a long time I was ashamed of the way I lived."
Dance hall girl: "You mean to say you reformed?"
Cowboy: "No, I got over being ashamed."

—*Goin' to Town* (1935)

J. W. Grant: "You bastard!"
Hired gun Henry "Rico" Fardan: "Yes, sir. In my case an accident of birth. But you, you're a self-made man."

—*The Professionals* (1966)

Fletch McCloud (Roy Rogers): "Ever hear what William Shakespeare said? 'All's well that ends well.'"
Cowboy Bob Seton (John Wayne): "Shakespeare, huh? He must have come from Texas. We've been saying that for years."

—*The Dark Command* (1940)

Trampas: "When I want to know anything from you, I'll tell you, you long-legged son of a—"
"The Virginian": "If you want to call me that, smile."

—*The Virginian* (1929)

Sheriff Bullock: "How is he, Doc?"
Doc: "Well, he suffered lacerations, contusions, and a concussion. His jugular vein was severed in three places. I counted four broken ribs and a compound fracture of the skull. To put it briefly, he's real dead."

—*Rancho Notorious* (1952)

"I like my coffee strong enough to float a pistol."

—Ernest Borgnine, *Jubal* (1955)

"I don't want trouble with anybody—unless I start it."

—"Wild Bill" Elliott, *The Showdown* (1950)

Coincidence? 40% of people who move to a new address change their brand of toothpaste at the same ti

WHEN YOU GOTTA GO...

Here's the BRI's quick, all-purpose language lesson. Now, no matter where you're traveling, you'll be able to ask the essential question: "Where is the bathroom?" Are you ready? Okay, now repeat after us...

Spanish: Donde ésta el baño?

Danish: Hvor er toilette?

Japanese: Torie wa doko desu ka?

Russian: Gde zdes tualet?

Hawai`I (Hawaiian): Ai hea lua?

Tâi-oân Hö-ló-oë (Taiwanese): Piän-só. tï tó-üi?

Italian: Dove e il bagno?

Cymraeg (Welsh): Ble mae'r toiled?

Magyar (Hungarian): Hol a mosdó?

Kiswahili (Swahili): Choo kiko wapi?

Dutch: Waar is het toilet?

Bahasa (Indonesian): Kamar kecil di mana?

Afrikaans: Waar is diebad-kamer? Waar is die toilet?

Româna (Romanian): Unde este toaleta?

Bosanski (Bosnian): Gdje je toalet?

French: Ou sont les toilettes?

C^estina: Kde je záchod?

Esperanto: Kie estas la necesejo?

German: Wo ist die Toilette?

Eesti (Estonia): Kus on väljakäik?

Íslenska (Icelandic): Hvar er snyrtingin?

Interlingua: Ubi es le lavatorio?

Polski (Polish): Gdzie jest toaleta?

Tagalog: Nasaan ang kasilyas?

Yiddish: vu iz der bodtsimer?

Cymraeg (Welsh): Ble mae'r toiled?

Latviski (Latvian): Kur atrodas vannas istaba?

Lietuvis (Lithuanian): Kur yra tualetas?

Srpski (Serbian): Gde je toalet?

Ivrit (Hebrew): eifo ha'sherutim?

Surveys say: Only about 1/4 of all American adults eat 3 meals a day.

NUDES & PRUDES

It's hard to shock anyone with nudity today. But stupidity is always a shock. These characters demonstrate that whether you're dressed or naked, you can still be dumber than sin.

NUDE..."In 1831, when Edgar Allen Poe was at West Point, parade dress instructions called for 'white belts and gloves, under arms.' According to legend, Poe took them literally. He appeared on parade ground, rifle balanced on his bare shoulder, wearing nothing but white belt and gloves. He was expelled."

PRUDE..."Madama de la Bresse directed that her life savings of 125,000 francs be used to buy clothing for naked Paris snowmen. In 1876 the courts upheld the validity of her bequest, making French snowmen the best dressed in the world." (*More Best, Worst, and Most Unusual*)

NUDE..."When state police in Ogdensburg, New York, caught William J. Hess, 39, burglarizing a greenhouse, he was wearing nothing. He replied that he was naked so that anyone who saw him in the greenhouse couldn't identify him by describing his clothing." (*Dumb, Dumber, Dumbest*)

PRUDE..."The Dallas grocery chain Minyard's pulled the November 1993 issue of *Discover* magazine from its shelves because of the cover photo of a sculpture of two apes, the 3.2-million-year-old *Australopithecus afarensis*, with their genitals exposed. The apes are believed to be our earliest ancestors. 'When it shows the genitals or the breasts,' Minyard's president Jay L. Williams said, 'we're going to pull it.'" (*Dumb, Dumber, Dumbest*)

NUDE..."In Greenfield, Wisconsin, owners of the Classic Lanes bowling alley decided to jazz up their sport with a little humor. Outside their building, they posted signs reading BOWL NAKED, BOWL FREE. Obviously, no one took them up on their offer...until April 16, 1996. That's the day 21-year-old Scott Hughes strolled into the bowling alley, rented a pair of shoes, and proceeded to take off his clothes. As a local church group watched in horror, Hughes went on to bowl a 225 game—wearing nothing but a cowboy hat and bowling shoes." (*Knuckleheads in the News*)

PRUDE... Francesca Nortyega, a well-known European reformer, willed her estate to a niece on the condition that she keep the family goldfish outfitted in pants.

NUDE... In 1995, San Francisco mayor Frank Jordan, running for re-election, tried to show he was a 'regular guy' by accepting a challenge from two disc jockeys to take a nude shower with them. Photos of the shower circulated all over the city. He lost in a landslide.

PRUDE..."East German swimmer Sylvia Ester set a world 100-meters record of 57.89 seconds in 1967—but officials refused to recognize it because she swam in the nude." (*World's Biggest Mistakes*)

NUDE..."Peter Archer, 47, was arrested for running naked down a street in Melbourne, Australia, but was released when police learned he was fleeing a mortuary where a doctor had officially pronounced him dead." (Portland *Oregonian*)

PRUDE..."Three small figurines in an exhibit at Dallas City Hall happened to be nude. So the thoughtful city officials, worried that the nudity might offend some viewers, had the figurines covered with tiny, handmade fig leaves." (*The 176 Stupidest Things Ever Done*)

NUDE... Irene Wachenfeldt, a Swedish high school teacher, illustrated a lesson on loving your body by taking her clothes off in class. "My body is good enough," she said. "I want you to feel the same about your bodies." When she was forced to quit, students objected. One wrote: "It was one of our best lessons."

PRUDE... Noah Webster, well known for his dictionaries, once published a censored version of the Bible as well. "Many words are so offensive, especially for females," he explained. He changed words like *teat* to *breast*, and *stones* (testicles) to *peculiar members*. It flopped.

BEGINNINGS

Of course you've heard of all the things listed below.
But you may not have heard how they got started.

SCOTCHGARD

In 1944, a laboratory assistant at the 3M company spilled an experimental chemical on her tennis shoes. She tried to wash the stuff off, but couldn't. As the weeks passed, she noticed that the chemical-stained part of her shoe remained clean while the rest of it collected dirt and grime. 3M researchers, who had been trying to find practical uses for the chemical, realized it was ideal as a fabric protector.

THE SODA STRAW

The first straws, made of parafinned paper, were introduced in 1888 by an inventor named Marvin Stone. They didn't catch on—the hand-rolled tubes cracked easily and were unsanitary. Then in the early 1900s—not long after concessionaire Harry Stevens introduced hot dogs to New York Giant baseball games—he noticed that when fans drank from their soda bottles, they had to take their eyes off the game for a moment. So he hired a paper maker to roll some straws out of paper, and began including one with every soda he sold. It increased his sales, and made straws a permanent part of American culture. In 1905, Stone's company came up with a machine to mass-produce them.

HIGHWAY DIVIDERS

Invented by Dr. June A. Carroll of Indio, California. Carroll lived near a particularly dangerous stretch of highway, so in 1912, she painted a stripe down the middle of the road for about a mile to help drivers stay on the right side of the road. The California Highway Commission liked the idea so much that it painted stripes down the middle of every paved road in the state.

KEEP HONKING ...I'M RELOADING

BRI member Debbie Thornton sent in this list of real-life bumper stickers. Have you seen the one that says...

Horn broken.
Watch for finger

He who laughs last thinks slowest.

What has four legs and an arm?
A happy pitbull

I love cats...they taste just like chicken.

Rehab is for quitters.

No radio—already stolen.

I don't suffer from insanity, I enjoy every minute of it.

Smile. It's the second best thing you can do with your lips.

Give me ambiguity... or give me something else.

We are born naked, wet, and hungry.
Then things get worse.

Always remember you're unique, just like everyone else.

Very funny Scotty.
Now beam down my clothes.

There are three kinds of people: those who can count... and those who can't.

Keep honking...
I'm reloading.

i suuport publik edekashun.

Make it idiot-proof and someone will make a better idiot.

Puritanism: The haunting fear that someone, somewhere may be happy.

It **IS** as bad as you think, and they **ARE** out to get you.

Cover me. I'm changing lanes.

I want to die peacefully in my sleep like my grandfather, not screaming and yelling, like the passengers in his car

Where there's a will, I want to be in it.

So many lawyers, so few bullets

The Earth is .02 degrees hotter during a full moon.

THE ANIMALS AT THE ZOO, Part 1

If you've ever gone to a zoo, you probably know what it's like to stare at animals for a few hours with no idea of what you're looking at. Why do they keep growling that way? Why are they digging like that? And so forth. We can't give you a complete rundown on every animal behavior, but here are a few tips that we hope will make your next visit to the zoo more interesting.

WATCHING LIONS

Lions are very social animals. They live in groups called prides, which normally consist of about 3 to 12 females and 2 to 4 males. There is one dominant male. They depend on each other for hunting, grooming, raising young, etc. Here are some things you might see them do:

Behavior: Peeing backward, onto a tree or wall (male).
What It Means: Marking a territory. Normally, males pee in a crouch. But when they want to mark an area, they spray backward onto a vertical object—sometimes even onto people watching them. If a zoo lion backs up to you with his tail raised, watch out.

Behavior: Excessive self-grooming (male).
What It Means: Stress. Male lions normally spend a lot of time grooming their manes and paws. But when they're under a lot of stress—which happens when they don't feel comfortable with other lions or with their surroundings—they do it more frequently.

Behavior: Lying on back with legs spread out.
What It Means: It's cooling off. A lion's fur is thinnest on its stomach, so it's letting the air circulate there.

Behavior: Yawning.
What It Means: Boredom? You might think so. But actually a lion's yawn, a familiar sight at zoos, is not a commentary on its life in

Ants don't sleep.

captivity. Even wild lions are habitual yawners. Yawning is simply a biological reflex that increases the flow of oxygen to the blood. You'll see lions yawn after waking from rest or just before feeding—a sign that they are gearing up to *do* something. And, yes, yawning is just as contagious among lions as it is among people.

Behavior: Roaring.

What It Means: In the jungle, it would be a territorial statement. In the zoo, it's more likely to be a response to some sort of loud noise. Interesting sight: Watch how one lion's roar will set off the rest of them. Soon, there will be a bunch roaring at the same time. It's as contagious as yawning.

OTHER ANIMALS

BEAR—Behavior: Pacing.

What It Means: Mental stress. Zoos have come a long way from the days when animals were displayed in caged cells. Today's zookeepers rely on the latest research, and their own creativity, to keep animals in good physical and mental shape. But the sad truth is that even the best efforts do not guarantee results. Bears in captivity are particularly likely to show signs of under-stimulation, such as pacing. One way that zookeepers try to keep animals spirited is by reducing "handouts" at mealtime. The animal is encouraged to work for its food. In the case of bears, honey placed inside a log often does the trick of challenging them, keeping them in touch with wild food-gathering instincts.

CROCODILE—Behavior: Biting each other's tails.

What It Means: Are they fighting or playing? Animals play rough, so sometimes it's hard to tell whether two animals engaged in aggressive physical contact are angry or having a good time. But with crocodiles, it's no mystery: they're not getting along. Playful or friendly behavior is virtually nonexistent among crocs. Most of the day, they tolerate each other at best (though, they *will* practice cooperative hunting and feeding). The rules of their biting battles are pretty basic: lock your opponent's tail in your jaw, and you win.

For more of "The Animals At The Zoo," see page 257.

Got gas? 40% of all the indigestion remedies sold in the world are bought by Americans.

THE TOP 10 HITS OF THE YEAR, 1960–1963

Here's another installment of BRI's Top Ten of the Year list.

1960

(1) Theme From "A Summer Place" —*Percy Faith*
(2) He'll Have To Go —*Jim Reeves*
(3) Cathy's Clown —*The Everly Brothers*
(4) Running Bear —*Johnny Preston*
(5) Teen Angel —*Mark Dinning*
(6) It's Now Or Never —*Elvis Presley*
(7) Handy Man —*Jimmy Jones*
(8) I'm Sorry —*Brenda Lee*
(9) El Paso —*Marty Robbins*
(10) The Twist —*Chubby Checker*

1961

(1) Tossin' And Turnin' —*Bobby Lewis*
(2) I Fall To Pieces —*Patsy Cline*
(3) Michael —*Highwaymen*
(4) Crying —*Roy Orbison*
(5) Runaway —*Del Shannon*
(6) My True Story —*Jive Five*
(7) Pony Time —*Chubby Checker*
(8) Will You Love Me Tomorrow? —*The Shirelles*
(9) Take Good Care of My Baby —*Bobby Vee*
(10) Runaround Sue —*Dion*

1962

(1) The Twist —*Chubby Checker*
(2) I Can't Stop Loving You —*Ray Charles*
(3) Mashed Potato Time —*Dee Dee Sharp*
(4) Roses Are Red (My Love) —*Bobby Vinton*
(5) Big Girls Don't Cry —*Four Seasons*
(6) Johnny Angel —*Shelley Fabares*
(7) The Loco-Motion —*Little Eva*
(8) Let Me In —*Sensations*
(9) Stranger On The Shore —*Mr. Acker Bilk*
(10) Soldier Boy —*Shirelles*

1963

(1) Sugar Shack —*Jimmy Glimer & the Fireballs*
(2) Surfin' U. S. A. —*Beach Boys*
(3) The End of the World —*Skeeter Davis*
(4) Rhythm of the Rain —*Cascades*
(5) He's So Fine —*Chiffons*
(6) Blue Velvet —*Bobby Vinton*
(7) Hey Paula —*Paul And Paula*
(8) Fingertips (Part 2) —*Little Stevie Wonder*
(9) My Boyfriend's Back —*The Angels*
(10) It's All Right —*Impressions*

The underside of a horse's hoof is called a frog.

THE LAST LAUGH: EPITAPHS

Some unusual epitaphs and tombstone rhymes, sent in by our wandering BRI tombstone-ologists.

In England:
Anna Lovett
Beneath this stone & not above it
Lie the remains of Anna Lovett;
Be pleased good reader not to shove it,
Least she should come again above it.
For 'twixt you & I, no one does covet
To see again this Anna Lovett.

In Topeka, Kansas:
Tim McGrew
Here lies Sheriff Tim McGrew who said he would arrest Bill Hennessy or die—He was right.

In London, England:
Anonymous
Beneath this silent stone is laid
A noisy antiquated maid
Who from her cradle talked to death,
And ne'er before was out of breath.

In England:
Edgar Oscar Earl
Beneath this grassy mound now rests
One Edgar Oscar Earl,
Who to another hunter looked
Exactly like a squirrel.

In Cleveland, Ohio:
Anonymous
I thought it was a mushroom when
I found it in the woods forsaken;
But since I sleep beneath this mound,
I must have been mistaken.

In Northumberland, England:
Matthew Hollingshead
Here lieth Matthew Hollingshead,
Who died from cold caught in his head.
It brought on fever and rheumatiz,
Which ended me—for here I is.

In Boston, Mass.
Owen Moore
Owen Moore:
Gone away
Owin' more
Than he could pay.

In Tombstone, Ariz.
John Timothy Snow
Here lies John Timothy Snow, who died fighting for a lady's honor. (She wanted to keep it)

In Wolverhampton, England:
Joseph Jones
Here lies the bones
Of Joseph Jones
Who ate whilst he was able
But, once o'er fed
He dropt down dead and fell beneath the table.
When from the tomb
To meet his doom,
He rises amidst sinners;
Since he must dwell in Heav'n or Hell
Take him—which gives best dinners.

The original Godzilla costume weighed 220 lbs. It was made of urethane and bamboo.

A COMIC STRIP IS BORN

Ever wonder how the creators of your favorite comic strips came up with the idea? Uncle John got curious and did some research. Here are a few of the stories he found.

THE FAR SIDE

Background: In 1976, jazz guitarist Gary Larson was on the verge of getting a dream gig with a big band in Seattle...but they hired somebody else. Crushed with disappointment, Larson spent the weekend drawing animal cartoons (something the "frustrated biologist," as he called himself, had done since he was a kid). On Monday, he took his drawings to a small California wilderness magazine to sell, and to his surprise, the magazine bought them all.

A Strip Is Born: Meanwhile, he kept drawing. To pay the rent, he took a job as an animal cruelty investigator with the Seattle Humane Society. (In true "Far Side" fashion, he ran over a dog on the way to the interview.) One day, while Larson was on assignment, a reporter for the *Seattle Times* noticed the drawings in his notebook. She asked if she could show them to her editor...who hired Larson to do a cartoon called "Nature's Way." Unfortunately, it ran right next to the children's crossword puzzle. Parents complained about its warped humor, and it was cancelled.

Luckily, Larson had just shown his cartoons to an editor at the *San Francisco Chronicle*. The editor immediately bought the strip. The only thing he changed was the name. "Nature's Way" became "The Far Side."

DILBERT

Background: Scott Adams' career as an artist didn't look promising. He got the lowest grade in a drawing class at college, and had cartoons rejected by *Playboy*, *The New Yorker* and a long list of comic strip syndicators. He was stuck in cublicle-land, working first at the Crocker National Bank for eight years, then at Pacific Bell for nine.

A Strip Is Born: In the late 1980s, while he was still at Pac Bell, he decided he wanted to earn a living as a cartoonist. He invented

"Dilbert" and sent samples to six comic strip syndicates. Four rejected him, one suggested he take drawing lessons, and one—United Features—offered him a contract. But since "Dilbert" wasn't a hit yet, Adams kept his day-job.

The turning point came in 1993. "I asked the syndicate for ideas on what they would like me to write more about," Adams recalls. "They said, 'Do more on downsizing, more on things getting harder in the workplace.'" To find out what people were thinking in cubicles around America, Adams began posting his e-mail address in every strip. The feedback he got helped him make "Dilbert" the first comic strip to capture the frustrations of modern office workers. In 1995, he was finally able to leave Pac Bell and become a fulltime cartoonist. Today, "Dilbert" is in over 1,000 newspapers; about 20% of his story ideas still come from readers.

CALVIN & HOBBES

Background: Bill Watterson graduated from college in 1979, and immediately got a job as a political cartoonist for the Cincinnati, Ohio *Post*. He was fired after six months. So in 1980, he tried a new career—as a comic strip artist. His first effort was called "Spaceman Spiff," about a character who "wore flying goggles, smoked a cigar, and explored space in a dirigible." It was rejected by every syndicate.

A Strip Is Born: Five years and several flops later, he finally got someone interested in his work. The United Features Syndicate picked out two minor characters in a strip he'd submitted—the lead character's little brother and a stuffed tiger who came to life—and paid Watterson to develop a strip about them. He called them Calvin (after theologian John Calvin) and Hobbes (after the pessimistic philosopher Thomas Hobbes). United Features actually rejected the finished product, so Watterson took it to Universal Press Syndicate. They liked it. "Calvin and Hobbes" debuted on November 18, 1985, and didn't bow out until ten years later, at the end of 1995. At that time it was America's most popular strip, appearing in 2,400 newspapers.

"There is no deodorant like success."—***Elizabeth Taylor***

Estimated cost for having your whole body tattoed: $30,000 to $50,000.

CELEBRITY GOSSIP

Here's this edition's installment of the BRI's cheesy tabloid section—a bunch of gossip about famous people.

SEAN CONNERY

Believes in reincarnation. According to one report, he's convinced that in a past life, he was "an alcoholic railroad builder in Africa who lived with two native women, both of whom bore him sons, and who died of alcohol poisoning."

CHARLES LINDBERGH

• When Lindbergh took his first flying lesson, he learned two things: (1) how to fly, and (2) that he was afraid of heights.

• To cure himself of vertigo, he first tried "wing walking" (climbing on the wings of a biplane while it was in flight), which didn't work, and then parachute jumping, which did.

• "When Lindbergh crossed the Atlantic," Jack Mingo writes in *The Juicy Parts*, "he didn't carry a radio because it added too much weight. His navigation was an iffy thing. At one point near the end of his journey he spotted a fishing fleet, dove his plane down to within shouting distance, cut the engines, and screamed, 'Which way to Ireland?'"

PABLO PICASSO

Picasso wasn't breathing when he was born, and his face was so blue that the midwife left him for dead. An uncle revived him by blowing cigar smoke up his nose.

DONALD TRUMP

• In his book *Trump: The Art of the Comeback*, Trump confesses to being a "clean-hands freak" who washes his hands whenever he can and who hates shaking hands with strangers, especially when the stranger has just come from the restroom, "perhaps not even having washed his hands."

• One year Trump visited the Bronx's Public School 70 (located in a poor neighborhood) for the school's annual Principal for a Day event. On his way out, Trump dropped a $1 million bill in the bake sale cash box. (It was fake, of course—Trump's idea of a joke.)

WILLIAM SHATNER

Swears he's seen a UFO. "You'd almost think he was joking," writes Tim Harrower in the Portland *Oregonian*, "but, no, Shatner was serious when he reported that a silver spacecraft flew over him in the Mojave Desert as he pushed his inoperative motorcycle. He also claims to have received a telepathic message from the beings in the craft advising him which direction to walk."

PRESIDENT LYNDON BAINES JOHNSON

• "It was well known," biographer Robert Dallek writes in *Flawed Giant: Lyndon Johnson and His Times*, "that he had ongoing affairs with a secretary, a beautiful Hispanic woman people called the 'chili queen,' and a woman at his ranch dubbed the 'dairy queen'.... When the wife of television newscaster David Brinkley accepted an invitation to visit Lyndon and Lady Bird at the ranch on a weekend her husband couldn't be there, Johnson tried unsuccessfully to get her into bed."

• Johnson could be extremely abusive to his aides, even the Secret Service officers sworn to defend him with their lives. Once, while driving across a field at the LBJ Ranch in Texas, Johnson stopped to relieve himself. "One of the Secret Service men standing near him 'felt warm water on his leg,'" Dallek writes. "He looked down and said, 'Mr. President, you are urinating on me.' And Johnson's response was, 'I know I am...it's my prerogative.' "

HENRY FORD

• One of his closest friends was Thomas Edison, and he was with the inventor when Edison died. At the moment of death, Ford captured Edison's last breath in a bottle. It was one of his most prized possessions.

• Once while fiddling with a microscope, Ford had a close-up look at some granulated sugar crystals...and was horrified by their sharp points. He swore off of sugar for the rest of his life, fearing it would slice up his internal organs.

Until President Kennedy was killed, it wasn't a federal crime to assassinate the President.

WEIRD MEDICAL CONDITIONS

You never know what's going to happen, right? Like, you might get stuck on that seat, have to call 911, and wind up in the next edition of the Bathroom Reader*....Or you might find you've got one of these conditions. Don't laugh—it could happen to YOU!*

THE STENDHAL SYNDROME

Diagnosed In: Florence, Italy, 1982

Medical Report: "Some visitors to Florence panic before a Raphael masterpiece. Others collapse at the feet of Michelangelo's statute of David," reports the Reuters News Service. "At least once a month on average, a foreign tourist is rushed to the psychiatric ward of Florence's Santa Maria Nuova Hospital suffering from acute mental imbalance, seemingly brought on by an encounter with the city's art treasures.

"Psychiatrists call it the Stendhal Syndrome, after the French writer who recorded a similar emotional experience on his first visit to the city in 1817. After viewing some of the city's famous art, he wrote: 'I felt a pulsating in my heart. Life was draining out of me, while I walked fearing a fall.'

"More than half the patients are tourists from European countries. Italians, on the other hand, seem to be immune to the condition, along with the Japanese, who are apparently so organized in their sight-seeing that they rarely have time for emotional attacks."

MUSCLE DYSMORPHIA SYNDROME

Diagnosed In: The United States, 1997

Medical Report: According to the *New York Times*: "Some bodybuilders appear to be suffering from an emotional disorder that is, in effect, the opposite of anorexia. Despite their muscular bodies and being in tiptop shape, they are convinced that they look puny.

"Their preoccupation with their bodies can become so intense that they give up desirable jobs, careers and social engagements so they can spend many hours a day at the gym bulking up. Some often refuse

Average growing time for Christmas trees to reach proper height: 7 to 10 years.

to be seen in a bathing suit out of fear that others will regard their bodies as too small and out of shape.

"The first description of the disorder, called *muscle dysmorphia*, appeared in an issue of the journal *Psychosomatics*."

KORO

Diagnosed In: Indonesia

Medical Report: According to *Fenton & Fowler's Best, Worst and Most Unusual*: "Indonesian men occasionally fall prey to an obsessive fear that their penis is withdrawing into the body and that, if they do not take the matter into their own hands, so to speak, the process will ultimately kill them. The prescribed treatment is to grasp the disappearing organ and hold on for dear life until it stops receding.

"Since a typical bout of the malady, called *koro*, can last for hours or even days, the embarrassed victim must often ask friends, wife, witch doctor, and others to spell him in holding onto the vanishing member while he rests. He may also use a small, specially-designed, notched box. The disease is purely psychological, of course, but the 'treatment' frequently leaves victims exhausted, temporarily impotent, and black and blue about the privates."

THE JERUSALEM SYNDROME

Diagnosed In: Jerusalem, Israel, 1994

Medical Report: According to the Associated Press: "A new condition is affecting visitors to the holy city of Jerusalem. Upon arriving there, people become convinced they are biblical figures reborn—including Moses, Jesus and Abraham.

"Yari Bar-El, the psychiatrist who has treated 470 of the tourists for the syndrome, chalks it up to the approach of the year 2000. 'We know that every millennium there's an increase of religious feelings,' he explains, adding that 'most patients recover in a week.'"

SEINFELD SYNCOPE

Diagnosed In: United States, 1998

Medical Report: According to *TV Guide*: "This newly identified medical condition caused a 62-year-old man to laugh so hard while watching *Seinfeld* that he became unconscious and fell face first into his dinner."

Fart fact: The average person passes 1 to 3 pints of gas a day, in 14 different episodes.

BRITS VS. AMERICANS A WORD QUIZ

We both speak English, but we don't necessarily use the same words. For instance, the British call trucks "lorries." See if you can match the British words to their American counterparts. Words are from I Hear America Talking, *by Stuart Berg Flexner*

BRITISH

1) Tower Block
2) Booter
3) Note
4) Fringe
5) Graughts
6) Caravan
7) Track
8) Cash Desk
9) Polka Dots
10) Candy Floss
11) Boarding
12) Motion
13) Accumulator
14) Fascia (panel)
15) Cubbyhole
16) Pantechnicon
17) Lie-by
18) Verge
19) Chucker Out
20) Push Chair
21) Wing
22) Patience
23) Sponge Bag
24) Braces
25) Spanner

AMERICAN

a) Cotton Candy
b) Checkout Counter
c) Moving Van
d) Dash (board)
e) Battery
f) Tread
g) Shaving kit
h) Stroller
i) Fender
j) Bangs (of hair)
k) Bill (paper money)
l) Billboard
m) Bouncer
n) Shoulder (of a road)
o) High-rise Apartment
p) Chocolate Chips
q) Horn, Siren
r) Trailer
s) Rest Area
t) Bowel Movement
u) Glove Compartment
v) Suspenders
w) Checkers
x) Wrench (tightening tool)
z) Solitaire (a card game)

Answers

1-o, 2-q, 3-k, 4-j, 5-w, 6-r, 7-f, 8-b, 9-p, 10-a, 11-l, 12-t, 13-e, 14-d,
15-u, 16-c, 17-s, 18-n, 19-m, 20-h, 21-i, 22-z, 23-g, 24-v, 25-x

Poll results: Nachos is the food most craved by Moms-to-be.

GOING ABROAD

Sandie Timco sent in a review of book called Going Abroad, *by Eva Newman. When we read the review, we knew it was perfect for us. Why? It's about using the bathroom in other countries. Here are few excerpts from it.*

THE SQUAT TOILET
Toilet facilities fall into two general categories, squat and sit. Surprisingly to many Westerners, a large part of the world actually prefers the position of squatting.

Just what is a squat toilet and how is it used? The example illustrated is the kind of squat toilet frequently encountered.

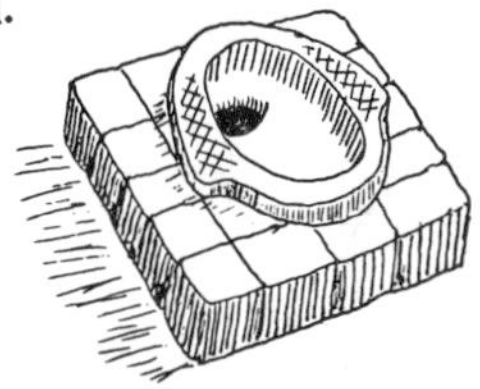

[Editor's note: To cleanse after using a squat toilet, many people splash water on their rear (a water basin is often provided). If there is no water nearby, use toilet paper, but dispose of it in a trash can.]

SQUATTING IN TURKEY
My own first encounter with an unfamiliar toilet was in Turkey, when I saw my first squat toilet. What a mystery! How do you manage? It seemed apparent from the faucet and pitcher next to the toilet that water was involved, but how was it used? Since there was no handle for flushing, what did you do?

I was much too embarrassed to ask a local person and even too embarrassed to mention the problem to my traveling companions. They, knowing no more than I, never alluded to the problem. So we muddled through, so to speak.

When I used toilet paper, I was chagrined to find the toilet was clogged on my next visit. Since it appeared that my use of paper was causing the problem, sometimes I'd throw water at my private parts, hoping for the best and thoroughly wetting my clothing. But nothing seemed to work! And I very likely left behind a path of clogged toilets and distressed toilet owners.

INDIA MYSTERY
It was not until a few years later in India that the mystery of

squat toilets was solved for me. After a thirty-five hour airplane ride, my friend and I arrived in Bangalore with a good case of jet lag and exhaustion. Our gracious Indian hosts showed us to our room and bath.

Waiting for us in the bathroom was a half-and-half toilet. I ventured to try it first. Sitting was too uncomfortable for me because there is no seat and the facility was too high for my feet to touch the ground. Amazingly, it seemed apparent to me that my standing on the "feet part" of the toilet and squatting would be more appropriate.

My shoes, with their slippery soles, allowed one of my feet to slide into the toilet. When I came out of the toilet with a soggy foot, my friend screamed with laughter.

Her turn was to come. My friend emerged from the same toilet mumbling that she needed to practice her aim as she dried her feet.

THE MYSTERY SOLVED

Our hysterics caused our host to inquire the next morning if we were having a problem. I think that since he had entertained Americans before, he suspected the truth. He was so concerned and kind we confessed our errors and ignorance. He explained all; the remainder of our six weeks' visit was spent in complete confidence. We had overcome the major obstacle to a happy stay in the real India. In fact, we came to like using squat toilets and to use water for cleansing afterward.

What is the attraction? One well-traveled leader of adventure tours summed up his feelings this way: The beauty of squatting is that your anatomy never has to touch places where many other anatomies have traveled.

PIG'S DELIGHT

After a delicious lunch of pork vindaloo in Goa, India, a traveler sought and found very clean stalls of squat toilets nearby. They were so spotless he was reluctant to use them.

But use them he must. He readied himself and as he was about to squat, to his horror, a pig's snout appeared in the toilet hole's opening. It seems the toilet's drain was a cement chute that ran to the ground in back of the facility, and pigs disposed of the refuse. This pig had become overly anxious.

As he exited, the traveler thought again about his lunch of pork vindaloo.

OH, MARLENE!

Here are a few thoughts from Marlene Dietrich, the great actress from the 1930s and 1940s.

"If there is a supreme being, he's crazy."

"My legs aren't so beautiful, I just know what to do with them."

"Tenderness is greater proof of love than the most passionate of vows."

"In America sex is an obsession. In other parts of the world, it's a fact."

"The average man is more interested in a woman who is interested in him than he is in a woman with beautiful legs."

"A man would prefer to come home to an unmade bed and a happy woman than to a neatly made bed and an angry woman."

"Once a woman has forgiven a man, she must not reheat his sins for breakfast."

"It's the friends you can call up at 4:00 a.m. who matter."

"They thought of us glamour girls as they used to think of color photography. When the story was weak, they shot it in color as a cover-up. If the feminine lead was a weak role, they cast a glamour girl in it. But if you tried to find the girl's part on paper, it wasn't there."

"Most women set out to change a man, and when they have changed him, they do not like him."

"It is a joy to find thoughts one might have, beautifully expressed by someone wiser than oneself."

"How do you know when love is gone? If you said that you would be there at seven and you get there by nine, and he or she has not called the police yet—it's gone."

"Superstitions are habits rather than beliefs."

"Victory is joyful only back home. Up at the front it is joyless."

A coffee tree yields about one pound of coffee in a year.

INSIDE THE X-FILES

Is the truth really out there? Our investigation into the TV phenomenon The X-Files *has turned up some fascinating pieces of information.*

HOW IT STARTED

Inspiration: The highest-rated TV movie of the 1972–73 season was a low-budget thriller called *The Night Stalker*. In it, a wise-cracking Las Vegas reporter named Carl Kolchak discovers that the serial killer terrorizing his city is really a vampire. Of course, no one believes him...and when he finally defeats the killer, all evidence vanishes. Only *he* realizes the dark truth—everyone else thinks he's a kook.

A year later, Kolchak returned in a film called *The Night Strangler*—this time chasing a killer zombie in Seattle. Once again, Neilsen ratings were high, and ABC commissioned a series for the 1974–75 season: *Kolchak: The Night Stalker*. It wasn't a huge success, but it did attract a cult following. One avid fan was a California teenager named Chris Carter. "It really shook me up to think there might be a twilight world of blood-sucking creatures," he recalls. "It made a big impression on me."

The TV Experience Ten years later, Carter was in the TV biz himself. After kicking around for awhile, he finally signed a deal to develop new programs for the fledgling Fox Network. "When I got to Fox in 1992," he explains, "I had the luxury of being asked what I would like to do. So I said I wanted to create a scary show, something as dark and mysterious as I remember *Kolchak* was when I was a kid."

Two other influences played into his work:

• *The Avengers*, an English spy program of the mid-1960s that featured a bantering man/woman team. They had an extraordinary chemistry that never turned into romance. Carter loved them.

• America's growing obsession with UFOs and the supernatural. Carter wasn't a "believer," but in 1991 he'd had a conversation with a Yale professor who claimed that as many as 3% of the American population actually thought they'd been abducted by aliens. Carter was

Average number of Santas hired by a U.S. shopping mall: 3.73.

shocked. "I realized there was a topicality to this theme of the unknown," he says, "and *The X-Files* grew out of that fascination."

THE STARS

David Duchovny (Agent Fox Mulder) planned to be an English Lit. professor, but while working on his doctorate in English Literature at Yale in 1985, he got a part in a Löwenbraü beer commercial. He made $9000—twice the annual salary of his teaching assistantship—and was hooked.

• After that, he had a variety of small roles in TV and films. He figured he was a break or two away from movie stardom when the *X-Files* pilot script showed up. He wasn't interested in more TV, but thought he'd get a free trip and a few weeks of work from it. He was so uninterested in the part that when producer Chris Carter told him to wear a tie to the audition, he wore one covered with pink pigs. Carter jokes, "I think that got him the job."

Gillian Anderson (Agent Dana Scully) landed a role in the off-Broadway play *Absent Friends* six months after graduating from college in 1990...and won the Theatre World Award as the "outstanding new talent of 1990-91" for it.

• Before reading the *X-Files* pilot script, she vowed never to do TV. But she was broke, and "couldn't put it down." Her audition was only the second time she'd ever been in front of a camera...and Duchovny toyed with her. "I already knew I had the part, so I played the scene in a kind of sarcastic way," he says, "—much more sarcastic than it was written—and Gillian was just completely thrown by it....She was shocked that anybody would talk to her that way."

• It turns out that was exactly the reaction Chris Carter was looking for. He wanted to hire her, but Anderson recalls that Fox protested. "They wanted somebody leggier, somebody with more breasts, somebody drop-dead gorgeous." Carter hired her anyway.

INSIDE FACTS

The Truth Is Out There?

The pilot episode ("The X Files") was supposedly based on a real incident. That claim hasn't been made for any other episodes...but stories are often based on real events. For example:

• In "Young at Heart," Barnett grows a "salamander-like" hand. Carter's inspiration: a news story about a London researcher "who grew an extra limb on a salamander's back."

• The toxic fumes given off by characters in "The Erlenmeyer Flask" and "Host" episodes were inspired by the unexplained fumes that came from a woman patient in a Riverside, California, hospital in 1994, making doctors and nurses seriously ill.

• According to the *Fortean Times*, the episode called "Humbug" was inspired by "the real-life killing of a sideshow character called 'Lobsterboy.'"

Close Encounters

Gillian Anderson barely held onto her job in the initial season. First she had trouble learning her lines and mastering the show's scientific jargon. Then she had a hard time with the grueling schedule. About six months into the first season she got married...and came back from her honeymoon pregnant. She was sure she'd be fired. She told Duchovny first. "It looked like his knees buckled," she says. "I think he said, 'Oh, my God.'"

A few weeks later, she told Carter. His reaction? Depends on who you ask. According to on-the-set sources, "He went ballistic. He wanted to get rid of her." But Carter says: "I never, ever considered replacing her." In any case, she stayed. During pregnancy, her condition was covered up with loose-fitting lab coats. When her due date hit, she had an emergency C-section. Ten days later, she was back to work.

What's In A Name?

Fox Mulder: Fox was the name of a boyhood friend of Carter's. Mulder is his mother's maiden name.

Dana Scully: Fans assumed she was named after UFOlogist Frank Scully. But Carter says the inspiration was L.A. Dodgers announcer Vin Scully.

Episode titles: Carter intentionally keeps them mysterious. "If titles come in that I don't think are up to our standard of vagueness or seriousness," says Carter, "I ask the writer to change them." One episode title—"Piper Maru"—sounds obscure...but it's really just the name of Anderson's daughter.

NEVER SAY NEVER

A few pearls of wisdom from 599 Things You Should Never Do, *edited by Ed Morrow.*

"Never accept a drink from a urologist."
—Erma Bombeck

"Never hit a man with glasses. Hit him with something much bigger and heavier."
—Anonymous

"Never insult seven men if you're only carrying a six shooter."
—Harry Morgan

"Never judge a man by the opinion his wife has of him."
—Bob Edwards

"Never eat Chinese food in Oklahoma."
—Bryan Miller

"Never get caught in bed with a live man or a dead woman."
—Larry Hagman

"Never hunt rabbit with dead dog."
—Charlie Chan

"Never miss a chance to have sex or appear on television."
—Gore Vidal

"Never put off till tomorrow what you can get someone else to do today."
—Douglas Ottati

"Never put off until tomorrow what you can do the day after tomorrow."
—Mark Twain

"Never put off until tomorrow what can be avoided altogether."
—Ann Landers

"Never keep up with the Joneses. Drag them down to your level. It's cheaper."
—Quentin Crisp

"Never take a job where the boss calls you 'Babe.'"
—Brett Butler

"Never trust a man who has only one way to spell a word."
—Dan Quayle, quoting Mark Twain

"Never expect to steal third base while keeping one foot on second."
—American Proverb

Why do puppies lick your face? They're instinctively searching for scraps of food.

THE TOP 10 HITS OF THE YEAR, 1964–1967

Here's another installment of BRI's Top Ten of the Year list.

1964

(1) I Want To Hold Your Hand —*The Beatles*
(2) She Loves You —*The Beatles*
(3) Hello, Dolly —*Louis Armstrong*
(4) Pretty Woman —*Roy Orbison*
(5) I Get Around —*Beach Boys*
(6) Louie, Louie —*The Kingsmen*
(7) My Guy —*Mary Wells*
(8) We'll Sing in the Sunshine —*Gale Garnett*
(9) Last Kiss —*J. Frank Wilson & The Cavaliers*
(10) Where Did Our Love Go —*Diana Ross & the Supremes*

1965

(1) (I Can't Get No) Satisfaction —*The Rolling Stones*
(2) I Can't Help Myself (Sugar Pie, Honey Bunch) —*Four Tops*
(3) Wooly Bully —*Sam The Sham & The Pharoahs*
(4) You Were On My Mind —*We Five*
(5) You've Lost That Lovin' Feelin' —*The Righteous Brothers*
(6) Downtown —*Petula Clark*
(7) Help! —*The Beatles*
(8) Can't You Hear My Heartbeat? —*Herman's Hermits*
(9) Turn, Turn, Turn —*The Byrds*
(10) My Girl —*The Temptations*

1966

(1) The Ballad Of The Green Berets —*Sgt. Barry Sadler*
(2) Cherish —*The Association*
(3) (You're My) Soul And Inspiration —*The Righteous Brothers*
(4) Reach Out I'll Be There —*The Four Tops*
(5) Monday, Monday —*The Mamas & The Papas*
(6) Last Train To Clarksville —*The Monkees*
(7) California Dreamin' —*The Mamas & The Papas*
(8) You Can't Hurry Love —*The Supremes*
(9) Good Vibrations —*The Beach Boys*
(10) These Boots Are Made For Walkin' —*Nancy Sinatra*

1967

(1) To Sir With Love —*Lulu*
(2) The Letter —*The Box Tops*
(3) I'm A Believer —*The Monkees*
(4) Windy —*The Association*
(5) Ode To Bille Joe —*Bobbie Gentry*
(6) Light My Fire —*The Doors*
(7) Somethin' Stupid —*Nancy Sinatra and Frank Sinatra*
(8) Happy Together —*The Turtles*
(9) Groovin' —*The Rascals*
(10) Incense & Peppermints —*The Strawberry Alarm Clock*

Supermarket survey: 90% of the U.S. population rode in a grocery carts when they were kids.

BEGINNINGS

You've heard of all the products listed below.
Here's a look at how they were invented.

THE CLUB

In 1985, Jim Winner, Jr. bought a brand-new Cadillac with all the whistles and bells, including GM's sophisticated new antitheft system. He added a car alarm to go with it, but it didn't do any good—the car was stolen a short time later. Winner thought back to his Army days, when he used to secure his jeep by running a thick chain through the steering wheel and around the brake pedal to keep his friends from driving off with it. He decided to make a simpler, similar device—one that fastened only to the steering wheel—for civilian use. He tested 50 prototypes in bad neighborhoods before settling on a design for The Club.

WIRE COAT HANGERS

Albert Parkhouse worked for the Timberlake Wire and Novelty Co. at the turn of the century. The company had a lot of employees, but not enough hooks for everyone to hang their coats and hats on. One morning in 1903, Parkhouse became so frustrated looking for a hook that he grabbed a piece of wire, bent it in half and twisted the two ends together to make a hook, then shaped the rest of the wire so that he could hang his coat on it. Timberlake patented the idea and made a fortune; according to his relatives, Parkhouse did not.

THE ZAMBONI

Frank Zamboni owned an ice skating rink in Paramount, California in the early 1940s. He hated paying five men for the 1-1/2 hours it took to smooth out the ice every night, and after seven years of experimenting, he finally invented a machine that could do it in 15 minutes. Olympic skating star Sonja Henie practiced at Zamboni's rink; she made the machines famous when she paid Zamboni $10,000 for two of them and brought them with her on her nationwide tour. By 1960, Zambonis were in use at the Winter Olympics.

SAY UNCLE!

Uncle John would like to take a few minutes to talk about some of the other *famous "uncles" in American history.*

UNCLE SAM, *a symbol of the United States*

Birth: Sam Wilson owned a meat-packing plant in Troy, New York. When the War of 1812 broke out, the government contracted him to supply meat to troops stationed nearby. He started stamping crates for the army with a big "U.S." But when a government inspector visited the plant and asked a worker what the initials meant, the worker shrugged and guessed it stood for his employer, "Uncle Sam."

Everyone's Uncle: The nickname spread among the soldiers. Soon, all army supplies were said to come from "Uncle Sam." Then a character called Uncle Sam began showing up in newspaper illustrations. The more popular he got, the more patriotic his outfit became. In 1868, Thomas Nast dressed Uncle Sam in a white beard and Stars-and-Stripes suit for a political cartoon. Nast borrowed the look from a famous circus clown named Dan Rice.

UNCLE TOM, *title character of* Uncle Tom's Cabin

Birth: Harriet Beecher Stowe wanted the title character of her novel, *Uncle Tom's Cabin*, to be "simple, easygoing and servile"...but also "noble, high-minded, and a devout Christian." She found inspiration in conversations with her cook, a free woman who was married to a slave in Kentucky. As Stowe explained in an 1882 letter to the Indianapolis *Times*, the cook said her husband

> was so faithful, his master trusted him to come alone and unwatched to Cincinnati to market his farm product. Now this, according to the laws of Ohio, gave the man his freedom, *de facto*. But she said her husband had given his word as a Christian, his master promising him his freedom. Whether he ever got it, I know not.

Everyone's Uncle: The book was published in 1852 and quickly became one of the best-selling novels of the 19th century. It played an important role in arousing anti-slavery passions that resulted in the Civil War. When Lincoln met Stowe, he greeted her by asking, "Is this the little woman whose book made such a great war?" Over time, "Uncle Tom" became a derogatory term to African-Americans, referring to someone too servile, or who cooperated too closely with whites—not entirely fair, since Uncle Tom was ultimately flogged to death by slave owner Simon Legree after he refused to reveal the hiding place of two female slaves.

UNCLE REMUS, *narrator of a popular series of folk tales*

Birth: Joel Chandler Harris grew up in the South after the Civil War listening to folk tales told by former slaves. As an adult, he began collecting them and publishing them. One of the most helpful people he talked to was an elderly gardener in Forsyth, Georgia, called Uncle Remus. Harris made him the narrator of his books

Everyone's Uncle: In the enormously popular *Uncle Remus: His Songs and His Sayings* (published in the late 1800s), Uncle Remus, a former slave, entertains his employer's young son by telling him traditional "Negro tales" (believed to have come from Africa) involving Brer Rabbit, Brer Fox, and Brer Wolf. Harris' books preserved the tales in print form and introduced them to a worldwide audience. Disney's animated *Song of the South* made Uncle Remus a part of modern American pop culture (Zip-a-dee-doo-dah!).

UNCLE FESTER, *crazed character from the* Addams Family *TV series*

Birth: The ghoulish family in Charles Addams' *New Yorker* cartoons was never identified by (first) name—so it was never clear exactly who the bald fiend in the family portraits was. But in 1963, Addams agreed to let ABC make a TV sitcom out of his characters. All he had to do was give the characters names and family relationships. The bald guy officially became Morticia's Uncle Fester.

Everyone's Uncle: The TV show was a Top 20 hit in 1964-65. Fester was brought to life by Jackie Coogan, who had been the first child star of the silent film age. In 1923, he was the biggest box office star in the country, but his appeal faded as he got older. By 23 he was broke and out of work. After a tragic life that included arrests for drugs and booze, Coogan made a comeback. He showed up for the *Addams* audition with a huge walrus mustache and hair on the sides of his head. Told that Fester was hairless, he returned the next day shaved completely bald and got the part.

STRANGE BREWS

Are Bud and Miller too bland? You can always try one of these…

CALLING HOMER SIMPSON…

"A brewery in Bulgaria recently announced that brewmaster Yordan Platikanov has developed a beer that neutralizes any residual uranium 134 or strontium in the body after exposure to nuclear radiation. Platikanov said the new beer should be urged on nuclear power plant workers relaxing at the end of a shift." **—Universal Press**

BEER FOR THE BATH

"The Kloser brewery in Nuezelle, Germany, announced it would soon begin selling dark beer concentrate for foam baths and eczema treatment. The new product differs from beer only in that the yeast is left in, creating its skin-soothing quality. Said owner Helmut Fritsche, 'You can bathe in it or drink it. Whoever wants to, can do both.'"
—The Edge,* Portland *Oregonian

ANCIENT BEER

"An Egyptologist, two scientists and Britain's largest brewer announced plans to brew an ale from a recipe dating back 3,500 years to the time of Tutankhamun. 'Tutankhamun Ale' will be based on sediment from old jars found in a brewery housed inside the Sun Temple of Nefertiti.…The team gathered enough materials to produce just 1,000 bottles of the ale. 'We are about to unveil a great Tutankhamun secret,' said a spokesman at Newcastle Breweries. '—the liquid gold of the Pharaohs. It's a really amazing inheritance they have left us—the origins of the beer itself.'" ***—San Francisco Examiner***

HEAVY METAL BEER

"Mötley Crüe promoted a new album with a bright, blue-colored beverage called Motley Brüe, a drink 'for people who are done with the whole drugs and alcohol thing but still want to have fun.'" ***—TV Guide***

The average American credit card holder owes almost $ 3,900.

THE FORGOTTEN MEN

U.S. vice presidents are the forgotten men of politics...and sometimes that's just as well; some pretty strange characters have been elected vice president over the years. Ever heard of any of these ex-veeps? We'll bet you haven't.

RICHARD MENTOR JOHNSON (served with Martin Van Buren, 1837–41)

Background: Democratic congressman from Kentucky. Described by one witness as "the most vulgar man of all vulgar men in this world." His personal affairs scandalized Washington society. He married three times, each time to a slave woman. When his second wife ran off with the man she truly loved, Johnson had her captured, then sold her at a slave auction.

VP Achievements: The only VP ever elected by Congress rather than by popular vote (he was so disliked that he couldn't get enough electoral votes). He was ahead of his time in one way—he cashed in on his newfound celebrity by opening a tavern and spa on his Kentucky farm. During his term, he chose to stay there and manage it most of the time, rather than live in Washington.

WILLIAM RUFUS DE VANE KING (served with Franklin Pierce, 1853)

Background: Democrat from Alabama. Known more for his effeminate clothing and demeanor than his politics. In 1834, he struck up a lasting friendship with future president James Buchanan, with whom historians speculate he had a homosexual relationship.

VP Achievements: On Inauguration Day, he was in Cuba trying to recover from tuberculosis, and was too sick to make it to Washington. He did make it to his home state for a victory celebration—and then died. The length of his term as VP: six weeks. This made him the only bachelor VP, the only VP to be sworn in outside the country, and the only one never to enter Washington, D.C., during his term. No one lost any sleep finding a replacement. The VP position remained vacant until the next election, which Buchanan won.

HANNIBAL HAMLIN (served with Abraham Lincoln, 1861–64)

Background: Republican senator from Maine. Described by one historian as "a keen opportunist with a short attention span." Once Lincoln was nominated, the Republicans needed someone from the east to balance the ticket. Hamlin's qualifications: He had political experience but wasn't controversial. In fact, he had almost no legislative record. He looked forward to the vice presidency, because it would "be neither hard nor unpleasant."

VP Achievements: Perhaps the most invisible VP ever. Being Lincoln's VP during the Civil War should have earned him a prominent spot in history books. But Lincoln quickly lost faith in his colleague's political skills and completely ignored him. Hamlin went home to his farm in Maine, sulking, "I am the most unimportant man in Washington." He only went back there once each year to open each new session of Congress, then returned to Maine. Lincoln dumped him in 1864 in favor of Andrew Johnson.

GARRET AUGUSTUS HOBART (served with William McKinley, 1897–99)

Background: Republican from New Jersey. Lost in his only bid for office (U.S. Senate) before becoming VP. Got the nomination because, as one of the richest men in the country, he had been willing to spend a lot of money on Republican causes.

VP Achievements: According to some historians, Hobart was one of the most influential VPs ever. No one has ever heard of him because he preferred wielding power behind the scenes. Most of his deals went down during intimate parties at his rented D.C. mansion, where senators were treated to cigars, liquor, and poker in exchange for their votes.

WILLIAM ALMON WHEELER (served with Rutherford B. Hayes, 1877–81)

Background: Republican congressman from New York. According to one historian, "The most boring of all the Republican vice presidents, and friends, that is saying something." Had a reputation for complete honesty—which made him a rarity in 1876.

VP Achievements: The only VP nominated as a joke. According to Steven Tally in *Bland Ambition*:

Because presidential nominee Rutherford B. Hayes was from Ohio, the delegates to the Republican convention of 1876 needed to pick someone from the important state of New York. They really didn't care who it was; it was just the vice presidency, after all, and most of the delegates had to be getting home. The delegates from New York began joking about which of them would take the nomination. Somebody yelled to future vice president Chester Arthur, "You take it, Chet!" and somebody else said, "You take it, Cornell!" The delegates were nearly beside themselves with merriment when one of the delegates said, "Let's give it to Wheeler!"

They thought this was such a good one that they presented the nomination to the floor. Wheeler's nomination was approved by acclamation, and according to a newspaper account of the event, "the delegates did not wait to continue the applause, but rushed off in every direction for the hasty dinner...and the out-speeding trains." This prompted the presidential nominee Hayes to write to his wife, "I am ashamed to say, who is Wheeler?"

THOMAS MARSHALL (served with Woodrow Wilson, 1912–1920)

Background: Democratic governor from Indiana. Diminutive man described as "120 pounds of 'glad to see ya, how ya doin'?'...a shorter version of George Bailey from *It's a Wonderful Life*." He claimed he wasn't surprised to be nominated vice president, because "Indiana is the mother of vice presidents, the home of more second-class men than any other state."

VP Achievements: First vice president to publicly treat the office as a joke. Asked how he got elected, he credited an "ignorant electorate." After the election, he sent President Wilson a book inscribed, "From your only vice." (Wilson was not amused.) When groups visiting the Capitol peered into his office, he would tell them to "be kind enough to throw peanuts at me."

According to *Bland Ambition*, however, Marshall's major achievement "came after a particularly tedious catalog of the nation's needs by a particularly bellicose senator—What this country needs is more of this! What this country needs is more of that! Marshall leaned toward an associate and said, 'What this country needs is a really good five-cent cigar!' The coining of this phrase may stand as the greatest accomplishment of a vice president in the nation's history."

Franklin Roosevelt was related to 5 other presidents by blood, and 6 others by marriage.

THE WORLD'S TALLEST BUILDINGS, PART II

On page 50, we told you the story of Elisha Graves Otis, inventor of the world's first safety elevator—which makes him one of the fathers of the modern skyscraper. Here's the story of another key figure in the quest to touch the sky...without ever leaving the ground.

BOOMTOWN

If ever a city needed tall buildings in a hurry, it was Chicago in the 1880s. Located in the center of America's farmland, with rail links to every coast, it was a natural hub of commerce for the entire continent, and one of the fastest growing cities in the country. The population more than doubled between 1880 and 1890, and commercial land prices shot up even faster: An acre of prime commercial real estate that cost $130,000 in 1880 was worth $900,000 by 1890. Building across the landscape became so expensive that people were forced to begin thinking of ways to build straight up into the air.

Out of the Ashes...

The Great Chicago Fire of 1871 made the need for tall buildings urgent even before the 1880s. The fire raged for only two days, but it wiped out one-third of all the buildings in the city—including most of the financial district. The fire was so devastating that when architect William LeBaron Jenney began work on the Home Insurance Building twelve years later, rebuilding was still underway.

MAN OF STEEL

Jenney was an uninspired architect—"a rather heavy-handed designer," one critic says, "who never turned out anything of great beauty." And if he hadn't had a noisy parrot, he might be forgotten today. Instead, he is the man historians consider the father of the modern skyscraper.

According to legend, Jenney was working on his design for the Home Insurance Building one afternoon in 1883 when the bird began making so much noise that he couldn't concentrate. He got so angry that he grabbed the heaviest book he could find and pounded furiously on the bird's steel-wire cage to shut it up.

The cage should have broken after such abuse, Jenney thought afterwards, but it didn't. It didn't even dent. If steel cages were so strong, he realized, why not make buildings out of steel? Why not build the Home Insurance Building with steel?

BRICK BY BRICK

By the early 1880s, buildings were still rarely taller than six or seven stories, and it wasn't just because people hated slow elevators or climbing stairs. Bricks, the standard construction materials of the time, were too heavy to build much higher than that. To support a tall structure, the lower walls would have to be so thick that there would be little floor space left. Besides, why use so many bricks to add just one floor when the same number of bricks could be used to construct an entire building someplace else?

Steel, on the other hand, is so much lighter and can carry so much more weight than brick that you can build more than 100 floors before you run into the same type of problem.

REACH FOR THE SKY!

Jenney was one of the first people to realize that steel made it possible to construct buildings with a strong inner "skeleton" to support the building's weight from the inside—so the outer walls didn't have to be built heavy and thick. As George Douglas writes in *Skyscrapers: A Social History in America*,

> In this great decisive step in architectural history, Jenney had perceived the advantages of a building whose exterior wall becomes a mere curtain or covering that encloses the building but does not support it. All the support is provided by the interior framing...in a way, one might say this was a new kind of building that had no wall, only a skin.

And thanks to the invention of the safety elevator, for the first time it was possible to transport people to the upper floors quickly and safely.

Ugly Duckling

The Home Insurance building stood ten stories tall when finished, but that was the only thing interesting about it. Otherwise, it was plain and undistinguished. It didn't even inspire other architects, let alone the public. However, even if it had been beautiful, it wouldn't have attracted much attention: Ten-story buildings didn't tower over their neighbors the way modern skyscrapers do. Douglas writes:

> By a strange irony of history, the importance of the Home Insurance Building did not dawn on either the general public…or the Chicago architects working with Jenney on other building projects….It was only years later that that critics and historians came to view the Home Insurance Building as the first real skyscraper.

CHICAGO STYLE

Nevertheless, the Home Insurance Building was the right building in the right city at the right time.

Chicago needed to replace as much office space as quickly, as economically and as efficiently as possible, and skyscrapers were made to order for the task: buildings like the Home Insurance Building provided more usable floor space for the money, materials, and land spent than was possible with any other construction method.

There was another bonus: Since the steel skeleton reduced the number of interior walls to a minimum, the precious office space inside could be partitioned however the tenants wanted it; when they moved away, the office space could be re-partitioned to suit the new tenants. That kind of versatility was ideal for a city that was reinventing itself day by day.

Numerous skyscrapers were built in Chicago over the next several years, including the Tacoma Building, the Rand McNally Building, and the tallest of them all, the Masonic Temple—a 21-story edifice that stood an amazing 302 feet high. It was the tallest building in the world.

Into the Dustbin…

It turned out that these large buildings created new problems: they didn't allow in as much light and air as smaller buildings, and they could be unsafe in fires. Landlords of smaller buildings were afraid skyscrapers would suck tenants away and cause rent prices to collapse.

By 1892, even the city government had turned against skyscrapers. Not long after the Masonic Temple was finished, the city passed a

One in three snake bite victims is drunk. One in five is tattooed.

new height limitation of 130 feet on all future buildings—less than half the height of the temple. The limit was raised to 260 feet in 1900, but the die was cast: Chicago, birthplace of the skyscraper, would soon take a back seat to New York as home to the tallest buildings on earth.

As for the Home Insurance Building, it was demolished in 1934 to make way for the Field Building, the last skyscraper built in Chicago before the Great Depression halted new construction for more than a decade.

Part III of the World's Tallest Buildings is on page 186.

*   *   *   *

DID YOU HEAR THE ONE ABOUT...

Muriel B. Mihrum sent us this article from the Wilmington,
N.C. Star News. *It's by Dave Peterson, their outdoor columnist.*

Did you hear the one about the black bear caper in Louisiana?

It seems that someone reported a bear clinging to small branches in the top of a tall pine. County officers responded and confirmed that there was, indeed, a bear in that tree.

Meanwhile, game wardens and wildlife biologists had been alerted, because the black bear is not common in that part of the state and has even been considered for the endangered list....To save the bear, wildlife people said they needed a veterinarian, a tranquilizer gun, and a substantial net beneath the tree.

The vet arrived and delivered the tranquilizer darts, but there was no visible reaction from the bear. We were now into about the eighth hour of rescue efforts and the area was ringed with 50 or more avid spectators.

After the tranquilizer darts failed, they decided that the only reasonable option was to cut the tree in a manner that would cause it to fall slowly to soften the blow to the bear.

When the tree came down, everyone rushed to secure the bear and it was at that point when faces turned red. It wasn't a bear! They had spent over eight hours rescuing a large black garbage bag that had blown into the tree.

Highest annual per capita consumption of Spaghetti-Os in the U.S.: Grand Rapids, Michigan

STRANGE LAWSUITS

Here are a few more real-life examples of unusual legal battles.

THE PLAINTIFF: Gloria Sykes, 25-year-old resident of the San Francisco Bay area.

THE DEFENDANT: The City of San Francisco.

THE LAWSUIT: Sykes was hit by a San Francisco cable car while crossing the street. The only visible injuries were a few cuts and bruises. But later, she claimed, she realized that the accident had turned her into a nymphomaniac. She sued, seeking compensation for neurological and psychological damages.

VERDICT: She was awarded $50,000.

THE PLAINTIFF: Anoki P. Sultan.

THE DEFENDANT: Roman Catholic Archbishop James Hickey.

THE LAWSUIT: Sultan blamed the church for allowing the devil to take over his body. He knew the devil was present, because he hadn't been able to hold a job, had dropped out of school, smoked cigarettes, and had committed other unspeakable acts. He sued, asking for either $100 million or an exorcism.

VERDICT: Case dismissed.

THE PLAINTIFF: Mukesh K. Rai, a devout Hindu living in California.

THE DEFENDANT: Taco Bell.

THE LAWSUIT: In January 1998, Rai ordered a bean burrito at a Ventura, California Taco Bell. They gave him a beef burrito instead. He took a bite, then realized the mistake. When he complained, he was told: "So you ate meat. What's the big deal?" He sued for severe psychological damage and emotional distress because cows are sacred in the Hindu religion, and may not be eaten. "This is the equivalent of eating his ancestors," his lawyer told reporters.

VERDICT: Not settled out of court yet (but it will be).

ON THE CABLE

Cable television was introduced in the 1950s as a way to bring distant TV signals to rural areas. It wasn't until the 1970s that people thought of using it to expand programming—and even then, experts said it would never have a large audience; after all, who would pay for TV when they could get it for free? Today, most of us who watch cable TV don't realize how new it is...or where the stations we watch came from. Maybe in a future Bathroom Reader *we'll do a long piece on how cable made its big breakthough. In the meantime, here are thumbnail histories of some of the better-known cable channels. (There's more on page 318.)*

HOME BOX OFFICE (HBO)

Background: In 1965, a small company called Sterling Communications won the exclusive rights to provide cable service to lower Manhattan. Their selling point: Better reception. But people weren't buying. After spending $2 million in two years—and still picking up only a few hundred customers—the company was in trouble. Time, Inc., a minor partner in the operation, loaned Sterling enough money to keep it afloat. But in 1970, Time decided the company was losing too much. Desperate to keep his business going, Sterling's founder came up with a new concept: "The Green Channel."

On the Air: The idea was simple: rent first-run movies from Hollywood studios, the way theaters do—but show them on television. Add in some sports events, and consumers would finally have a reason to pay for cable service. The cost of the movies would be high but could be covered by selling the service to other cable companies. Intrigued, Time gave Sterling enough money to test the idea, and the channel (now called HBO) went on the air in 1972. It started with a market-test of 325 homes in Wilkes-Barre, Pennsylvania. By the 1980s, it had become Time's largest source of profit.

TURNER BROADCASTING SYSTEM (TBS)

Background: Ted Turner was twenty-four in 1963 when his father committed suicide. He took over the family's billboard/advertising company and saved it from bankruptcy. In 1970, he bought a small Atlanta UHF television station that ran network reruns and old movies. A few years later, he purchased the rights to Atlanta Braves baseball games and built his network around them. Meanwhile, in 1975 the FCC issued a ruling that independent TV stations could send their signals outside local areas to distant markets. This opened the door for the growth of cable, and Turner walked through.

On the Air: He immediately bought space on the first orbiting telecommunications satellite (owned by RCA) and began broadcasting his newly-christened TBS "SuperStation" to cable systems from coast to coast. Almost overnight, his little UHF station doubled its audience to two million households. Baseball was TBS's main attraction, and Turner realized that he couldn't afford to lose the rights to the Braves. So he bought the team. With them, he flourished.

USA NETWORK

Background: In 1975, United Artists and Columbia Cablevision joined forces to create an all-sports station, the Madison Square Garden Sports Network.

On the Air: They hired a 34-year-old consultant, Kay Kaplovitz, to set the network up. Two years later, the station made history by naming Koplovitz its president—the first woman to head a national TV network. She changed its name to USA and moved to diversify programming. Her strategy was a success. In 1981, she proudly announced that USA had become the first advertiser-based cable network to turn a profit, having earned "a few pennies" that year. Today, sports aren't a part of their programming at all.

THE ENTERTAINMENT AND SPORTS PROGRAMMING NETWORK (ESPN)

Background: Before cable, sports fans had to wait until the weekend to find sports on TV. William Rasmussen, the announcer on local Connecticut broadcasts of the World Hockey Association's Hartford Whalers, guessed that die-hard fans would pay to have sports brought into their living rooms every day. So he signed up for space on the RCA telecommunications satellite (which beamed signals to cable stations). Then he tried to raise money to pay for it. By the time ESPN debuted on September 7, 1979, the Getty Oil Company had bought 85% of the network for $10 million.

On the Air: ESPN's first broadcasts were of University of Connecticut games, but plans were in the works for bigger things: The network contracted with the National Collegiate Athletic Association (NCAA) to telecast hundreds of NCAA events nationally. College athletics remain the station's bread and butter, though it now provides some coverage of professional sports and off-the-wall events like the Strong Man competition. It's now owned by Disney.

LIFETIME

Background: Billed as "the first woman's cable network," Lifetime arose in 1984 out of the ashes of two failing cable stations: Daytime (a diet and talk-show channel) and the Cable Health Network.

On the Air: Lifetime premiered as a mixed bag of talk and call-in shows featuring, among others, Regis Philbin, Richard Simmons, and sex therapist Ruth Westheimer. Dr. Ruth was a hit, but little else was. Losses of $36 million in the first two years proved that women weren't interested. In fact, a poll of viewers revealed that some believed Lifetime was a religious channel. In 1988, Lifetime hired a new head of programming, who switched the focus to drama and reruns of shows like *Moonlighting* and *L.A. Law*. The formula worked. Today, about 70% of Lifetime's viewers are female.

TURNER NETWORK TELEVISION (TNT)

Background: TBS and CNN were well-established in the mid-1980s when Ted Turner made two financial decisions that sent him deep into debt. First, he failed in a hostile takeover attempt of CBS. Then he paid $1.6 billion to acquire 3,650 films from the MGM library, including *The Wizard of Oz* and *2001: A Space Odyssey*. Some analysts estimated he'd overpaid for the films by a half-billion dollars.

On the Air: Beleaguered by unpaid bills, on the verge of losing control of his empire, Turner made a surprising decision: He started yet another cable channel—TNT—and offered many of the MGM movies on it. One problem: Many of the films were in black and white, and contemporary audiences prefer color. So Turner colorized the films, over the objections of directors like Woody Allen and Steven Spielberg. (Congress even held hearings on the subject.) The controversy turned into the fledgling network's biggest publicity break. It debuted in 1988 with *Gone with the Wind*, carried by more cable systems than any new network in history.

The 1st presidential news conference shown on TV was in 1955. Eisenhower was president.

VIDEO TREASURES

How many times have you found yourself at a video store staring at the thousands of films you've never heard of, wondering which ones are worth watching? It happens to us all the time—so we decided to offer a few recommendations for relatively obscure, quirky videos you might like.

SOLDIER OF ORANGE (1978) *Drama / Foreign*

Review: "Rutger Hauer became an international star as a result of his remarkable performance in this Dutch release, in which he plays one of four college buddies galvanized into action when the Nazis invade the Netherlands. This is an exceptional work; an exciting, suspenseful, and intelligent war adventure." (*Video Movie Guide*) *Stars*: Rutger Hauer, Jeroen Krabbe, Edward Fox, Susan Penhaligon. *Director*: Paul Verhoeven.

MONA LISA (1986) *Drama*

A sort of noir mystery in the tradition of Chinatown.

Review: "A wonderful, sad, sensitive story of a romantic, small-time hood who gets personally involved with the welfare and bad company of the high-priced whore he's been hired to chauffeur." (*Video Hound's Golden Movie Retriever*) *Stars*: Bob Hoskins, Cathy Tyson, Michael Caine. *Director*: Neil Jordan.

COMFORT AND JOY (1984) *Comedy*

One of Uncle John's favorite Christmas movies.

Review: "Quirky, fun little comedy. When a mild-mannered Scottish disk jockey's girl moves out on him, his world begins to fall apart. He decides to find more meaning in his life by throwing himself into a noble struggle to reconcile two groups battling over territorial rights for their ice cream trucks. Full of dry wit and subtle humor. Sophisticated viewers are more likely to find this good fun." Music by Mark Knopfler of Dire Straits. (*Illustrated Guide To Video's Best*) *Stars*: Bill Paterson, Eleanor David, C.P. Grogan, Alex Norton. *Director*: Bill Forsyth.

BABETTE'S FEAST (1987) *Foreign / Drama*

Review: "Exquisite, delicately told tale of two beautiful young minister's daughters who pass up love and fame to remain in their small

Cats can make over 100 different vocal sounds; dogs can make about ten.

Dutch village. They grow old, using religion as a substitute for living life...and then take in Parisian refugee Audran, a woman with a very special secret. Subtle, funny and deeply felt, with several wonderful surprises, an instant masterpiece that deservedly earned a Best Foreign Film Academy Award. [Director] Axel wrote the screenplay, from an Isak Dinesen short story." (*Leonard Maltin's Movie & Video Guide*) *Stars*: Stephane Audran, Jean-Phillippe Lafont, Gudmar Wivesson, Jarl Kulle, Bibi Andersson, Birgitte Federspiel, Bodil Kjer. *Director*: Gabriel Axel.

HOW TO GET AHEAD IN ADVERTISING (1989) *Certifiably weird comedy.*

Review: "A cynical, energetic satire about a manic advertising idea man who becomes so disgusted with trying to sell pimple cream that he quits the business. Ultimately he grows a pimple of his own that talks and begins to take over his life. Acerbic and hilarious." (*Video Hound's Golden Movie Retriever*) *Stars*: Richard E. Grant, Rachel Ward, Richard Wilson. *Director*: Bruce Robinson.

BAGDAD CAFE (1988) *Comedy / Drama*

Review: "This delightfully off-beat comedy-drama concerns a German businesswoman who appears in the minuscule desert town in California called Bagdad. She and the highly strung owner of the town's only diner-hotel have a major culture and personality clash. Jack Palance as a bandanna-wearing artist is so perfectly weird he practically walks off with the film." (*Video Movie Guide*) *Stars*: Marianne Sägebrecht, C.C.H. Pounder, Jack Palance. *Director*: Percy Adlon.

HOUSE OF GAMES (1987) *Mystery*

Review: "A very unusual and fascinating thriller. An uptight pop psychiatrist and best-selling female author decides to rescue one of her clients from a charismatic con artist. Instead, she is nearly conned out of $6,000 of her own money and she has also become fascinated with this man. She is both drawn to him and challenged by him. And, she quickly gets in over her head....Quickly the twists and cons get so thick that she doesn't know who is conning who. A slick thriller well worth watching, but pay attention." (*Illustrated Guide To Video's Best*) *Stars*: Lindsay Crouse, Joe Mantegna, Lilia Skala, Mike Nussbaum, J.T. Walsh. *Director*: David Mamet.

The Pacific island of Nauru's economy is based almost entirely on bird droppings.

I REMEMBER ED WOOD

Ask any film buff to name the worst directors of all-time, and you can be sure Ed Wood's name will come up. He's become a legend for films like Plan 9 from Outer Space*—a movie so bad it needs to be seen just to be believed. This piece was written by someone who knew him—in fact, the reluctant star of* Plan 9*, Gregory Walcott.*

The Connection

Early in our marriage, Barbara and I lived in a cottage just across the street from the First Baptist Church of Beverly Hills. Ed Reynolds, a chubby little man who attended the church, had come out to Hollywood from Alabama to make Biblical films. He talked to me occasionally, knowing I was in the movie industry, about his "calling" to produce religious movies with life-embracing themes. I tried not to encourage him, knowing he had no background in film production. Naive individuals like Reynolds are easy bait for Hollywood hucksters.

Reynolds' Big Break

About a year later, Reynolds came to me and said he was going to finance a film starring Bela Lugosi. He wanted me to play the young romantic lead. I said to him, "But Ed, Bela Lugosi is DEAD!"

Reynolds said, "Well, that's not a problem. There's a very ingenious director, Ed Wood, who has some excellent footage of Lugosi, and he has written a very clever screenplay around that film."

"But Ed, I thought you wanted to make Biblical pictures?"

"Yes! That's the ultimate plan. But Biblical pictures with big sets, large casts and costumes are very expensive. This fellow, Wood, has convinced me that by making a few exploitation films, I can build up my bankroll to where I can then make big budget Biblical films."

I had never heard of Ed Wood, so I asked to see the script. It was the most atrocious piece of writing I had ever seen. A child could've written better dialogue. I said, "Ed this is a terrible script, and I hate to see you get involved in this project and lose your money."

"No, no! I want you to meet the director," he insisted. "I'll arrange a luncheon."

Reynolds was dazzled by Hollywood and couldn't be dissuaded.

Before the meeting, I looked into Wood's background, and discovered he had done a few cheesy low-budget pictures. It was incongruous that sweet, sincere Reynolds, who wanted to produce inspirational Biblical motion pictures, would be connected with Wood, whose movies could only be booked in fleabag theaters on back streets.

Meeting the Auteur

At the luncheon, I found Wood to be a charmingly handsome man, who gushed about how perfect I was for the role. He assured me I would be working with a top-notch Hollywood crew and a good cast.

Wood resembled Errol Flynn, and was clearly a smooth promoter. In fact, he started attending Reynolds' church and showed an interest in becoming a convert to the faith. This pleased Reynolds, convincing him that Wood was sincere and a godsend. I was there the night Ed Wood was baptized. He stood in the pool, resplendent in a white robe. His boyish face had the look of an angel. As he was immersed into the baptismal waters of the church, Ed Reynolds beamed in satisfaction, and said stoutly, "Amen!"

Taking the Plunge

I reluctantly agreed to do the film, *Plan Nine From Outer Space*, as a favor to Ed Reynolds, working at scale wages on a four-day schedule.

The first day I reported to work on a tiny sound stage—behind a sleazy bar and a disreputable hotel. I knew right away I had made a mistake. The sets looked like something a 6th-grade class had hastily put together. The crew seemed fairly normal, but the cast members were a bizarre assemblage of Wood's cronies: hopeful actors, former wives, an astrologer, an over-the-hill wrestler, a few cross-dressers, and his chiropractor.

The set had the ambiance of an old-time carny side-show, not a professional movie sound stage. I went home that first day, and I remember distinctly saying to my wife, "Honey, this has got to be the worst film ever made."

Unfortunately my assessment was prophetic, and the movie turned out to be a debacle. Poor Ed Reynolds could get no distributor to release the picture, and he lost his investment. A couple of years later he died, a broken man at the early age of 52.

A Cult Film

The film was eventually released to television and shown during late-night ghetto hours. Amazingly enough, it picked up an audience; it was so shockingly bad that it was actually funny.

A freaky Edward D. Wood phenomenon began. Even Tim Burton, director of the *Batman* mega hits was so fascinated by the quirky auteur that he made a movie of his life story in 1994. The film, *Ed Wood*, received favorable reviews but limited box office success. It did, however, add to Wood's growing international fame.

But Why?

I am still puzzled as to why people are attracted to Ed Wood's ghastly legacy and his ludicrously inept films. Perhaps it's like the fascination one finds looking at a macabre auto wreck. Perhaps Wood appeals to people who feel lost, or who rebel against society's stereotypes.

I think my son, Todd, may have hit upon the real reason: "It's that thing we fear, in ourselves, that we, too, are not really talented, and in time that truth will be revealed."

I do say, I have to admire Wood for his flint-faced determination to do the thing he loved the most, making movies, and his uncanny ability to complete the projects, no matter how tasteless and poorly made. Who knows, maybe effort should be recognized as well as art.

R.I.P.

In his later years, Wood dashed off dirty magazine stories to survive and drank heavily. Evicted from his rat-hole apartment, he moved in with a friend in whose bed the 54-year-old Wood died quietly and unexpectedly in December 1978. His ashes were scattered in the ocean off the coast of Southern California.

Identity crisis? Approximately 10% of Jewish households have Christmas trees.

ED WOOD'S MASTERPIECE

As a follow-up to Greg Walcott's piece about Ed Wood (immediately preceding this), we thought we'd include a few comments from critics about Plan 9 from Outer Space.

ONLY HUBCAPS

"Some say [*Plan 9 from Outer Space*] is the worst movie anyone ever made. Certainly it's the worst movie Ed Wood ever made. And nobody but Wood could have made it. The lunacy begins with a portentous introduction from our old friend Criswell, the clairvoyant. 'Greetings my friends,' Criswell reads from his cue card. 'We are all interested in the future because that's where you and I are going to spend the rest of our lives.' While we're still mulling over the meaning of that statement, Wood hits us with the heavy-duty special effects—UFOs flying over Hollywood Boulevard. Actually, they're only hubcaps, superimposed on a pseudo-sky."

—*The Worst Movies of All Time,* by Michael Sauter

ATTACK OF THE UNDEAD

"God knows what the first eight "Plans" were, but Plan 9 is a doozy....Aliens Dudley Manlove and Janna Lee (today a successful scriptwriter) were sent by The Ruler to raise the dead so that they'd attack the living. That's just about what Wood tried to do with his dead friend Bela Lugosi, billed as the star of the film although he died *prior* to production. Wood had a couple of minutes of footage of Lugosi from an aborted project, so he simply inserted the snippets into this film and repeated them over and over so that Lugosi had adequate screen time. Lugosi's character—The Ghoul Man—was played in the rest of the movie by a chiropractor, an extremely tall fellow who spends his screen time with a cape covering his face so we won't know he's an impostor. The ruse doesn't work, but I don't think Wood really cared."

—*Guide for the Film Fanatic,* by Danny Peary

If you shake a can of mixed nuts, the larger nuts go to the top.

BEYOND RIDICULE

"Words such as amateurish, crude, tedious and aaarrrggghhhh can't begin to describe this Edward D. Wood film with Bela Lugosi in graveyard scenes made shortly before his death....

The unplotted plot by Wood has San Fernando Valley residents troubled by UFOs of the worst encounter. Humanoid aliens Dudley Manlove and Joanna Lee land their cardboard ship with a ninth plan to conquer the world (the first eight failed, you see). They resurrect corpses, including Vampira, Tor Johnson and Lugosi's double. The results are unviewable except for masochists who enjoy a good laugh derived from watching folks making fools of themselves."

—***Creature Features Movie Guide Strikes Again,*** **by John Stanley**

MASTERFUL SPECIAL EFFECTS

"The graveyard set provides the film with many of its eerie moments, thanks to a number of dead tree branches and cardboard tombstones; in one scene a policeman accidentally kicks over one of the featherweight grave markers.

"Despite the resourcefulness of the director, there are slight technical shortcomings in the final version of Plan Nine. Even Wood's staunchest defenders will admit that the Old Master seemed to have a tough time with lighting. In one scene, as Mona McKinnon runs in horror from Bela Lugosi's double, she goes directly from a graveyard at midnight to a nearby highway at high noon. This same confusion between night and day occurs several times in the course of the film."

—***The Golden Turkey Awards,*** **by Harry and Michael Medved**

CHEAP, CHEAP, CHEAP

"Money was always a problem for Wood. Budgets were routinely nonexistent, forcing him to film on the cheap, scrimping...as best he could....How cheap was *Plan 9*? The flying saucers are hubcaps suspended by wires. In several scenes the movie jumps from daylight to nighttime and back. And outdoor lawn furniture doubles as bedroom furniture....In all of the literature about *Plan 9* (and there's reams of the stuff) one question about the movie has never been answered. If Plan 9 was to revive the dead, what were the other eight plans?

—***Why The People of Earth Are "Stupid,"*** **by Tom Mason**

It takes five minutes to execute someone in a gas chamber.

FOUNDING FATHERS

You already know their names. Here's who they belonged to.

Jerome Smuckers. Started out selling apple butter in Orrville, Ohio in 1897; in 1923 he branched out to jams and jellies.

Abraham and Mahala Stouffer. Cleveland, Ohio restaurateurs. Their Stouffer's restaurants were so popular that they began freezing entrees for customers to eat at home. By 1957, they were selling frozen foods in supermarkets; and by the late 1960s they were suppling frozen dinners for the Apollo space program.

John Deere. In 1837, Deere invented the first practical steel plow, which unlike iron plows, cut through black, sticky prairie soil without bogging down in the thick muck. Today John Deere is the largest agricultural machinery manufacturer in the world.

Jack Mack. Mack and his brother Augustus were wagon builders in Brooklyn at the turn of the century. In 1900, they built the first bus in the U. S. It was used to carry tourists around Brooklyn's Prospect Park. The bus was so reliable—it logged more than 1 million miles over 25 years—that Jack and Augustus were swamped with orders. They and three other brothers formed the Mack Brothers Company a short time later. Jack designed the company's first truck in 1905.

The Smith Brothers. The first commercial typewriters were available in 1873, but it wasn't until 1895 that someone invented a typewriter that allowed you to see the words as you were typing. When Union Typewriter Co. balked at making the new machine in 1903, Lyman, Wilbert, Monroe, and Hurlbut Smith left the company and founded the L.C. Smith Brothers Typewriting Co. In 1925 they merged with the Corona Typewriting to become Smith-Corona.

Herman Fisher and Irving Price. Together with Helen Schelle, they founded the Fischer-Price toy company in 1930 to make toys out of Ponderosa Pine. Their first big hit: Snoopy Sniffer, a "loose-jointed, floppy-eared pull toy who woofed when you pulled his wagging spring tail," in 1938. The company made its first plastic toys in 1949.

INTERNATIONAL LAW

Believe it or not, these laws are real.

In England, it's illegal to name your pet "Queen" or "Princess" without the Queen's permission.

If you aren't a member of the royal family in Japan, it's illegal for you to own a maroon car.

In Equatorial Guinea, you can name your daughter anything you want—except Monica.

In India, women—but not men—are allowed to marry goats.

Old English law: if an object is smaller than a husband's little finger, he can beat his wife with it.

In Canada, if a debt is higher than 25¢, it's against the law for you to pay with pennies.

In Vancouver, British Columbia, the speed limit for tricycles is 10 miles per hour.

In Baluchistan, Pakistan, the law allows a man to "acquire" a wife by trading in his sister.

In Athens, Greece, driving on public roads while "unbathed" or poorly dressed can cost you your driver's license.

If a man is wearing a hat in Cheshire, England, the law requires him to raise it when a funeral passes.

You can keep cows in sheds in the Northern Territories of Canada, and you can keep chickens in sheds. But you can't keep cows *and* chickens in the same shed.

Makes sense: in London, England, it's illegal to operate a motor vehicle while sitting in the back seat.

In Australia, the pictures of convicted drunk drivers are published in newspapers with the caption, "He's drunk and in jail."

Cigarettes are legal in Nicaragua; cigarette *lighters* aren't.

Boxing is illegal in China (too brutal); capital punishment isn't.

ELEMENTARY, MY DEAR SHERLOCK

Here are a few of the more interesting comments author Arthur Conan Doyle had Sherlock Holmes make in his books.

"Eliminate all other factors, and the one which remains must be the truth."

"I never guess. It is a shocking habit—destructive to the logical faculty."

"You can never foretell what any one man will do, but you can say with precision what an average number will be up to."

"As a rule, the more bizarre a thing is, the less mysterious it proves to be."

"Life is infinitely stranger than anything which the mind of man could invent."

"There is nothing more deceptive than an obvious fact."

"You know my method. It is founded on the observance of trifles."

"It is always dangerous to reason from insufficient data."

"Crime is common. Logic is rare."

"Any truth is better than indefinite doubt."

"I cannot agree with those who rank modesty among the virtues."

"It is stupidity rather than courage to refuse to recognize danger when it is close upon you."

"Mediocrity knows nothing higher than itself; but talent instantly recognizes genius."

"I can discover facts, Watson, but I cannot change them."

"A man always finds it hard to realize that he may have finally lost a woman's love, however badly he may have treated her."

"The most difficult crime to track is the one which is purposeless."

MENTAL AEROBICS

Here's something else to do while you're sitting there—exercise your mind. We've adapted some standard mental exercises for bathroom readers, so when you're feeling sluggish, or just haven't woken up yet, you can use this time to make yourself more alert.

STRETCH YOUR MIND

Use this exercise to warm-up or refresh your mental muscles, anytime during the day.

Complete some or all of the following seven steps. If you can, try saying them out loud.

1. Count backwards from 100 to zero, quickly.

2. Recite the alphabet, assigning a word for each letter (like, "A, apple; B, ball; etc."). Do this quickly.

3. List 20 names of men you know, assigning a number to each ("1, Brian; 2, Pete, etc."). Quickly.

4. Do the same thing as #3, but list 20 women you know assigning a number to each ("1, Jennifer; 2, Andrea; etc."). Quickly.

5. Name and number 20 foods as quickly as you can ("1, burger; 2, cookies, etc.").

6. (Feeling much more alert by now!) Choose one letter of the alphabet and name 20 words that begin with that letter as quickly as you can AND number them ("1, news; 2, nice, etc.").

7. Close your eyes and count to 20 slowly, then open them. Your mind is now geared-up to meet whatever mental challenges you might face today.

TAKE CREATIVE LEAPS

One way to become more creative is to change your normal routine. Experts say that most big shifts in our lives come from a lot of little shifts. Don't underestimate their potential!

Try some of the following:

1. Wipe with your opposite hand!

2. Walk out of the bathroom backwards.

3. If you normally flush while you're sitting, wait until you stand up; if you normally flush standing up, do it while sitting.

4. Put your pants on the way you normally do, paying attention to which leg you put in first. Take them off again. Put them back on using the "wrong" leg first.

5. Turn on the faucet. Now turn it off; turn it on again, using the *other* hand.

6. Wear your watch on the opposite wrist.

7. Brush your teeth with the opposite hand.

...Or come up with some more of your own.

MENTAL SPRINT

Helps increase creativity and sharpness.

1. Flip to any other page in this book (make sure you dog-ear or leave your finger on this one so that you can find it again).

2. Select the first noun that you see on that page (e.g., "ball").

3. Look at your watch.

4. For the next minute or two (or longer), list as many words or phrases that you can relate to that noun ("ball: bounce, play, games, red, etc."). Don't stop to think or analyze, just go as quickly as you can.

To enhance results, do this exercise aloud...if you dare.

AND IF NONE OF THESE WORK...

Here are some good excuses for sleeping on the job:

1. "They told me at the blood bank this might happen."

2. "Whew! I musta left the top off the liquid paper."

3. "This is one of the seven habits of highly effective people!"

4. "Oh, I wasn't sleeping! I was meditating on our mission statement and envisioning a new paradigm!"

If you're over 100 years old, there's an 80% chance you're a woman.

RANDOM AMERICANA

A few bits of info we've put aside to entertain you.

PURVIS' FOLLY

"The first person ever to belch on national radio was Melvin Purvis, head of the Chicago office of the FBI. Purvis was the guest on a show sponsored by Fleischmann's Yeast, in 1935, and in the middle of reading a commercial, the famed G-man emitted a loud burp. For many years thereafter, Fleischmann's Yeast was nicknamed 'Purvis' Folly.'"

—***The Book of Strange Facts and Useless Information*, by Scot Morris**

LUCKY DOG

"The Crystal Beach Cyclone in Buffalo, New York, was once considered the most terrifying of all roller coaster rides. A nurse was kept on duty at all times. The first drop in the ride featured an 85% turn to the right that caused patrons to lose hats, coats, teeth, and wigs, and to careen into each other, sometimes cracking ribs. However, in its 20 years of existence, there was only one fatality—in 1943. A man stood up to remove his suit jacket as the coaster started. His arms locked, and he couldn't sit back down. He was thrown from the car and run over. His heirs sued, claiming that the lap bar didn't hold him. The judge put a dog in the coaster to test it, the dog emerged healthy and happy, and the suit was denied. Turns out, the dog, a British bulldog, belonged to the park's maintenance supervisor and rode the coaster daily."

—***The Worst of Everything*, contributed by Paul Ruben**

AMERICAN KNOW-HOW

"A baby conceived with the help of a $2.95 turkey baster was born on Mother's Day. Julie Johnson, 34, of Cary, N.C., volunteered to be a surrogate mother for her sister, Janet, after Janet's $15,000 in vitro failed. So Julie stood on her head and received the sperm via the sterilized kitchen baster. "I figured gravity couldn't hurt," she said. Her sister added, "We're going to be completely honest with the kid. We'll tell him Aunt Julie had to have him because we couldn't.

—***San Francisco Examiner***

Wettest city in the U.S.; Quillayute, Washington. Driest: Yuma Arizona.

ORIGIN OF THE WHITE HOUSE, PART II

Here's the second part of our story of how the White House was built. Part I is on page 97.

BUILDING THE HOUSE

The cornerstone for the president's house was laid on October 13, 1792 (nobody knows for sure where—the exact location was not recorded), and work on the four-foot-thick outer walls began. They were built by masons and slave laborers, all of whom lived in shanties on the property because there was no place else in the as-yet unbuilt city for them to live. (At one point, a brothel was set up on the White House grounds, for their "convenience.")

The exterior would be faced with freestone, a form of sandstone that was chosen because it can be cut like marble. But freestone is also very porous and is highly susceptible to water damage, so the masons sealed the stone with a wash of salt, rice and glue. It was the building's first coat of white paint; soon it would be nicknamed the "White House."

STOP AND GO

Work on Washington, D.C. was moving slowly due to shortages of skilled labor, raw materials, and—especially—dollars, thanks to the disappointing land sales in the district and a Congress that was reluctant to commit any extra money.

The White House had more than its share of its own problems: Despite all the cuts that had been made, it was still way over budget, and when the Congress learned in 1798 how much money had been spent, it refused to pay any more. When the roof was finished the building was sealed up and abandoned, sitting empty for more than a year until new funds could be raised to pay for the interior.

The Wet House

When work resumed, an architect named Benjamin Henry Latrobe examined the structure to determine its structural soundness. He

On average, it takes 660 days from conception for an elephant to give birth.

found that the structural timbers, which weren't the highest quality of wood to begin with, had been exposed to so much cold, dampness, and rain during the seven years of construction that they were now dangerously decayed. But there was no money to replace them, so Latrobe repaired them as best he could and work on the house continued.

By now the White House was hopelessly behind schedule. "We do not believe it will be possible to prepare the building for the reception of the President until October or November next," the commissioners wrote in February 1800.

FIRST NIGHT

George Washington didn't live to even *see* the finished White House, let alone live in it. He left office in 1797 and died two years later, at about the same time the exterior walls were completed.

The White House was still unfinished when Washington's successor, John Adams, arrived in Washington, D.C., but he moved in anyway on November 1, 1800. The rest of the federal government—which consisted of 130 federal employees—moved to the new capital a month later.

A WORK IN PROGRESS

"Unfinished" is the polite way to describe the condition of the White House. The roof leaked, the ceilings were crumbling, and the windows were so loose that rain and wind blew into just about every room. "Not one room or chamber is finished," First Lady Abigail Adams wrote. "It is habitable only by fires in every part....This is such an inconvenience that I know not what to do!" The White House didn't even have an enclosed yard, so she took to hanging her wet laundry in the unfinished East Room.

The exterior looked even worse. As Ethel Lewis writes in *The White House*, the grounds were strewn with "dump heaps, old brick kilns, and water holes giving off evil odors...it looked more like a ruin than a Presidential Palace." The workers and slave laborers were still living in shanties on the lawn, and it would be nearly a month before the White House had an outhouse.

IN AND OUT

But the Adamses would suffer for only four months—in 1800, Adams lost the presidential election to his political rival, Thomas Jefferson. Adams avenged the defeat three different ways:

(1) He stayed up late on Inauguration eve appointing judges that he thought would be embarrassing to Jefferson.

(2) He boycotted the Inauguration the following morning.

(3) He moved out of the White House as required, which meant that Jefferson would have to move in.

Jefferson preferred to stay at Monticello whenever possible, but he also did a lot to improve the White House. He removed the shanties, landscaped the grounds, installed a fence, and filled the mansion with fashionable furniture. And for safety's sake, "mixed in with the fine furniture," Ethel Lewis writes, "were eight fire buckets."

By the time Jefferson left office in 1809, the White House was finally a comfortable home, though not by today's standards—there was no electricity, no telephones, no central heating, no air conditioning, and there was only the most primitive system of running water, designed by Jefferson himself. There weren't even any closets (in those days few people owned more than a cedar chest full of clothes, and built-in closets were unheard of).

By 19th-century standards, the White House would do just fine...but not for long—in 1814 British soldiers burned it to the ground, leaving the mansion's white stone walls an empty shell.

For more on the history of the White House, turn to page 259.

*   *   *

CAN'T HOLD A CANDLE TO IT

Q: *Why do some flames burn blue while others burn yellow?*

A: "It's a matter of how much oxygen is available to the burning fuel. Lots of oxygen makes blue flames, while a limited amount of oxygen makes yellow ones." (From *What Einstein Didn't Know*, by Robert L. Wolke)

All the gold ever mined could be molded into a cube 60 feet high and 60 feet wide.

KNOCK YOURSELF OUT!

"Knock yourself out" usually means something like, "Have a good time." But these people took the phrase literally.

STANLEY PINTO

Usually a skilled professional wrestler, he got tangled in the ropes in a Providence, Rhode Island, match. Trying to get free, he pinned his own shoulders to the mat for three seconds. The referee counted him out.

HARVEY GARTLEY

"In 1977, Gartley fought Dennis Oulette in a Golden Glove boxing competition. Gartley was counted out in a knock-out 47 seconds after the opening bell. Oulette never made contact with Gartley. The young Gartley was so excited during the match that he 'danced himself into exhaustion and fell to the canvas'—knocking himself out and losing the fight." (*Oops*)

THE USS *SCORPION*

The last U.S. nuclear submarine lost at sea sank with two nuclear weapons on board. Apparently, one of *Scorpion's* conventional torpedoes became activated and threatened to explode. To save the ship, the crew ejected it. But the torpedo "became fully armed, and sought its nearest target—the *Scorpion*."

HMS *TRINIDAD*

Sailing in the Arctic in 1941, the British ship fired a torpedo at a German destroyer—forgetting the effect that the icy water would have on the oil in the torpedo's steering mechanism. The torpedo curved, and in less than a minute it was headed straight at the *Trinidad*. It blasted right into the ship's engine room and put HMS *Trinidad* out of action for the duration of the war.

SPANISH AIR FORCE JET

"In 1979, a Spanish Air Force jet was participating in a target practice run near a hillside in Spain. The jet's gunfire ricocheted off the mountain and blew up the plane." (*Oops*)

Four most common arrests in the U.S.: drunk driving, theft, drugs, drunkeness.

BOBBY CRUICKSHANK.

"It was the final round of the 1934 U.S. Open," write Ross and Kathryn Petras in *The 176 Stupidest Things Ever Done*, "and the pressure was on. Cruickshank was two strokes ahead of his competitors. He had to make the next hole in four strokes to keep his lead.

"Cruickshank's drive off the tee was fine. But his following approach shot was too weak. With horror, he watched the ball sink with a splash into the stream in front of the green.

"A split second later, the ball bounced back out of the water—apparently ricocheting off of a submerged rock—and rolled onto the green only ten feet from the hole.

"It was a miracle. With a whoop, Cruickshank tossed his club in the air, tipped his hat, and yelled to the heavens, 'Thank you, God!' Unfortunately, the club landed on his head. It knocked him down and upset his balance for the rest of the day. He lost the lead and came in third."

HENRY WALLITSCH

In 1959, Wallitsch fought a heavyweight match against Bartolo Soni in Long Island, New York. In the third round, he took a wild swing at Soni and missed. The force of his swing made him lose his balance, and he fell through the ropes head-first. His chin hit the floor so hard, it knocked him out.

JACK DOYLE

In the mid-1930s, Doyle was considered a promising heavyweight boxer. When a reporter declared him "the next heavyweight champion," he stopped training—and didn't even fight for a year and a half. In October, 1938, after the long lay-off, he announced he was was going to fight Eddie Phillips—and he was taking this bout very seriously.

He arrived a half hour late for the match. Then, in the second round, "he swung such a mighty punch that, when Phillips stepped sideways, Doyle knocked himself out, plunged through the ropes and landed next to the time keeper who solemnly counted to ten." (*The Return of the Book of Heroic Failures*)

DUMB CROOKS

Here's proof that crime doesn't pay.

HI, THIS IS A ROBBERY. HERE'S MY I.D.

DALLAS, Texas—"Ronnie Darnell Bell, 30, was arrested in Dallas for attempting to rob the Federal Reserve Bank. According to police, Bell handed a security guard a note that read: *This is a bank robbery of the Dallas Federal Reserve Bank of Dallas, give me all the money. Thank you, Ronnie Darnell Bell.* The guard pushed a silent alarm while an oblivious Bell chatted amiably, revealing to the guard that only minutes earlier he had tried to rob a nearby post office but that 'they threw me out.'"

—*The Edge, The Portland Oregonian,* 6/18/98

TAKE THE MONEY AND...?

BALTIMORE, Maryland—"Bank robbers usually take the money and run. Not Jeffrie Thomas, police said. Thomas, 35, walked into a Signet Bank on Monday and handed the teller a note demanding money. When police arrived and asked which way he went, employees pointed to a man counting cash near a teller's station. It was Thomas, adding up the take, police said. Thomas, who was unarmed, was taken into custody."

—*The Baltimore Sun,* 4/13/97

HOT TIPS

DADE COUNTY, Florida—"On several break-ins, Ronald Bradley, 21, carefully wore gloves. But...he wore golf gloves—the kind that left his fingertips naked. He was sent to prison for three years."

—*Sports Illustrated,* 6/20/78

A HELPFUL ATTITUDE

MINNEAPOLIS, Minnesota—"Suspected purse-snatcher Dereese Delon Waddell in suburban Minneapolis last winter stood on a police lineup so the 76-year-old female victim could have a look at him. When police told him to put his baseball cap on with the bill facing out, so as to be presentable, he protested, 'No, I'm gonna put it on backwards. That's the way I had it on when I took the purse.'"

—Jay Leno's Police Blotter

CAREFUL DRIVER

SYRACUSE, New York—"In 1992, Philip S. Whaley, Sr., was captured and charged with grand larceny and other crimes after a twenty-eight-minute chase involving numerous route changes. For all twenty-eight minutes, Whaley signaled every single turn that he made. Said an officer, 'We knew exactly where he was going.'"

—America's Least Competent Criminals

MISSING PIECES

GRAPEVINE, Texas—"In 1993, 24-year-old David Bridges stole a television set so he could watch the Dallas Cowboys. He was arrested when he went back a second time, to get the remote control."

I'LL BE RIGHT OVER, OFFICER

PANAMA CITY, Florida—"Brandon Lamont Dawson, 20, was captured after police found a pager he'd left in his car following a homicide, traced it to Dawson, called him on the phone, and asked him to come to retrieve the device. He was arrested when he walked into the Panama City police station."

—*TV Guide*, 12/13/97

DUMB DRIVE-IN

VIRGINIA BEACH, Viginia—"A man charged with auto theft came to court in, of all things, a stolen car.

"Tony Brite appeared in court Friday like he was supposed to, then left with two companions after his preliminary hearing. A detective followed Brite outside, then watched as the three got into a new Volvo with New York license plates.

"Suspicious, Detective Gary Nelson ran a check on the plates and was told they belonged to a Mercedes. The Volvo had been stolen the day before from a Virginia dealership. Nelson followed the Volvo into a convenience store parking lot across the street from Virginia Beach's First Precinct. All three were arrested peacefully."

—From a 1997 wire service report

Driest inhabited place on earth: Aswan, Egypt, which receives 0.02 inches of rain per year.

FAMILIAR PHRASES

Here are more origins of some everyday phrases.

THE WHOLE NINE YARDS

Meaning: Everything; the whole shebang.

Origin: "Curiously enough, the nine yards does not refer to distance gained or lost in any kind of athletic contest....The reference is to the amount of cement contained in one of the rotating cement-mixer trucks used by construction companies. When emptied, it would discharge *the whole nine yards*, thereby completing its mission." (From the *Morris Dictionary of Word and Phrase Origins*, by William and Mary Morris)

IT'S ALL GREEK TO ME

Meaning: Something doesn't make sense.

Origin: "During the Middle Ages, as for centuries thereafter, any educated Englishman or woman knew Latin, but only a minority also knew Greek. A major reason was that Greek uses its own alphabet, so before even starting to learn the language you have to learn the letters. The phrase itself comes from Shakespeare's *Julius Caesar*." (From *Loose Cannons & Red Herrings*, by Robert Claiborne)

MIND YOUR P's AND Q's

Meaning: To be on your best behavior.

Origin: According to Edwin Radford and Alan Smith in *To Coin a Phrase:* "The most likely origin of this traditional warning is the practice of tavern owners 'chalking up' the pints and quarts consumed by a thirsty customer in the course of an evening." Customers had to keep track of how much they'd drunk...and how much they owed.

BULL IN A CHINA SHOP

Meaning: To be clumsy, especially in a delicate situation.

Origin: A common expression in English since the 1830s—and probably a political one. In 1834, China terminated trade with John Bull

The five animals most frequently mentioned in the bible are sheep, lambs, lions, oxen, & rams.

(England). This, says Robert Hendrickson in *Animal Crackers*, "had something to do with the coining of the phrase—perhaps through a political cartoon showing an angry John Bull threatening to destroy a 'China' shop if trade wasn't resumed." He adds: "The 'china' in the phrase refers to the fine porcelain from China brought to Europe from the Far East as early as the 16th century."

TO REST ON YOUR LAURELS

Meaning: To be content with success already achieved; stop going after more glory.

Origin: "For centuries, wreaths of laurel were used to crown victors, great poets, and people who had achieved distinction. This 'evergreen' was chosen to signify that they will be remembered for all time (hence the term 'poet laureate'). Once someone had been crowned, they didn't have to prove themselves anymore—and could 'rest on their laurels.'" Another meaning: Traditionally, "anyone who aspired to greatness placed laurel leaves under their pillow—literally resting on their laurels—to acquire strength for victory, or inspiration for their poetry." (From *Everyday Phrases*, by Neil Ewart)

LEFT IN THE LURCH

Meaning: Left far behind, often in difficult circumstances.

Origin: "The key word apparently comes from the French *lourche*, a 16th century game said to have resembled backgammon. To be 'in the lurch' started off as a way of saying a player was far behind in a game" and evolved into a term that could apply to any situation. (From *The Dictionary of Clichés*, by James Rogers)

THE DIE IS CAST

Meaning: A final decision has been made.

Origin: "The term comes from Suetonius's account of Julius Caesar's invasion of Italy in 49 B.C. When Caesar crossed the River Rubicon into Italy, thereby advancing against [Pompey] and the Roman Senate, he supposedly said, '*Jacta alea est*' (The dice have been thrown), meaning that now there was no turning back." (From *Fighting Words*, by Christine Ammer)

First women to win a Nobel Prize: Marie Curie, for Physics, in 1903.

CRUM'S LEGACY

Here's an edible tale from our food editor, Cousin Jeff.

BACKGROUND

Cornelius "Commodore" Vanderbilt was born on May 27, 1794 and grew up on Staten Island. His father eked out a living carrying cargo across New York Harbor in the family skiff. When Cornelius was 14, he quit school to help...and by the time he was 16, he'd saved enough to buy a small ferry of his own

During the War of 1812, he made his first fortune, carrying troops and supplies to forts in the New York area. In 1829, at age 35, he started a steamship line; 25 years later, thanks to passengers lured by the 1849 Gold Rush, he was one of the richest men in the world.

I SAY POTATO...

Vanderbilt's wealth allowed him to live lavishly. He built a number of stately homes, one of which was near Sarasota Springs in upstate New York. In 1853, while summering there, his tactless, imperious manner led to the creation of a favorite American snack.

In those days, potatoes were usually served baked, boiled, or mashed; oil was too expensive to waste on frying them. But when Vanderbilt had dinner at Moon's Lake House, he told the waiter to bring him fried potatoes like the ones he'd tasted in France. He gave detailed instructions on how to prepare them.

The chef, George Crum, had the ego of a master chef—reinforced by the fact that he was a proud Native American, a chief in the Algonquin tribe. He made the fries as directed. Vanderbilt sent them back. They were too large and not crisp enough. The chef prepared another batch, but they, too, were sent back. They were still too big and not crisp enough. Furious, Crum sliced the next potatoes paper thin, dipped them in hot fat, and dusted them with salt. Vanderbilt loved them—they were better than French fries! He offered to finance a restaurant if Crum wanted to go into business for himself.

Vanderbilt did not believe in charity; but a few years before his death he gave $1 million to a struggling college in Nashville, Tennessee. Vanderbilt University is his monument...but George Crum's is even greater. He gave the world potato chips.

THE SECRETS OF NOSTRADAMUS

Could Nostradamus have predicted his own influence four centuries after his death? This 16th-century soothsayer is still as popular as ever, more than 400 years after he made his famous predictions. This profile is from our book Uncle John's Indispensable Guide to the Year 2000.

BACKGROUND Michel de Nostradame was born in 1503 in St. Remy, France. He was trained as a physician and gained a reputation for "remarkable healing powers" during the Black Plague. But when his wife and two infant sons died of the plague, he gave up medicine and began wandering aimlessly through the south of France.

About this time, Nostradamus began experiencing visions and discovered his "powers of prophecy." According to legend, he spontaneously knelt before a monk named Felice Peretti—who later became Pope Sixtus V—and insisted that one day the monk would head the Catholic Church.

In 1550, after years of studying magic and astrology, Nostradamus began publishing an almanac filled with predictions. Thanks to his almanacs, his reputation as a psychic spread. And in 1558, he published the book that sealed his reputation: *Centuries*—a series of 1,000 quatrains (four-line verses) that purported to predict events until the year 3797.

SUPERSTARDOM

One quatrain in particular catapulted Nostradamus to psychic superstardom in his own time:

> The young lion will overcome the old one
> On the field of battle in combat:
> He will put out his eyes in a cage of gold,
> Two wounds one, then die a cruel death.

As it turns out, a few years later the reigning French monarch,

J. Edgar Hoover liked to fire FBI agents whose palms were sweaty when shaking hands.

Henry II (the "old lion"), was mortally wounded in a riding tournament by a young captain of the Scottish guard (the "young lion").

The details of the event were so similar to the quatrain that the king's wife, Queen Catherine de Medici, was sure Nostradamus had prophesied it. She invited him into her royal circle, and he began devising royal horoscopes and offering advice based on astrological events. His advice was apparently good. According to *The Book of Predictions:* "In his own day Nostradamus was acknowledged as the greatest seer alive." Stewart Robb writes in *Prophecies on World Events by Nostradamus* that "his neighbors held him in awe and respect. Kings, princes and prelates beat a path to his door; he was never in want."

By the time he died in 1566, Nostradamus was a legend. And tales of his death only added to his stature. On the night he died, he reportedly told a pupil that "tomorrow at sunrise I shall not be here." He also supposedly arranged for a marble plaque to be buried with him. When his coffin was exhumed in 1700 to move his remains to a newer tomb, the story goes, the plaque was discovered on his skeleton. On it the date "1700" was inscribed.

NOSTRADAMUS'S PREDICTIONS

Amazingly, *Centuries* has never been out of print. After the Bible, it's the oldest continuously published book in history—still widely read, interpreted...and believed.

The genius of its prophesies—and the reason they've lasted so long—is that most can be interpreted any way a reader wants. So thousands of "experts" over the years have been able to use them to "prove" Nostradamus anticipated practically every major event in Western history. He's credited with predicting the reigns of Napoleon and Hitler, the assassinations of the Kennedy brothers, even the rise of Saddam Hussein.

But how accurate was he really? Here are a few of his quatrains, selected at random, along with a contemporary analysis. See what you think.

Quatrain: "The great man will be struck down in the day by a thunderbolt / The evil deed predicted by the bearer of a petition / According to the prediction another falls at night time / Conflict in Reims, London, and pestilence in Tuscany."

Analysis: In *Nostradamus and the Millennium*, John Hogue cites this quatrain as a prediction of John and Robert Kennedy's assassinations. He says the first line is a reference to JFK; the second line refers to psychic Jeanne Dixon's attempt to forewarn JFK(!); the third to Robert Kennedy; and the fourth to events going on at the time of RFK's death.

Got that? Let's try another.

Quatrain: "Liberty will not be recovered / A bold, black, base-born iniquitous man will occupy it / When the material of the bridge is completed / The Republic of Venice will be annoyed by Hister."

Analysis: In *Prophecies on World Events by Nostradamus*, Stewart Robb says that although *Hister* is an ancient Latin term for the Danube River, it is also an anagram for the name *Hitler* (one letter change is permitted with anagrams). So it refers to a bridge across the Danube that the Nazis built in 1941. Shortly after, he says, Nazis began infiltrating Italy—the "Republic of Venice."

About the Hister-Hitler connection: There are a number of quatrains with references to Hister. During World War II, some scholars theorized that Hister is a misspelling of Hitler and suggested Nostradamus intentionally scrambled it to avoid trouble. But as one critic asks: "Why hide the name of a man who didn't even exist yet?"

ON THE OTHER HAND...

According to *The Book of Predictions*, Nostradamus gave a surprisingly detailed prediction of the rise and fall of Napoleon in a series of quatrains. They say he foretold of "an Emperor born near Italy" named "Pau. nay. loron"—an anagram for *Napaulon Roy*—who "for 14 years will rule with absolute power." (Napoleon did.)

The last of the Napoleon quatrains quoted in the book goes: "The captive prince, conquered, to Elba / He will pass the Gulf of Genoa by sea to Marseilles / He is completely conquered by a great effort of foreign forces...Will end his life far from where he was born / Among 5,000 people of strange customs and language / On a chalky island in the sea." Napoleon *was* exiled to Elba after being beaten by the British at Waterloo.

So who knows? Maybe every once in a while, Nostradamus really did tap into the future. To see what he predicted for 2000, check out "Nostradamus Today" on page 390.

World's heaviest primates: "morbidly" obese humans. After that: gorillas, at 485 lbs.

BRAIN TEASERS

BRI member Tim Harrower sent us these puzzles and dared us to solve them. They were a favorite in the BRI "research lab," so we're "passing" them on to you. See page 461 for the answers.

1. A married couple goes to a movie. During the film, the husband strangles the wife. No one notices—and he's able to get her body back home without attracting attention. How did he do this?

2. A man goes to a party, drinks some punch, and then leaves early. Everyone else at the party who drinks the punch dies of poison. Why didn't the man die?

3. One day Kerry celebrates her birthday. Two days later, her older twin brother Terry celebrates his birthday. How could this be, when they were born a half-hour apart?

4. How quickly can you find out what is unusual about this paragraph? It looks so ordinary that you would think that nothing is wrong with it at all—and, in fact, nothing is. But it *is* a bit odd. Why? If you study it and think about it, you may find out, but I am not going to assist you in any way. You must do it without coaching. No doubt, if you work at it for long, it will dawn on you. Who knows?

5. It's the ninth inning. The pitcher delivers; the batter hits a deep fly ball. The outfielder starts to catch it—then deliberately lets it fall from his glove. Why?

6. John's mother has three children. The oldest is a boy named Herbert, who has brown eyes—everyone calls him Herb. Next youngest is a girl named Penelope. Everyone calls her Penny. The youngest child has green eyes and can wiggle his ears. What is his first name?

7. Three men decide to share a hotel room for the night. The desk clerk charges them $30. They each pay $10. After they go to their room, the desk clerk realizes the room is only $25, so he gives a bellhop $5 to take up to the men. On his way up, the bellhop decides to tip himself $2 for his trouble. In the room, he gives each man $1—which means that each guy actually paid $9 for the room.

So: 3 x $9 = $27; the bellhop kept $2; that adds up to $29. Where did the other dollar go?

What's going on here? Why doesn't the math add up right?

8. An hour later, two women check into another room. The room is $30; they each pay $15. Again, the desk clerk realizes the room is only $25, so he gives the bellhop $5 to take up to the women. This time, the bellhop keeps $3 for himself and gives $1 to each of the two women. So each woman actually paid $14 for the room.

So: 2 x $14 = $28; the bellhop kept $3; that adds up to $31.

And that's where the missing dollar shows up again.

9. A man lies dead in a room with 53 bicycles in front of him. What happened?

10. Bob and Carol and Ted and Alice all live in the same house. One night, Bob and Carol go to a movie; when they return, Alice is lying dead on the floor in a puddle of water and glass. It's obvious that Ted killed her—but Ted is never arrested or punished. How could this be?

11. A deaf-mute goes into a hardware store. He wants to buy a pencil sharpener, so he walks up to the clerk, sticks a finger in his ear and rotates his other hand around his other ear. The next customer is a blind man. How does he let the clerk know he wants a pair of scissors?

BAD PUNS

From Best Book of Puns, *by Art Moger*

- They say all sheep are alike—actually, they have mutton in common.
- Many folks believe that legalized gambling has made Atlantic City a bettor place.
- Adam and Eve lived appley ever after.
- A soldier hid inside a cannon to avoid guard duty, but he was finally discharged.

THE TOP 10 HITS OF THE YEAR, 1968–1971

Here's another installment of BRI's Top Ten of the Year list.

1968

(1) Hey Jude —*The Beatles*
(2) Love Is Blue —*Paul Mauriat*
(3) Honey —*Bobby Goldsboro*
(4) People Got To Be Free —*Rascals*
(5) (Sittin' On) The Dock Of The Bay —*Otis Redding*
(6) Sunshine Of Your Love —*Cream*
(7) This Guy's In Love With You —*Herb Alpert*
(8) The Good, The Bad, And The Ugly —*Hugo Montenegro*
(9) Mrs. Robinson —*Simon & Garfunkel*
(10) Woman, Woman —*Gary Puckett & the Union Gap*

1969

(1) Sugar, Sugar —*The Archies*
(2) Aquarius/Let The Sunshine In —*The Fifth Dimension*
(3) I Can't Get Next To You —*The Temptations*
(4) Honky Tonk Women —*The Rolling Stones*
(5) Everyday People —*Sly & The Family Stone*
(6) Dizzy —*Tommy Roe*
(7) Hot Fun In The Summertime —*Sly & The Family Stone*
(8) Get Back —*The Beatles*
(9) Build Me Up Buttercup —*The Foundations*
(10) Crimson & Clover —*Tommy James & The Shondells*

1970

(1) Bridge Over Troubled Water —*Simon And Garfunkel*
(2) (They Long To Be) Close To You —*The Carpenters*
(3) American Woman —*Guess Who*
(4) War —*Edwin Starr*
(5) Raindrops Keep Fallin' On My Head —*B.J. Thomas*
(6) Ain't No Mountain High Enough —*Diana Ross*
(7) Let It Be —*The Beatles*
(8) Get Ready —*Rare Earth*
(9) I'll Be There –*The Jackson Five*
(10) Band Of Gold —*Freda Payne*

1971

(1) Joy To The World —*Three Dog Night*
(2) Maggie May —*Rod Stewart*
(3) It's Too Late/I Feel The Earth Move —*Carole King*
(4) How Can You Mend A Broken Heart —*Bee Gees*
(5) One Bad Apple —*The Osmonds*
(6) (The Lament Of The Cherokee Reservation Indian) Indian Reservation —*The Raiders*
(7) Take Me Home, Country Road —*John Denver*
(8) Go Away Little Girl —*Donny Osmond*
(9) Just My Imagination (Running Away With Me) —*The Temptations*
(10) Knock Three Times —*Dawn*

About 10% of U.S. households pay their bills in cash.

ABOMINABLE FACTS

Here's an interesting scenario: You're climbing Mt. Everest, and nature calls. You find a cave, take out your Bathroom Reader, *and are lost in "thought" when suddenly, a big hairy creature appears in front of you. It's the Abominable Snowman! What do you do? Well, that's up to you—but our advice is, go ahead and give him the book. You can always get another one back in the States, and he's got nothing to read while he's...uh...you know. No wonder he's abominable.*

HOW HE GOT HIS NAME

Abominable Snowman is a great name, but it actually means nothing; it was a mis-translation.

In 1921, Lt. Col. Charles Kenneth Howard-Bury was climbing in the Himalayas when he spotted a number of "dark forms" moving about on a snowfield above his party. But they were too far away to tell for sure what they were, and by the time the climbers reached the snowfield, the animals were gone. All that was left was a trail of some very large footprints.

Barking up the wrong tree

Howard-Bury thought the forms were large grey wolves; the sherpas with him described the animals as *Meto-Kangmi* or "snow creatures," a generic term used to describe a number of familiar animals that might have made the tracks.

Howard-Bury reported his findings to Katmandu, Nepal, and from there they were transmitted to London. In the process, something changed: *meto-kangmi* became *metch-hangmi*, which means "abominable snowman"—a meaningless, but intriguing phrase.

As Ivan Sandersen writes in *Abominable Snowmen*, "The result was like the explosion of an atom bomb. Nobody, and notably the press, could possibly pass up any such delicious term."

Articles on the "snowman" appeared in newspapers around the globe, turning the abominable snowman from a sleepy regional mystery into something that people were talking about all over the world. Ironically, because the creature was popularly referred to as a

Real estate agent's rule of thumb: To estimate what a house

"snowman," it was assumed that it's white. Actually, people who claim to have seen it say its long, shaggy hair is reddish.

THE FIRST REPORT OF FOOTPRINTS

In 1889, Major L.A. Waddell, an English explorer, stumbled onto a trail of giant footprints in the snow while trekking through the Himalayas. The footprints were discovered on a mountain more than 17,000 feet above sea level. His native guides told him that they belonged to the *Yeti*, a vicious ape-like creature known to eat humans. The guides advised him to run downhill if attacked, because the creature's long hair blocked its vision when it ran downhill.

THE FIRST EVIDENCE

Eric Shipton, a mountain climber, was flying home from an expedition to Mount Everest in 1951. The flight out of Karachi, Pakistan, was uneventful—until the stewardess notified him that a throng of reporters would be waiting for him when the plane landed in London. He couldn't figure out what they wanted. Then he realized they were interested in some photos he'd taken on the Menlung Glacier and sent back home.

The photos in question had, in fact, captured the attention of the entire world. They depicted huge footprints in the snow—more than 13 inches wide and 18 inches long—that apparently belonged to a two-legged animal much larger than a human being. The only problem: no such animal is known to exist in the Himalayas. People speculated that Shipton had finally found proof that the *Yeti*, or *abominable snowman* exists.

RUSSIAN SIGHTINGS

• In 1958, Dr. Alexander Pronin of Leningrad University reported seeing a humanoid creature in the Pamir mountains near Kiev in the Soviet Union. He watched the creature for more than three minutes before it ran away, and then saw it again the next day.

• In 1988, the Soviet news agency TASS reported that some researchers had come within 35 yards of an abominable snowman in the Pamir mountains. After the sighting the researchers planned a second trip into the region, but no further sign of the creature was ever found.

will sell for, ask the owner what it's worth and subtract 10%.

THE HILLARY EXPEDITION

In the late 1960s, Sir Edmund Hillary, the first man to conquer Mt. Everest, returned to the Himalayas to study human physiology at high altitudes. Before he left, he announced that he would investigate the question of the abominable snowman.

Sure enough, Hillary found some "Yeti tracks" in the snow. But as it turns out, they weren't made by a Yeti. In the shade, the tracks were small and had clearly been made by a fox...but wherever the tracks emerged from the shade and into the sunlight, they melted into enlarged, distorted footprints, creating the illusion that they had been made by an animal much larger than a fox. Hillary also noticed that when he let his own footprints melt, some of them grew to nearly a foot wide and two feet in length.

Later in the trip Hillary borrowed a "Yeti scalp" from a Buddhist monastery and had it examined. It turned out to be from a goatlike animal called a serow. Then he examined fur purportedly taken from a Yeti. It was from a Tibetan blue bear.

By the time he returned from the Himalayas, Hillary was convinced that Yetis were purely legendary animals.

THE SLICK EXPEDITION

In 1958, explorer Tom Slick visited the Pangboche monastery in Nepal and photographed a large, shrivelled hand that was kept there.

In 1959, the thumb and other parts of the hand were smuggled out of the country. Dr. Osman Hill of the London Zoological Society performed blood tests that showed the skin was "not human or from any known primate." Dr. Hill became convinced they were Neanderthal.

In 1991, the *Unsolved Mysteries* TV show had the fragments analyzed at the University of California biology laboratories in Los Angeles; these tests showed that the skin was not human, but that it was "close to human." In May 1991, someone broke into the Pangboche monastery and stole a Yeti skullcap and what was left of the Yeti hand. The monastery burned down a few months later.

Coincidence? Conspiracy? To this day, there is not a single shred of tangible, incontrovertible evidence that the Yeti exist. But many people believe it's just a matter of time.

Henry Ford, father of the Model T, is also father of the charcoal briquet.

RUMORS

Why do people believe wild, unsubstantiated stories? According to some psychologists, "rumors make things easier than they are." And besides, they're fun. Here are a few you might have heard.

RUMOR: If you mail your old sneakers to Nike, they'll send you a new pair free.

HOW IT SPREAD: Over the Internet, in 1998. An announcement sent via e-mail claimed Nike had started the promotion "to help make playgrounds for the underprivileged from old tennis shoes." It said: "Pass this e-mail to everyone you know so that everybody can help out." It also listed a mailing address for what it called the "Nike Recycling Center."

THE TRUTH: It was a fake. The address belonged to a Nike warehouse. Nike now receives an average of 100-150 pairs of old shoes a day at the warehouse, and public-minded corporations like Time-Warner began collecting old shoes for Nike until they learned it was a hoax.

RUMOR: Don't throw rice at weddings. Birds eat it, it expands in the stomachs, and they explode.

HOW IT SPREAD: Via the Ann Landers advice column. In 1996 Landers fell for the rumor and published a warning in her column. "Please throw rice petals instead," she implored her readers. "Rice is not good for the birds."

THE TRUTH: The USA Rice Federation, which admittedly has a vested interest in keeping the rice flying, sent an angry letter to Landers. "This silly myth pops up periodically, and it is absolutely unfounded," spokeswoman Mary Jo Cheesman insists.

RUMOR: The pre-printed label on your federal tax forms contains a secret code that tells the IRS auditors whether or not to audit you. If you throw the label away, you won't be audited.

HOW IT SPREAD: From one worried (and hopeful) taxpayer to another, especially in the weeks leading up to April 15.

THE TRUTH: The label is actually there to reduce processing costs, lower the risk for error, and speed the delivery of tax refunds. "It does contain coding information," says Mary Turville, an accountant with the National Society of Accountants, "but it has to do with mail routes and the form package you used in the past. There is no way to trace your tax return from the label."

RUMOR: When the TV show *Green Acres* went off the air in 1971, the cast and crew killed Arnold the Pig and ate him at the farewell barbecue.

HOW IT SPREAD: In 1995 *Starweek* magazine published a letter from a *Green Acres* fan who wrote to complain about the alleged incident. "Arnold was a valuable member of the cast," the letter writer said. "Just because he was a pig was no reason to eat him. I had fond memories of *Green Acres*, but not now. I hope the cannibals burn in hell! Forever!" From there, the story took on a life of its own.

THE TRUTH: At least twelve different pigs played Arnold, and according to trainer Frank Inn, they all lived to old age and died of natural causes. Similar rumors circulated about the pigs that starred in the 1995 film *Babe*.

RUMOR: There's a seeing-eye dog in Germany named Lucky. He has led four of his owners to their deaths so far, but the agency that places him is making plans to give him to a *fifth* owner...without revealing Lucky's checkered past. "It would make Lucky nervous," trainer Ernst Gerber supposedly explained.

HOW IT SPREAD: The story is attributed to a newspaper called the *Europa Times*. It appeared in 1993. Since then it has spread via the Internet and word of mouth. "I admit it's not an impressive record," Gerber supposedly told the newspaper, explaining:

> Lucky led his first owner in front of a bus, and the second off the end of a pier. He actually pushed his third owner off a railway platform...and he walked his fourth owner into heavy traffic, before abandoning him and running away to safety. But, apart from epileptic fits, he has a lovely temperament. And guide dogs are difficult to train these days....

THE TRUTH: It's a complete fabrication.

SCOOBY-DOO, WHERE ARE YOU?

Who's the most famous made-for-TV cartoon character ever? It could be Scooby.

HOUSE OF MYSTERY

In 1969, Fred Silverman, daytime programming director at CBS, asked Bill Hanna and Joe Barbera, TV's most prolific animators, to develop an animated series called *House of Mystery*. It was supposed to be a supernatural/whodunit series based loosely on a combination of a 1940s radio show called *I Love a Mystery* (considered by critics to be the best radio serial ever) and the 1959–1963 sitcom *Dobie Gillis*, which centered around a group of teenagers.

Hanna-Barbera quickly created the characters. The show, was called *Mysteries Five*, then renamed *Who's S-s-s-cared?* It was to revolve around four teenagers and their dog (who at that time only had a small part). Silverman took the idea to New York and presented it to the top CBS brass. To his surprise, they rejected it. The reason: it was too frightening for little children. That posed a big problem to Silverman: he had already reserved his best Saturday morning slot for the show. He was determined to change their minds.

THE CHAIRMAN COMES THROUGH

Silverman spent most of his flight back to L.A. trying to figure out how on earth he would be able to sell the show. Finally, to relax, he put on his headphones. The first thing he heard was Frank Sinatra singing "Strangers in the Night"...which ends with the nonsense lyrics, "Scooby-Dooby-Doo." Silverman suddenly had an inspiration—*that* could be the dog's name. And if he made the dog the star of the show with the other characters supporting him, it would be funny rather than scary.

The CBS executives bought it, and Scooby Doo was born.

Cool customers: The U.S. eastern seaboard consumes almost 50 % of all ice cream sandwiches.

WHO'S WHO?

The final cast of characters for the show included:

• **Scooby-Doo**, a Great Dane. Don Messick, who voiced everyone from Bamm-Bamm to Papa Smurf in Hanna-Barbera cartoons, had to invent a new type of speech for Scooby. "I had to come up with what I call 'growl talk,'" he said. "The words were there. Joe [Barbera] liked things starting with R's, for the dogs especially. He got that from watching Soupy Sales in the early days." (Go ahead, say "Rooby-Rooby Roo"—you know you want to.)

• **Norville "Shaggy" Rogers**, Scoob's best friend, was based on Bob Denver's characterization of Maynard G. Krebs in *Dobie Gillis*. He was voiced by Top 40 deejay Casey Kasem. (Famous quote: "Zoiks!")

• **Velma Dinkley** (voice: Nicole Jaffe), the brains of the outfit, was blind as a bat without her glasses. Seemed to know every language on earth. (Famous quote, whenever she figured out a clue: "Jinkees!")

• **Daphne Blake** (voice: Heather North), the wealthy redheaded beauty who seemed to have no purpose on the show at all. Occasionally, she'd accidentally stumble on a clue. (Famous quote: "Oops!")

• **Freddie Jones** (voice: Frank Welker), the good-looking leader of the gang, who always made Shaggy do the dangerous stuff. (Famous quote: "We'll split up. Velma, you go with Scooby and Shaggy, and I'll go with Daphne.") Hm-m-m—maybe Daphne *did* have a purpose.

THE NUMBERS

The show was an instant success. It took over Saturday morning in the 1970s and eventually set a still-unbroken record as the longest-running continuously-produced children's animated show. Eighteen years passed before television was without some new incarnation of *Scooby-Doo*. In all, there were eleven different series with the name "Scooby Doo" in them. The most recent series (1990) was *A Pup Named Scooby-Doo*. Ten other dogs appeared in the series, all related to Scooby. The most famous, but least liked, was Scooby's nephew, Scrappy-Doo. According to a recent poll on the Internet, Scrappy was the most annoying cartoon character of all time.

Time-killer: Check out the Internet to find numerous recipes for Scooby snacks.

Good taste: Mosquitoes prefer children to adults, blondes to brunettes.

HOW THE BALLPOINT PEN GOT ROLLING

Look carefully at the point of a ballpoint pen. There's a tiny little ball there, of course, which transports the ink from the ink reservoir onto the paper. It looks simple. But actually developing a workable ballpoint pen wasn't easy. Here's the story of how it became a "Bic" part of our lives, from Jack Mingo.

BACKGROUND

On October 30, 1888, John J. Loud of Massachusetts patented a "rolling-pointed fountain marker." It used a tiny, rotating ball bearing that was constantly bathed on one side in ink. That was the original ballpoint pen. Over the next thirty years, 350 similar ballpoint patents were issued by the U.S. Patent Office—but none of the products ever appeared on the market.

The main problem was getting the ink right. If it was too thin, the pens blotched on paper and leaked in pockets. If it was too thick, the pens clogged. Under controlled circumstances, it was sometimes possible to mix up a batch of ink that did what it was supposed to do... until the temperature changed. For decades, the state-of-the-art ballpoint would (usually) work fine at 70° F, but would clog at temperatures below 64° and leak and smear at temperatures above 77°.

OUR HEROES

That's how it was until the Biro brothers came along. In 1935, Ladislas Biro was editing a small newspaper in Hungary. He constantly found himself cursing his fountain pen; the ink soaked into newsprint like a sponge and the pen's tip shredded it. Eventually, he recruited his brother Georg, a chemist, to help him design a new pen. After trying dozens of new designs and ink formulations, the brothers — unaware that it had already been done at least 351 times before— "invented" the ballpoint pen.

A few months later, while they were vacationing at a Mediterranean resort, the brothers began chatting with an older gentleman about their new invention. They showed him a working model, and he was impressed. It turned out that the gentleman was Augustine Justo, the president of Argentina. He suggested that the Biros open a pen factory in his country. They declined...but when World War II began a few years later, they left Hungary and headed to South America. The Biros arrived in Buenos Aires with $10 between them.

Surprisingly, Justo remembered them and helped them find investors. In 1943, they set up a manufacturing plant. The results were spectacular—a spectacular failure, that is. They'd made the mistake everyone else had made—depending on gravity to move the ink onto the ball. That meant the pens had to be held straight up and down at all times. Even then, the ink flow was irregular and globby.

A PEN SAVED IS A PEN EARNED

Ladislas and Georg returned to the lab and came up with a new design. The ink was now siphoned toward the point no matter what position the pen was in. The Biros proudly introduced their new improved model in Argentina—but the pens still didn't sell. They ran out of money and stopped production.

That's when the U.S. Air Force came to the rescue. American flyers, sent to Argentina during the war, discovered that Biro ballpoints worked upside down and at high altitudes. So the wartime U.S. State Department asked American manufacturers to make a similar pen. The Eberhard Faber Company paid $500,000 for the American rights in 1944, yielding the Biro brothers their first profitable year ever.

RIPOFF CITY

About this time, a Chicagoan named Milton Reynolds saw a Biro pen in Argentina. When he returned to the U.S., he discovered that similar pens had been patented years earlier. Since the patents had expired, he figured he could get away with copying the Biro design. He began stamping out pens and selling them for $12.50 each through Gimbels department store in New York City. They were such a novelty that Gimbel's entire stock—a total of 10,000 pens—sold out the first day. Other manufacturers jumped on the bandwagon.

The Reynolds Pen Company hired swimming star Esther Williams to show that the pen would write underwater. Other manufacturers showed their pens writing upside down or through stacks of a dozen pieces of carbon paper. But despite the hoopla, ballpoint pens still weren't dependable. They plugged up or leaked, ruining many documents and good shirts. People bought one, tried it, and—frustrated—vowed never to buy another ballpoint as long as they lived. Sales plummeted.

LA PLUME DE MARCEL

Meanwhile, Marcel Bich, a French manufacturer of penholders and cases, watched with professional interest as the ballpoint industry took off and then crashed. He was impressed by the ballpoint pen's innovative design, but appalled by the high cost and low quality. He realized that if he could come up with a dependable, reasonably priced pen, he could take over the market. So he licensed the Biro brothers' patents, and began experimenting.

For two years, he bought every ballpoint pen on the market and systematically tested them, looking for their strengths and weaknesses. Then in 1949, Bich unveiled his triumph: an inexpensive ballpoint with a six-sided, clear plastic case. It wrote smoothly and didn't leak or jam. They were a huge hit in Europe.

Looking ahead, he knew that his name would eventually be a problem in America. Rather than risk having his product referred to as a "Bitch Pen," he simplified his name so it would be pronounced correctly no matter were it was sold—"Bic."

CONQUERING AMERICA

In 1958, Bic set up shop in the U.S. As it turned out, it wasn't his name that proved a problem—it was those shoddy pens people had bought a decade earlier. The American public had come to trust expensive pens, but refused to believe a 29¢ pen would really work.

So Bic launched an ad campaign to demonstrate that his pens would work the "first time, every time." He flooded the airwaves with TV commercials—many live—showing that Bic pens still worked after "being shot from guns, drilled through wallboard, fire-blasted, and strapped to the feet of ice-skaters and flamenco dancers." He also began selling them in grocery stores, and little shops near schools, where he knew students would see them.

The result: By 1967, Bic was selling 500 million pens—60% of the U.S. market. His competitors also began selling cheap, high-quality pens...and ballpoints were changed forever.

As *Time* magazine said in 1972: "Baron Bich has done for ballpoints what Henry Ford did for cars."

giant crayon 35' wide and 100' taller than the Statue of Liberty.

HE SAID, SHE SAID

Ronald B. Schwartz collected these gems in his book,
Men are Lunatics, Women are Nuts!

"There's no such thing as a man...Just a little boy in a man's body."

—Elvis Presley

"If you want anything said, ask a man. If you want anything done, ask a woman."

—Margaret Thatcher

"If you want to resist the feminist movement, the simple way to do it is to give them what they want and they'll defeat themselves. Today, there are women who don't know if they want to be a mother, have lunch, or be secretary of state."

—Jack Nicholson

"A man's home may seem to be a castle on the outside; inside, it's often his nursery."

—Clare Booth Luce

"I require three things in a man. He must be handsome, ruthless, and stupid."

—Dorothy Parker

"As long as you know that most men are children, you know everything."

—Coco Chanel

"The best way to get most husbands to do something is to suggest that perhaps they're too old to do it."

—Shirley MacLaine

"If men can run the world, why can't they stop wearing neckties? How intelligent is it to start the day by tying a little noose around your neck?"

—Linda Ellerbee

"Talking with a man is like trying to saddle a cow. You work like hell, but what's the point."

—Gladys Upham

"Men are gluttons for punishment. They fight over women for the chance to fight with them."

—Vincent Price

* * *

"Marriage is a three ring circus: engagement ring, wedding ring, and suffering." ***—Anonymous***

The BBC reported in 1964 that Ringo Starr had his toenails removed. It was really his tonsils.

THE WORLD'S TALLEST BUILDINGS, PART III

Here's the story of how New York became the skyscraper capital of the world. *(Part II is on page 138.)*

NEW YORK'S FIRST SKYSCRAPER

In 1888, a young silk manufacturer named John Noble Stearns bought a skinny strip of land in lower Manhattan. He wanted to build something on it, but wasn't sure what. He just knew he wanted to make a lot of money.

It happened that Stearns' architect was familiar with the skeleton-construction method becoming popular in Chicago. He suggested constructing an 11-story building 159 feet long, 158 feet tall...but only 21-1/2 feet wide. Stearns liked the idea, and work on the Tower Building, New York's first true skyscraper, began.

White Elephant

The Tower Building was so flat and thin that many people were afraid it would blow over in the first high wind. Stearns' friends laughed at him when the building went up, and they refused to go inside when it was finished. Nobody wanted to be in it when it finally fell over.

But when several months passed and the Tower Building didn't collapse, people began venturing in and climbing to the eleventh floor, one of the highest points in the entire city. New York's love affair with tall buildings had begun.

UP, UP AND AWAY

The subsequent growth of the New York City skyline mirrored the improvements in elevator technology. From 1841 to 1894, the tallest building in the city was Trinity Church on lower Broadway, which had a steeple 284 feet high. For a few cents you could climb the rickety wooden staircase inside the steeple and take in the highest view the city had to offer.

But in the 1890s, after the Otis brothers had perfected the first electric elevator, a burst of new construction completely transformed the business district of Manhattan. In 1894, the 17-story Manhattan Life Insurance Building became the first to top Trinity Church, making it the tallest building east of Chicago. It was quickly followed by scores of other skyscrapers, including the 21-story American Surety Building, the 23-story American Tract Society Building, and the 32-story Park Row Building—which, at 391 feet, finally beat out Chicago to make New York City the home of the tallest building on Earth.

THE SKYSCRAPER RACE

The Park Row Building was only the beginning. As George Douglas writes in *Skyscrapers: A Social History in America:*

> New York hadn't seen anything yet. In the years between 1900 and the First World War...skyscrapers rose like tall grasses on the summer prairie....New York business leaders came to see in the skyscraper not only convenient and economical office space, but a possible means of corporate glory and aggrandizement. A great tower, obviously, could not only house management but glorify it.

The Singer Building

In the 1890s, the Singer Sewing Machine Company built a 10-story office building at Broadway and Liberty St. in Manhattan. They added to the building repeatedly over the years, and in 1906 announced the addition of a 612-foot-tall, 47-story tower that would be "higher than all existing skyscrapers by 200 to 300 feet."

The building also boasted every state-of-the-art convenience the early 1900s had to offer: centralized steam heat complete with individual thermostats, a central vacuum cleaning system, hot and cold running water in every office, and 16 elevators—more than in any other building in the world.

The tower opened on May 1, 1908, and held the title of the world's tallest building for a mere 18 months. Sixty years later this precious architectural gem set another record: it became the tallest building ever demolished, when it was razed to make way for the "banal and colorless" United States Steel Building.

The Metropolitan Life Building

Next on the list of "tallest buildings in the world" was the Metropoli-

Peter Dowdeswell holds 25 records for speed-eating, including eating 1 lb. of eels in 13.7 seconds.

tan Life Building, which in 1909, became the first office building to pass the 700-foot mark. It was 88 feet higher than the Singer Building.

The land and the building cost an astronomical $6 million, a shocking sum that was difficult for Metropolitan's conservative shareholders to stomach. But the head of Metropolitan justified the expense by explaining that since the building was fully occupied, it cost almost nothing in the long run...and generated invaluable free advertising for the company.

Metropolitan capitalized on its headquarters in ways the Singer company never dreamed of: It made the massive lantern at the very top of the pointed roof into its corporate symbol, as well as the inspiration for the company's slogan, "The light that never fails." And on election night in 1908, it even used the beacon to beam the results of the presidential election out to the rest of the city.

The Metropolitan Building still stands, and is still the home office of the Metropolitan Life Insurance Company.

JUST THE BEGINNING

Both the Singer Tower and the Metropolitan Life Tower were impressive sights to behold, but the first building to really capture the public's imagination—and cement its love affair with the skyscraper—was the Woolworth Building, a magnificent 60-story edifice that to this day is considered one of the most beautiful skyscrapers ever built.

For that story, turn to page 206.

*   *   *   *

RANDOM "THOUGHTS"

"It is wonderful to be here in the great state of Chicago."
—Former U. S. Vice-President Dan Quayle

"The streets are safe in Philadelphia. It's only the people that make them unsafe."—**Former Philadelphia Mayor Frank Rizzo**

Just one in three consumers pays off his or her entire credit card bill every month.

THE TOP 10 HITS OF THE YEAR, 1972–1975

Here's another installment of BRI's Top Ten of the Year list.

1972

(1) The First Time Ever I Saw Your Face —*Roberta Flack*
(2) Alone Again (Naturally) —*Gilbert O'Sullivan*
(3) American Pie —*Don McLean*
(4) I Gotcha —*Joe Tex*
(5) Candy Man —*Sammy Davis, Jr.*
(6) Without You —*Nilsson*
(7) Lean On Me —*Bill Withers*
(8) Brand New Key —*Melanie*
(9) Baby Don't Get Hooked On Me —*Mac Davis*
(10) Daddy, Don't You Walk So Fast —*Wayne Newton*

1973

(1) Tie A Yellow Ribbon Round The Old Oak Tree —*Tony Orlando and Dawn*
(2) Bad, Bad Leroy Brown —*Jim Croce*
(3) Let's Get It On —*Marvin Gaye*
(4) Killing Me Softly With His Song —*Roberta Flack*
(5) My Love —*Paul McCartney / Wings*
(6) Why Me —*Kris Kristofferson*
(7) Will It Go Round In Circles —*Billy Preston*
(8) Crocodile Rock —*Elton John*
(9) You're So Vain —*Carly Simon*
(10) Touch Me In The Morning —*Diana Ross*

1974

(1) The Way We Were —*Barbra Steisand*
(2) Seasons In The Sun —*Terry Jacks*
(3) Come And Get Your Love —*Redbone*
(4) Love's Theme —*Love Unlimited Orchestra*
(5) Dancing Machine —*Jackson Five*
(6) The Loco-Motion —*Grand Funk Railroad*
(7) The Streak —*Ray Stevens*
(8) TSOP —*MFSB*
(9) Bennie And The Jets —*Elton John*
(10) One Hell Of A Woman —*Mac Davis*

1975

(1) Love Will Keep Us Together —*The Captain & Tennille*
(2) Rhinestone Cowboy —*Glen Campbell*
(3) Philadelphia Freedom —*Elton John*
(4) Shining Star —*Earth, Wind & Fire*
(5) My Eyes Adored You —*Frankie Valli*
(6) Before The Next Teardrop Falls —*Freddy Fender*
(7) Fame —*David Bowie*
(8) One Of These Nights —*Eagles*
(9) Laughter In The Rain —*Neil Sedaka*
(10) Thank God I'm A Country Boy —*John Denver*

obert Moses, the man responsible for most major highways in New York, never learned how to drive.

YOUR GOVERNMENT AT WORK

Concerned about the government's priorities? Now you can breathe a sigh of relief, knowing your tax dollars are being well-spent on things like...

• **Real estate.** "In 1986 the National Park Service bought a half acre of land in southwest Washington, D.C., for $230,000. In 1988 someone discovered that the Park Service already owned the land—they bought it in 1914." (*Great Government Goofs*)

• **Streamlining the Pentagon.** "During the 1980s Department of Defense efficiency experts saved between $27 million and $136 million each year! However, the efficiency experts cost between $150 million and $300 million each year." (*Stupid Government Tricks*)

• **Physical fitness.** "When $122 million was allocated for an addition to the Dirksen Office Building in Washington, D.C., it went to give the senators a third gymnasium." (*Goofy Government Grants & Wacky Waste*)

• **Reimbursement.** "According to a 1989 report by the State Department Watch, a private watchdog organization, the Department of State issued eighteen thousand travel expense checks without getting corroborating evidence for the expenses. One check for $9,000 was issued to 'Ludwig van Beethoven,' whose Social Security number was listed as '123-45-6789.'" (*Stupid Government Tricks*)

• **Sociology.** "$84,000 [was] approved by Congress for a project to discover why people fall in love." (*Great Government Goofs*)

• **Fighting Poverty.** $5 million was approved by Congress as an interest-free loan to Sears, Roebuck under the federal "antipoverty" funds program. (*Great Government Goofs*)

• **Space travel.** "The National Aeronautics and Space Administration spent $23 million to build a prototype toilet for the space shuttle—a 900% increase over the original estimate. Why the overrun? The astronauts wanted a manual flush rather than an automatic one." (From *Goofy Government Grants & Wacky Waste*)

Last 2 European countries to let women vote: Switzerland (1971) and Leichtenstein (1984).

• **Natural history.** "$107,000 was appropriated by Congress for a project to study the sex life of the Japanese quail." (*Great Government Goofs*)

• "The Illinois Department of Conservation spent $180,000 to study the contents of owl vomit." (*Great Government Goofs*)

• **Medical research.** "In 1993 the Physicians Committee for Responsible Medicine termed 'outlandish' a $3 million federally funded research project to determine whether marijuana will make rabbits more susceptible to syphilis and mice more prone to contract Legionnaires' disease." (*Stupid Government Tricks*)

• **On-the-spot research.** "More than $7 million is spent each year by politicians on junkets to popular vacation spots around the world. It's called 'business travel.' As a matter of fact, when the government's fiscal year is about to run out, there's an estimated 48% increase in government business travel." (*Goofy Government Grants & Wacky Waste*)

* * * *

AND SPEAKING OF DUMB...

News of the Weird reports that "Annette Montoya, 11, of Belen, New Mexico, and her parents were arrested for forgery after Annette, in the company of her father, attempted to open a bank account with a $900,000 check. The girl told sheriff's deputies that she earned the money doing 'some yard work.' During the interrogation, she crossed her heart and said, 'Hope to die if I'm lying.'"

From the BRI files: Lagos, Nigeria—Two small buses collided when their drivers tried to slap each others' hands in greeting, the News Agency of Nigeria reported. Seven people died; the two drivers were among them.

Longest snake in the world: the Royal Python (no relation to Monty), which tops out at 35 feet.

DAEDALUS AND ICARUS

This Greek tale about man's first attempt to fly is still used today to illustrate both the dangers of hubris and the impetuous nature of youth. This version is from Myths and Legends of the Ages.

On the island of Crete, during the reign of King Minos, there lived a most skillful artisan named Daedalus. Daedalus was the greatest inventor and craftsman of his time, and his fame spread to the far corners of the world.

It was Daedalus who built the famous labyrinth in which King Minos kept that terrible beast, the Minotaur. This labyrinth was a building with hundreds of winding halls and passages so complicated that no one who went into it could ever find his way out again.

But although Daedalus performed great services for King Minos, the king feared him. Minos was afraid that Daedalus, with his great wisdom and skill, might someday gain the throne of Crete. So King Minos imprisoned Daedalus and his young son, Icarus, in a dark stone tower.

But no locks could hold Daedalus! For he could open them all. And one dark night, Daedalus and Icarus escaped from the tower.

After they had fled, Daedalus and Icarus did not find it so easy to escape from Crete. You see, Crete is an island, and King Minos had his soldiers search every ship that left its shores.

Daedalus and Icarus lay in hiding in a cave along the seashore. One bright day, Daedalus was idly watching the seagulls soaring and swooping over the water in their search for food. Suddenly, an idea struck him.

"King Minos may control the land and the sea," he cried, "but he does not control the air. That is how Icarus and I shall escape."

Then Daedalus set to work to study the birds and learn the secret of their flight. For endless hours he watched the birds flying. He caught a bird and studied the clever structure of its wings. Then he put to use his knowledge and skill to copy the wings of a bird. The boy, Icarus, spent his days trapping the seagulls and plucking their feathers. Daedalus took the feathers which his son had obtained, and sewed them together with marvelous skill. Soon, wings began to take shape, so wonderfully made that, except for their great size, they looked exactly like the real wings of a bird. And then Daedalus took these wings, and with melted wax attached them to a wooden framework.

When he had made a pair of wings for himself and a pair of wings for his son, Daedalus fastened them in place. A wing was strapped to each arm. Then Daedalus proceeded to teach his son to fly, just as a mother bird teaches her young. How happy and excited young Icarus was when he found that he could fly through the air, that he could circle and float on the wind! He was impatient to be off.

Finally the time came when Daedalus felt they were ready to make the escape from Crete. He turned to his young son and said, "Icarus, listen carefully to my words. Follow close behind me in your flight. Do not fly too low or the dampness from the sea will cling to your wings and make them too heavy for you to lift. Do not fly too high or the sun will melt the wax of your wings."

Then Daedalus kissed his son fondly and began to rise into the air. Icarus followed his father. As the two of them flew across the sky, people looked up in amazement. The ploughmen in the fields gazed upward, the shepherds marveled! They thought they were watching the flight of gods.

At first, Icarus stayed close behind his father. But then, exalting in his new-found power, he flew off on little side trips. Soon he forgot everything his father told him and flew high into the heavens.

Then the blazing sun did its work and the wax of his wings melted. Icarus fluttered his arms, but there were not enough feathers left to beat the air. He called his father, but in vain. Down he fell into the sea!

Daedalus sped to the aid of his son, but when he saw the feathers floating on the ocean, he knew to his grief that Icarus had been drowned. So ended man's first attempt to fly; for Daedalus, heartbroken at the loss of his son, flew on to Sicily, took off his wings and never flew again.

First baseball game on TV: the Brooklyn Dodgers vs. the Philadelphia Eagles, August 26, 1939.

NAME YOUR POISON

You may not like the products...but it's always interesting to find out where familiar brand names come from.

Pall Mall cigarettes: Named for one of the most fashionable streets in London. The British pronunciation is "Pell Mell."

Cutty Sark scotch: Named after the clipper ship that won a trans-Atlantic sailing race in the 1870s.

Lucky Strike cigarettes: Dr. R. A. Patterson, a Virginia doctor, gave the name to plug tobacco that he sold to miners during the California Gold Rush of 1856. It was first introduced as a cigarette in 1917.

Bourbon whiskey: When Louis XVI of the Bourbon dynasty of France assisted the struggling colonists during the Revolutionary War, they named a region of Virginia and Kentucky Bourbon County in his honor. The county later became the birthplace of bourbon whiskey.

Chesterfield cigarettes: Named after the 4th Earl of Chesterfield, 18th-century trend-setting socialite. The Chesterfield couch and jacket are also named after him.

Old Crow scotch: Named in 1835 after Dr. James Crow, the Scottish surgeon and chemist who introduced sanitation and modern distillation methods to the domestic whiskey industry.

Kent cigarettes: Herbert A. Kent, a Lorillard Tobacco Company executive, was so popular at the office that the company named Kent cigarettes after him in 1952.

White Horse scotch: Originally served in the White Horse Inn in Edinburgh, Scotland.

I. W. Harper whiskey: When Isaac W. Bernheim and his brother started a whiskey business in 1872, they named their product I. W. Harper—I. W. for Bernheim's initials...and Harper after their star salesman. The firm's customers already called it Mr. Harper's whiskey. Bernheim figured there was no point in tampering with a well established name.

PREDICTIONS FOR THE YEAR 2000

For a century, people have been speculating about what life would be like way off in the future—in the year 2000. Now that it's almost here, we can see just how bizarre some of those predictions were. These quotes were compiled for our book Uncle John's Indispensable Guide to the Year 2000.

THE DREAM HOUSE OF 2000

"[Using] wonderful new materials far stronger than steel, but lighter than aluminum...houses [in the year 2000] will be able to fly.... The time may come when whole communities may migrate south in the winter, or move to new lands whenever they feel the need for a change of scenery."

—Arthur C. Clarke,
***Vogue*, 1966**

"Keeping house will be a breeze by the year 2000. Sonic cleaning devices and air-filtering systems will just about eliminate dusting, scrubbing and vacuuming. There may be vibrating floor grills by doors to clean shoes, and electrostatic filters will be installed in entrances to remove dust from clothes with ultrasonic waves."

—Staff of the *Wall Street Journal*,
***Here Comes Tomorrow!* (1966)**

"When [the housewife of 2000] cleans house she simply turns the hose on everything. Why not? Furniture—(upholstery included), rugs, draperies, unscratchable floors—all are made of synthetic fabric or waterproof plastic. After the water has run down a drain in the middle of the floor (later concealed by a rug of synthetic fiber), [she] turns on a blast of hot air and dries everything."

—Waldemarr Kaempfert,
***Popular Mechanics*, 1950**

Wet Glaze, Gum Swamp, and Convalescent Corral were all battles in the Civil War.

COMMUTING

"[In 2000], commuters will go to the city, a hundred miles away, in huge aerial buses that hold 200 passengers. Hundreds of thousands more will make such journeys twice a day in their own helicopters."

—Waldemar Kaempfert,
***Popular Mechanics*, 1950**

"[Commuters will] rent small four-seater capsules such as we find on a ski lift. These capsules will be linked together into little trains that come in to the city. As the train goes out towards the perimeter of the city, the capsule will become an individual unit. One can then drive to wherever he may want to go."

—Ulrich Frantzen,
Prophecy for the Year 2000

A Seattle executive could commute 300 miles to Los Angeles with ease. "He might board his reserved-seat air-cushion coach at 8:15 A.M. It would lift off the roadbed, whirl around an 'acceleration loop' and plunge into the main tube running from Seattle to San Diego. Little more than half an hour later, the car would peel off onto the 'deceleration loop' in downtown Los Angeles. By 9 a.m. the executive would be at his desk."

—Mitchell Gordon,
***Here Comes Tomorrow!* (1966)**

THE WORLD OF WORK

"By 2000, the machines will be producing so much that everyone in the U.S. will, in effect, be independently wealthy. With government benefits, even nonworking families will have, by one estimate, an annual income of $30,000–$40,000 (in 1966 dollars). How to use leisure meaningfully will be a major problem."

—*Time*, February 25, 1966

"By the year 2000, people will work no more than four days a week and less than eight hours a day. With legal holidays and long vacations, this could result in an annual working period of 147 days [on] and 218 days off."

—*New York Times*,
October 19, 1967

First four countries to have television: England, the U.S., the U.S.S.R., and Brazil.

CAUGHT IN THE SPOTLIGHT

Everyone wants to be famous these days—but sometimes people forget that it's not always a good idea. Take these guys—they hopped into the limelight. .and ended up making headlines they wished they hadn't.

HEADLINE: *Man Wins Largest Prize in Game Show's History. .and Free Trip to Jail*

The Story: In December 1987, a man identifying himself as "Patrick Quinn" went on the TV game show *Super Password* and won $58,600, the largest one-day jackpot in the show's history.

Caught: The show aired on January 8, 1988...and within minutes phones at the *Password* offices began to ring. "We started getting calls from people...saying, 'That's not Patrick Quinn, there is no Patrick Quinn,'" executive producer Bob Sherman told reporters.

The man was actually Kerry Ketcham, who was wanted by the Secret Service for faking a $100,000 life insurance claim on his wife (who had not died). When Ketcham showed up at the *Super Password* offices to pick up his check, he was arrested. He pled guilty to two counts of mail fraud...and forfeited his winnings from the show. Reason: he gave a false name when applying to be a contestant.

HEADLINE: *Man Loses Nearly $10 million in Lottery; Wins Prison Sentence.*

The Story: On October 19, 1990, a real estate executive named Joseph A. Sutera won the "Mass Millions" prize in the Massachusetts lottery, collecting a jackpot of $9,916,540 to be paid out in annual installments over 20 years.

Caught: Years earlier, Sutera had swindled hundreds of seniors in Connecticut, Rhode Island, New Hampshire, and other states out of their retirement savings in bogus real estate deals. When Sutera won the lottery, more than a thousand swindled retirees spotted his name in news stories. So many claims were filed against the winnings that Sutera was forced into bankruptcy. A federal judge awarded Sutera's winnings to his victims in 1994. By then, Sutera was already serving a five-year prison sentence on federal fraud charges.

HEADLINE: *Large Donor at Political Fundraiser Earns a Seat at President Bush's Table...and a Ticket to Jail.*

The Story: On April 28, 1992, Los Angeles businessman Michael Kojima contributed $500,000 to a Republican Party Fundraiser called "The President's Dinner" for then-President George Bush, who was pushing "Family Values" as a major theme in his campaign. That made Kojima the largest contributor at the event (which raised a record $9 million in one night, the largest political fundraiser ever) and earned him a spot at President Bush's table. He appeared in photographs and news footage broadcast around the world.

Caught: Los Angeles prosecutors immediately recognized Kojima as the man dubbed "America's Most-Wanted Deadbeat Dad," wanted on a fugitive warrant for failing to pay more than $200,000 in child support to two of his five ex-wives. According to the *Los Angeles Times*, Kojima "had eluded investigators for four months, moving frequently and living under assumed names."

Authorities arrested him a few days later as he was preparing to leave on vacation with his sixth wife. But rather than turn the money over to Mrs. Kojima and her children, Republican fundraisers put the $500,000 in an escrow account and asked a judge to decide who should get the money, while maintaining that the party "has a valid interest in and is entitled to the political contributions." In the end, the GOP got to hang on to about half of the money.

HEADLINE: *Hijacked Honeymooners Receive Key to City; Trip to Prison.*

The Story: In 1977, Jerry and Darlene Jenkins of Burlington, Vermont, were honeymooning in New York City when a mentally ill man hijacked their car and took them on a terrifying ride that ended when the car jumped a curb and plowed into a crowd of people, killing one pedestrian and injuring 12 others.

New Yorkers were so shocked by the senselessness of the crime that they showered the couple with dinner invitations, tickets to Broadway plays, and free hotel rooms paid for by the *New York Daily News*, the New York Telephone Company, and other big corporations. Mayor Abraham Beame even had the couple over to City Hall, where he presented them with a public apology and an engraved silver plate.

Caught: The incident made headlines all over the country, including Burlington, Vermont—where law enforcement officials recognized Jerry Jenkins as the man who was wanted for passing more than $2,500 worth of bad checks in area stores. And, as *The Washington Post* reported a week later, "there was some question as to whether the couple was even married. His woman companion, who previously identified herself as his 21-year-old bride, Darlene, apparently left New York for parts unknown." Jenkins was arrested.

ON THE OTHER HAND...

HEADLINE: *Viewers of "America's Most Wanted" TV Show Nab Another Desperado.*

The Story: David Adams, a Tennessee man wanted in connection with a number of fraud and arson cases, was nabbed at a Nashville country fair after two women recognized him from an "America's Most Wanted" episode that had aired two days earlier. The women alerted park rangers, who took Adams into custody.

Caught: "David Adams" turned out to be actor Christopher Cotton, the man hired by "America's Most Wanted" to portray the crook in the show's crime reenactment sequences.

Cotton showed proof of identification to the rangers, but it didn't win his release—at least not right away. According to news reports, "Adams had often used fake identification and disguises to elude authorities, so the authorities had to take Cotton into custody until a photo and fingerprints could be compared."

"I guess it's an occupational hazard," Cotton told reporters, "but I never expected it. You never know how people are going to react to television."

Most sought after Cracker Jack prizes: toy rings. Reason: they're often used as engagement rings

BEGINNINGS

At the BRI, we enjoy finding out where things come from. Here are some items we picked at random:

THE SQUARE HANDKERCHIEF

Among her many eccentricities, Marie Antoinette hated the fact that handkerchiefs came in so many sizes and shapes. She decided that she liked the square ones the best, and, in 1785, she had her husband, Louis XVI, issue a law that henceforth, "the length of handkerchiefs shall equal their width, throughout my entire kingdom." Non-square handkerchiefs have been hard to find ever since.

ERASERS

In 1770, an American friend gave renowned English scientist Joseph Priestly a ball made out of a material Priestly had never seen before. He observed that the material, which was sap from a South American tree, could rub away pencil marks from paper, so he called it "rubber." It wasn't until the discovery of vulcanized rubber in 1839 that rubber erasers became practical, and even then it took another 20 years before a Philadelphia inventor named Hyman Lipman patented the first pencil with an eraser.

AIRLINE STEWARDESSES

Before 1930, only men served on airplane crews. Then, Ellen Church, a nurse and student pilot, convinced United Airlines that having females on board would help ticket sales...but not for the reason you'd think: "Don't you think it would be good psychology to have women up in the air?" she asked the directors. "How is a man going to say he is afraid to fly when a woman is working on the plane?" United agreed and told her to hire seven women. The women had to be under 5'4" and 115 pounds, age 25 or less, single, and—*registered nurses*. Their wage: $125 a month for each 100 hours in the air. On top of serving passengers, the first stewardesses also had to help the crew clean the plane, load the baggage, gas the plane, and push it from the hanger.

RED BARNS

BRI-member Douglas Ottati sends us this information: "Why are barns painted red? In the early nineteenth century, farmers learned that the color red absorbed sunlight extremely well and was useful in keeping barns warm during winter. The farmers made their red paint from skim milk mixed with the rust shavings of metal fences and nails."

GUIDE DOGS

It probably seems as though seeing-eye dogs have been around forever. Actually, they are a 20th-century development.

Near the end of World War I, a doctor and his dog were walking the grounds of a German military hospital with a soldier who'd lost his sight in the war. The doctor stepped inside the hospital for a minute. When he returned, he found that the dog had led the soldier around the grounds on its own. That inspired him to do some experiments. When the doctor showed that he had successfully trained dogs to lead the blind, the German government lent its support. Later, an American named Dorothy Eustis visited Germany to see the trained dogs, and wrote an article about it in *The Saturday Evening Post*. In 1929, the first school for seeing-eye dogs was set up in the U.S.

BASEBALL'S "MOST VALUABLE PLAYER" AWARD

According to *Wheels of a Nation*, by Frank Donovan, the award started out as an effort to publicize a now-forgotten car called the Chalmers: "Hugh Chalmers announced in 1910 that he would give a car to the champion batters of each league. He was delighted when Ty Cobb, a Detroiter, won the American League championship. But his elation turned to fury when Cobb promptly sold his prize."

THE RUBBER BAND

In 1820, Thomas Hancock, an Englishman, was given a bottle made of rubber by some Central American Indians. He cut it into strips and created the first rubber bands (although he sold them as garters and waistbands).

MYTH AMERICA

Here are a few "facts" about the Wild West that you may have heard...which are 100% baloney. Most of the information is from Bill Bryson's excellent book, Made in America.

THE MYTH: Cowboys talked like cowboys—they said things like "get along little dogie," and "I've got an itchy trigger finger."

THE TRUTH: A lot of the words associated with cowboys were invented by novelists and movie scriptwriters, and not until long after the age of the cowboy had passed. Motherless calves were not called *dogies* until 1903, jails didn't become *hoosegows* until 1920, and the expressions *bounty hunter*, *gunslinger*, and *I've got an itchy trigger finger* were all invented in Hollywood.

MYTH: Settlers travelled west in huge Conestoga wagons pulled by horses.

THE TRUTH: Conestoga wagons were too heavy, and horses were too weak, for the long trip west. Settlers used smaller, nimbler wagons called *prairie schooners*, and they pulled them with mules or oxen, which were stronger and hardier than horses.

MYTH: Wagon trains travelled in straight, single-file lines across the prairies.

THE TRUTH: The trip across much of America was so dusty, Bryson writes, that whenever possible, wagons "fanned out into an advancing line up to ten miles wide to avoid each other's dust and the ruts of earlier travelers."

MYTH: If your wagon train was attacked by Indians, the way you defended yourself was by circling the wagons.

THE TRUTH: Another invention of Hollywood filmmakers, who liked the way circled wagons looked on film. The wagons didn't circle, Bryson writes, "for the simple reason that the process would have been so laborious and time consuming to organize that the

The 5 smartest primates, after humans: Chimpanzees, Gorillas, Orangutans, Baboons, Gibbons.

participants would very probably have been slaughtered long before the job was accomplished." Some wagon trains did circle when they stopped at night, but not specifically for protection. They needed a way to corral the animals.

MYTH: If you wanted to make it as a gunfighter in the Old West, you had to be man enough to take a bullet in the shoulder or thigh, and keep on shooting.

THE TRUTH: Taking a bullet "like a man" is such a standard plot device in cowboy novels that, as one film critic put it, "One would think that the human shoulder was made of some self-healing material, rather like a puncture-proof tire." Actually, most people who were shot never got up again. Bullets were slower and softer in the 19th century—which sounds nice, but can actually make them more lethal. Instead of shooting straight through the body and exiting quickly out the other end, they tend to bounce around like a pinball, then exit "with a hole like a fist punched through paper," Bryson writes. "Even if they miraculously missed the victim's vital organs, he would almost invariably suffer deep and incapacitating shock and bleed to death within minutes."

MYTH: As marshall of Dodge City, Wyatt Earp helped tame the Wild West.

THE TRUTH: Earp was never the marshall of Dodge City. He did serve two terms as *deputy* marshall, but according to historian Peter Lyon in *American Heritage*, the only reason he took the job was because it was good for his gambling career. "Every professional gambler needed a star," Lyon writes. "The badge of office permitted its wearer to carry a gun....Only peace officers were permitted to carry guns in Dodge City; all others were obliged to check their weapons in racks provided for that purpose." Wyatt wasn't even an honest card player, let alone a standup lawman, which may be why he wanted a gun. According to historian Floyd Streeter, Earp had a reputation for being "up to some dishonest trick every time he played."

"There's two ways for a fellow to look for adventure: By tearing everything down, or building everything up." —**The Lone Ranger**

Snowiest city in the U.S.: Blue Canyon, California.

THE TOP 10 HITS OF THE YEAR, 1976–1979

Here's another Top Ten of the Year list.

1976

(1) Silly Love Songs —*Paul McCartney / Wings*
(2) Don't Go Breaking My Heart —*Elton John / Kiki Dee*
(3) Disco Lady —*Johnnie Taylor*
(4) December, 1963 (Oh, What A Night) —*The Four Seasons*
(5) Kiss And Say Goodbye —*The Manhattans*
(6) Play That Funky Music —*Wild Cherry*
(7) 50 Ways To Leave Your Lover —*Paul Simon*
(8) Love Machine, Pt. 1 —*Miracles*
(9) Love Is Alive —*Gary Wright*
(10) A Fifth Of Beethoven —*Walter Murphy & The Big Apple Band*

1977

(1) Tonight's The Night —*Rod Stewart*
(2) I Just Want To Be Your Everything —*Andy Gibb*
(3) Best Of My Love —*Emotions*
(4) Love Theme From "A Star Is Born" —*Barbra Streisand*
(5) I Like Dreamin' —*Kenny Nolan*
(6) Angel In Your Arms —*Hot*
(7) Don't Leave Me This Way —*Thelma Houston*
(8) Higher and Higher —*Rita Coolidge*
(9) Torn Between Two Lovers —*Mary MacGregor*
(10) Undercover Angel —*Alan O'Day*

1978

(1) Shadow Dancing —*Andy Gibb*
(2) Stayin' Alive —*The Bee Gees*
(3) You Light Up My Life —*Debby Boone*
(4) Night Fever —*The Bee Gees*
(5) Kiss You All Over —*Exile*
(6) How Deep Is Your Love —*The Bee Gees*
(7) Baby Come Back —*Player*
(8) (Love Is) Thicker Than Water —*Andy Gibb*
(9) Three Times A Lady —*The Commodores*
(10) Boogie Oogie Oogie —*A Taste Of Honey*

1979

(1) My Sharona —*The Knack*
(2) Bad Girls —*Donna Summer*
(3) Reunited —*Peaches And Herb*
(4) Da Ya Think I'm Sexy? —*Rod Stewart*
(5) Le Freak —*Chic*
(6) Y.M.C.A. —*The Village People*
(7) Hot Stuff —*Donna Summer*
(8) I Will Survive —*Gloria Gaynor*
(9) Ring My Bell —*Anita Ward*
(10) Sad Eyes —*Robert John*

Uh-Oh. The population of the earth has more than doubled since 1950.

THE CLASSIFIEDS

Have you ever been in a place where all you can find to read in the bathroom is an old newspaper? Try this: just flip to the classifieds and look for funny goofs like these. Most were collected by Richard Lederer for his book Fractured English.

FOR SALE

An antique desk suitable for lady with thick legs and large drawers.

GREAT DAMES FOR SALE

Four-poster bed, 101 years old. Perfect for antique lover.

Pit Bull For Sale: Owner deceased.

Eight puppies from a German Shepherd and an Alaskan Hussy.

WANTED

Looking for hanging cage for my daughter. Must have exercise wheel.

Unmarried girls to pick fresh fruit and produce at night.

Girl wanted to assist magician in cutting-off-head illusion. Salary and Blue Cross.

Preparer of food. Must be dependable, like the food business and be willing to get hands dirty.

Man wanted to work in dynamite factory. Must be willing to travel.

Hard working, experienced farm woman. Household and field work; know how to cook; must own tractor—send photo of tractor.

Hair-cutter. Excellent growth potential.

MISCELLANEOUS

Lost: Beagle, partly blind, hard of hearing, castrated; answers to the name of Lucky.

For rent: 6-room hated apartment

Illiterate? Write today for free help.

The license fee for altered dogs with a certificate will be $3 and for pets owned by senior citizens who have not been altered the fee will be $1.50.

Free—Three Kittens: Siamese coloring. Will do yard work. To a loving home only.

Oldest TV show still on the air: *Meet the Press,* which first aired on November 6, 1947.

THE WORLD'S TALLEST BUILDINGS, PART IV

Here's the story of how FW Woolworth used nickels and dimes to pay for one of the most popular skyscrapers ever constructed. (Part III on page 186.)

KING OF COMMERCE

At the turn of the century, Frank Winfield Woolworth was one of the richest merchants in the world. And every penny of his fortune was earned in nickels and dimes.

Woolworth had opened the world's first "5 & 10 Cent Store" in 1879. As the name implied, he priced everything at either a nickel or a dime—and started a revolution in retailing. With that kind of pricing, he didn't need skilled (or high-salaried) salespeople; customers just picked out what they wanted and brought it to the register. Shoppers flooded his store with business. Woolworth had five stores by 1886, 28 by 1895, and 59 by 1900. In 1910, he merged with several rivals to create a retailing empire with more than 600 stores.

MONUMENT TO EXCESS

In 1909, Woolworth decided to build a magnificent world headquarters to commemorate his rags-to-riches story. He bought a plot of land on Broadway in lower Manhattan and commissioned architect Cass Gilbert to build what would later be dubbed a "cathedral of commerce"—the tallest building in the world.

Woolworth had an enormous ego, which is one reason he wanted his building to be taller than the Metropolitan Tower. But he may have had a more personal reason for knocking Metropolitan out of the #1 slot: revenge. Earlier in his career, Metropolitan had turned Woolworth down for a loan. Dwarfing the Metropolitan Tower with his own Woolworth building would be his way of evening the score.

Opposition

The Woolworth building would eventually become one of the most

Switzerland has the highest per-capita consumption of soft drinks in the world.

beloved buildings in the world; but during construction it made a lot of enemies. The industry journal *Engineering Record* was a particularly adamant critic, and in its pages it argued that construction of the building should be halted. It warned of what would happen to New York if buildings as tall as the one Woolworth proposed continued to be built.

> There is no such excuse...for the rearing of this great pile, shutting off the light of its neighbors, darkening the streets, and containing a population of several thousand people whose concentration on a little piece of ground will add another heavy burden to the transportation facilities in the vicinity.

The *Record's* complaints were ignored and the construction went forward. But this and similar warnings would soon prove accurate, and would change the quality of life in cities forever.

TAKING CHARGE

Woolworth obsessed over every detail of construction. As George Douglas writes in *Skyscrapers: A Social History in America:*

> [Woolworth] argued with Gilbert about the width of corridors, the layout of offices, the style of radiators, the light fixtures, the elevators, and everything else that came to his attention. When it was time to pick out the plumbing fixtures, Woolworth himself visited the offices of the Sanitas Manufacturing Company to look at the line of toilets and other bathroom fixtures available. He personally picked out the levers that he wanted for the urinals in the men's rooms.

Woolworth spared no expense to make his building one of the most opulent skyscrapers ever built.

> The main entrance on Broadway was a magnificent arch treated to rich Gothic detail and filigree. The lobby might well have served as the entrance to a Turkish sultan's palace or harem. The walls were of golden marble from the Isle of Skyros....For his own private offices Woolworth had ransacked the galleries and auction houses of Europe, and, impressed by Napoleon's tastes and zest for power, he emulated the decor of Napoleon's palace at Compiegne.

Another item gracing the lobby was a sculpture of Woolworth himself, holding a nickel.

The building was also a technological marvel. There were air cush-

Most-studied foreign languages in the U.S.: 1)Spanish 2)French 3) German 4)Italian 5) Japanese

ions at the bottom of every elevator shaft, a restaurant and a swimming pool in the basement. The exterior of the building was illuminated with 80,000 light bulbs. "Highest, Safest, Most Perfectly Appointed Office Structure in the World," one advertisement read, "Fireproof Beyond Question, Elevators Accident Proof."

BRAVE NEW WORLD

The building was finished in 1913 and opened its doors for business on April 24. It was 60 stories high and more than 800 feet tall; it cost $13.5 million to build—every penny of which Woolworth paid in cash. From the White House, President Woodrow Wilson himself pushed the button that illuminated the exterior. The Woolworth Building was now officially the tallest building on Earth, and it would remain so until 1930.

It was also one of the most important skyscrapers ever built. "Before that day in 1913," George Douglas writes, "the skyscraper had been a thing of architectural and engineering curiosity. Now at last it was clearly revealed as one of the great wonders of the modern world."

Feeling high? Part V of "The World's Tallest Buildings" is on page 248.

*   *   *   *

RANDOM "THOUGHTS"

"It isn't pollution that's harming the environment. It's the impurities in our air and water that are doing it."

—Former U.S. Vice-President Dan Quayle

"China is a big country, inhabited by many Chinese."

—Former French President Charles de Gaulle

ART IMITATES LIFE

Ever wonder where screenwriters get their ideas? Sometimes it's from news stories like these.

In Real Life: "Ed Gein was a soft-spoken, hard-working handyman in a small town in Wisconsin. His entire life was dominated by his stern, repressive mother, Augusta, and after her death, he turned her room into a shrine.

"In the fall of 1957, a policeman investigating the disappearance of a local shopkeeper checked up on the last purchase listed in her receipt book—the sale of a can of antifreeze to Ed Gein." The officer went to Gein's house to ask about it and found the woman's body—along with female "masks" made from other bodies he'd apparently unearthed from a local cemetery. (*It's a Weird World,* by Paul Hagerman).

On Screen: Gein was the inspiration for the character of Norman Bates, played by Anthony Perkins in Alfred Hitchcock's classic thriller, *Psycho*.

In Real Life: Geoffrey Francis Bowers was an attorney with the world's largest law firm, Baker & McKenzie. In 1986, he was dismissed because he had AIDS and filed a lawsuit against them charging discrimination. He died while the case was still being tried but was posthumously awarded $500,000 by a jury.

On Screen: His life-and-death story became *Philadelphia*, the Oscar-winning 1993 drama starring Tom Hanks. But when Bowers' parents complained that their son's life story had been appropriated for the movie without permission, Tri-Star denied it was him. The family sued for $10 million. They settled out of court, with Tri-Star admitting publicly that Hanks's character was, indeed, Bowers.

In Real Life: "In 1961," according to the *Fortean Times*, "the small California seaside resort of Rio del Mar, near Santa Cruz, was bombarded by hordes of crazed birds. They pecked people, smashed into houses or cars, knocked out car headlights, broke windows, chased people around the streets and staggered around vomiting pieces of anchovy over local lawns. Eight people were nipped.

On Screen: Two years later, in 1963, director Alfred Hitchcock—who had been living in a nearby town at the time (and had called local newspapers for information)—released *The Birds*, starring Rod Taylor and Tippi Hedren. The film was based partly on a Daphne du Maurier story...and partly the strange occurrence at Rio del Mar.

In Real Life: In 1936, the small town of Hollister, California, began an annual motorcycle race called the Gypsy Tour. They stopped it in 1947, when 4,000 bikers from a group called the Angelenos showed up for the event, took over the town, and reportedly turned it into a bottle-throwing riot. Photos of the bikers that ran in *Life* magazine shocked the nation. They also shocked some of the witnesses, who said the photos had been faked and the story grossly embellished by reporters.

On Screen: Whether or not it really happened, the story inspired John Paxton to write the screenplay for the immensely popular 1953 film, *The Wild One*, starring Marlon Brando as "Johnny," the motorcycle gang leader. It made him a teen/screen idol. In 1997, Hollister tried to resurrect the Gypsy Tour as a nostalgia event.

In Real Life: Kim Peek's brain was damaged during fetal development, and it left him with "diminished motor capacities." His parents had no idea he had any special talents until 1984, when he was thirty-three years old. That's when a screenwriter named Barry Morrow interviewed him. After the interview, Morrow asked Peek's father: "Do you know that he knows all the ZIP codes in the United States?" It turned out that Kim could also remember incredibly detailed information about history, sports, geography, and many other subjects.

On Screen: Morrow used the interviews to write *The Rain Man*, starring Tom Cruise and Dustin Hoffman. The success of the film influenced Peek. For the first time, he felt confident enough to interact with people. He even gave speeches in which he urged tolerance for people who are different.

Fear of cancer is known as "cancerophobia;" fear of heart attacks is know as "cardiophobia."

GONE, BUT NOT FORGOTTEN

You can see them in museums or in books—but you won't see them on the road, because no one makes them anymore. Here's some info about four automobile legends.

THE RICKENBACKER (1922–1927): One of the first cars named for a celebrity. Before World War I, Eddie Rickenbacker was one of the most famous race car drivers in the United States. After the war he was even more famous as "America's first hero in the air," a title he earned by shooting down 26 German airplanes in dogfights. When he returned home, a group of Detroit businessmen backed him in his own car company. Rickenbacker's cars boasted six-cylinder engines with two flywheels instead of one, which made them among the smoothest-running automobiles on the road.

FATE: In 1927, huge losses forced the company to close its doors. Ironically, the last Rickenbacker designs were sold to the German automaker Audi; Rickenbacker himself became president of the Indianapolis Speedway.

THE OAKLAND (1908–1931): An early luxury car manufacturer. It was nearly bankrupt by the second year of its existence, but General Motors saw its potential. They bought it in 1909, and every year from 1910 to 1926, the Oakland was one of the 15 best-selling cars in the country. Its biggest claim to fame was its 1924 "True Blue" model—the first car ever mass-produced that *wasn't* painted black.

FATE: Oakland was headquartered in Pontiac, Michigan. In 1926, the division introduced a new, lower-priced car called the Pontiac that quickly overshadowed the Oakland, selling 140,000 cars in 1927 to Oakland's 50,000. GM discontinued the Oakland in 1931 and renamed the division Pontiac in 1933.

THE HUPMOBILE (1908–1930s): Founded by Robert C. Hupp, who was quickly recognized as one of the most gifted auto-makers of his day. "I recall looking at Bobby Hupp's roadster at the first show where it was exhibited," Henry Ford remarked years later, "and wondering whether we could ever build as good a small car for as little money." The company's most famous design was its 1934 model—one of the first ever designed with aerodynamics in mind. But its biggest claim to fame today is the fact that it's the only car ever commemorated on U.S. money. That's a Hupmobile in the illustration on the back of the $10 bill.

Fate: Hupmobile had reliable sales until it moved upmarket, building larger, more luxurious cars to earn higher profits. The strategy backfired during the Great Depression, when auto industry sales plunged more than 75%. Hupmobile never fully recovered, and in 1940 it abandoned automaking altogether, diversifying into electronics, auto parts, kitchen appliances, and other businesses.

THE MAXWELL (1904-1925): In 1903, John Maxwell designed his own automobile and joined with Benjamin Briscoe, owner of a sheet metal plant in Detroit, to form the Maxwell-Briscoe Motor Company. Briscoe hoped to become a major player in the auto industry. He copied General Motors, forming a holding company and buying other car companies, but for him, the strategy didn't work. His United States Motor Company bought up 150 different automakers...and then, in 1912, went belly-up. The Maxwell Motor Company managed to stay afloat until 1920, but by then it was $35 million in debt and there were more than 26,000 unsold Maxwells gathering dust in warehouses all over the country.

Fate: In 1921, the bankers who controlled Maxwell hired Walter P. Chrysler, a former president of Buick who'd developed a reputation as a "doctor" for sick companies, to turn Maxwell around. Chrysler wasted no time—he sold off the 26,000 Maxwells by slashing prices to $5 over cost; then he used the money to engineer a new car he named the "Good Maxwell," to counter consumer fears that Maxwells weren't well-built. Somehow, it worked—Maxwell sold nearly 49,000 cars in 1922 and earned more than $2 million in profits.

In 1924, Chrysler introduced the Chrysler Six, Maxwell's first six-cylinder car. It sold so well that Chrysler discontinued the Maxwell models the following year, and on June 6, 1925 reorganized Maxwell as the Chrysler Corporation.

THE CREAM OF THE CRUD

It may be hard to believe, but these recordings are real. We guarantee it. Who made them...and why? We'll never know. Some mysteries are beyond human understanding.

THE WORLD'S WORST RECORDINGS

"Music to Make Automobiles By"
Volkswagen made this recording "to inspire their workers." It features the exciting sounds of an auto assembly line, backed with an orchestra. (We mentioned this in the *Giant BR*, but it really does belong here too.)

"Granny's Mini-skirt"
A bluegrass "rap" song from Irene Ryan, who played Granny on *The Beverly Hillbillies*. According to the lyrics, she decided to learn to Twist and Jerk, and started wearing a mini-skirt. Only trouble is, the sight of her knobby knees is makin' ol' Grandpa sick.

"Buddy Ebsen Says Howdy in Song and Story"
Another atrocity from a *Beverly Hillbillies* alumnus. *Critic's comment*: "Jed Clampett goes a-shootin' at some tunes, and up from his throat comes a-bubblin' crud."

"Elvis' Greatest S--t"
A bootleg album on the Dog Vomit label, with the *National Equirer* shot of Elvis in his coffin on the front cover. It contains the absolute worst of Elvis Presley. Tracks include: "Old McDonald Had a Farm," "Song of the Shrimp," "Fort Lauderdale Chamber of Commerce," and "Dominic the Impotent Bull."

"Sound Effect of Godzilla One" (Japanese import)
Critic's comment: "You can drop the needle anywhere and basically you'll hear Godzilla going 'Rarr...Rarr.' That's it."

"Sound Effects: U.S. Air Force Firepower"
Stuart Swezey, who actually owns a copy of this one, says, "[It has]

tracks like 'Mass napalm attack by F-100s' and 'Psychological warfare, public address from C-47,' where they announce [with helicopter sounds in the background] 'Clear the village! We are about to strafe and bomb it!'"

"Laverne & Shirley Sing!"

According to the authors of *Hollywood Hi-Fi*, "An entire album of early '60s girl group tunes, as interpreted by Cindy Williams (who can almost carry a tune) and Penny Marshall (who sounds like a lovelorn goose honking for a mate). Since they are shown on the cover eating Popsicles, a more accurate title might've been *Laverne and Shirley Suck*."

"Bobby Breaux and the Pot-Bellied Pig"

Drummer Bobby Breaux collaborated with a 450-lb boar named Rebel after noticing he grunted in tunes. Features "Amazing Grease" and "Hava Nasquela." Breaux backed the pig up on drums and synthesizer.

"The Sound of Combat Training"

Recorded live at the United States Army Training Center, Fort Knox, Kentucky. Tracks include: "Innoculation," "Mess Hall," and "Gas Chamber Exercise."

"The Crepitation Contest" (The Power of Positive Stinking)

A whole album of nothing but farting. From the liner notes: "If you put your fingers in your ears, you can't hold your nose. If you hold your nose, you'll have to listen...."

NORAD Tracks Santa

A Cold War classic recorded in 1962. NORAD's (North American Air Defense) job was to protect us from enemy air attack. According to Ken Sitz, who owns a copy: "Interspersed with standard Christmas music are NORAD reports on Santa Claus—basically, whether or not he's going to be shot down!"

And don't miss..."Muhammed Ali Fights Mr. Tooth Decay: A Beautiful Children's Story."

IRONIC, ISN'T IT?

More irony to put the problems of your day-to-day life in proper perspective.

BUREAUCRATIC IRONY

• In 1974, the Consumer Product Safety Commission ordered 80,000 buttons promoting toy safety. They said: "For Kids' Sake, Think Toy Safety." The buttons were recalled when the agency found out they had "sharp edges, parts a child could swallow, and were coated with toxic lead paint."

• "The town council of Winchester, Indiana, passed an anti-pornography law, but the editors of the town's only newspaper refused to publish it on the grounds that the statute itself was pornographic. Unfortunately, a law does not take effect in Winchester until it has been published in the newspaper." (*Fenton and Fowler*)

• When the public clamored for campaign finance reform, a columnist in *USA Today* reported that Republicans favored "a let-the-good-times-roll proposal that would eliminate all contribution limits....This bill is called the (I'm not making this up) Doolittle Bill, named for its sponsor, California GOP Rep. John Doolittle." (*USA Today*, October 1, 1997)

• Shortly after passing a bill that prohibited pornography on the Internet, the House of Representatives released the Starr Report...on the Internet.

IRONIC APPEARANCES

• "On the night of September 20, 1996, author Bertil Torekul gave a lecture to an audience of 300 in the Stifts-och Landsbibliotek Library in Linkoping, Sweden. He spoke about...book-burning. The fire alarm sounded about a minute after he finished his speech. The Linkoping library burned to the ground." (*Fortean Times*)

• "After the world premiere at England's Leeds Playhouse of *The Winter Guest*, a play featuring a community cut off by a blizzard, the audience found themselves snowbound and were put up for the night in the theater." (*Fortean Times*)

IRONIC FIRES

• In 1613, the town of Quimper, France, was burned down by its fire equipment. The fire started in a canvas fire bucket. (*Ripley's Believe It Or Not*)

• "To warn the public about Fourth of July brush fires, sheriff's deputies and firefighters gathered at a remote bomb-disposal range outside San Diego to blow up thousands of illegal fireworks for the news media. Sparks from the demonstration fell onto a nearby hill, causing a ten-acre brush fire that required 50 firefighters, two water-dropping helicopters and a bulldozer to extinguish." (*Dumb, Dumber and Dumbest*)

• On December 31, 1903, the Iroquois Theater in Chicago burned down. Thirty days earlier, it had opened with much fanfare as the "World's First Fireproof Theater."

IRONIC DEATHS

• Dr. Alice Chase, who wrote *Nutrition for Health* and other books on the science of proper eating, died recently...of malnutrition. (*Fenton and Fowler*)

• "Dr. Stuart M. Berger, an author of best-selling diet and health books who contended that his weight-loss programs would result in increased longevity, died on February 23, 1994. At the time, he was 40 years old and weighed 365 pounds." (*Dumb, Dumber, and Dumbest*)

• "The famous physician, Semmelweis, who fought against operating room contamination by unclean doctors, died of an infection caused by cutting his hand with dirty dissection instruments." (*Oops*)

• J. I. Rodale, publisher of books on health and nutrition, appeared on *The Dick Cavett Show* in 1971, when he was 72 years old, and predicted he would live to be 100. Later in the show, Cavett noticed Rodale appeared to have fallen asleep. Actually, he was dead.

DELICIOUS IRONY

• "In 1996, a landslide near Los Angeles broke a sewer line and sent tons of human waste into the Pacific Ocean, closing the stretch of beach where the TV show 'Baywatch' was filmed." (From news services.)

About 40% of U.S. adults say they "change into something more comfortable" to watch TV.

UNCLE JOHN'S PAGE OF LISTS

For years, the BRI has had a file full of lists. We've never been sure what to do with them...until now.

5 FILMS THAT FEATURE FARTS

1. *Airplane!* The pilot is affected by mild food poisoning.
2. *Blazing Saddles*. Bean-eating cowboys toot up a storm by the old campfire.
3. *Amadeus*. Mozart rips one mockingly after caricaturing Salieri at the piano.
4. *Le Grande Bouffe*. A character farts himself to death.
5. *Fanny and Alexander*. Uncle Karlchen astonishes children by blowing out candles.

—From *The Research Book of Bodily functions*

THE 7 DEADLIEST DOGS

1. Pit bull
2. German shepherd
3. Chow
4. Malamute
5. Husky
6. Wolf hybrid
7. Akita

6 WORDS YOUR DIGITAL CLOCK CAN SPELL

1. ZOO (2:00)
2. S.O.S. (5:05)
3. SOB (5:08)
4. SIS (5:15)
5. BOO (8:00)
6. BOB (8:08)

7 LAWS OF TV

1. The hero will always find a parking space.
2. Police never wait for backup.
3. If a woman is running away from someone, she will trip and fall.
4. Cars will explode in all accidents, no matter how slight.
5. Haunted houses are never locked.
6. If a hero jumps hundreds of feet into water, it will always be deep enough.
7. Nobody on TV has time to watch TV.

—From *Reader's Digest*

6 THINGS THE AVERAGE RAT CAN DO

1. Wriggle through a hole no larger than the diameter of a quarter.
2. Scale a brick wall as though it had rungs.
3. Swim a half mile and tread water for 3 days.
4. Gnaw through lead pipes and cinder blocks
5. Multiply so fast, a pair could have 15,000 descendants in a year.
6. Plummet five stories to the ground and scurry off unharmed.

—From *Hodge Podge*

4 GRAFFITI FROM GRACELAND

1. Elvis, no matter where you go, there you are.
2. Elvis, I'm having your baby 29 Sept.'91.
3. Elvis, can I use your bathroom?
4. Elvis, you came, you saw, you conquered, you croaked.

AMERICA'S ALL-TIME BIGGEST CROOKS

How quickly we forget. The S&L scandal was the biggest rip-off in U.S. history—it cost every family several lifetimes' worth of wages. But have you heard about it in the news lately? To help combat "national amnesia," we've decided to include this S&L "Rogues' Gallery." Here are the stories of some of the conspirators who made the S&L scandal possible, from It's a Conspiracy...*by the National Insecurity Council.*

BACKGROUND S&Ls were traditionally one of the sleepiest sectors of the financial world; until the early 1980s, they took in the savings of middle-class depositors and lent them out as home mortgages to members of the community. Federal laws and regulations prevented S&Ls from doing much else. They didn't pay high interest, but their deposits were safe because they were insured by the federal government.

Then, in 1982, came deregulation. Suddenly, S&L executives were free to lend money to whomever they wanted (even to themselves) and could spend it on whatever investments they pleased—no matter how risky.

Free from regulatory oversight, many S&Ls were bought up by real estate speculators, corrupt business people, and even the Mafia. The new owners spent depositors' money on exorbitant salaries, multimillion-dollar loans to their friends, wild parties, wildcat real estate deals, junk bonds, and other high-risk ventures. They didn't care if the S&Ls lost money: The deposits were insured, and the executives pocketed a huge transaction fee every time they made a loan—whether or not the loan was ever paid off.

Within two years of deregulation, however, the S&L industry was broke. In 1980, the industry was worth $32 billion; by 1982, it was worth less than $4 billion and falling fast; by 1990 it was more than $500 billion in the red—and guess who paid for it?

Here are a few of the conspirators who stuck you with the bill for their multibillion-dollar spending spree:

CHARLES KEATING, Lincoln Savings and Loan (Irvine, California)

Highlights: In 1984, Keating bought Lincoln Savings and Loan with cash he made with Michael Milken's junk bonds, "fired senior staff, and hired a slick crew of salespeople to push his worthless paper on elderly Southern Californians." He falsely claimed his bonds were guaranteed by the federal government and instructed his sales staff to focus on the "weak, meek, and ignorant. [They're] always good targets." (*Inside Job*)

Outcome: Within five years, Keating—and 11 of his relatives on the staff, who received more than $34 million in salaries and other perks—had run Lincoln into the ground. When Lincoln crashed in 1989, it lost the $230 million that had been invested in the bonds by some 23,000 people, most of them seniors. At least one of the victims (an 89-year-old who wrote, "There's nothing left for me") committed suicide. Lincoln's end would have come much sooner, were it not for the help of "the Keating Five," U.S. Senators Cranston, DeConcini, Glenn, Riegle, and McCain, who pressured regulators to leave Lincoln alone. Their payoff was more than $1.3 million in campaign and other contributions. By the time regulators finally seized Lincoln in 1989, the bailout cost taxpayers $2.5 billion. Keating was sentenced to ten years in prison.

EDWIN "FAST EDDIE" McBIRNEY, Sunbelt Savings and Loan (Dallas, Texas)

Highlights: McBirney liked to spend Sunbelt's deposits entertaining business associates at a palatial suite at the Las Vegas Dunes. He flew them into town on a private 727 and provided them with prostitutes. At one lavish party, he fed his guests broiled lion and antelope; at a Halloween fiesta, he had a warehouse decorated as an African jungle and hired a magician to make an elephant disappear. McBirney also owned seven airplanes.

Outcome: Sunbelt collapsed, and in the summer of 1990, the FSLIC sued McBirney for $500 million. He later pled guilty to four counts of bank fraud and tax evasion. The bailout of Sunbelt was estimated to cost taxpayers $1.7 billion.

5 most popular lunches in U.S. schools: pizza, chicken nuggets, tacos, burritos and hamburgers.

DUAYNE CHRISTIANSEN, North American Savings and Loan (Santa Ana, California)

Highlights: Christiansen, a dentist who began wearing all-white suits after he bought North American, spent an enormous amount of depositors' money decorating his office: it was made completely of marble (including the desk), and the entrance boasted 14-foot-high copper doors.

Outcome: Christiansen was killed in a mysterious car accident in June 1988—the day before regulators seized North American Savings and Loan. In broad daylight, he drove his Jaguar into a freeway abutment. Three days earlier he had rewritten his will, leaving everything to his girlfriend. Regulators estimate that he looted more than $40 million from North American; the money was not recovered. North American's bailout was estimated to cost taxpayers $209 million. (*Inside Job*)

DONALD P. MANGANO and JOHN L. MOLINARO, Ramona Savings and Loan (Ramona, California)

Highlights: Some of Ramona's deposits were used to finance condos built by Mangano's construction company and carpeted by Molinaro's carpet store. Another portion of the depositors' funds was kept in the trunk of a car parked behind the S&L. According to one report, when regulators seized Ramona, they discovered an office with a fake wall and, behind that, "a secret passageway leading to the basement. From there it connected to a tunnel at the end of which, they said, was an alley behind the bank and a car packed with food, cash, and guns." Investigators speculate that Mangano and Molinaro were taking precautions in case of a lightning raid by federal regulators. When FBI agents caught Molinaro "trying to get to the Cayman Islands on a dead man's passport," he told them "he had deposited $3 million in First Cayman Bank." (*Inside Job*)

Outcome: Ramona collapsed in 1986, more than $70 million in debt. The feds estimate that the two men alone looted more than $24 million from the S&L.

ERWIN HANSEN, Centennial Savings (Guerneville, California)

Highlights: Hansen invested a considerable amount of the S&L's

49er faithful: The town of Ismay, Montana has changed its name to Joe, Montana.

money on his offices, including $48,000 on a desk and $98,000 on other decorations. He also liked cars. He bought a $77,000 Mercedes stretch limousine for Centennial and in one afternoon alone bought five cars for himself and his family. But his larger extravagance was The Stonehouse, an old stone building he refurbished into a $2 million corporate headquarters—only to abandon it after four months. He complained that the building was too cold and said, "It reminded me of a mortuary." (*Inside Job*)

Outcome: Centennial collapsed in August, 1985; Hansen died mysteriously two years later—one day before he was scheduled to begin cooperating with the Justice Department against other Centennial officials. The coroner ruled that he died from a cerebral aneurysm. Centennial's bailout was estimated to cost taxpayers as much as $165 million.

DON DIXON, Vernon Savings and Loan
(Vernon, Texas)

Highlights: Dixon used Vernon depositors' money to buy a $2 million Swiss chalet, a $1 million San Diego beach house, a fleet of airplanes, a Rolls Royce/Ferrari dealership, and a $40,000 painting he eventually gave to Pope John Paul II. Dixon also bought the sister ship of the presidential yacht *Sequoia,* which he anchored in Washington, D.C., and used to entertain politicians.

Outcome: Vernon collapsed in 1987, with more than 97% of its loans in default. Convicted on twenty-three counts of fraud and "misapplication of funds," Dixon was sentenced to five years in prison. Cost to taxpayers: $1.3 billion. (*Savings & Loan Scandal Trading Cards*)

RECOMMENDED READING

• *Savings & Loan Scandal Trading Cards*, by Dennis Bernstein and Laura Sydell (Eclipse Enterprises, Forestville, California)

• *Inside Job: The Looting of America's Savings and Loans*, by Stephen Pizzo, Mary Fricker, and Paul Muolo (HarperCollins, 1991)

What do snails and sports cars have in common? Retractable antennae.

FAMILIAR PHRASES

Here are more origins of everyday phrases.

CLOSE, BUT NO CIGAR

Meaning: Nice try, but not quite!

Origin: "In the old-time fair or carnival, local lads were invited to exhibit their strength or skill by throwing baseballs at targets, pounding with a mallet to raise a weight, and so on—and the prize was a cigar. Since these devices were almost always rigged, the ambitious youths seldom won. The concessionaire would encourage them to further efforts (at a nickel a time) with, 'Close, but no cigar!'" (From *Loose Cannons and Red Herrings*, by Robert Claiborne)

THE BIG CHEESE

Meaning: An important or self-important person.

Origin: Sounds like it comes from a big wheel of cheese, but actually is derived from *chiz*, the Persian and Urdu word meaning "thing." It also might have been a play on the word "chief."

SPICK AND SPAN

Meaning: Neat and well turned out.

Origin: "This expression was first used to describe ships fresh from the shipwrights and carpenters. A spick was a 'spike' or 'nail,' and span was a 'wood chip.'" (From *To Coin a Phrase*, by Edwin Radford and Alan Smith)

THE WHOLE SHEBANG

Meaning: Everything.

Origin: "Shebang"—from the Irish word *shebeen*—was coined in America by Irish immigrants. According to the *Morris Dictionary of Word and Phrases*, "A shebeen in Ireland was a very lowly public house, one where drinks were sold without a license....[It] was regarded as a relatively valueless piece of real estate, and the expression 'I'll give you so much for the whole shebeen' became current. Gradually the original reference was lost and shebeen—now shebang after the trip across the Atlantic—came to mean any kind of...business affair."

OOPS! II

More examples of Murphy's Law—anythng that can *goe wroong will!*

COME AND LISTEN TO A STORY...

"[Using] the very latest equipment, Texaco workmen set about drilling for oil at Lake Peigneur in Louisiana during November, 1980.

"After only a few hours of drilling they sat back expecting oil to shoot up. Instead, however, they watched a whirlpool form, sucking down not only the entire 1,300-acre lake, but also five houses, nine barges, eight tugboats, two oilrigs, a mobile home, most of a botanical garden and ten percent of nearby Jefferson Island, leaving a half-mile-wide crater. No one told them there was an abandoned salt mine underneath.

"A local fisherman said he thought the world was coming to an end."

—***The Return of Heroic Failures***

DETAILS, DETAILS

"A group of Russian counterfeiters produced a near-perfect run of bogus 50,000-ruble bank notes (worth about $22). Once they went into general circulation, officials agreed that it was an excellent job and [the bills] appeared to be genuine currency. Their only error was misspelling 'Russia.'"

—***Dumb, Dumber, Dumbest***

AND WAS THAT IN 1492...OR 1865?

"Ads that ran in national newspapers last week for the forthcoming movie *Jefferson in Paris* used images of the Constitution of the United States.

"Then it was learned at Walt Disney Co., where the film and ad were created, that neither Thomas Jefferson nor Nick Nolte, who plays him in the movie, had written the Constitution.

"'We all walked in Monday morning and said, "Oh, s--t, it should

What is businessman Oliver Pollock's claim to fame? He invented the dollar sign in 1778.

have been the Declaration of Independence!' an unnamed Disney executive told *Newsweek*.

"The magazine notes that Disney is the company that planned to build a Virginia theme park to celebrate American history."

—***San Francisco Chronicle***

SO MUCH FOR THE "MEDIA ELITE"

"On June 9, 1978, Mr. Bob Specas was ready to beat a domino record by knocking down 100,000 dominoes in a row. The media was there to broadcast the historic event. A TV camera recorded his progress as Specas set up the last dominoes for his performance.

"97,497...97,498...97,499. Then a TV cameraman dropped his press badge...and the dominoes went off."

—***The 176 Stupidest Things Ever Done***

HAPPINESS IS A STRANGE GUN

"When police in Saginaw, Michigan, pulled over a motorist on a traffic violation, they made a discovery: the guy was carrying a pistol in his car. Despite his protestations that he had never seen the weapon before, the cops knew their duty and they arrested him. Imagine the officers' embarrassment when they had to let the suspect go the following day with an apology! Seems the gun had dropped out of a cop's holster into the car when they were questioning the motorist about the traffic charge."

—***Oops***

ALL IN THE FAMILY

"Ian Lewis, 43, of Standish, Lancashire (England), spent 20 years tracing his family tree back to the 17th century. He traveled all over Britain, talked to 2,000 relatives and planned to write a book about how his great-grandfather left to seek his fortune in Russia and his grandfather was expelled after the Revolution. Then he found out he had been adopted when he was a month old and his real name was David Thornton. He resolved to start his family research all over again."

—***Strange Days*, by the editors of *Fortean Times***

Pink plastic lawn flamingoes were inspired by a 1957 photo in a National Geographic magazine.

WHY DO WE CRY TEARS?

Here's one answer to that question, written by Ben Patrusky. We found it in a book called The Day Lightning Chased the Housewife.

WHY CRY?

Your dog dies. You win the beauty pageant. You break up with someone you love. Your daughter gets married. You lose your job. Your best friend has a serious accident.

How do you handle such stressful episodes? Chances are you cry. Shedding tears seems to bring about a terrific emotional release.

Why?

No one can say for sure. Humans apparently shed a variety of tears. There are the tears we secrete all the time, those to help keep our eyes properly moistened. Then there are irritant tears, the kind we spill when peeling an onion or coping with smog. Finally, there are emotional tears, the stuff we trickle in response to grief, joy, frustration, or other stresses.

CRY BABIES

Curiously, of all the earthly creatures, only humans seem to shed emotional tears. That makes such tearing a late evolutionary development. Tears of emotional stress also appear relatively late in infant development. Unhappy newborns often cry tearlessly until they are several days old or even until weeks after they are born. But challenge them with an eye irritant, and they can spill tears at birth.

Charles Darwin proposed what appears to be the first scientific theory to explain emotional tearing. In his book *The Expression of the Emotions in Man and Animals*, [he claims] it was the total act of crying that relieved suffering and made people feel better— not the secretion of tears, which, he contended, was an incidental and in itself purposeless accompaniment to the catharsis.

About three decades ago another theory surfaced, this one promulgated by anthropologist Ashley Montagu. According to Montagu, the tears that went with sobbing did indeed have survival value in that they helped to protect us against disease. He argued that sobbing—

gasping and convulsive catching of breath—dried out nose and throat membranes, thereby increasing vulnerability to bacterial invasion. Tears, which also drain into the nasal passages, served to offset this tendency towards dryness....

ANOTHER IDEA

Dissatisfied with both theories, William H. Frey II, a biochemist and director of the psychiatry research laboratories at the St. Paul-Ramsey Medical Center in Minnesota, suggested another hypothesis. He proposed that tears may help to rid the body of chemicals produced by emotional stress. According to Frey, when we need relief, we may literally "cry it out." He argued that all other excretory functions—urinating, sweating, exhaling, defecating—are involved in removing excess or toxic products from the body. Why shouldn't the same hold true for emotional tears?

CRY ME A RIVER

On the face of it, Frey's theory seems most plausible. But for now it remains purely speculative. None has been verified or refuted in the lab. Frey's hypothesis, however, seems most amenable to experiment. As such, the Minnesota investigator recently [1989] began a series of trials aimed at testing its validity. One thing he's doing is having volunteers watch tear-jerkers; his favorite is *The Champ*, a movie about a down-and-out boxer and a little boy. He compares these emotion-provoked tears with irritant tears collected from the same subjects while they peel onions. If Frey's theory has merit, then there should be a significant difference in the chemistry of these two varieties of tears. Results from a group of over 80 subjects suggest there are. Emotional tears contain a greater concentration of protein than do irritant tears.

But there's no telling what, if anything, this protein difference means. Are there differences in protein kind as well as quantity? Are there specific proteins associated with emotion? If so, how do they relate to the hormones or other agents that mediate our emotions? Is there a specific substance associated with each emotion? Is there one agent, for instance, that makes us feel anger, another, elation, and yet a third, grief? Only time and research will tell.

To be continued in our next edition.

When pitched, the average major league baseball rotates 15 times before it's hit by the batter.

THERE ONCE WAS A LADY FROM FRANCE...

Limericks have been around since the 1700s. Here are a few of the more "respectable" ones that readers have sent us.

A certain young chap named
Bill Beebee
Was in love with a lady named
Phoebe;
'But,' he said, 'I must see
What the clerical fee
Be before Phoebe be Phoebe
Beebee.'

There was a young artist called
Saint,
Who swallowed some samples
of paint;
All shades of the spectrum
Flowed out of his rectum
With a colorful lack of
restraint.

A flea and a fly in a flue
Were imprisoned, so what
could they do?
Said the fly: 'Let us flee,'
Said the flea: 'Let us fly!'
So they flew through a flaw in
the flue.

When a jolly young fisher
named Fisher
Went fishing for fish in a
fissure,
A fish, with a grin,
Pulled the fisherman in;
Now they're fishing the fissure
for Fisher.

There was young fellow called
Cager,
Who, as the result of a wager,
Offered to fart
The whole oboe part
Of Mozart's *Quartet in F Major.*

The fabulous Wizard of Oz
Retired from business becoz
What with up-to-date science,
To most of his clients,
He wasn't the Wizard he woz.

There was an old spinster from
Fife,
Who had never been kissed in
her life:
Along came a cat,
And she said "I'll kiss that!"
But the cat meowed: "Not on
your life!"

I sat next to the Duchess at tea,
Distressed as a person could be.
Her rumblings abdominal,
Were simply phenomenal,
And everyone thought it was me!

Said an eminent, erudite ermine:
"There's one thing I cannot
determine:
When a dame wears my coat,
She's a person of note—
When I wear it, I'm called only
vermin."

2 people most admired by teenagers in 1983: Eddie Murphy and Ronald Reagan, in that order.

HELLO, DOLLY

Besides music, singer Dolly Parton is known for three things. The third is her straight talk. Here's a bit of what she has to say.

"I'm not offended by all the dumb blonde jokes, because I know I'm not dumb...and I also know that I'm not blonde."

"One of the surest signs that a woman is in love is when she divorces her husband."

"It's important that, though I rely on my husband for love, I rely on myself for strength."

"I was the first woman to burn my bra—it took the fire department four days to put it out."

"I buy all those (fitness) videos —Richard Simmons, Jane Fonda. I love to sit and eat cookies and watch 'em."

(On her acting) "I'm never going to be a Meryl Streep. But then, she'll never be a Dolly Parton either."

"I've never left the Smoky Mountains, I've taken them with me wherever I go, and (pointing to her chest) I'm not referring to these either."

"You'd be surprised how much it costs to look this cheap."

"Radio doesn't seem interested in old folks like me, [even though] I feel like I'm doing the best work of my career right now. They say wisdom comes with age. Well, so does talent."

"The way I see it, if you want the rainbow, you gotta put up with the rain."

"I've got more confidence than I do talent, I guess. I think confidence is the main achiever of success."

"If people think I'm a dumb blonde because of the way I look, then they're dumber than they think I am. If people think I'm not very deep because of my wigs and outfits, then they're not very deep."

"I look just like the girl next door...if you happen to live next door to an amusement park."

It takes about a week to make a jellybean.

STEINEM SPEAKS

Some of Gloria Steinem's comments about women are controversial…but whether you agree with them or not, you'll find them thought-provoking.

"I have yet to hear a man ask for advice on how to combine marriage and a career."

"Men should think twice before making widowhood women's only path to power."

"Some of us are becoming the men we wanted to marry."

"A woman without a man is like a fish without a bicycle."

"Jacqueline Onassis has a very clear understanding of marriage. I have a lot of respect for women who win the game with rules given you by the enemy."

"Law and justice are not always the same. When they aren't, destroying the law may be the first step toward changing it."

"Women may be the one group that grows more radical with age."

"Every country has peasants—ours have money."

"We can tell our values by looking at our checkbook stubs."

"Women age, but men mature."

On why she never married:
"I can't mate in captivity."

"One day, an army of gray-haired women may quietly take over the earth."

"Someone once asked me why women don't gamble as much as men do, and I gave the common sense reply that we don't have as much money. That was a true but incomplete answer. In fact, women's total instinct for gambling is satisfied by marriage."

"It may eventually turn out that men and women have similar degrees of aggressiveness, but for the next fifty years or so, until the sex roles are… reformed, women will be a good and peaceful influence in politics."

Take your height and divide by eight. That's how "tall" your head is.

GOING ABROAD

On page 123, we shared an excerpt from Eva Newman's book Going Abroad. *Here are some more funny stories of her...experiences.*

While on an early morning animal viewing adventure in East Africa, nature may call and the guide will carefully search the landscape with his binoculars—for hungry lions. It is only after the area is secure from danger that the guide will release the passengers from the truck, with women to one side and men to the other.

Now what to do? Obviously, surrounded by such natural beauty, you are reluctant to pollute the landscape. You do not want to see young lions romping about in toilet paper.

The first step is to find some soft soil. If no shovel is available, dig a hole with the heel of your boot (people on safari usually wear boots or other sturdy footwear).

Squat and use the hole! Now, using the heel of your boot, kick the loose soil back over the hole until it's covered. If a rock is available, you can further secure the hole by placing a rock over it.

In some areas, this procedure is called digging a "cat hole." And don't leave behind any "paper flowers."

If you are in a desert region, or if the soil is too hard to dig, some people dispose of the toilet paper by bagging or burning. Since there is little rain in deserts, paper will not decompose for decades. Do we really want someone to have to deal with our dirty paper twenty years from now?

Note that using these holes in high winds is perilous. Be sure your feet are upwind of your rear.

* * *

On a recent trip to Thailand, I was visiting a large and imposing tourist attraction in a big city. Despite careful investigation, I was unable to locate a toilet. It was necessary to ask.

Not speaking the language, I decided one of the guards who dealt often with tourists would understand "toilet" in English. Sure enough, the guard did seem to understand and indicated with waving hands that I was to go down the street and around the corner.

I followed his instructions but found the street around the corner to be lined with a tall wall and parked cars. I cruised the block—but no toilet. Again I asked a local, "toilet?" She indicated I was to return the way I had come. Again, nothing. My instinct was that these people were far too kind and generous to be playing tricks on a stupid tourist. I knew there had to be a toilet.

I returned to the ticket booth of the tourist attraction and asked again. This time they indicated the same direction, but said "bus." I repeated, "Bus?" They nodded. Ah, it was at a bus stop. I returned to the same block. Oh yes, there was a bus. I walked around it. No toilet.

But I noticed something odd about the bus. Against its front was a row of large potted plants, as if the bus wasn't going anyplace. The door of the bus was open—and what was that familiar odor? A toilet?

I hesitantly approached the open door and asked the attendant for the toilet. Yes, she said and motioned me in. Sure enough, it was a bus of only toilets. It was used by both sexes. There were small (very small) closed stalls in the middle and urinals in the rear.

Each stall had its own water tap and a chemical-flush squat toilet. In the front of the bus was a wash sink and a desk for the attendant. How ingenious.

* * *

In Hong Kong...after dining in a local noodle shop, I inquired for the facility. The manager was apologetic as he told me that the toilet might not meet my standards.

I told him that I did not care as I was in desperate need. He showed me through the kitchen, where helpers were washing dishes with a hose connected to an outside faucet.

We stopped at a small room off the kitchen. It had only a cement floor and a hole in the back wall at ground level! He told me to use the floor as I must and the kitchen ladies would hose the floor.

After this adventure I was very thankful I had my usual gamma globulin shot, together with every other kind of shot that offered health protection.

On average, which lives longer—a spider or a dolphin? Spiders live 4-7 years; dolphins 3-4.

BIRTHDAY TRADITIONS

In her book Happy Birthdays Around the World, *Lois Johnson explains how people in other countries celebrate their birthdays. A few examples:*

CHINA. "A baby's birthday is celebrated when he is thirty days old, and when he is a year old. Then there are no more celebrations until the tenth birthday. After that, every tenth year is celebrated for as long as the person lives. The most important date is the thirtieth anniversary, when a child becomes an adult."

NIGERIA. "Many children follow the old tribal custom of celebrating their birthdays as an age group, instead of having an individual birthday. The custom began in very early times, when there was no calendar. The only way the people had of marking their birthdays was by the reign of a certain king, or by some important event. People then, who were born during one of these periods, became an age group, and celebrated their birthdays together."

THAILAND. "According to tradition, if the parents of the child can afford it, the father and mother buy as many birds or fish, sometimes both, as their child is years old, plus one extra animal for the child to 'grow on.' After sprinkling each animal with blessed water, the boy or girl lets the birds fly free, and returns the fish to the waters of the river or canal. This ceremony is believed to insure the favor of the gods for the coming year."

INDIA. "On this day, the Hindu child does not have to go to school. Hindus believe that a special day such as a birthday is meant for prayer and celebration."

KOREA. "A baby's first birthday is celebrated with great ceremony. The same sort of custom that is followed in other Asian countries is observed in Korea. The mother and father lay all kinds of articles on a table—pencils, pieces of money, books, and strips of cloth. The baby is then set down in the middle, and whatever the baby reaches for is supposed to show what his future skills will be. "

GREAT BRITAIN. "Sometimes well-meaning classmates may follow the British custom of 'bumping.' To wish the birthday child well, some of his friends will pick him up by the ankles while others will lift him under the armpits, and then they 'bump' him on the ground as many times as he is years old—with, of course, an extra 'bump' to grow on."

SRI LANKA. "The first birthday celebration comes when a Sri Lankan baby is thirty-one days old. Then, customarily, a close relative brings the baby a special gift. For a boy baby, it may be a gold chain; for a girl, gold arm bangles. The parents also present the new baby with a charm, made of copper in a scroll design, which is rolled into a gold-enclosed cylinder or tube. This charm is worn all through the person's life and is supposed to protect them from harm."

* * *

GOOD OL' AMERICAN INGENUITY

"Paragon Cable in New York recently began a new approach to customers with delinquent accounts. Instead of cutting off service altogether, which would create additional expense to restart when the customer paid up, Paragon merely fills the customers entire 77-channel lineup with C-SPAN. Paragon said the project had been successful."

—*U.S. News & World Report,* July 31, 1995

BANDS THAT NEVER EXISTED

You've heard the expression, Don't believe everything you hear? Well, it turns out the rule also applies to rock bands.

THE MASKED MARAUDERS

In 1969, Greil Marcus wrote a story for *Rolling Stone* magazine claiming that the biggest rock stars of the day had gotten together and recorded an album. "This is indeed what it appears to be," he wrote, "John Lennon, Mick Jagger, Paul McCartney, and Bob Dylan, backed by George Harrison and a drummer as yet unnamed—the 'Masked Marauders.' The album was recorded with impeccable secrecy in a small town near the site of the original Hudson Bay Colony in Canada." The magazine even printed a Masked Marauders album cover with the article.

The Truth: Marcus made the whole thing up. When the article generated attention, he cashed in on it, hiring some "musicians" to record an album—complete with songs like "Mammy" and "I Can't Get No Nookie." It was an outrageous rip-off, but nothing on the album cover indicated that it was a joke. So people who believed what they read in *Rolling Stone* and rushed out to buy the album had no idea they were really getting a tone-deaf fake.

MILLI VANILLI

In 1990, Arista Records released *Girl, You Know It's True*, the debut album for a pop duo Milli Vanilli, made up of Fabrice Morvan, a Frenchman, and Robert Pilatus, a German.

It was a spectacular hit, selling more than 10 million copies worldwide—including 7 million in the United States. The album won several American Music Awards, as well as the 1990 Grammy for best new artists. "Musically," Pilatus told reporters, "we are more talented than any Bob Dylan. Musically, we are more talented than Paul McCartney. Mick Jagger, his lines are not clear. He don't know how he should produce a sound. I'm the new modern rock 'n' roll. I'm the new Elvis."

The battle hymn of the Ethiopian army used to be "The St. Louis Blues."

The Truth: In December, 1989, a rap singer named Charles Shaw informed a *New York Newsday* reporter that Morvan and Pilatus hadn't even sung on their album. He retracted the claim a few weeks later (it turned out that he was paid $150,000 for the retraction), but Milli Vanilli's horrible live performances fueled suspicions that they weren't the genuine article. Finally in November, 1990, Milli Vanilli's producer, Frank Farian, confirmed it. The pair, it turned out, had been hired because they would add sex appeal to the music videos.

Morvan and Pilatus were stripped of their Grammy and were even named in a class action suit filed by angry fans. They eventually regrouped as "Rob and Fab: The German and the French," but the new act bombed.

THE ARCHIES

When the *Archie* comic strip became a half-hour CBS cartoon show in 1968, sales of everything connected to *Archie* characters, from lunch boxes to comic books, skyrocketed. The executives who created the show wanted to sell records, too. So, they hired Don Kirshner, the man behind the Monkees' hits, to put together a group that would make records as the Archies. The band released an album in 1968. Their first single, "Bang Shang-A-Lang," was a modest success, but their second single, "Sugar, Sugar"—a song the Monkees had turned down in 1967—was the biggest selling record of 1969, with total sales of over $4 million.

The Truth: There was no band. Kirshner had endured so many problems with the Monkees that the last thing he wanted was another group. He simply hired two studio singers—Ron Dante (who provided the voices for Archie, Jughead, and Moose) and Toni Wine (who sang the Veronica and Betty parts)—and recorded everything with them.

A number of "Archies" bands toured the country claiming to be the genuine article, but the "real" Archies never toured. It wasn't from lack of trying: "At one point they wanted me to dye my hair and put freckles on and go out as Archie," Dante remembers. "I said, 'Oh boy, is this a career move or what?'"

* * *

"On behalf of all white people, I'd like to say we're sorry about Vanilla Ice." —***Dennis Miller***

THE BAD BOYS OF 2000

At the end of the 19th century, plenty of articles were written speculating on what life would be like 100 years away, in the year 2000. We read a lot of them for our book Uncle John's Indispensable Guide to the Year 2000, *but this was the weirdest. Apparently, "Uncle Richard" had a regular children's column in the* Chicago Tribune. *This piece ran on December 30, 1900, under the title, "Uncle Richard Tells of the Bad Boys of the Year 2000."*

Your Uncle Richard has told you of the bad boys of many lands, and from history's dawn down to the present. He will now peer ahead into the gray mists that veil the future and tell you what is on the cards for the year 2000, and whether or not it will repay you to sit around and wish that you could be a boy at that time.

In the first place, it would not be a good idea to wish to be a bad boy in that year, for there will be no bad boys then. Inventions will have been made so wonderful that the bad boy will have to become a nice sweet child...or step off the earth.

Teachers in the schools will have wonderful instruments on the desks that will record the name of everybody who whispers, and all the teacher will have to do to bring swift punishment will be to press a certain button on the desk, and a current of electricity will shoot through the victim, and make him think he is a human pincushion.

Fond parents who wish their offsprings to rise in the morning will not have to shout up the back stairs fifteen or twenty times and finally threaten to come "right up there now with this apple tree switch, do you hear me?" No, indeed. The parent of the year 2000 will press a small button in the sitting room, and the bed in which the boy is sleeping will have convulsions, and the boy will be hurled clear across the room. An electric spanker will then do a few stunts, and the boy will be glad to make haste in stirring himself suitably for appearance in polite society. If the boy sulks when he is downstairs his mother will punish him by not permitting him to sail with Jimmy Jones in his new airship in the afternoon.

No bad boy will run away from home to kill Indians, for there will be no Indians at that time except the ones who play football...besides, nobody is going to run away if they know their fond mama is going to pursue them with the velocity and ease of the great bald eagle. For individual flying machines will be in great vogue that year, and mamas, as well as papas, will flit about through the air with great ease, and when they spy their offspring they will pounce down on him from some dizzying height, and bat him over the head with an aluminum wing if he says he won't promise never to smoke again.

There will be very few horses in the year 2000 and all of them will be in the dime museums, so that the small boy will have nothing to curry except the family flying machine. All the milk will be manufactured downtown and there will be no cows to drive. The milk will be forced through hydrants to the consumers and nobody will have to go after it. The fond mother will say: "James, turn on the milk at the milk-drant and let it flow for a while so that it will be cool." Will that not be an easy thing?

There will be no chores to do in the year 2000. An electric ax will split the wood and an electric shovel will put the coal into the buckets which an electric carrier will convey to the furnace. Does not all this seem too good to be true?

Of course there will be school in the year 2000, but learning will be much easier. Instead of studying in the books about the capitals, children will simply step into the teacher's airship and be taken on a trip through most of the world's capitals—Berlin, Paris, London—returning hurriedly and going again the next day. All the adding and multiplying and silly things like that will be done by machines, and history will be learned from watching moving pictures of the events to be considered in the day's lesson. Of course, now and then some wicked boy may tie an aluminum can to a dog's tail, but the dog will probably be an electric dog, so he will not mind it at all.

Does not all of this seem like a dream? Well, dear children, you have guessed correctly, and as Uncle Richard's pipe has gone out, he will now wake up. So, good-bye.

GREASY, GRIMY GOPHER GUTS

We were looking for some new ways to entertain you, when someone came up with the idea of a singalong/poetry reading. You know, while you're sitting in there, you can make some...uh...other kinds of noise. But we wondered—what should we include? That's when Aunt Jenny came up with a book called Greasy, Grimy Gopher Guts, *compiled by Joseph Sherman and T.K.F. Weisskopf. Its full of those ditties you used to know when you were in 1st grade. Sing it out, now! (Explain it to your family later.)*

(Sung to the tune of
"The Old Grey Mare")
Great green gobs of greasy,
grimy gopher guts,
Mutilated monkey meat,
Little birdies' dirty feet.
Great green gobs of greasy,
grimy gopher guts,
And I forgot my spoon.

Jingle Bells, Santa smells,
A million miles away.
Stuffed his nose With Cheerios
And ate them all the way—
hey!

I'm gonna go eat worms.
Big ones and little ones,
Ishy guishy squishy ones,
I'm gonna go eat worms.
I'm gonna die,
Everybody cry,
I'm gonna eat some worms.

Eeny meeny miney moe,
Catch your teacher by the toe.
If he squirms, squeeze it tight
Then you take a great big bite.

'Twas the night before
Christmas
And all through the garage,
Not a creature was stirring,
Not even the Dodge.
The tires were hung by the
chimney with care.
In hopes that St. Nicholas
would fill them with air.

Little Miss Muffet
Sat on a tuffet
Eating her curds and whey.
Along came a spider
And sat down beside her
And she ate that, too.

Mary had a little lamb.
She fed it castor oil.
And everywhere that Mary went,
It fertilized the soil.

(To be sung to the tune of
"The Star-Spangled Banner")
Oo-oh say can you see
Any bedbugs on me?
If you do, pick a few—
'Cause I got them from you.

NEVER SUCK ON A CHOPSTICK

Planning on traveling abroad? Many cultures frown on behavior we consider "normal"—fingerpointing, yawning without covering your mouth, even eating while walking on the street. Here is a list of rude or vulgar behavior from around the world...which just might help you avoid touching off an international incident.

China: Never suck on your chopsticks.

Russia: Never squeeze through a theater aisle with your backside turned to the people sitting there.

Turkey: Don't talk to elderly people in a louder-than-normal voice.

Thailand: Avoid stepping on doorsills. (It's believed that a domestic deity lives in them.)

Taiwan: Never move an object with your foot.

Chile and Bolivia: Don't pour wine with your left hand.

Bali: Never take pictures of topless or nude bathers.

Arab countries: Don't sit so that the sole of your shoe ("the lowest and dirtiest place on your body") is pointing at someone.

Germany: Never shake hands while your other hand is in your pocket.

Poland: Don't drink everything in your glass if you hadn't intended getting a refill.

Indonesia: Never touch anyone's head.

Japan: Don't scribble on someone's business card.

Brazil: Don't give the "O.K." sign—it's considered obscene.

Chile: Don't slap your fist into the palm of your hand.

Portugal: Never use your bread to soak up the juices from your meal.

Kenya: Never accept a gift with your left hand.

India: Don't whistle in public.

Iran: Never blow your nose in public.

England: Don't start a conversation with "What do you do?"

Ireland: Avoid discussion of religion or politics.

Iceland: Never use a person's last name when greeting them.

Florida has more tornados per square mile than any other state.

YOU'RE MY INSPIRATION

It's always fascinating to find out who, or what, inspired familiar characters. Here are some we've come across.

DON CORLEONE, the Mafia leader in *The Godfather*, Mario Puzo's bestselling novel.

Inspired by: Puzo's mother. "Like the don," he explains, "she could be extremely warm and extremely ruthless....[For example], my father was committed to an insane asylum. When he could have returned home, my mother made the decision not to let him out—he would have been a burden on the family. That's a Mafia decision."

MOBY DICK, the Great White Whale, title character of Herman Melville's classic novel.

Inspired by: Mocha Dick, a real white sperm whale that was the terror of the seas in the first half of the 19th century. (He was named for Mocha Island, near Chile.) Mocha Dick was said to have wrecked or destroyed nearly thirty whaling boats and killed thirty men, beginning in 1819. Historians say Melville first read of him in an 1839 issue of *Knickerbocker* magazine.

WINNIE THE POOH, Christopher Robin's stuffed bear.

Inspired by: A Canadian black bear. In 1914, Harry Colebourne, a Canadian soldier, was traveling east on a troop train headed for England and World War I. When the train stopped in White River, Ontario, Harry bought a black bear cub from a hunter. He called it Winnie, after his hometown of Winnipeg, and took it to England as a mascot.

Colebourne was eventually stationed in France, and while he was gone, he loaned Winnie to the London Zoo. By the time he returned, the bear had become so popular that he decided to leave it there.

A few years later, a four-year-old named Christopher Milne

brought his favorite stuffed bear, Edward, to the zoo. Christopher saw Winnie and became so excited that he decided to rename Edward. "Pooh" was his nickname for a swan he loved—he appropriated it for the bear, and Edward became Winnie the Pooh.

MARY, the classic nursery rhyme character ("Mary had a little lamb, its fleece was white as snow...").

Inspired by: An eleven-year-old girl in Boston, Massachusetts. In 1817, a young man named John Roulstone saw young Mary Sawyer on her way to school...followed by a pet lamb. He thought it was so amusing, he jotted down a little poem about it.

Thirteen years later, Mrs. Sarah Josepha Hale added 12 more lines to the poem and published the whole thing under her own byline. Today there's some controversy about the authorship of the poem...but not the inspiration.

OLIVER BARRETT IV, the romantic hero in *Love Story*, a #1 bestselling book by Erich Segal and a hit movie in the 1970s.

Inspired by: Two students Segal knew at Harvard in the 1960s. The side of Barrett that was "the tough, macho guy who's a poet at heart" was fashioned after Tommy Lee Jones (now an actor). The side that "had a controlling father and was pressured to follow in the father's footsteps" was inspired by Jones's roommate—Al Gore.

MICKEY MOUSE, the most famous cartoon character in history.

Inspired by: A real mouse...and maybe actor Mickey Rooney. The mouse, whom Disney called Mortimer, was a pet that the cartoonist kept trapped in a wastebasket in his first art studio in Kansas City. Rooney, a child movie star, says in his autobiography that *he* inspired the mouse's new name, in the early 1920s:

> One day I passed a half-open door in a dirty old studio and peeked in. A slightly built man with a thin mustache...looked up and smiled. "What's your name, son?"
>
> "Mickey.... What are you drawing?"
>
> "I'm drawing a mouse, son." Suddenly he stopped drawing, took me by the shoulders, and looked me in the eye. "Did you say your name was Mickey?"
>
> "Yes sir."
>
> "You know what I'm going to do?...I'm going to call this mouse Mickey—after you."

Do you talk to your car? According to polls, more women do than men.

THE CURSE OF THE WEREWOLF, PART I

We've all heard the werewolf legend, seen it in films and on TV. In real life, it's called Lycanthropy. Here's a little of its history.

ANIMAL TALES

Nearly every society has legends about people who change into animals. In Russia there are stories of were-bears. In Africa, they have were-leopards, were-hyenas, and were-hippos. In Asia there are tales about were-tigers, elephants, crocodiles, snakes, and even sharks.

Why are these animals singled out? "In almost all cases," Nancy Garden writes in her book, *Werewolves*, "the animal has these characteristics: 1) It is commonly found in the area; 2) It is feared by the inhabitants; and 3) It has been known to attack people and/or farm animals."

In Europe, wolves fit that profile: As the population grew over the centuries, Europeans settled in parts of the continent where wolves had roamed freely. As the wildlife that wolves depended on for food began to disappear, they often preyed on livestock. And when food was *really* scarce, they might even go after humans. As late as 1875, an estimated 160 people were attacked by starving packs of wolves in Russia. So it's not surprising that when Europeans told scary stories by the fireside, wolves were a common subject. Their spooky habit of howling at the moon made them that much more fearsome.

THE WEREWOLF TRIALS

No one (or at least *hardly* anyone) believes in werewolves today, but in the Middle Ages, they were taken quite seriously. "Of all the world's monsters," says Daniel Cohen in his book, *Werewolves*, "the werewolf is the one that has been most widely believed in, and the most widely feared."

Here are some of the things people commonly believed:

• A person could become a werewolf in a number of ways: if he was cursed, drank water from a wolf's pawprint, ate the meat of an animal killed by a wolf, wore a girdle made of wolfskin, or used a magic salve. "The business about becoming a werewolf after being bitten by another werewolf is basically a creation of the movies," says Cohen. "'Real' werewolves didn't just bite people, they tore their victims to pieces and ate them."

• In some versions of the legend, the werewolf remained human, but took on wolf characteristics, such as fur, fangs, and paws. In other variations, the person literally turned into a wolf.

• Werewolves could be killed any way that a normal wolf could be killed.

DEMON WOLVES

It was commonly accepted that werewolves were in league with the devil. Even educated churchmen who didn't believe human beings could really transform into other animals assumed that the devil was involved. "They often said that the devil created the 'illusion' of transformation," Cohn writes. "He made people 'think' they had turned into wolves, and made the victim 'think' they were being attacked by the creature."

Some "authorities" believed a real wolf could be turned into a werewolf when the spirit of an evil person entered it. "It was possible therefore," Cohen explains, "for an evil person to be asleep in his bed at night, or even locked in a cell under the eyes of his jailers, and yet his spirit could roam free as a werewolf. As a result, a lot of people were convicted of being werewolves even after it was proven that they were nowhere near the place where the werewolf had allegedly committed its crimes."

This was serious business. In Europe, as late as the 18th century, if you were suspected of being a werewolf you could be put on trial and then put to death. Untold thousands *were* put to death—between 1520 and 1630, an estimated 30,000 cases of "werewolfery" trials were recorded in central France alone, and thousands more trials took place in other parts of Europe.

"The Curse of the Werewolf, Part II" is on page 351.

State sport of Maryland: Jousting.

TABLOID SECRETS

This article is adapted from a fascinating book called Grossed-Out Surgeon Vomits Inside Patient—An Insider's Look at Supermarket Tabloids, *by Jim Hogshire. (The author worked on tabloids, and the title is a headline he once wrote.) We never realized how carefully the* Enquirer, Globe, *etc.—popular bathroom reading material—are put together.*

ALWAYS JUDGE A TAB BY ITS COVER

Daily newspapers make the majority of their money from advertisers...[and subscribers.] But supermarket tabloids rely on the cover price for at least 80% of their profits. *The National Examiner*, with its million-plus circulation, has never had more than 23,000 people subscribing—despite the substantial discount for doing so.

• It's that way at all the tabloids. Marketing studies show that most tabloid buyers do not intend to purchase one before arriving in the checkout line and spend fewer than four seconds looking at a cover before deciding to buy.

• A cover can be rejected in a second. Studies in which lasers were aimed at customer's eyes reveal that a person's gaze does not often drop below the top half of the page. Sometimes it goes no further than the title.

THE COVER

[So] editors use the cover as their most powerful tool. "It's the only selling point you have. It's your only promotion billboard; it's your only selling point," says one.

• "It may look like garbage but that's the way we want it to look," said Cliff Linedecker, former assistant editor at *The National Examiner*. "We always try to make the cover look like a circus poster."

• The paper might look haphazard, but the formula is exacting. A "gee-whiz" is the banner headline at the top that announces a 7-year-old girl had a baby on a rollercoaster. "Hey, Marthas" are stories that combine impact with the ability to hold a reader's interest. In tabloid circles these win as much praise as Pulitzer-winning articles in the mainstream press. The classic "Hey, Martha!" story is "Headless Body Found in Topless Bar."

A killer whale's heart beats 30 times a minute under water, 60 times a minute on the surface.

• Also crucial to a good cover is a "must-buy" headline. "People see a headline like 'Marilyn Monroe Was a Dyke!' and say, 'Aw, Christ, I gotta buy that one,'" *Examiner*'s Billy Burt said. "Every editor every week sits down and tries to come up with a 'must-buy' headline that'll catch people's attention."

INSIDE THE TABLOID

Filling the pages of a supermarket tabloid is a formulaic process and can be handled with an almost assembly-line approach. Staff writers typically crank out far more stories per week than appear in the paper to create a healthy backlog. Noncelebrity stories have lead times of at least three weeks. Even the most trivial of stories may go through a half-dozen rewrites before the editors are satisfied. Nothing appears in a tabloid story by accident.

• Tabs' budgets may call for a certain percentage of Bigfoot stories, or a certain number and type of diet articles. Whenever a need arises, editors simply reach into a large file cabinet known as the bin and retrieve whatever story fits the hole they have to fill. If it's a 6-inch UFO story, it's there. If they need a 12-incher on a miracle cure at Lourdes, no problem.

• There is no exact science to what goes into a tabloid, yet correct timing seems to play a role. Thus, vinegar and mayo diets might appear only twice a year. Even though Elvis is a proven seller, he cannot be reincarnated at will. The time must be ripe.

• Celebrity photos are guaranteed to appear in the same places in a tabloid, and the "mix" of stories is almost like a recipe, with certain genres appearing in certain places in the magazine. "Everybody keeps experimenting with the mix," Burt said, "but there are some things you know are good sellers, like diet stories, or a good medical story that affects everybody....Bible stories are also a staple."

TV & CELEBRITIES

"Back in the 1970s," Burt continued, "there was the traditional tabloid mix of health, love, money, celebrity, plus the psychic bit. But it's changed. It's only since the tabloids started getting really good color that they really promoted the main picture, and now that's always a celebrity."

Half of all Americans over the age of 55 have no teeth.

• Burt recalled earlier days of tabloids when part of the mix was to feed off popular television shows. He felt it was one of the key components that made the *Enquirer* and others so successful. "That was when television was at its peak and you had the celebrities. You had Charlie's Angels and every week you could rotate Farrah Fawcett, Jaclyn Smith, Cheryl Ladd, Kate Jackson. Look at Joan Collins. *Dynasty* and all these major soaps had millions of people watch every week, and they really wanna know what's going on in the stars' lives. Do they screw around like they do on the show?"

• The arrival of cable TV has so diluted this once lucrative pool of recognizable celebrities that tabloids have had to work hard to find stars to take their places. But the pickings are slim. In the '80s and '90s "tabloid TV" began to reverse the trend and feed off the supermarket tabloids. Almost every day tabs are called up by producers of shows like *Hard Copy*, *Inside Edition* and *A Current Affair*. Ironically, calls come in just as often from the network news shows.

REVERSE LOGIC

"The tabs used to feed off television. Now television's feeding off the tabloids. *Nightline*—Ted Koppel gets his best ratings, *20/20* gets their best ratings, when they do tabloid stories. Of course the greatest thing is to hold [the tabloid] up and say, 'Look at this piece of s--t. We would never do a story like this.' And then they repeat the story!" Burt said.

• "*The Examiner* once ran a story about Randy Travis possibly being gay. He was on *Entertainment Tonight* with Mary Hart, saying, 'I'm not gay,' but he gives them a full interview. They show the cover of the paper and that says he is gay. They ask him if he is gay and he says he's not gay. But they perpetuate the whole bloody thing. If it's libel then what are they doing going around repeating the libel?!"

• Because of the dearth of sure-selling TV characters, tabloids have had to search for their stories where they've always been—whatever interests the reader. Inevitably, readers turn to tabloids for comfort and titillation. They go there to be assured the world outside is worse than they can imagine and that, in the end, a humdrum life doesn't mean they're a failure.

Consensus reality is really reality, after all.

Slow food: The average French citizen eats 500 snails a year.

THE TOP 10 HITS OF THE YEAR, 1980–1983

Yet another installment of BRI's Top Ten of the Year list.

1980
(1) Call Me —*Blondie*
(2) Another Brick In The Wall —*Pink Floyd*
(3) Rock With You —*Michael Jackson*
(4) Magic —*Olivia Newton-John*
(5) Crazy Little Thing Called Love —*Queen*
(6) Do That One More Time —*Captain & Tennile*
(7) Coming Up —*Paul McCartney*
(8) Funkytown —*Lipps, Inc.*
(9) It's Still Rock And Roll To Me —*Billy Joel*
(10) The Rose —*Bette Midler*

1981
(1) Bette Davis Eyes —*Kim Carnes*
(2) (Just Like) Starting Over —*John Lennon*
(3) Lady —*Kenny Rogers*
(4) Endless Love —*Diana Ross & Lionel Richie*
(5) Jessie's Girl —*Rick Springfield*
(6) Celebration —*Kool & The Gang*
(7) Kiss On My List —*Daryl Hall & John Oates*
(8) Keep On Loving You —*Reo Speedwagon*
(9) I Love A Rainy Night —*Eddie Rabbitt*
(10) 9 To 5 —*Dolly Parton*

1982
(1) Physical —*Olivia Newton-John*
(2) Eye Of The Tiger —*Survivor*
(3) I Love Rock N' Roll —*Joan Jett & The Blackhearts*
(4) Centerfold —*J. Geils Band*
(5) Ebony And Ivory —*Paul McCartney & Stevie Wonder*
(6) Don't You Want Me —*Human League*
(7) Hurts So Good —*John Cougar*
(8) Jack And Diane —*John Cougar*
(9) Abracadabra —*Steve Miller Band*
(10) Hard To Say I'm Sorry —*Chicago*

1983
(1) Every Breath You Take —*Police*
(2) Billie Jean —*Michael Jackson*
(3) Down Under —*Men At Work*
(4) Flashdance...What A Feeling —*Irene Cara*
(5) Beat It —*Michael Jackson*
(6) Total Eclipse Of The Heart —*Bonnie Tyler*
(7) Maneater —*Daryl Hall & John Oates*
(8) Maniac —*Michael Sembello*
(9) Baby Come To Me —*Patti Austin with James Ingram*
(10) Sweet Dreams (Are Made Of This) —*Eurythmics*

No laughing matter: William Shakespeare invented the expression, "Laugh it off."

PART V: THE CHRYSLER BUILDING

*Part V of the World's Tallest Buildings is the story of a skyscraper that's still regarded by many as the most beautiful building ever built.**(For Part IV, see page 206.)*

TOP THIS

By the late 1920s, the Woolworth Building had held the title of "world's tallest building" for more than a decade. But its reign clearly wouldn't last much longer—skyscrapers were going up all over Manhattan, and many of their owners publiclv asoired to be the new record-holder.

However, no one knew who would actually pull it off—it was a "rule" in this building competition that the heights of prospective skyscrapers be kept secret to prevent rival architects from planning even taller structures.

One man who was determined to own the world's tallest building was Walter P. Chrysler, a former machinist's apprentice who had worked his way up to vice president at General Motors—and then left to head his own successful auto company.

For years Chrysler had wanted to build a skyscraper. But it wasn't until he took a trip to France that he finally decided how tall it should be. "Something that I had seen in Paris kept coming back to me," he later explained. "I said to the architects, 'make this building higher than the Eiffel Tower.'"

GETTING OFF THE GROUND

Chrysler's architect, William Van Alen, knew that two former partners of his, H. Craig Severance and Yasuo Matsui, were designing a building for the Bank of Manhattan at 40 Wall St. He didn't know how high it was going to be, and they weren't about to tell him. So Van Alen announced that the Chrysler Building would be 925 feet tall, expecting them to make their design just tall enough to beat it. He was right—as it neared completion it became clear that 40 Wall Street was going to be 927 feet tall, a scant two feet higher than the Chrysler Building's announced height.

MAKING A POINT

Now Van Alen knew what number to beat, and he had an idea about how to do it.

In its original plans, the 71-story Chrysler Building was topped by a hollow 142-foot art-deco dome. Van Alen used it as a sort of Trojan Horse. While construction went on as planned *outside*, a new construction crew was operating in secret inside the dome, building a 123-foot high spire.

Just as 40 Wall St. was nearing completion, Van Alen had the workers lift the spire up through the hole in the top of the dome and bolt it into place. The spire pushed the Chrysler Building's height to 1,048 feet, making it the first building to pass the 1,000 foot mark—as well as the tallest building in the world. It was also the first building to be built taller than the Eiffel Tower, just as Walter Chrysler had asked.

HIGH WATER MARK

The Chrysler building is considered by many to be the most beautiful skyscraper ever built, the pinnacle of art deco architectural design. Van Alen incorporated numerous automotive themes into the building's exterior. At each corner of the base of the tower at the 31st floor, he placed a gargoyle in the form of a winged helmet of Mercury—the symbol on Chrysler's radiator caps at the time. And on the 61st story he added eagle's-head gargoyles that were modeled after the hood ornament on the 1929 Chrysler Plymouth.

One architectural historian describes the building as "the skyscraper of skyscrapers. It is perhaps the sort of building one might dream in a primitive dream....Its silvery tower kindles the imagination of those who believe there is some life and glory in urban existence. The Chrysler Building remains one of the most appealing and awe-inspiring of the skyscrapers. It has few equals anywhere."

The Chrysler Building's beauty has endured for decades, but its status as the world's tallest building only lasted a year. Even as it was opening for business, the construction of the Empire State Building was already underway.

Part VI of the World's Tallest Buildings is on page 301.

Smallest post office in the United States: Ochopee, a town in the western Everglades.

TITANIC COINCIDENCES

There's something almost mystical about the Titanic. There are so many bizarre coincidences associated with it, you'd think it was an episode of The Twilight Zone.

THE TITAN/TITANIC

In 1898, a short novel called *The Wreck of the Titan or Futility*, by Morgan Robertson, was published in the U.S. It told the story of the maiden voyage of an "unsinkable" luxury liner called the *Titan*. Robertson described the boat in great detail.

The *Titan*, he wrote, was 800 feet long, weighed 75,000 tons, had three propellers and 24 lifeboats, and was packed with rich passengers. Cruising at 25 knots, the *Titan*'s hull was ripped apart when it hit an iceberg in April. Most of the passengers were lost because there weren't enough life boats. Robertson apparently claimed he'd written his book with the help of an "astral writing partner."

Eerie Coincidence: Fourteen years later, the real-life *Titanic* took off on its maiden voyage. Like the fictional *Titan*, it was considered the largest and safest ship afloat. It was 882.5 feet long, weighed 66,000 tons, had three propellers and 22 life boats, and carried a full load of rich passengers. Late at night on April 14, 1912, sailing at 23 knots, the *Titanic* ran into an iceberg which tore a hole in its hull and upended the ship. At least 1,513 people drowned because there weren't enough lifeboats.

THE TITANIAN/TITANIC

In 1935, a "tramp steamer" was heading from England to Canada. On watch was a 23-year-old seaman named William Reeves. It was April, the month when the *Titanic* hit an iceberg and went down. As the *Reader's Digest Book of Amazing Facts* tells it:

> Young Reeves brooded deeply on this. His watch was due to end at midnight. This, he knew, was the time the Titanic had hit the iceberg. Then, as now, the sea had been calm. These thoughts swelled

and took shape as omens...as he stood his lonely watch....He was scared to shout an alarm, fearing hs shipmates' ridicule. But he was also scared not to.

Eerie Coincidence: All of a sudden, Reeves recalled the exact date of the *Titanic* accident—April 14, 1912—the day he had been born. That was enough to get him to act.

He shouted out a danger warning, and the helmsman rang the signal: engines full astern. The ship churned to a halt—just yards from a huge iceberg that towered menacingly out of the night.

More deadly icebergs crowded in around the tramp steamer, and it took nine days for icebreakers from Newfoundland to smash a way clear.

The name of the ship Reeves saved from a similar fate to the *Titanic's*? The *Titanian.*

THE LUCKLESS TOWERS

Talk about coincidences! BRI member Andrew M. Borrok (hope we got that right—the fax is hard to read) submitted the following excerpt just as Uncle John was writing this piece. Obviously we had *to include it. Thanks!*

The stoker on the *Titanic* was named Frank Lucks Towers. Charles Pelegrino writes in his book, *Her Name, Titanic:*

Though he would survive this night (*Titanic*) without injury, his troubles were just beginning. In two years he'd be aboard the *Empress of Ireland* when it collided with another ship, opening up a hole in the *Empress'* side. (Note: it was the worst peacetime maritime disaster—over 2000 lost.) It would be an usually hot night, and all the portholes would be open as she rolled onto her side in the St. Lawrence River. In minutes she would be gone—yet miraculously, Frank Towers was going to survive—virtually alone. He'd take his next job aboard the *Lusitania,* (sunk by German U-boats in 1915) and would be heard to shout "Now what!" when the torpedo struck. He'd swim to a lifeboat, vowing every stroke of the way to take up farming.

His story was destined to inspire a young writer to script a teleplay entitled *Lone Survivor*. The teleplay was so well received that it paved the way for a series. The writer's name was Rod Serling and the series became *The Twilight Zone.*

The 1st live televised murder was in 1963, when Jack Ruby killed JFK's assassin, Lee Harvey Oswald.

URBAN LEGENDS

In our last Bathroom Reader *(the* Giant 10th Anniversary *edition), we ran a piece on urban legends. Since then, we've come across so many more good ones that we just had to include them. Remember the rule of thumb: if a story sounds true, but also seems too "perfect" to be true, it's probably an urban legend.*

THE STORY: Two speeding semi trucks crash head on in a heavy fog. The drivers survive, but the two trucks are too smashed together to separate, so the towing company tows them to the junkyard in one piece. A few weeks later, junkyard workers notice a terrible smell coming from the wreck. They pry the cars apart...and discover a Volkswagen beetle with four passengers crushed flat in between the two trucks.

THE TRUTH: Urban legends featuring small cars smashed by big vehicles are so numerous that they're practically a category by themselves. What keeps them alive is the general fear of meeting a similar fate.

THE STORY: Rock Hudson and Jim Nabors (TV's *Gomer Pyle*) were married in a secret Hollywood ceremony.

THE TRUTH: According to Rock Hudson biographer Sara Davidson, Hudson and Nabors barely knew one another. Davidson says she believes the rumors were started "by some gay guys who as a joke sent out invitations to the wedding of Nabors and Hudson." The invitations were mistakenly taken seriously, and the rumors became so pervasive that Nabors and Hudson "made a point of not being seen together at Hollywood events."

THE STORY: In a South African hospital, a number of patients have died mysteriously while convalescing in a particular bed. The hospital investigated...and discovered that the cleaning lady had been inadvertently killing a patient every time she polished the floor.

HOW IT SPREAD: On the Internet, in 1996. The e-mail was supposedly taken from a June 1996 *Cape Times* article headlined "Cleaner Polishes Off Patients." The story follows:

"It seems that every Friday morning a cleaner would enter the ward, remove the plug that powered the patient's life support system, plug her floor polisher into the vacant socket, then go about her business. When she had finished her chores, she would plug the life support machine back in and leave, unaware that the patient was now dead. She could not, after all, hear the screams and eventual death rattle over the whirring of her polisher.

"We are sorry, and have sent a strong letter to the cleaner in question. Further, the Free State Health and Welfare Department is arranging for an electrician to fit an extra socket, so there should be no repetition of this incident. The enquiry is now closed."

THE TRUTH: Rumors of death-by-cleaning-lady incidents floated around South Africa for years before reporters at a South African newspaper named *Die Volksblad* decided, in 1996, to see if there was any truth to them. They ran an article asking relatives of any of the victims to come forward. No one did...but another South African paper picked up the story—and finally the *Cape Times* mistakenly ran the story as an actual occurrence, rather than a regional newspaper's attempt to track down an urban legend.

THE STORY: A medical school student prepares to work on a cadaver during her gross anatomy laboratory. She lifts the cover off of the body...and discovers that the cadaver is an ex-boyfriend.

THE TRUTH: Finding out that the cadaver assigned to you is a friend, relative or loved one is a fear as old as medical school anatomy classes themselves. Tales of such a thing happening have been traced back hundreds of years. One version, involving the English novelist Laurence Sterne, dates back to 1768.

Note: It actually did happen at least once. In 1982, a student at the University of Alabama School of Medicine learned that the body of her great aunt was one of the nine cadavers assigned to her anatomy class. The state anatomy board replaced it with another body.

*　　*　　*　　*

"Nothing in education is so astonishing as the amount of ignorance it accumulates in the form of inert facts." —**Henry Adams**

ASPIRIN: THE MIRACLE DRUG

Here's more on the history of aspirin.
The first part of the story is on page 60.

MID-LIFE CRISIS

In 1950, aspirin earned a place in the *Guinness Book of World Records* as the world's best-selling painkiller. But if the medical community had paid attention to Dr. Lawrence Craven, an ear-nose-throat specialist, in 1948, aspirin would have been recognized as much more than that.

Dr. Craven had noticed that when he performed tonsillectomies, patients who took aspirin bled more than the ones who didn't. He suspected the aspirin was inhibiting the ability of blood to clot, something that might be useful in preventing strokes and heart attacks—both of which can be caused by excessive clotting of the blood.

Craven decided to test his theory. He put 400 of his male patients on aspirin, then watched them over several years to see how many had heart attacks. Not one did, so Craven expanded his research. He began following the histories of 8,000 regular aspirin-takers, to see if any of *them* had a heart attack. None of them did, either.

Dr. Craven published his findings in a medical journal. But nobody listened. "The medical community shunned his findings," says Dr. Steven Weisman. "He wasn't a cardiologist, he wasn't in the academic community and he was publishing in a lesser-known journal."

ASPIRIN SCIENCE

The biggest problem was that as late as 1970 nobody had any idea how aspirin worked. That year John Vane, a researcher with London's Royal College of Surgeons, discovered what Dr. Craven had known intuitively—that aspirin blocks an enzyme that causes blood platelets to stick together, which is what happens when blood clots.

By inhibiting clotting, aspirin helps to prevent strokes, heart attacks, and other cardiovascular ailments.

Not long afterwards, researchers in Sweden discovered that aspirin also blocks the production of *prostaglandins*, hormone-like chemicals that affect digestion, reproduction, circulation, and the immune system. Excess levels of prostaglandins can cause headaches, fevers, blood clots, and a host of other problems. Scientists quickly began to discover that aspirin's ability to block the prostaglandin production makes it an effective treatment for many of these problems.

WONDER DRUG

For the first time in 70 years, researchers were beginning to understand aspirin's potential beyond reducing pain, fever and inflammation. Thousands of studies have since been conducted to test aspirin's effectiveness against a number diseases, and many more are planned.

The results have been astounding. In 1980, the U.S. Food and Drug Administration (FDA) recommended aspirin to reduce the risk of stroke in men experiencing stroke symptoms. In 1985, it recommended aspirin to heart attack patients as a means of reducing the risk of second heart attacks. One 1988 heart attack study was so successful that researchers shut it down five years early so that the test subjects who weren't taking aspirin could begin to take it. In 1996, the FDA recommended administering aspirin *during* heart attacks as a means of lowering the risk of death.

And that's only the beginning. Aspirin is believed to lower the risk of colon cancer by as much as 32%, and scientists are also exploring aspirin's ability to slow the progression of Alzheimers disease, cataracts, diabetes, numerous other forms of cancer, and even HIV, the virus that causes AIDS.

"No little white pill does everything, that's for sure," says the University of Pennsylvania's Dr. Garret Fitzgerald, one of the world's top aspirin experts. "But the strength of the evidence for aspirin working where it has been shown to work is probably greater than the strength of the evidence for any drug for human disease."

First meal eaten on the moon: 4 bacon squares, 3 sugar cookies,

Bathroom Reader Warning: Aspirin isn't for everyone. Consult a doctor before taking aspirin regularly. Aspirin is still an acid, and it can irritate the lining of the stomach and cause pain, internal bleeding and ulcers. "'An aspirin a day' does not apply to everyone," says Dr. Paul Pedersen, a doctor of internal medicine. "It's not like apples."

• **Also:** In 1986, scientists established a link between aspirin and Reye's syndrome, a rare but sometimes fatal disease that strikes children suffering from acute viral infections like influenza and chicken pox.

ASPIRIN FACTS

• Americans take an estimated 80 million aspirin a day—about the same amount as the rest of the world combined. 30-50% of them are taken as preventative medicine for cardiac disease.

• How you take aspirin depends on where you live: Americans prefer pills; the English like powders that dissolve in water; Italians like fizzy aspirin drinks, and the French like aspirin suppositories.

• Roughly 6% of Americans cannot take straight aspirin because it irritates their stomachs. That's where coated or "buffered" aspirin comes in—each pill is treated with a special, slow-to-dissolve coating that prevents the aspirin from being absorbed by the body until it has left the stomach and gone into the intestines.

• One of the remaining unsolved aspirin mysteries is why it only works on you when you're sick. "If your body temperature is normal, it won't lower it," says Roger P. Maickel, a professor of pharmacology at Purdue University. "If you don't have inflammation, it doesn't have any antiarthritic effects on your joints. It's beautifully simple to work with, yet the damn thing does everything."

MIGRAINE MATERIAL

What did Felix Hoffman, inventor of aspirin, have to show for his work? Not much—aspirin made the Bayer family fabulously wealthy, and it earned Felix Hoffman's supervisor, Heinrich Dreser, enough money to retire early. Hoffman was not so lucky—he was entitled to royalties on anything he invented that was patented, but since aspirin was never successfully patented in Germany, the really big bucks eluded him.

peaches, pineapple-grapefruit drink, coffee.

THE ANIMALS AT THE ZOO, Part 2

Here's more info on animal-watching at the zoo, from Beastly Behaviors, *by Janine M. Benyus*

WATCHING ELEPHANTS

The typical elephant herd is made up of adult females and the young of both sexes. It is a very tight-knit group. In the wild, adult males wander by themselves or congregate in small bachelor groups. Bulls are extremely irritable, unpredictable, and dangerous when in "must" (heat). For this reason, many zoos refuse to keep them.

Behavior: Elephants do most of their "talking" with their trunks. Here's what the different trunk positions mean.

Position: Hanging straight down.

What It Means: The elephant has nothing in particular on its mind. This is how it holds its trunk while going about its normal, everyday business.

Position: Held up in "tea spout" position (U-curve in the middle, pointed outward at the tip).

What It Means: It's the elephant's sniffing position. Usually, an elephant's first reaction to something new is to try to pick up its scent.

Position: Hanging down with tip curled in.

What It Means: Fear or submission.

Position: Thrust straight outward.

What It Means: Aggression. Threat. Elephants hold their trunks this way when they're charging.

Behavior: Touching each other's trunk.

What It Means: Greeting. Take note of the ears as one elephant approaches another. If they're high and folded, it's going to be a friendly encounter.

Behavior: Flapping their ears.

What It Means: The elephant is cooling itself. Its favorite way to beat the heat, though, is to roll in mud.

Behavior: Trumpeting.

What It Means: Excitement. Elephants get vocal only when they're excited. Generally, the more excited they are—either with joy or anger—the longer and louder they'll trumpet. At zoos, they'll give a short, sharp toot when they're impatient to be fed.

Behavior: Bold trumpeting; lots of rubbing and bumping against each other. Could be accompanied by urinating and defecating.

What It Means: The scene may sound and look scary, but it's probably a celebration. Elephants reunited after a long separation can become very raucous. It's just their way of telling each other, "It's great to see you. I missed you."

OTHER ANIMALS

DOLPHINS

Behavior: Rubbing.

What It Means: Affection. When you see dolphins nuzzling, you probably think they're expressing care for one another. And you're right. Dolphins use touch as a way to bond. They also use rubbing to remove social tensions, and parasites, such as barnacles, from each others' skin. A dolphin may rub its body, fluke, or flippers against a neighboring dolphin. Or two dolphins may engage in a full-body rub or pat each other repeatedly in a "pat-a-cake" maneuver.

OSTRICHES

Behavior: Pretending to feed.

What It Means: Think of it as a way for a male and female to test their compatibility during a complicated courtship ritual. Together, the couple will peck at the ground. Though it might look like they're feeding, they're not. It's more like a dance—with their goal being to move in unison.

Each year, 30,000 people in the U.S. are seriously injured by exercise equipment.

TEARING DOWN THE WHITE HOUSE

The White House wasn't always a national treasure. A number of presidents once seriously considered tearing it down or turning it into a museum and building a new residence somewhere else. But today, that's unthinkable. Here's why.

NOT ENOUGH SPACE

At first, most Americans didn't think there was anything particularly special about the White House. Few had ever seen it or had any idea what it looked like, and even the families who lived there found it completely inadequate.

When it was built, the White House was the largest house in the country (and it remained so until after the Civil War). But it served so many different purposes that little of it was available for First Families to actually live in. The first floor, or "State Floor," was made up entirely of public rooms; and half of the second floor was taken up by the president's offices, which where staffed by as many as 30 employees. The First Family had to get by with the eight—or fewer—second-floor rooms that were left.

By Lincoln's time, the situation was intolerable. Kenneth Leish writes in *The White House*, "The lack of privacy was appalling. The White House was open to visitors daily, and office seekers, cranks, and the merely curious had no difficulty making their way upstairs from the official rooms on the first floor."

THE LINCOLN WHITE HOUSE

Lincoln was so uncomfortable with the situation that he had a private corridor (since removed) constructed. This at least allowed him to get from the family quarters to his office without having to pass through the reception room, where throngs of strangers were usually waiting to see him.

He also received a $20,000 appropriation to improve the furnishings of the White House, which had become, as one visitor put it, "bare, worn and spoiled," like "a deserted farmstead," with holes in the carpets and paint peeling off of the walls in the state rooms.

Lincoln was busy with the Civil War, so he turned the matter over to his wife, who spent every penny and went $6,700 over budget. Lincoln was furious, and refused to ask Congress to cover the balance. "It would stink in the nostrils of the American people," he fumed, "to have it said that the President of the United States had approved a bill overrunning an appropriate [amount] for *flub dubs* for this damned old house, when the soldiers cannot have blankets."

The new furnishings did not last for more than a few years. When Lincoln was assassinated in 1865, the White House fell into disarray. "Apparently," writes The White House Historical Society, "no one really supervised the White House during the five weeks Mrs. Lincoln lay mourning in her room, and vandals helped themselves."

SAVING THE HOUSE

Ironically, at the same time the White House was being ransacked, it was gaining a new respect with Americans...attaining an almost shrine-like status.

National tragedy turned the White House into a national monument. It wasn't just the White House anymore—it was the place where the great fallen hero, Lincoln, had lived. Photography had only been invented about 30 years earlier. Now for the first time, photos of the White House circulated around the country. It became a symbol of the presidency...and America.

The Founding Fathers had assumed that future presidents would add to, or even demolish and rebuild the official residence as they saw fit. But after 1865, no president would have dared to suggest tearing it down.

Feeling patriotic? There's more on the White House on page 395.

* * * *

"I'll be glad to be going—this is the loneliest place in the world."

—***President William Howard Taft, on leaving the White House***

WHY ASK WHY?

Sometimes, answers are irrelevant—it's the question that counts. These cosmic queries are from a variety of readers.

Why do psychics have to ask your name?

Why don't sheep shrink when it rains?

How much deeper would the ocean be without sponges?

What happens if you get scared half to death twice?

Despite the cost of living, have you noticed how it remains so popular?

How do you tell when you run out of invisible ink?

Did ancient doctors refer to IVs as "fours"?

Why are they called "apartments" when they're all stuck together?

If bankers can count, how come they have eight windows and only four tellers?

Is Dan Quayle's name spelled with an *e* at the end?

Why do we play in recitals and recite in plays?

If the #2 pencil is so popular, why is it still #2?

If most car accidents occur within five miles of home, why doesn't everyone just move 10 miles away?

Why can't I set my laser printer on "stun"?

If all the world is a stage, where is the audience sitting?

Why do they call them "hemorrhoids" instead of "asteroids"?

Why is the alphabet in that order? Is it because of that song?

If you write a book about failure and it doesn't sell, is it a success?

Would a fly without wings be called a *walk*?

If white wine goes with fish, do white grapes go with sushi?

If the funeral procession is at night, do folks drive with their lights off?

Why is the celtuce plant called a celtuce? It tastes a little like celery, a little like lettuce.

TWO FORGOTTEN INVENTORS

Here's a look at two people who made great inventions, only to see the credit go to someone else.

FORGOTTEN INVENTOR: John Fitch
CLAIM TO FAME: He had been George Washington's gunsmith at Valley Forge, and had skills as a silversmith, brass founder, surveyor and clockmaker. But he should have been known as the man who invented the steamboat—not Robert Fulton. He built his first model of a "boat propelled by steam" in 1785, and successfully tried out a full-size version the following year. He obtained exclusive rights in five states for mechanically-propelled boats and, by 1790, was operating regularly scheduled services between Philadelphia, Pennsylvania and Trenton, New Jersey.
HIS LEGACY: Over the years Fitch's debts piled up and squatters took over his lands. He died sad and broke in 1798 at the age of 55, five years before Fulton "invented" the steamboat. Congress later honored Fitch with a mural in the U.S. Capitol, but Fulton is still the one who gets all the credit.

FORGOTTEN INVENTOR: Nathan B. Stubblefield
CLAIM TO FAME: Stubblefield was the real inventor of the radio—not Marconi. He first demonstrated a "wireless telephone" for a few friends on his farm in 1890, when Marconi was still a teenager. He filed no patent at the time, he "just went on tinkering." On January 1, 1902 (less than a month after Marconi had transmitted the letter "S" across the Atlantic in Morse code), he finally got around to doing a demonstration for the public. About 1,000 friends and neighbors watched as, "speaking softly into a two-foot-square box, he was heard at half a dozen listening [stations] around town." Later that year, he gave a better-publicized and better-attended demonstration in Washington, D.C., from a steam launch on the Potomac River.

Most popular soap opera in the world: Mexico's *The Rich Also Cry.*

Marconi, known today as the father of radio, actually pioneered *wireless telegraphy*, the transmission of Morse code. Stubblefield sent *voices* and *music* (played by his son) over the air, and he did it years before Marconi sent his first dots and dashes. In a 1908 patent he described how to put radios in horseless carriages, making him the father of the car radio—another invention he did not capitalize on.

INTO THE DUSTBIN: None of Stubblefield's inventions, "including a battery devised for radios," made him much money. His marriage broke up, his house burned down. Still he continued to work on new inventions. But we don't know much about them—Shortly before his death Stubblefield destroyed all his inventions and burned their plans. He was a lonely, impoverished hermit when he was found starved to death in a shack near his hometown of Murray, Kentucky in 1928. His body went into an unmarked grave.

* * * *

AND SPEAKING OF THE DUSTBIN OF HISTORY...

Here's another historic figure who's been swept out of the history books:

FORGOTTEN FIGURE: Captain James Iredell Waddell, Confederate war hero and commander of the warship *Shenandoah.*

CLAIM TO FAME: Under Waddell's command, the *Shenandoah* disrupted Yankee whaling operations in the Pacific, captured numerous Union vessels, destroyed over $1 million worth of shipping, and took more than 1,000 prisoners.

Much of this success came *after* General Lee's surrender at Appomattox on April 9, 1865. Even when Waddell learned of the surrender, he chose to ignore it, believing the South would keep fighting a guerrilla war.

INTO THE DUSTBIN: Waddell made plans to attack San Francisco by sea. But on his way there, the *Shenandoah* met up with a friendly British merchant ship, whose captain informed Waddell that the war was definitely over. Realizing he would be tried and probably hanged for piracy if he made port in America, Waddell and crew sailed for England. The *Shenandoah* surrendered to the British in Liverpool on November 6, 1865.

FAMOUS FOR BEING NAKED

Here are a few celebrities who are remembered for not wearing any clothes. (Or for looking like they weren't.)

CHERI BRAND, child model.

Famous For: Posing for the original portrait of Little Miss Coppertone, the girl whose bottom is exposed because a dog is pulling down her bathing suit.

The Bare Facts: In 1953, a Miami advertising agency hired graphic artist Joyce Ballentyne to design the logo for Coppertone suntan lotion. For models, she used her 3-year-old daughter Cheri and a cocker spaniel she borrowed from a neighbor. The image appeared in ads on billboards all over the U.S., accompanied by slogans like "Don't be a paleface," and "Tan, don't burn." The image became a pop icon, as well as one of the most recognized logos in the country. Today, it's a reminder of innocent 1950s and of summer vactions past.

Brand, now a health club manager, is proud to be a part of pop culture. "If I get teased, I suppose I would blush," she says, "but what child doesn't have a photo like that in their album. Mine just happens to be more public."

Little Miss Coppertone faded as a corporate symbol in the late 1970s as deep tanning became synonymous with skin cancer, but the company brought her back in 1987 when it launched Water Babies, a sunscreen for children. The character's new role: "teaching the importance of sun protection to kids."

ANNETTE KELLERMAN, a Hollywood actess in 1916.

Famous For: Being the first person to appear completely naked in a feature film, in 1916.

The Bare Facts: The film was called *A Daughter of the Gods*, and was filmed on location in Jamaica. In one memorable scene Kellerman, formerly a professional swimmer, jumps from a 100-foot-high tower into a pool supposedly filled with alligators, then crashes against some rocks and falls down a waterfall. She is nude the entire time.

The average coach airline meal costs the airline $4.00. The average first class meal: $50.

Amazingly, the film was so bad that not even the novelty of film nudity could save it. William Fox, head of the Fox Film Corporation, hated it so much that he re-edited it himself, then removed the director's name from it and barred him from the premiere.

ADAH ISSACS MENKEN, stage actress of the 1860s

Famous for: Performing as the "Naked Lady" of the theater. She toured the world with a play called *Mazeppa,* in which she wore in a loose-fitting tunic that showed off her "uncovered" calves (actually flesh-colored tights).

The Bare Facts: Ironically, the woman known internationally as the "Naked Lady" always appeared fully clothed. She wore a skimpy, loose-fitting tunic over flesh-colored tights, which, as Edward Marks writes in *They All Had Glamour*, "were completely unknown in 1861. The audiences thought they were gazing on bare skin."

In 1860, a theater owner in Albany, NY decided to spice up the well-known play *Mazeppa.* Until then, the play's highlight had always been when a live horse performed a stunt onstage. To make it more exciting, the theater owner tied the provocatively dressed Adah to the horse. A star was born. As one historian writes:

> Adah, whose acting career had gotten off to a slow start due to lack of talent, found herself completely at home in the role of celebrity. She took *Mazeppa* to New York, where she opened to rave reviews, then went to wow 'em out west. Adah's curvaceous calves did the trick. Neophyte journalist Mark Twain was smitten. Mormon leader Brigham Young, though expressing shock, managed to sit through the whole show.

Menken traveled to Europe, where she was equally popular. The *London Review* observed that Adah looked like "Lady Godiva in a slip," noting that "of course, respectable people go to see the spectacle and not her figure." At one performance Napoleon III, the King of Greece, the Duke of Edinburgh were all in attendance; Charles Dickens considered her a close friend.

Then in 1868, at the height of her fame, she collapsed onstage. A month later she was dead of tuberculosis.

15 million gallons of wine were destroyed in the 1906 San Francisco earthquake.

THE BIRTH OF THE BURGER

BRI member and food editor, Jeff Cheek, contributed this fascinating history of the hamburger.

WILD HORSEMEN

In the 13th Century, wild, nomadic horsemen known as Tartars overran most of Asia and Eastern Europe. They had a distinct way of preparing meat: slice off a large chunk of horsemeat or beef and slip it under a saddle. A day of hard riding would tenderize it. Then it was chopped up and eaten raw.

This custom was introduced into the area we now call Germany by traders traveling down the Elbe River to Hamburg.

The German people did not eat horsemeat—but they did start serving ground, raw beef flavored with garlic, spices and a raw egg. (Today, it's called *steak tartare*, and is still popular in Europe.) And for those who preferred cooked beef, the raw beef patties became the first hamburger steaks. But they weren't the hand-held sandwiches we call hamburgers. Those came hundreds of years later.

BIRTH OF THE BURGER

It began around 1879, in a restaurant near the docks of the Hamburg-Amerika Line in Germany. Owner Otto Kuase began serving a sandwich American sailors loved: two slices of buttered bread, pickle strips, and a fried beef patty with a butter-fried egg on top. Add a mug of good German beer, and this sandwich made an excellent, inexpensive dinner.

So many Yankee seamen came to his restaurant for the sandwich that Kuase listed it on his menu as "American Steak." When the sailors returned home, they taught restaurants along the Eastern Seaboard how to make it. Soon, all a customer had to say was "bring me a hamburger." The name stuck, even when the recipe changed.

THE BURGER STARTS SIZZLING

In 1904, to celebrate the centennial of the Louisiana Purchase, St.

The U.S. Army accidentally ordered an 82-year supply of freeze-dried tuna salad mix for troops in Euro

Louis staged a huge World's Fair. There were hundreds of vendors selling foods—including German immigrants peddling their native fare. This included a new version of the old hamburger. The slices of bread were replaced with dinner rolls, which fit the round meat patty. Butter was expensive, so the rolls were smeared with the cheaper Heinz ketchup. The butter-fried egg was replaced by slices of onion, tomato, and pickles.

The new hamburger was inexpensive because cheaper cuts of beef could be used...and it was an instant success. People from all over the country attended the fair, and returned home ready to eat more.

THE BUN

There was one flaw—the dinner rolls made burgers harder to eat. So for another dozen years or so, people kept using the traditional slices of bread. Then an enterprising cook in Wichita, Kansas invented the last component of the modern hamburger: he created a round, soft bun that absorbed the juices of the meat patty.

His name was J. Walter Anderson. He was working as a short order cook when he made his discovery. Soon after, he bought an old trolley and converted it into a five stool diner, specializing in burgers at 5¢ each. This was in 1916, but it was a real bargain even then. In 1920, Anderson added two more diners, stressing their cleanliness with the name White Castle Hamburgers. Others followed and White Castle became the first national hamburger chain.

THE NAME'S THE SAME?

At the beginning of World War I, Kaiser Wilhelm had a treaty with Belgium guaranteeing its neutrality. When he sent his armies through Belgium to attack France, the U.S. protested—and the Kaiser replied that the treaty was just "a scrap of paper." It was a public relations disaster—anti-German hysteria swept the world. In Britain, the Royal Family changed its name from the House of Saxe-Coburg to the English-sounding House of Windsor. On American menus, *sauerkraut* became "victory cabbage" and *hamburger steak* became Salisbury Steak. But against pressure to call burgers "ground meat patty sandwiches," burger-lovers held their ground. Today, a hamburger is still a hamburger.

FIREWORKS FACTS

Next July 4th, you'll have something new to talk about.

A FLASH IN THE PAN

The first fireworks were hollowed out bamboo stalks stuffed with black powder. The Chinese called them "arrows of flying fire," and shot them into the air during religious occasions and holidays to ward off imaginary dragons.

According to legend, the essential ingredient—black powder—was first discovered in a Chinese kitchen in the 10th century A.D. A cook was preparing potassium nitrate (a pickling agent and preservative) over a charcoal fire laced with sulfur. Somehow the three chemicals—potassium nitrate, charcoal, and sulfur—combined, causing an explosion. The meal was destroyed, but the powder, later known as gunpowder, was born.

SAFETY FIRST

According to the fireworks industry's own estimates, as many people have been killed by 4th of July fireworks as were killed in the Revolutionary War. Nearly all of the victims were killed setting off their own fireworks, not watching public displays. And most fatalities occurred before World War II, when fireworks were almost completely unregulated. The carnage became so widespread that the 4th of July actually came to be known as the "Bloody Fourth" and even the "Carnival of Lockjaw," due to the large number of people who died from infected burns.

Then in the 1930s, several organizations began a campaign to outlaw fireworks. Pressured by the *Ladies' Home Journal* (which printed photographs of dozens of maimed victims), the federal government and individual states outlawed just about every kind of firework imaginable...to the point where many states now ban them entirely. Since then, the number of firework-related injuries plummeted. Today, the Consumer Safety Commission ranks them as only the 132nd most-dangerous consumer item, behind such things as beds, grocery carts, key rings, and plumbing fixtures.

Fattest newspaper ever printed: *New York Times*, October 17, 1965 at 946 pages. It weighed 7-1/2 lbs

COLORS

• Because black powder burns at a relatively low temperature, for more than 800 years fireworks burned only with dull yellow and orange flames. It wasn't until the 19th century that pyrotechnicians discovered that mixing potassium chlorate into the powder made it burn much hotter, enabling it to burn red when strontium was added, green when barium was added, and bright yellow when sodium was added.

• White was impossible to produce until the mid-1800s, when scientists developed ways to add aluminum, magnesium, and titanium to black powder.

• Blues and violets (caused when copper and chlorine are added) are the hardest colors to create; even today, fireworks manufacturers judge their skills according to how well their blues and violets turn out.

FIREWORKS LINGO

Here are some names the fireworks industry gives to its creations:

• **Willows:** Fireworks with long colorful "branches" that stream down towards the ground.

• **Palm Trees:** Willows that leave a brightly-colored trail from the ground as they're shot into the air.

• **Chrysanthemums:** Fireworks that explode into perfect circles.

• **Split comets:** Fireworks that explode into starlets, which explode again into even more starlets.

• **Salutes:** A bright, white flash, followed by a boom.

• **Triple-break Salutes:** Salutes that explode three times in rapid succession.

• **Cookie-Cutters:** Created by filling the inside of a cardboard container with black powder and gluing individual starlets to the outside. When the black powder charge explodes, the starlets explode in the same shape as the cookie-cutter. Shapes include stars, hearts, ovals, etc.

When Sir Henry Royce died in 1933, the "RR" Rolls-Royce monogram was changed from red to black.

THE FORGOTTEN HERO OF FLAGPOLE-SITTING

Ever heard of flagpole-sitting? At the height of his fame in 1930, the greatest flagpole-sitter of all, "Shipwreck Kelly," claimed he had spent a total of 20,613 hours "in cloudland." Perched atop flagpoles on tall buildings he endured 14,000 hours of rain and sleet, 210 hours in temperatures below freezing, 47 hours in snowstorms. He climbed poles for more than 20 years, and what he started never stopped. Ever since Kelly's time, others have sat on flagpoles in search of the publicity that once surrounded the self-described "luckiest fool alive." Here's the story from Bill Severn's A Carnival of Sports.

L'IL ORPHAN ALVIN

Alvin Anthony Kelly, born in New York's tough "Hell's Kitchen" district in 1893, ran off to sea at the age of thirteen. He was supposedly called "Shipwreck" because of his boast that he had survived several ship sinkings during his years as a sailor. But friends admitted his nickname came from his career as a professional boxer, when opponents dropped him to the canvas so often that fans began chanting, "Sailor Kelly's been shipwrecked again!"

In the early 1920s, the five-foot seven-inch Irishman got a job with a skyscraper construction crew walking steel girders. Discovering that he had no fear of high places, he decided to become a professional stunt man. He balanced on rooftops, climbed walls as a human fly, put on exhibitions as a high diver, and finally drifted to Hollywood.

In 1924, a Los Angeles theater owner hired him to sit on a flagpole atop the theater as a publicity stunt. Kelly stayed on the pole most of a day, drew a big crowd, pocketed a good fee, and at the age of thirty-one began a new career.

A STAR IS BORN

Americans in the Roaring Twenties turned out by gawking thousands to stare up at what was then something completely new. "Shipwreck Kelly" on his flagpole, like a man pronged on the point of a giant toothpick, was a headline-making curiosity. Pictures of him captured such newspaper space for his sponsors that Kelly soon was earning a hefty $100 a day. He was a one-man sporting spectacle.

But not for long. Dozens of others got into the act, swarming up flagpoles from coast to coast. Some of his many imitators borrowed not only the game but also his name, calling themselves "Shipwreck Kelly." He once counted seventeen other "Shipwrecks" in operation at the same time.

POLE POSITION

Kelly took flagpoling seriously. When he sat atop a pole for days, his perch was a small 13" wooden disc. He slept in five-minute catnaps with his thumbs locked into holes bored in the pole. Any wavering while he dozed would bring a sharp twinge of pain and alert him instantly so he wouldn't fall off.

When he stood, which was harder and more dangerous, it usually was only for hours instead of days, on an even smaller perch, a tiny six- to eight-inch platform. There were stirrups or rope slings to hold his legs, but no other support to keep him standing.

His food and other necessities were hauled up in a basket on a rope pulley, and the same rope was used to haul down a washbasin and pot that were also needed by a man stranded on a flagpole without bathroom facilities. A covering blanket, discreetly used, afforded privacy.

ABOVE THE LAW

By 1927, the craze he started had so many rivals up on poles that police in Boston, Los Angeles, and several other cities moved to arrest them as public nuisances. Kelly himself later had some brushes with the law. New York police, for example, ordered him down from one pole over a midtown hotel because he was attracting crowds that choked Times Square traffic. But his prestige as the nation's number one flagpoler usually won him tolerance. Mayors and other public officials were happy to pose for pictures with him and bask in his publicity.

CHILD'S PLAY

In 1929, he set a then "world's record" for flagpole-sitting by staying aloft twenty-three days at a Baltimore amusement park. When he came down, the crowd-roaring acclaim made him such a hero to the young that the whole city blossomed with juvenile pole-sitters. Boys and girls from the age eight upward took to the tops of trees and backyard poles at such a rate that in a single week reporters counted twenty-five young disciples of "Shipwreck Kelly" at roost.

As the epidemic spread, newspapers and national magazines sounded editorial alarms, and public moralists demanded a mobilization of parents to apply hairbrushes and straps to the posterior of pole-sitting young America. But for the most part, the young pole-perchers were encouraged by adults eager to share their notoriety.

RECORD BREAKER

Kelly accomplished the greatest feat of his own pole-sitting career the next summer at Atlantic City. On June 21, 1930, he climbed atop a 125-foot mast above the New Jersey shore resort's Steel Pier, hoping to stay on his 13-inch perch long enough to beat his previous record of twenty-three days aloft. When he had smashed the record on July 14, he decided to stay up a little longer.

He kept busy answering hundreds of fan mail letters basketed up to him, making nightly pole-top radio broadcasts, and sending messages down to the boardwalk crowds below to tell them how much he was enjoying the cool ocean breeze. There was more than a breeze at times; storm winds whipped and swayed his flagpole, and he endured thunderstorms and hail.

Finally, on August 9, he decided to come down and prepared himself to greet his public. A girl *The New York Times* called "one of the prettiest of barberettes" was pulled up the rope to give him a shave, haircut, and manicure.

HERO'S WELCOME

Twenty thousand cheering people were on hand when he made his slow descent that afternoon, and there was a flood of congratulatory telegrams from prominent Americans. Kelly had trouble using his feet when he first touched ground, but was able to shake hands with the official dignitaries who welcomed him back to earth and to pose for newsreel cameramen.

He had been on his flagpole for 1,177 hours, more than forty-nine days, which was a record nobody broke for nearly another decade. Kelly himself never equaled it again.

A MAN APART

Kelly went on flag-poling through the Thirties and into the Forties, but his fame gradually faded as a new crop of pole-sitters came along. On October 11, 1952, Kelly collapsed on the sidewalk and died of a heart attack, not far from Madison Square Garden where his name once had been up in lights. Under his arm was a scrapbook of old news clippings from...when he had been a headliner. In the nearby furnished room where he had been living...police found a single duffel bag of personal belongings, mostly...flagpole-sitting gear.

Even in the 1970s, there were others still claiming new records, some for perching on high for as long as eight months. But many did their sitting on broad platforms, in tents, huts, and with all the conveniences of home, which "Shipwreck Kelly" would have called not flagpole-sitting at all.

* * * *

Strange Scholarships

Want some help with college tuition? You might qualify for one of these. In 1994, it was announced that:

• The Frederick & Mary F. Beckley Fund for Needy Left-handed Freshmen offers up to $1,000 for left-handers who want to go to Juanita College in Pennsylvania.

• The National Make It Yourself with Wool scholarship offers $100-$1,000 to knitters.

• The Dolphin Scholarship Foundation offers $1,750 to the children of WWII submarine veterans.

• The John Gatling Scholarship Program offers $6,000 to anyone with the last name Gatlin or Gatling who wants to go to the University of North Carolina.

• Tall Clubs International offers two scholarships of $1,000 each for females 5'10" or taller, and males 6'2" or taller.

Given the opportunity, deer will chew gum. And marijuana. No word on which they like most.

WORD ORIGINS

Ever wonder where words come from? Here are some interesting stories.

CURFEW

Meaning: A prescribed time to leave certain places.

Origin: "In medieval times the danger from fire was especially great because most buildings were made of wood. With a wind blowing, a single burning house could start a conflagration. Hence the practice developed of covering fires before retiring for the night. During the reigns of Williams I and II, a bell was sounded at sunset to give notice that the time had come to extinguish all fires and candles. This came to be called 'curfew,' a word borrowed almost directly from the French *couvre feu*, which, in translation, is 'cover the fire.'" (From *The Story Behind the Word*, by Morton S. Freeman)

SHAMPOO

Meaning: Soap for washing hair.

Origin: "Early travelers in India were intrigued by a native custom. Sultans and nabobs had special servants who massaged their bodies after hot baths. From a native term for 'to press,' such a going-over of the body with knuckles was called a 'champo' or 'shampoo.'" (From *Why You Say It*, by Webb Garrison)

ALIMONY

Meaning: An allowance made to one spouse by the other for support pending or after legal separation or divorce.

Origin: "The word *aliment* means food. This traces to the Latin *alo*, 'nourish.' So the way the many divorce laws are written now, if a wife sues for release from her bonds, she expects alimony, which, etymologically, is really 'eating money.'" (From *Word Origins*, by Wilfred Funk)

CANNIBAL

Meaning: A person who eats humans.

Origin: "When Christopher Columbus landed in Cuba, he asked the natives what they called themselves. In their dialect they said that they were Canibales, or people of Caniba. (This was a dialectal form of *Caribe*, and the Cuban natives were *Caribes*.) Later explorers used either name, Canibales or Caribes, in referring to any of the people of the West Indies. All of these people were very fierce; some were known to eat human flesh. Less than a century after Columbus's voyages, all Europeans associated the name Canibales with human-eaters." (From *Thereby Hangs a Tail,* by Charles Earle Funk)

ONION

Meaning: A pungent, edible vegetable.

Origin: "In Latin there is a word *union* which is translated as 'oneness' or 'union.' The word onion is derived from this...because it consists of a number of united layers. There is also another interesting analogy between 'union' and 'onion.' The rustics about Rome not only used the word *unio* to mean onion, but they also thought it a suitable designation for a pearl. And even today a cook will speak of 'pearl onions' when she means the small, silvery-white variety." (From *Word Origins*, by Wilfred Funk)

HORS D'OEUVRE

Meaning: A small treat served before a meal.

Origin: "These tasty treats before a fancy meal get their name from a French expression meaning 'outside of work.' Preparing the meal was part of the ordinary labor of the kitchen staff, and any extras for special occasions or feasts were not part of the regular chores." (From *Where in the Word?*, by David Muschell)

POSTMAN

Meaning: Deliverer of mail.

Origin: "The term 'post' to describe mail or message delivery originated in the 13th century with Marco Polo. He described Kublai Khan's network of more than 10,000 yambs, or relay stations, calling them in Italian *poste*, or 'posts.' They were located every 25 to 45 miles on the principal roads throughout the empire. In addition, at three-mile intervals between the *poste* there were relay stations for runners, who...wore wide belts with bells to signal the importance of their business." (From *Remarkable Words with Astonishing Origins*, by John Train)

To win at Bingo in the old days you had to ring a small bell. That's where the bing comes from.

WRETCHED REVIEWS

Doesn't it bother you when a movie you love gets a thumbs-down from those two bozos on TV? Us, too. The Critics Were Wrong, *by Ardis Sillick and Michael McCormick, compiles hundreds of misguided movie reviews like these.*

FRANKENSTEIN (1931)

"I regret to report that it is just another movie, so thoroughly mixed with water as to have a horror content of about .0001 percent....The film...soon turns into sort of comic opera with a range of cardboard mountains over which extras in French Revolution costumes dash about with flaming torches."

—*Outlook & Independent*

THE GRADUATE (1967) *Nomination for best actor*

"*The Graduate* is a genuinely funny comedy which succeeds despite an uninteresting and untalented actor (Dustin Hoffman) in the title role."

—*Films In Review*

LETHAL WEAPON (1987)

"As a thriller, it lacks logic. As a cop film, it throws standard police procedures, and with them any hope of authenticity, to the wind. As a showcase for the martial arts, it's a disappointment....And as action-adventure, it's pointlessly puerile."

—Johanna Steinmetz, *Chicago Tribune*

M*A*S*H* (1970)

"At the end, the film simply runs out of steam, says goodbye to its major characters, and calls final attention to itself as a movie—surely the saddest and most overworked of cop-out devices in the comic film repertory."

—Roger Greenspun, *New York Times*

ROCKY (1976) *Top box-office hit / Oscar winner for best picture and director / Nomination for best actor and screenplay*

"An overly grandiose script, performed with relentless grandiloquence....Up to a point I'm willing to overlook the egg on a guy's face, but, really, there's such a thing as too much—especially when they're promoting this bloated, pseudo-epic as a low-budget Oscar-bound winner."

—Washington Star

2001: A SPACE ODYSSEY (1968)

"Not a cinematic landmark. It compares with, but does not best, previous efforts at filmed science-fiction....It actually belongs to the technically-slick group previously dominated by...the Japanese."

—Variety

ANNIE HALL (1977) *Oscar winner for best picture and director*

"Woody Allen has truly underreached himself....His new film is painful in three separate ways: an unfunny comedy, poor moviemaking and embarrassing self-revelation....It is a film so shapeless, sprawling, repetitious and aimless as to seem to beg for oblivion."

—John Simon, *New York*

PSYCHO (1960) *Oscar nomination for best director*

"Hitchcock seems to have been more interested in shocking his audience with the bloodiest bathtub murder in screen history, and in photographing Janet Leigh in various stages of undress, than in observing the ordinary rules for good film construction. This is a dangerous corner for a gifted moviemaker to place himself in."

—Moira Walsh, *America*

SATURDAY NIGHT FEVER (1977)

"Nothing more than an updated '70s version of the...rock music cheapies of the '50s. That is to say...more shrill, more vulgar, more trifling, more superficial and more pretentious than an exploitation film....A major disappointment."

—Variety

Are you one of the 33% of the population who can't snap their fingers?

THE WORLD'S SECOND DUMBEST OUTLAW

Here's another example of someone who's gone down in history as the worst there ever was.

"BLACK JACK" TOM KETCHUM (1862?–1901)

Background: Ketchum was an ordinary cowboy before turning to crime. He returned from a cattle drive one day and learned that his girlfriend had eloped with another man. The rejection pushed him over the edge.

Claim to Fame: Ketchum has been dubbed the "second stupidest outlaw who ever lived." He ran with members of Wyoming's notorious Hole-in-the-Wall gang, but bungled so many stick-ups that getting away with a few dollars was the best he usually managed.

He had a strange reaction to failure, as Jay Robert Nash explains in *American Eccentrics*:

> Whenever a caper of his went wrong, he would methodically beat himself on the head with the butt of his six-shooter snarling, "You will, will you? (slam!)...Now take that (pop)...and that (bang)!"
>
> Many of Black Jack's planned crimes turned into disasters, and if each member of his gang got $10 for his share, it could be considered a superior outing. Needless to say, Black Jack's gun and skull both took regular beatings.

But even stupid outlaws have their day. In 1898, Ketchum and his boys robbed a train in New Mexico of about $500. Not exactly a king's ransom, but it was enough to keep Ketchum coming back for more. He didn't bother to vary his routine even a little. Ketchum went after the same train, at exactly the same remote spot, a total of four times. On the fourth, lawmen were waiting for him. There was a shoot-out, and Ketchum was wounded and captured.

So why was Ketchum only the *second*-stupidest outlaw? Because his brother, Sam, was even dumber. While Black Jack was in prison, Sam masterminded yet another identical robbery of the same train. He got himself killed in the attempt.

Troubled waters: "Caribbean" is derived from the same root as "cannibal."

THE "ART" OF ROCK

What do rock stars really think of their "art?" Maybe not what you'd expect.

Q: "If you had to put into 25 words or less what it is you're trying to say when you get up on stage, what would it be?"
A: "LOOK AT ME!"

—Joe Strummer (the Clash)

"Rock 'n' roll is a bit like Las Vegas; guys dressed up in their sisters' clothes pretending to be rebellious and angry, but not really angry about anything."

—Sting

"I may be a living legend, but that sure don't help when I've got to change a flat tire."

—Roy Orbison

"Somebody said to me, 'But The Beatles were antimaterialistic.' That's a huge myth. John and I literally used to sit down and say, 'Now, let's write a swimming pool.'"

—Paul McCartney

"People got my face up on their walls. You turn on TV, that's my head. That's sick, man. I used to have a...McDonald's costume on. I used to make hamburgers."

—Mark White (Spin Doctors)

"If you want to torture me, you'd tie me down and force me to watch our first five videos."

—Jon Bon Jovi

"Mick Jagger would be astounded if he realized to many people he's not a sex symbol, but a mother image."

—David Bowie

"In rock 'n' roll, you're built up to be torn down. Like architecture in America, you build it up and let it stand for ten years, then call it shabby and rip it down and put something else up."

—Joni Mitchell

"Art is the last thing I'm worried about when I write a song. If you want to call it art, yeah, okay, you can call it what you like. As far as I'm concerned, 'Art' is just short for 'Arthur.'"

—Keith Richards

"To have a huge hit record with only three chords is one of the best tricks a writer can do."

—Burton Cummings (the Guess Who)

Franklin D. Roosevelt's 3 favorite foods: frog legs, pig knuckles, and scrambled eggs.

LUCKY FINDS

Here's a look at a few more lucky people who found some real valuable stuff.

GRANDMA'S GARBAGE

The Find: An old painting.

Where It Was Found: At grandma's house.

The Story: In 1964, a Connecticut woman happened to be visiting her grandparents' house on a day when they were throwing out some old junk. She saw an old painting she liked, and her grandparents let her have it. She hung it over her bed, where it stayed for the next 25 years.

In 1989, the woman took the painting into an art appraiser to see if it was worth anything. The appraiser offered her $1,000 for it. She refused. A little while later, he called and offered her $100,000. Now she was suspicious, and contacted an auction house. It turned out to be a rare work by the 19th-century artist Martin Johnson Heade. The painting sold at auction a few months later for $1.1 million.

STEPPING OUT

The Find: An animated cartoon film made in 1922.

Where It Was Found: In a film rental library in London, England.

The Story: In the mid-1970s, film collector David Wyatt paid two pounds (about $3) for a 7-minute-long, black-and-white silent cartoon titled "Grandma Steps Out."

Twenty years later, Wyatt showed the film to Russell Merritt, a film scholar working on a book called *Walt in Wonderland: The Silent Films of Walt Disney*. Merritt recognized "Grandma Steps Out" as the only known copy of "Little Red Riding Hood," Disney's first film—and one of the American Film Institute's ten "most-wanted" lost films. Disney drew the film when he was a 21-year-old commercial artist in Kansas City. Six years later he finished "Steamboat Willie," his first Mickey Mouse cartoon.

Wyatt's copy may have been a bootleg—which explains the new

title—but it's still the only copy of a film that, for decades, was assumed to be lost forever. Estimated value: priceless. "Its value historically is inestimable," says Scott MacQueen, at Walt Disney studios. "Not only is this the very first Disney cartoon, but there are also very few examples of work in Disney's own hand. It represents the beginning of the dynasty."

PICTURE PERFECT

The Find: A daguerreotype photograph of a young man, taken in 1847.

Where It Was Found: At an antique photograph auction in Pittsburgh, Pennsylvania.

The Story: In 1996, Paul and Maria Pasquariello saw an original daguerreotype at the auction. It was identified as a picture of George Lippard, an obscure 19th century novelist and historian, but they knew they'd seen the picture somewhere before. They were almost positive the picture was actually of the famous abolitionist John Brown.

But the Pasquariellos couldn't be sure—because this picture was of a young, cleanshaven man, and most pictures of Brown were taken when he was older and had grown an enormous beard.

That night they poured through history books until they finally found the same picture—a portrait of Brown described as coming from "a long lost daguerreotype."

The next day the Pasquariellos bought the daguerreotype for $12,075. Sotheby's later auctioned it to the Smithsonian Institute's National Portrait Gallery for $129,000, the highest price ever paid by the gallery for a photograph.

WHAT A DOLL

The Find: An old doll.

Where It Was Found: On a garbage heap in Bochum, Germany.

The Story: Five-year-old Nicole Ohlsen found the doll in some trash. Her mother was about to throw it away when she discovered a cache of diamonds inside. Estimated value: $72,000. The mother took the diamonds to the police, who told her no one had reported them missing—and let her keep them.

NATURE'S REVENGE

What happens when we start messing around with nature, trying to make living conditions better? Sometimes it works...and sometimes nature gets even. Here are a few instances when people intentionally introduced animal or plants into a new environment...and regretted it.

Import: Kudzu, a fast-growing Japanese vine.

Background: Originally brought into the Southern U.S. in 1876 for use as shade. People noticed livestock ate the vine and that kudzu helped restore nitrogen to the soil. It seemed like a perfect plant to cultivate. So in the 1930s, the U.S. government helped farmers plant kudzu all over the South.

Nature's Revenge: By the 1950s, it was out of control, blanketing farmers' fields, buildings, utility poles and—often fatally—trees. Today, utility companies spend millions of dollars annually spraying herbicides on poles and towers to keep them kudzu-free. And instead of helping plant kudzu, the government now gives advice on how to get rid of it.

Import: The mongoose.

Background: The small Asian mammals famous for killing cobras were brought to Hawaii by sugar planters in 1893. Their reason: They thought the mongooses would help control the rat population.

Nature's Revenge: The planters overlooked one little detail: the mongoose is active in the daytime while the rat is nocturnal. "In Hawaii today," says one source, "mongooses are considered pests nearly as bad as rats."

Import: The starling, an English bird.

Background: In 1890, a philanthropist named Eugene Schieffelin decided to bring every type of bird mentioned in Shakespeare's plays to New York City's Central Park. He brought in hundreds of pairs of birds from England. Unfortunately, most (like skylarks and thrushes) didn't make it. Determined to succeed with at least one species, Schieffelin shipped 40 pairs of starlings to Central Park and let them loose just before the mating season on March 6, 1890.

The average city dog lives three years longer than the average country dog.

Nature's Revenge: There are now more than 50 million starlings in the U.S. alone—all descendants from Schieffelin's flock—and they have become a major health hazard. They fly in swarms, littering roads and highways with their droppings, which carry disease-bearing bacteria that are often transmitted to animals and people. They've also become pests to farmers, screeching unbearably and destroying wheat and cornfields.

Import: The gypsy moth.

Background: In 1869, Leopold Trouvelot, a French entomologist, imported some gypsy moth caterpillars to Massachusetts. It was part of a get-rich-quick scheme: he figured that since the caterpillars thrive on oak tree leaves, which are plentiful there, he could crossbreed them with silkworm moths, and create a self-sustaining, silk-producing caterpillar. He'd make a fortune!

Unfortunately, the crossbreeding didn't work. Then one day, a strong wind knocked over a cage filled with the gypsy moth caterpillars. They escaped through an open window and survived.

Nature's Revenge: At first, the moths spread slowly. But by 1950, gypsy moths could be found in every New England state and in eastern New York. They've since spread to Virginia and Maryland—and beyond. Populations have become established as far away as Minnesota and California, probably due to eggs unknowingly transported by cars driven from the Northeast to those regions. They're not a major threat, but can cause severe problems: In 1981, for example, they were reported to have stripped leaves from 13 million trees.

Import: Dog fennel.

Background: At the turn of the 19th century, Johnny Appleseed wandered around the Ohio territory, planting apples wherever he went. It's not widely known that he also he sowed a plant called *dog fennel*, which was believed to be a fever-reducing medicine.

Nature's Revenge: It's not only *not* medicine, it's bad medicine; farmers are sick of it. "The foul-smelling weed," says the *People's Almanac*, "spread from barnyard to pasture, sometimes growing as high as fifteen feet. Today, exasperated midwestern farmers still cannot rid their fields of the plant they half-humorously call 'Johnnyweed.'"

ODDBALL FOOD NAMES

Can you imagine being offered a nice, big helping of Burgoo? Sounds appetizing, doesn't it?

ANADAMA BREAD

A Gloucester, Massachusetts, fisherman was married to a woman named Anna and every night, she fed him cornmeal and molasses for dinner. He got so sick of it that one evening he stormed into the kitchen, threw some yeast into the mix, and baked a sodden, lumpy loaf...muttering "Anna, damn 'er" the whole time. His Yankee-accented phrase came out as *Anadama*, giving the bread its name.

This story first appeared in print in 1915—and though it sounds like a tall tale, it's cited so often that most food historians believe it.

BURGOO

Politics and Burgoo go hand in hand in Kentucky. This Southern beef and fowl stew was cooked for people at political rallies. There are several versions about how it was created, but this one is the most colorful: During the Civil War, a Yankee soldier managed to kill a number of wild birds which he promptly made into a stew, using a copper kettle normally used for mixing gunpowder. He invited his buddies to join him, and-having eaten nothing but hardtack and bacon for days—they jumped at the offer. The soldier suffered from a speech impediment. When he was asked what the dish was, he tried to say "bird stew," but it came out as "Burgoo."

JANSSON'S TEMPTATION

In 1846, Eric Jansson fled Sweden to escape religious persecution for his radical theology. He and his followers settled in Illinois. Jansson told his followers that eating was a sin that turned their thoughts away from God, and he allowed them only a starvation diet. His downfall came when they found him consuming a rich dish of potatoes, onions, and cream, now known as Jansson's Temptation.

It takes a drop of ocean water more than 1,000 years to circulate around the world.

BAPTIST CAKE

Many churches settle for a symbolic sprinkling of holy water during baptism, but Baptists insist on full immersion. When deep-fried doughnut-like confections were introduced in New England in the 1920s, they were named Baptist Cakes because they were "baptized" in hot oil.

HOPPIN' JOHN

A New Orleans dish of cowpeas and rice, traditionally served on New Year's Day to ensure good luck in the coming year. The name dates back to 1819 and is derived from a New Year's ritual of having the children hop around the table before being served.

LIMPING SUSAN

A variation on Hoppin' John, with red beans substituted for cowpeas.

JOHNNY CAKE

Blame the Yankee accent for Johnny Cakes, too. In Colonial America, travelers would bake a supply of cakes to take on trips, called Journey Cakes. "Journey" comes out as "johnny" when pronounced with a broad, New England accent. In 1940, the Rhode Island Legislature ruled that only cakes made from flint corn could carry the proud title of Johnny Cakes. There is a Johnny Cake Festival in Newport every October...as well as a Society for the Propagation of the Johnny Cake Tradition.

MONKEY GLAND

A cocktail made with "orange juice, grenadine, gin and an anise cordial." According to food historian John Mariani:

> It became popular in the 1920s, when Dr. Serge Voronoff, a Russian emigre to Paris and director of experimental surgery at the Laboratory of Physiology of the College de France, was promoting the benefits of transplanting the sex glands of monkeys into human beings to restore vitality and prolong life....
>
> The cocktail, which facetiously promised similar restorative powers, may have been invented at Harry's New York Bar in Paris, by owner Harry MacElhone.

Mammal rule of thumb: if you eat meat, you have at least four toes on each foot.

STAR TREK: THE NEXT GENERATION

Uncle John's very first Bathroom Reader *came out in 1988—a year after* Star Trek: The Next Generation *debuted. In that book, we profiled the original* Star Trek. *Now, because readers have asked for it, we're finally getting around to writing about* TNG.

HOW IT STARTED

As soon as the original *Star Trek* became a syndicated hit in the early 1970s, Paramount and *Trek* creator Gene Roddenberry started planning a sequel (working title: "Star Trek II").

But in 1975, Paramount switched directions and decided to make a feature film instead. *Trek*'s writers worked for three years on the concept...but they couldn't come up with a script that the studio felt had a "big enough" plot to justify a full-length movie. So Roddenberry and his crew went back to work on the new TV series.

In 1978, three weeks before production of the show was supposed to begin, Paramount stepped in again—and cancelled it. The reason: *Star Wars* was making a killing at the box office, and studio execs decided a big-budget feature film would make more money than a TV series. By March 1978, all of the original cast of *Star Trek* had been signed to make *Star Trek: The Motion Picture.*

Resurrection. Eight years later, in 1986, two events inspired Roddenberry to resurrect "Star Trek II": A *Star Trek* 20th reunion party got Roddenberry's team excited about doing TV again; and *Star Trek IV: The Voyage Home*, the best of the *Trek* movies to that point, was a critical and box office success. It convinced Roddenberry that the time was right for a new small-screen *Star Trek*—but not a sequel. The new show, he decided, would have...

- A new cast. Creating all-new characters had two major advantages for Paramount: (1) It left the original *Star Trek* cast free to make feature films; and (2) a cast of unknowns would be cheaper.
- A new setting. Roddenberry figured about "a century after Kirk" (later refined to 78 years), which put it in the 24th century.

What is "sight of sleep phobia?" Fear of watching others go to sleep. Not many people have it.

• No "retread" Vulcans, Klingons, or other beings.

• A longer mission (ten years or more instead of the original five) and a different philosophy for the *Enterprise*. The vessel was to feel less like a battleship and more like a family-friendly exploration/peacekeeping craft with services to support its population.

Given the original *Trek*'s popularity, it seems logical to assume that one of the big networks grabbed the show, right? Wrong. No one wanted to foot $1 million per episode for sci-fi, which still didn't have a prime-time track record. Instead, Paramount ended up selling it directly to local stations. But once again, *Star Trek* proved that the network experts didn't understand the lure of good science fiction. It quickly became the most successful syndicated drama in television history.

INSIDE FACTS

High-priced Gamble

The Next Generation was TV's most expensive program in 1987, and the highest-priced syndicated show ever. In fact, by the second season, it already had pushed its budget to $1.5 million per episode. This led panicky execs to institute some unexpected cost-cutting measures. For example, in the third season, new crew uniforms were unveiled, at a cost of $3,000 each. To save money, no one on the set below the rank of ensign was allowed to have one.

Still on the Cheap

On the other hand, the special-effects budget was only about $85,000 per episode. When adjusted for inflation, that's less than the special effects of the original show. The result: some surprisingly low-budget effects were used. In one episode, for example, when they needed to show the surface of a sun, they used "vibrating dry oatmeal on a light box." In another, the corona of a sun was achieved by "bouncing a laser beam off of a beer can onto a piece of white cardboard." And to get the texture of a planet, visual-effects producer Dan Curry says, "I did a macro shot of a rock in my garden, with my camcorder."

A Bald Englishman?

Gene Roddenberry was looking for a Frenchman to play Captain Picard, but couldn't find the right actor. Then *Trek* producer Bob Just-

Poll result: Most popular sandwich to pack in kids' lunches? Peanut butter and jelly, of course.

man saw Patrick Stewart address a drama conference and decided he'd be perfect. But Roddenberry took one look at Stewart's photo and said, "I'm not going to have a bald Englishman for a captain." In the end, Stewart was the best they could find. They auditioned him wearing a toupee, but hated it. "That wasn't the Patrick we wanted," recalled Roddenberry. "He looked like a drapery clerk."

Name Game

• Geordi LaForge, the blind navigator played by Levar Burton, was named in tribute to George LaForge—a young, wheelchair-bound Trekkie who died in 1975 from complications related to muscular dystrophy.

• Wesley Crusher, the doctor's son, was named after Gene Roddenberry, whose middle name was Wesley. "He is me at 17," Roddenberry said. "He is the things I dreamed of being and doing."

Making Whoopi

No one believed it when Oscar winner Whoopi Goldberg sent word (through a friend) that she'd love to be on the show. Finally, she took a more direct route, phoning the *Star Trek* offices herself. "Since I was a little girl on the streets, *Star Trek* was always my guide to morality," she explained. She appeared as Guinan, hostess of the ship's lounge, in the first episode of the second season, and appeared in 26 more shows over the next six years.

Brief Notes

• It wasn't until the third season, when ratings were strong and the show was fully accepted by Trekkies, that Roddenberry began bringing in characters from the first series. Mark Lenerd, who played Sarek, Spock's father, was the first to cross over.

• Jonathan Frakes auditioned for the part of Riker seven times—and was actually the second choice for the role. The first choice blew his final audition so badly that Frakes got the job.

• Roddenberry eventually agreed to have a Klingon on the bridge because it showed that Starfleet had made "progress" in its relations with other worlds in the years since the first show.

LOONEY LAWS

Believe it or not, these laws are real.

In Kentucky, it's against the law to throw eggs at a public speaker.

In Shawnee, Oklahoma, it's illegal for three or more dogs to "meet" on private property without the consent of the owner.

In Hartford, Connecticut, transporting a cadaver by taxi is punishable by a $5 fine.

In Michigan, it's illegal for a woman to cut her own hair without her husband's permission.

You can ride your bike on main streets in Forgan, Oklahoma, but it's against the law to ride it backwards.

If you tie an elephant to a parking meter in Orlando, Florida, you have to feed the meter just as if the elephant were a car.

California law forbids sleeping in the kitchen...but allows cooking in the bedroom.

It's a felony in Montana for a wife to open a telegram addressed to her husband. (It's *not* a crime for the husband to open telegrams addressed to his wife.)

You can gargle in Louisiana if you want to, but it's against the law to do it in public.

In Maryland it's against the law for grandchildren to marry their grandparents.

It's against the law to anchor your boat to the train tracks in Jefferson City, Missouri.

In Columbus, Montana, it's a misdemeanor to pass the Mayor on the street without tipping your hat.

It's illegal to throw an onion in Princeton, Texas.

Kentucky law requires that every person in the state take a bath at least once a year.

It's against the law to pawn your wooden leg in Delaware.

That's where *testimony* comes from.

THE TOP 10 HITS OF THE YEAR, 1984–1987

Another installment of BRI's Top Ten of the Year list.

1984

(1) When Doves Cry —*Prince*
(2) What's Love Go To Do With It —*Tina Turner*
(3) Against All Odds (Take A Look At Me Now) —*Phil Collins*
(4) Footloose —*Kenny Loggins*
(5) Say Say Say —*Paul McCartney & Michael Jackson*
(6) Jump —*Van Halen*
(7) Owner Of A Lonely Heart —*Yes*
(8) Hello —*Lionel Richie*
(9) Ghostbusters —*Ray Parker, Jr.*
(10) Karma Chameleon —*Culture Club*

1985

(1) Careless Whisper —*Wham! featuring George Michael*
(2) Like A Virgin —*Madonna*
(3) Wake Me Up Before You Go-go —*Wham!*
(4) Everybody Wants To Rule The World —*Tears For Fears*
(5) I Feel For You —*Chaka Khan*
(6) Money For Nothing —*Dire Straits*
(7) I Want To Know What Love Is —*Foreigner*
(8) Out Of Touch —*Daryl Hall & John Oates*
(9) Crazy For You —*Madonna*
(10) Take On Me —*A-ha*

1986

(1) That's What Friends Are For —*Dionne & Friends*
(2) Say You, Say Me —*Lionel Richie*
(3) On My Own —*Patti Labelle & Michael Mcdonald*
(4) I Miss You —*Klymaxx*
(5) Broken Wings —*Mr. Mister*
(6) How Will I Know —*Whitney Houston*
(7) Party All The Time —*Eddie Murphy*
(8) Kyrie —*Mr. Mister*
(9) Burning Heart —*Survivor*
(10) Addicted To Love —*Robert Palmer*

1987

(1) Walk Like An Egyptian —*Bangles*
(2) Alone —*Heart*
(3) Shake You Down —*Gregory Abbott*
(4) I Wanna Dance With Somebody —*Whitney Houston*
(5) Nothing's Gonna Stop Us Now —*Starship*
(6) C'est La Vie —*Robbie Nevil*
(7) The Way It Is —*Bruce Hornsby & The Range*
(8) Here I Go Again —*Whitesnake*
(9) Livin' On A Prayer —*Bon Jovi*
(10) Shakedown (from *Beverly Hills Cop II*) —*Bob Seger*

HURRY UP AND PAY!

"In China," the New York Times *reports, "it's common for sales clerks to abandon their posts without notice, and to ignore—or even insult—customers." In 1995, as part of a national politeness campaign, the Chinese government banned 50 commonly-used phrases from retail stores. Here's a sample list.*

The busier I am, the more you bother me. How annoying!

Who told you not to look where you're going?

Didn't you hear me? What do you have ears for?

Get out of the way, or you'll get killed.

Are you finished talking?

If you're not buying, what are you looking at?

Are you buying or not? Have you made up your mind?

Go ask the person who sold it to you.

What are you yelling about?

Don't you see I'm busy? What's the hurry?

I can't solve this. Go complain to whoever you want.

I just told you. Why are you asking again?

Buy if you can afford it, otherwise get out of here.

Why didn't you choose well when you bought it?

Hurry up and pay.

Ask someone else.

Time is up, be quick.

The price is posted. Can't you see it yourself?

If you're not buying, don't ask.

Stop shouting. Can't you see I'm eating?

It's not my fault.

We haven't opened yet. Wait awhile.

I'm not in charge. Don't ask me so many questions.

Didn't I tell you? How come you don't get it?

Don't push me.

If you want it, speak up; if you don't, get out of the way.

Don't talk so much. Say it quickly.

You're asking me? Whom should I ask?

Don't stand in the way.

Why don't you have the money ready?

Woof! If your dog lives to age 11, you'll have spent more than $13,000 on him/her.

JAWS, JR.

They're just little fishes, but piranhas can turn you into a skeleton in a few seconds flat. Nice thought, huh?

THE NAME. The word "piranha" comes from the Tupi language of South America and means "toothed fish." In some local dialects of the Amazon region, the name for common household scissors is also "piranha."

NOT A SHARK. A piranha only has one row of upper and lower teeth, not several, as many sharks do. But its teeth are sharper than almost any shark teeth. When the piranha snaps them together, says one expert, "the points in the upper row fit into the notches of the lower row, and the power of the jaw muscles is such that there is scarcely any living substance save the hardest ironwood that will not be clipped off." Natives often use the teeth as cutting blades.

FISHING TIP. Piranhas are capable of biting through a fishing net. If caught on a hook, they usually die from the injury. So a good way to "bring them in alive" is to throw a chunk of meat in the water. The fish will bite into it so hard that you can lift bunches of them out of the water before they let go.

BEHAVIOR. Some things that attract piranhas are blood and splashing. Experts disagree over whether the fish will attack a calm, uninjured person, but piranhas are definitely territorial. That's why Amazon fishermen know that if they catch a piranha, they'd better try another spot if they expect to catch anything else.

DEADLY DIET. Surprisingly, only a few species of piranha are meat-eaters; many eat fruits and other plants that fall into the river. But those meat-eaters can do exactly what you think they can. In the 19th century, for example, Teddy Roosevelt wrote about his adventures along the Amazon. He claimed to have seen piranhas quickly make a skeleton of a man who had fallen off his horse and into the river.

MORE DUMB CROOKS

More proof that crime doesn't pay.

GIVING HIM THE SLIP

SAN FRANCISO, Ca.—"Talk about dumb, here's a beaut....A would-be San Francisco bank robber recently cased two different banks. He even picked up a deposit slip at one of them. But his carefully planned robbery began to fall apart when he presented a holdup note—written on the Bank of America deposit slip he'd picked up—to a teller at Wells Fargo.

"'Sorry, this is a Bank of America slip; we can't honor this. Why don't you try them? They're just down the street,' a quick-thinking teller said.

"Off went the robber to try his luck at the other bank.

"The teller called the cops, who happily greeted the would-be robber a few minutes later with open arms (and handcuffs) as he walked in the door."

—*San Francisco Chronicle*, Jan. 7, 1996

HOW DID YOU KNOW?

PITTSBURGH, Pa.—"MacArthur Wheeler, 46, was sentenced to 24 years in prison in Pittsburgh last month, a conviction made possible by clear photography from the bank's surveillance camera. Wheeler and his partner did not wear masks and, in fact, were not concerned about the camera at all, because they had rubbed lemon juice all over their faces beforehand, believing the substance would blur their on-camera images."

—Medford, Oregon *Mail Tribune*, February 22, 1996

BOOK 'EM!

BUFFALO, Okla.—"The only explanation police have is that the two teenagers must have gotten the bank mixed up with the library.

"It's the first attempted library robbery I ever heard of," policeman Ray Dawson said Thursday. Dawson said the teenagers held out an empty pillow case and told the library attendant, 'Put it in.'

"'Put what in?' the attendant asked.

"'The money. Put it in and nobody'll get hurt,' the youth demanded.

"The attendant, who said there was less than $1 in collected library fines in his petty cash box, ran out the door and escaped. The teenagers were arrested hours later in Garden City, Kansas."

—United Press International, 1975

OH, *THAT*

WANDSWORTH, England—"On July 20, 1979, an armed robber dashed into a little grocery store and told the proprietor 'Give me the money from your till or I will shoot.' The owner was perplexed. 'Where's your gun?' he asked. There was an awkward silence....Then the robber replied that he didn't actually have a gun, but if the owner gave him any trouble, he'd go out and get one and come back. After a moment, the crook quietly left."

—The Return of Heroic Failures

RIGHT ON SCHEDULE

VERNON, British Columbia—"Raymond Cuthbert entered a drugstore in Vernon, and announced that he and his partner would be back in half an hour ro rob the place. Employees called the Royal Canadian Mounted Police, who arrested Cuthbert and Robert Phimister when they returned as promised."

—Dumb, Dumber, Dumbest

COPS *AND* ROBBERS

CHICAGO, Ill.—"Terry Johnson had no trouble identifying the two men who burglarized her Chicago apartment at 2:30 A.M. on August 17, 1981. All she had to do was write down the number of the police badge that one of them was wearing and the identity number on the fender of their squad car. The two officers—Stephen Webster, 33, and Tyrone Pickens, 32—had actually committed the crime in full uniform, while on duty, using police department tools."

—Crime/16 Stupid Thieves

In 1948 four men took a cow to the top of the Matterhorn. They all froze to death.

THE POLITICALLY CORRECT QUIZ

As we pointed out in the last Bathroom Reader, *"political correctness" isn't as bad as it's made out to be—after all, there's nothing wrong with becoming more sensitive to people's feelings. On the other hand, people can get pretty outrageous with their ideas of what's "appropriate." Here are seven real-life examples of politically correct—or "incorrect"—behavior. How sensitive are you? Can you spot the "correct" one?* *(Answers on page 462.)*

1. In 1997, the "Beetle Bailey" comic strip moved toward political correctness when cartoonist Mort Walker wrote a story in which...

a) Cookie began offering vegetarian meals.

b) Sarge apologized for calling Beetle "dehumanizing" names.

c) After taking sensitivity training, General Halftrack admitted to being "sexist."

2. In 1993, Hempstead, Texas school officials banned pregnant girls from their high school's sixteen-member cheerleading squad. Then they rescinded the rule because...

a) They would have been illegally discriminating against the four pregnant cheerleaders on the squad.

b) An angry cheerleader threatened to sue them for not providing birth control.

c) Church groups picketed the school, protesting the implication that cheerleading causes pregnancy.

3. In February 1998, it was announced that the latest group to take offense at "insensitive" language was...

a) British sanitation workers, who objected to being called "garbage men."

b) Barroom bouncers in New York City, who began a letter-writing campaign to local newspapers to get them to use the term "crowd control engineers."

c) Meat shop owners in France, who objected to newspapers describing murderers as "butchers."

4. Political correctness goes both ways. In 1962, for example, a woman wrote to the Sears, Roebuck and Co. Catalog (then the world's largest) and complained that the women modeling maternity lingerie...

a) Should not be on display unless they are really pregnant.

b) Weren't wearing wedding rings.

c) Should be holding baby bottles, to take the focus off their breasts.

5. More reverse political correctness. In 1996, a Laurens, South Carolina man told reporters that he was shocked local African-Americans were so prejudiced. What was he referring to?

a) Their objection to a local school's "slave auction" fundraising event.

b) Their objections to a Ku Klux Klan "museum and apparel store."

c) Their objections to "flesh-colored" crayons being used in classrooms, and their insistence that "black" crayons be referred to as "flesh-colored" also.

6. At the University of Pennsylvania, a woman was asked to leave a meeting of a group called "White Women Against Racism" because...

a) She protested that the initials in the group's name spell out WAR (WWAR).

b) She was black.

c) She was a transsexual.

7. When Connecticut's Canine Control Office issued dog tags in the shape of a fire hydrant...

a) Firefighters objected that it ridiculed their profession.

b) Women called the office to object that it discriminated against female dogs.

c) Church groups called the office and complained that the tag's shape resembled a male sex organ.

THE ANIMALS AT THE ZOO, Part 3

Here's even more info for zoo-lovers and animal watchers.

WATCHING GORILLAS

Gorillas are highly intelligent, social animals. Groups are led by a dominant "silverback" male. Gorillas were once thought to be ferocious people-eating beasts. In reality, they're peaceful vegetarians.

Behavior: Chest beating.

What It Means: Usually excitement, but it depends on the context. A gorilla could thump his chest in the middle of play, for example, or as part of a threat display. The sound can travel as far as a mile.

Behavior: "Smiling." Teeth not bared.

What It Means: Invitation to play. Gorillas, especially young ones, like to have fun. As a sort of "come and get me" gesture, one gorilla will direct a happy face at another. Within seconds, the two may be chasing each other and wrestling.

Behavior: Inspecting and picking each other's skin and hair.

What It Means: Grooming. This practice is common among primates. It's important for group hygiene. But it's just as important for social bonding. You can learn a lot about the social structure of a gorilla group by observing who grooms whom.

Behavior: Various sounds.

What They Mean: All gorillas enjoy a good belch to express satisfaction with a meal. The silverback does most of the specialized vocalizing. He grunts when he wants to call the group together. He gives a call that sounds something like a dog's bark when he wants to hurry the group along to a different spot.

Behavior: Back riding.

What It Means: Foreplay. Mother gorillas will carry their babies on

Five oldest words still in use in the English language: Town, priest, earl, this, and ward.

their backs. Among grown gorillas, though, playing "horsey" means that the two are definitely an item.

Despite the male gorilla's reputation as the "Don Juan" of the animal kingdom, it's typically the female who is more sexually assertive. She's the one who climbs up onto her mate's back and rides him like a horse. If you're lucky enough to see this rare courtship display at a zoo, you won't need an interpreter to explain what's going on.

WATCHING GIRAFFES

Giraffes are the tallest land mammals, measuring 15–17 feet (male) or 13–15 feet (female) from horn tip to toe. Our fascination with these animals is nothing new. In ancient times, a giraffe was transported 2,000 miles along the Nile from southern Africa to a royal zoo in Egypt.

Behavior: Neck held erect while walking.

What It Means: Dominance. You can pick out the dominant bull from the rest of the herd by its proud walk. The other giraffes, in comparison, hold their necks lower, at an angle.

Behavior: Necking.

What It Means: Conflict. Giraffes are generally peaceful. When they do spar, they rub and wrap their necks together. You know the situation is getting serious when they begin to slam heads and jab with their horns.

Behavior: Mother nuzzling her young.

What It Means: Giraffe I.D. The mama giraffe is filing some very important information as she lovingly noses and licks a newborn. She's learning the youngster's distinctive smell and skin pattern. The information will come in handy some day when she needs to pick her kid out of the crowd.

Behavior: Nosing, rubbing, and/or licking each other.

What It Means: Bonding. Group harmony is important to giraffes. But giraffes don't necessarily spread their affection around equally. Researchers have found that certain herd members are touched more than others.

Wettest inhabited place on earth: Buenaventura, Columbia, with 265 inches of rain per year.

THE TOM AND JERRY STORY

The cartoon world's most famous cat and mouse are almost sixty years old. But with cable TV airing their cartoons daily, a whole new generation knows (and apparently loves) them.

BACKGROUND

In the late thirties, MGM had a full-time animation studio. But while Disney and Warner Brothers cartoons became more popular each year, MGM's list of cartoon flops kept growing. One reason was their disorganized and indecisive management. Another was weak characters; MGM had nothing to compare with Bugs Bunny or Mickey Mouse.

William Hanna and Joe Barbera, two young MGM animators, were convinced that the studio would soon fold, so they decided they might as well develop a cartoon of their own. After all, what did they—or MGM—have to lose? They picked a cat and mouse as their subjects because, as Joe Barbera put it, "half the story was written before you even put pencil to paper."

DON'T CALL US...

In 1940, they finished "Puss Gets the Boot" about a cat named Jasper trying to catch an unnamed mouse. The brass at MGM didn't care for it, but since they didn't have anything else in the works, they released it to theatres. To their surprise, the public loved it. It was even nominated for an Academy Award.

It was just what MGM needed. So Hanna and Barbera were shocked when MGM executives called them in and told them to "stop making the cat and mouse cartoons." Why? Because they "didn't want to put all our eggs in one basket."

"Of course," Barbera says wryly, "before 'Puss Gets the Boot,' MGM didn't have a single good egg to put in any basket." But orders were orders. Shortly after, however, MGM got a letter from a leading Texas exhibitor asking, "When are we going to see more of those

Top 5 male cat names in the U.S.: Tiger/Tigger, Smokey, Pepper, Max/Maxwell, and Simon.

adorable cat and mouse cartoons?" He was too important to ignore, so Hanna and Barbera were given the green light to develop the series.

WHAT'S IN A NAME?

Now that the team was going to make more cat and mouse cartoons for MGM, they needed names for their characters. Instead of painstakingly researching and developing a title for the pair, Hanna and Barbera asked fellow workers to put pairs of names into a hat. The pair they picked: "Tom and Jerry." An animator named John Carr won fifty dollars for the idea. MGM, on the other hand, made millions.

For seventeen years, Hannah and Barbara, still unknown to the public, made over 120 *Tom and Jerry* cartoons in the basement at MGM. Because their lead characters didn't talk, the cartoon's success was dependent on top-notch animation, plus writing that relied heavily on facial expressions and timing. This was all held together by composer Scott Bradley's complex music scores for each cartoon. *Tom and Jerry* cartoons won seven Academy Awards. Due to financial constraints at the studio, however, the series was dropped in 1958. Hanna and Barbera went on to create their own animation studio and churn out more made-for-TV cartoons than anyone in history, including *The Flintstones*, *The Jetsons*, *Yogi Bear*, and *Scooby Doo*.

MEANWHILE...

In 1963, five years after the last *Tom and Jerry* cartoon was made, legendary Warner Brothers animator Chuck Jones moved to MGM to resurrect the series. Not only did he have the unenviable task of toning down the violence in a cartoon that revolved around it, but by Jones' own admission, he didn't understand the characters. What came out was a wimpy copy of the *Roadrunner and Coyote* cartoons that didn't have the budget of the previous *Tom and Jerry* series. Not only were the plots and animation static, but Scott Bradley's carefully constructed scores were replaced by stock '60s music. After three unsuccessful years, MGM dropped the cat and mouse for good.

Since then, the series has been resurrected for TV in a number of different varieties (like *Tom and Jerry Kids*)...by Hanna-Barbera Studios.

The Netherlands has more burglaries per capita than any other country on earth.

PART VI: THE EMPIRE STATE BUILDING

It isn't the world's tallest skyscraper anymore, but the Empire State Building is still one of the most popular skyscrapers in the world, and as enduring a symbol of New York City as the Statue of Liberty. Here's the story of how it was built. (*Part V is on page 248.*)

FAMILY PLOT

In 1827, William Backhouse Astor, son of New York land baron John Jacob Astor, bought a large plot of farmland in what is now mid-Manhattan. He didn't do much with it; he just held on to it because he figured that one day it might be worth more than the $20,500 he paid for it.

By the mid-1850s, several of the Astors had built mansions on the property, including William's daughter-in-law, Caroline. Much of the surrounding area was still farmland and pasture, but that was okay—Mrs. Astor liked the peace and quiet.

PAIN IN THE ASTOR

As the years passed, the property surrounding the Astor mansions was also developed, first into mansions for other millionaires, and later into upscale shops and other commercial buildings. In 1893, Mrs. Astor's nephew, William Waldorf Astor, built a 13-story hotel right next door to her mansion. He named it the Waldorf, after himself.

The Waldorf soon became the finest hotel in New York, playing host to royalty, captains of industry, and visiting heads of state—but Mrs. Astor, the queen of New York society, was furious that her own flesh and blood had forced her to live next door to *transients*. So she struck back—she tore down her mansion and in its place, built a 16-story hotel whose only purpose was to steal business from the Waldorf. Like her nephew, Mrs. Astor named her hotel—the Astoria—after herself.

Eventually, Mrs. Astor and her nephew patched up their differences and began operating the hotels jointly as the Waldorf-Astoria. It was more than a hotel—it was the gathering-place for the city's high-

Heaviest U.S. president: William Howard Taft (332 lbs). Lightest: James Madison (100 lbs).

society. The millionaires who lived nearby would frequently drop in for dinner, drinks or tea while out on their daily strolls. But as time went on and the relentless commercialization of the neighborhood continued, many wealthy neighbors abandoned the area. With fewer and fewer of the city's elite living in walking distance, the hotel faded in importance. By the 1920s, the Waldorf-Astoria was passé; its fading velvet-tassle Victorian decor completely out of step with contemporary fashion. In 1929, the Astors sold the hotel(s) and some surrounding property to the Bethlehem Engineering Corporation for $16 million.

STARTING OVER

Bethlehem planned to demolish the building and replace it with a 55-story structure that would be the largest (though not the tallest) office building in the city.

But they couldn't arrange the financing. In September 1929, they sold the property to the Empire State Building Corporation.

Dynamic Duo

This new group of developers had financial and political clout that Bethlehem could only have dreamed of. Two of the most important members were John J. Raskob, a former vice president of General Motors, and Al Smith, the scrappy former governor of New York and Democratic presidential nominee.

Raskob was in charge of coming up with the money to build what was going to be called the Empire State Building. Smith was in charge of public relations. His job was to sell the building, not just to the public, but also to prospective tenants. He was the right man for the job—nicknamed "the Happy Warrior," he'd worked his way up from the sidewalks of New York City into the governor's mansion, and was one of the most popular politicians New York had ever seen. Besides, a lot of people owed him favors.

BACK TO THE DRAWING BOARD

Bethlehem had planned to make its 55-story building low and wide. Raskob and his partners figured that a taller, skinnier building would make more money. So they told their architectural firm, Shreve, Lamb & Harmon, to come up with a design for one.

"Bill, how high can you make it so that it won't fall down?" Raskob supposedly said to architect William Lamb. Lamb replied that it was possible to construct a building 80 stories tall or higher. When the architects asked what the building should look like, either Smith or Raskob (both men later claimed credit) pulled out a big pencil and pointed it skyward. "It should look like this," they supposedly said.

Competing with Chrysler

Raskob decided to build the biggest building on Earth, and not just for the bragging rights. He had a personal motive—revenge. Apparently, Raskob had once made a deal with Walter P. Chrysler to join the Chrysler company…and Chrysler had reneged. Now Mr. Chrysler was building his own world's-tallest-skyscraper several blocks away. As John Tauranac writes in *The Empire State Building*, "Raskob wanted a building that would literally and figuratively put Walter Chrysler's building in the shade."

The only problem *was* that nobody except Walter Chrysler himself knew how tall the Chrysler building was going to be, and he wasn't talking.

One-Upsmanship

When the Chrysler Building was finally completed at 1,048 feet, Raskob was free to make new plans. He had announced the height of the Empire State Building as 1,000 feet. But it was still on the drawing board. So he ordered Shreve, Lamb & Harmon to add 5 stories to the building, making it 85 stories and 1,050 feet tall—two feet higher than the finished Chrysler Building. At this stage, the Empire State Building called for a flat-topped building with no tower or spire on the roof. That would come a little later…and it, too, would outdo the Chrysler building.

TRIAL BALLOON

In December 1929, Al Smith announced a change in the design of the building that would increase the height from 1,050 feet to 1,250 feet. Smith wasn't talking about adding a flagpole. He was talking about constructing a mooring mast for dirigibles, which would enable the building to serve as a sort of downtown airport for lighter-than-air balloons. The airships would tie up to the building in much the same way that a ship ties up to a pier. Passengers

Geography quiz: Which country borders 16 other countries? China

would then disembark via a gangplank that extended from the airship to the mooring mast. The topmost floors of the Empire State Building would be arrival and departure lounges, ticket counters, and passenger services.

This may sound absurd today, but at the time, dirigibles seemed like the future of long-distance air travel. "No kidding," Smith told reporters. "We're working on the thing now." In September 1931, a small zeppelin actually did tie up to the mooring mast, and two weeks later a Goodyear blimp picked up a stack of newspapers from the top of the *New York Evening Journal* magazine and delivered them to the top of the Empire State Building. The stunt was an attempt to demonstrate that roof-to-roof deliveries might be a way to reduce congestion in the traffic-clogged streets below.

HOT AIR

Nobody knew whether the plan was really feasible, but that didn't stop Raskob and Smith. John Tauranac explains:

> No estimate of the additional cost of the project had been made at the time of the announcement, nor had feasibility studies been made or any market research done to determine whether people were actually willing to walk a gangplank from a dirigible to a mooring mast suspended almost 1,250 feet in the air. Nevertheless, Raskob had told Smith to proceed....The whole job was estimated at about $750,000, a paltry addition to the final costs.

The dirigible mast remained a part of the building's design and actually did get built. The idea of actually using it, however, was quietly dropped, and the landing gear that would have enabled dirigibles to use it was never installed. As for the space that was set aside for the ticket counter and passenger lounge, it was converted to "the world's highest soda fountain and tea garden."

As long as you're already visiting the Empire State Building, why not turn to the next installment, Part VII? It's on page 322.

IRONIC, ISN'T IT?

More irony to put the problems of your day-to-day life in proper perspective.

DELICIOUS IRONY

"A 1978 newsletter edited at a branch of Mensa, an organization for high-IQ people, had numerous misspellings—including the word, 'intelligense.'" ***—The Literary Life and Other Curiosities***

• "The U.S. Postal Service suffered a courtroom setback in 1992. USPS needed to get an expert-witness list to a Dayton, Ohio, judge by the next day in an unemployment discrimination case in order to be able to use the witnesses at trial. The list was sent from Washington, D.C., by the Postal Service's overnight Express Mail but did not arrive for ten days." ***—The Concrete Enema***

• "In 1993 near Alvin, Texas, Andrea Guerrero, 18, and her brother came across a man who was slumped over his truck and not breathing. Andrea saved his life by administering CPR until an ambulance arrived. At the time, Guerrero was on her way home from a CPR certification exam, which she had flunked." ***—The Concrete Enema***

• "[In 1986,] our *For What It's Worth Department* concludes that Orlando, Florida has one prejudiced jury! In the Orange County Courthouse, a jury of twelve...was stuck for twenty minutes in a courthouse elevator...On their way to the courtroom to hear a case against the Otis Elevator Company!" ***—Paul Harvey's For What It's Worth***

• "In 1978 Ray Wright of Philadelphia, Pennsylvania was promoting his burglar alarm business, leaving flyers on autos. They read, 'If you didn't see me put this on your windshield, I could just as easily have stolen your car.' While he busy advertising, someone stole his truck." ***—Encyclopedia Brown's Book of Facts***

EMBARRASSING IRONY

• "[In 1994,] author James Herriot, whose gentle accounts of the life of a British country veterinarian (such as *All Creatures Great and Small*) are sold throughout the world and have inspired a television series, was in the hospital yesterday after being attacked by a flock of sheep." **—News Report**

• "The always-so-correct British Broadcasting Corporation was severely embarrassed when news leaked out that they had paid white film extras up to five times as much as black extras during African location shooting of a documentary film series. Its title: *The Fight Against Slavery*." ***—The World's Greatest Mistakes***

• "Human Kindness Day took place in Washington, D.C. on May 10, 1975. At a press conference afterwards, police said there had been 600 arrests, 150 smashed windows, and 42 looted refreshment stands." ***—The Book of Heroic Failures***

IRONY FROM ABOVE

• "In 1979 the Allied Roofing and Siding Company of Grand Rapids, Michigan was engaged in cleaning snow from roofs in the area to prevent damage or collapse from the weight of heavy snow. But guess what roof did collapse from the weight of snow? The roof over the Allied Roofing and Siding Company." ***—The Book of Blunders***

• "In Jacksonville, the Riverside Chevrolet Company launched a sales campaign featuring the slogan, 'Look for it! Something BIG is going to happen!' A few hours later, the showroom ceiling collapsed on six new cars." ***—Not a Good Word About Anybody***

• "The American Institute of Architects held their 1979 annual conference in Kansas City, to be near the Kemper Arena, to which they had awarded their prize as 'One of the finest buildings in the nation.' On the first day of the conference, hordes of architects toured the inspired structure, with its wide spanning roof trusses, which *The Architectural Record* described as having 'an almost awesome muscularity.' On the second day, the roof of the $12 million building fell down. Twenty-six architects were hospitalized." ***—The Book of Heroic Failures***

According to scientific tests, the odors that most commonly arouse women sexually are:

THE TOP 10 HITS OF THE YEAR, 1988–1991

Here's another installment of BRI's Top Ten of the Year list.

1988
(1) Faith —*George Michael*
(2) Need You Tonight —*INXS*
(3) Got My Mind Set On You —*George Harrison*
(4) Never Gonna Give Up —*Rick Astley*
(5) Sweet Child O' Mine —*Guns N' Roses*
(6) Heaven Is A Place On Earth —*Belinda Carlisle*
(7) So Emotional —*Whitney Houston*
(8) Hands To Heaven —*Breathe*
(9) Could've Been —*Tiffany*
(10) Roll With It —*Steve Winwood*

1989
(1) Look Away —*Chicago*
(2) My Prerogative —*Bobby Brown*
(3) Every Rose Has Its Thorn —*Poison*
(4) Miss You Much —*Janet Jackson*
(5) Straight Up —*Paula Abdul*
(6) Wind Beneath My Wings (from *Beaches*) —*Bette Midler*
(7) Cold Hearted —*Paula Abdul*
(8) Girl You Know It's True —*Milli Vanili*
(9) Baby, I Love Your Way/Freebird Medley —*Will To Power*
(10) Giving You The Best That I Got —*Anita Baker*

1990
(1) Hold On —*Wilson Phillips*
(2) Nothing Compares 2 U —*Sinead O'Connor*
(3) It Must Have Been Love (from *Pretty Woman*) —*Roxette*
(4) Poison —*Bell Biv Devoe*
(5) Vogue —*Madonna*
(6) Another Day In Paradise —*Phil Collins*
(7) Vision Of Love —*Mariah Carey*
(8) Hold On —*En Vogue*
(9) Cradle Of Love (from *Ford Fairlane*) —*Billy Idol*
(10) Blaze Of Glory (from *Young Guns II*) —*Jon Bon Jovi*

1991
(1) (Everything I Do) I Do It For You (from *Robin Hood*) —*Bryan Adams*
(2) I Wanna Sex You Up (from *New Jack City*) —*Color Me Badd*
(3) Gonna Make You Sweat —*C&C Music Factory*
(4) One More Try —*Timmy T.*
(5) Rush Rush —*Paula Abdul*
(6) Unbelievable —*EMF*
(7) I Like The Way (The Kissing Game) —*Hi-Five*
(8) More Than Words —*Extreme*
(9) The First Time —*Surface*
(10) Baby Baby —*Amy Grant*

pumpkin pie, lavender, cucumbers, baby powder, and Good 'n' Plenty candy.

TO TELL THE TRUTH...

We found this in It's a Conspiracy *by the National Insecurity Council. Apparently, no one has a monopoly on lying in government.*

"The charge has been made that the United States has shipped weapons to Iran as ransom payment for the release of American hostages in Lebanon, that the United States undercut its allies and secretly violated American policy against trafficking with terrorists. Those charges are utterly false."

—Ronald Reagan, 1986

"The agency does not violate U.S. law."

—CIA spokesperson

"There is no truth, no truth whatever, to the widely circulated suspicions of immoral conduct."

—Ted Kennedy,
referring to the incident at Chappaquiddick

"There was no blacklist....That was a lot of horseshit...The only thing our side did that was anywhere near blacklisting was just running a lot of people out of the business..."

—John Wayne,
unclear on the concept

"We are not telling lies or doing any of these disinformation things."

—Ronald Reagan,
discussing Iran-Contra

"The CIA had nothing to do with the [Chilean] coup, to the best of my knowledge and belief, and I only put in that qualification in case some madman appears down there who, without instructions, talked to somebody."

—Henry Kissinger,
denying U.S. involvement in the overthrow of Chile's President Allende

"80 percent of air pollution comes not from chimneys and auto exhaust pipes, but from plants and trees."

—Ronald Reagan, 1979

"I didn't say air pollution. I said oxides of nitrogen."

—Ronald Reagan, 1980

"Your President is not a crook."

—Richard Nixon

More than 10 % of the world's annual production of salt is used to de-ice American roads.

IS IT KOSHER?

Everyone has heard the term "kosher." In American slang, that means "on the up-and-up." Most people also know it's actually a religious term—a part of Judaism. But what does it really mean? Even many less-observant Jews aren't 100% sure.

KOSHER BASICS

Kosher means "fit" or "acceptable" in Hebrew. According to the Torah, or Old Testament (Leviticus, chapter 11), only certain types of animals are considered kosher and can be eaten. In addition, three verses (Exodus 23:19, 24:26, and Deuteronomy 14:21) forbid the cooking of a baby goat in its own mother's milk.

From these origins, the rabbis in the Talmud (the book of ancient writings that are the basis of religious authority for Orthodox Jews) developed a detailed set of requirements for raising, slaughtering, preparing, storing, cooking, and eating animals.

For Jews who "keep kosher" (many do not), everything from the animal's birth to its consumption at mealtime must be done in accordance with these rules. And for a processed food to be labelled kosher, it must be certified by a rabbi who has overseen all of the ingredients...as well as the manufacturing process and equipment.

WHAT FOOD IS KOSHER?

It's detailed, but here are some general rules:

Meat: Animals must be raised without hormones and growth stimulants, and must be slaughtered quickly to minimize pain. Within three days of slaughter, kosher butchers are required to de-vein meat, salt it, and rinse it three times in fresh, flowing water to remove blood—which people are forbidden to eat.

Kosher: Any animal that chews its cud *and* has split hooves (e.g., cows); fish with both fins and scales; all birds except scavengers and birds of prey.

Non-kosher: Pigs, rabbits, shellfish, reptiles, invertebrates, amphibians and underwater mammals.

Milk: Meat and dairy products must be kept completely separate from one another. They not only have to be stored apart, but cooked and eaten with separate dishes, utensils, pots and pans. (Glass dishes, which are non-porous, can be used for anything.) Especially devout Jews wait six hours after eating meat before eating a milk product, so that the foods don't mix even in their stomachs.

Pareve Foods: *Pareve* is Yiddish for "neutral." Eggs, fish, tofu, and fruits and vegetables are neither dairy nor meat and can be eaten with either milk or meat (if prepared with neutral utensils)

KOSHER COMPLICATIONS

Some rules governing how kosher foods must be manufactured and prepared make it hard to tell if a food really *is* kosher. For example: kosher foods can't be produced on the same assembly lines as non-kosher foods. So if a "kosher" spaghetti sauce is manufactured on the same assembly line as spaghetti sauce containing non-kosher meat, it's not kosher. And nondairy creamers that contain sodium caseinate, a milk derivative, are considered a dairy product; they can't be used in drinks served at meals where meat is served.

It's almost impossible for consumers to tell on their own whether a food is truly kosher. That's why more than 400 Rabbinical Supervision agencies have sprung up to evaluate foods, by overseeing the manufacturing process and certifying it to be kosher. The oldest and largest of these is the Union of Orthodox Jewish Congregations of America. Foods they certify have a letter U in a circle on the package. Another organization, The Committee for the Furtherance of Torah Observations, uses a K in a circle.

KOSHER FACTS

• As of 1997, there were 20,000 kosher products on U.S. store shelves, representing 30% of all packaged foods in supermarkets and 40% of packaged foods in health food stores.

• Roughly 7,000,000 consumers spend $3 billion a year on kosher foods, and the market is growing at a rate of 11% a year.

• Ironically, a majority of certified kosher foods (about 76% of them) are sold to non-Jews who are concerned about food safety, or whose religions have similar food restrictions.

The Great Smoky Mountains National Park gets the most visitors of any national park.

LENO-ISMS

Some late-night comments from a guy with a really big chin.

"The essential difference between men and women is that men think the Three Stooges are funny, and women don't."

"The Supreme Court has ruled they cannot have a Nativity scene in Washington, D.C. This wasn't for any religious reasons. They couldn't find three wise men and a virgin."

"In New York crime is getting worse. I was there the other day. The Statue of Liberty had both hands up."

"I looked up the word 'politics' in the dictionary and it's actually a combination of two words: 'poli,' which means many, and 'tic,' which means bloodsuckers."

"A new report from the government says raw eggs may have salmonella and may be unsafe. In fact, the latest government theory says it wasn't the fall that killed Humpty Dumpty—he was dead before he hit the ground."

"On Presidents' Day you stay home and you don't do anything. Sounds like Vice Presidents' Day!"

"I heard that Evelyn Wood just lost a lawsuit. A guy sued her because his eyeball blew out at ten thousand words a minute."

"The atheists have produced a Christmas play. It's called *Coincidence on 34th Street.*"

"The reason there are two senators for each state is so that one can be the designated driver."

"Scientists believe that monkeys can be taught to think, lie, and even play politics within their community. If we can just teach them to cheat on their wives we can save millions on congressional salaries."

"It was reported that sex is good for people who suffer from arthritis—it's just not that pleasant to watch."

ANIMAL SUPERSTITIONS

Superstitions are intriguing, even if you don't believe in them. Here are some very old ones relating to animals, collected by Edwin and Mona Radford in their book, Encyclopedia of Superstitions.

"A strange dog following you is good luck. A dog howling is a sure sign of death."

"If a rooster crows near the door with his face towards it, it is a sure prediction of the arrival of a stranger."

"Good luck will attend anyone upon whose face a spider falls from the ceiling."

"If a cat sneezes, it is a sign of rain. If a cat sneezes three times, a cold will run through the family."

"Living pigeons cut in half and applied to the feet of a man in fever will cure him."

"To cure illness in a family, wash the patient and throw the water on a cat. Then drive the cat out of doors, and it will take the illness with it."

"If blind people are kind to ravens they will learn how to regain their sight."

"If you find a hairy caterpillar, you should throw it over your shoulder for good luck."

"If a dog passes between a couple who are going to be married, much ill-luck will result to them."

"Mice, minced, given to a sufferer, will cure the measles."

"Dried rat's tails will cure a cold."

"If a white weasel crosses your path, it presages death or misfortune; but if one runs in front of you, you will be able to beat all your enemies."

"If a cat sneezes near a bride, it means she will have good luck in her wedded life."

"When mice swarm into a house hitherto free from them, a member of the household will die."

"If the rooster crows at midnight, the Angel of Death is passing over the house."

"If a man should kill a glowworm, it will endanger his love affair, and may cause the death of his beloved."

Nickname for Leisure World, a city for seniors in Orange County California: "Heaven on hold."

MORE LEGENDARY BETS

Some bets achieve the status of legends because of the unexpected results they produce. Here are two classic examples of bets that got out of hand...and became folklore.

THE BOTTLE HOAX OF 1749

The Wager: In the first week of 1749, the Duke of Portland bet the Earl of Chesterfield that if he were to advertise the public performance of something obviously impossible, "there'd be enough fools in London to fill the theater and pay handsomely for it." Chesterfield took him up on it.

The Duke then placed this ad in the London papers:

> At the New Theater in the Haymarket, on Monday next, is to be seen a Person who performs most surprising things....He presents you with a common Wine Bottle, which any of the spectators may first examine; this Bottle is placed on a Table in the midst of the Stage, and he (without any equivocation) goes into it, in the sight of all the Spectators, and sings in it. During his stay in the bottle, any person may handle it, and see plainly that it does not exceed a common Tavern Bottle.

The Result: The Duke won. Soon all London was talking about the upcoming event. The theater was sold out well in advance of the day—with people paying as much as 7 shillings, 6 pence a seat to see it. But, obviously, there wasn't anything to see and things got ugly quickly. After about 20 minutes, when it became apparent that they'd been had, the audience rioted...they destroyed the theater, stealing everything in it...and then they burned the building down. The Duke had covered his tracks, and the true story of the bet didn't leak out until several years later.

THE BERNERS STREET HOAX OF 1809

The Wager: A well-known practical joker of his day, Thomas Hook, was walking in a quiet residential neighborhood near London with a friend. He pointed to a particularly quiet-looking house on Berners Street, No. 54, and bet that "within a month, that house will be the talk of London." His friend took him up on it.

According to one account: "Hook went into action. No. 54, he discovered, was occupied by an elderly widow, a Mrs. Tottingham—and he rented a room in the house opposite. Then he wrote and posted more than a *thousand* letters—it took him two weeks—and when 'zero hour' dawned, he and his friend were sitting in their window to watch the fun."

The Result: Hook won. Here's how Curtiss MacDougall describes it in his book, *Hoaxes*:

> It began early in the morning, with the arrival of about a dozen chimney sweeps from all parts of London, summoned by a letter to sweep the chimneys of No. 54. While the agitated housemaid was still arguing heatedly with these disappointed men, there converged upon No. 54 several coal-carts, each with a ton of coal, "as per your esteemed order." Then came a van-load of furniture, a consignment of beer, in barrels, a huge chamber organ (carried by six men), a cart-load of potatoes, and even a hearse, with a train of mourning-coaches. Shopkeepers of all kinds—confectioners, wig-makers, opticians, clockmakers, fancy-goods dealers, dressmakers and many more—arrived in large numbers, all bringing samples of their wares. Two fashionable doctors and a dentist did their best to struggle through the ever-growing crowd and pay professional visits to the unfortunate Mrs. Tottingham—who could really have done with medical attention, for she was on the verge of hysterics.
>
> By this time, Berners street was choked up with carts, furniture, barrels of beer, and a large crowd. The police had been called out—and to make matters worse, all sorts of notables began to arrive, all headed to No. 54. The Duke of York, Commander-in-Chief of the Army, came in reply to a pathetic note telling him that a brother-officer was lying dangerously ill at No. 54, and begged a parting interview. The Lord Chief Justice came—so did the Archbishop of Canterbury, the Governor of the Bank of England, and the Lord Mayor of London. Apparently, he'd been victimized by a very similar letter to the one that bagged the Duke of York.
>
> One gets the impression that if it had been possible, 'the architect of this most outrageous deception' would probably have been hanged, drawn, and quartered. As it was, nothing happened to them—because, while everybody suspected a lot, nothing could be proved. Still, Hook left his Berners Street lodging very quietly as soon as the mob had been dispersed, and he wasn't seen in London for a long time afterwards.

Middle-class malaise: The higher the income, the more likely an American man will cheat on his wife.

WHY WE HAVE SPRING AND WINTER

Here's another Greek/Roman tale from Myths and Legends of the Ages. *This one tells us how springtime and winter were created.*

Far down under the surface of the earth lay the lands of Pluto, god of the underworld. Pluto, who despised light and avoided cheer, rarely left his dark and gloomy kingdom. But one day, he paid a short visit to the surface of the earth.

As he sped along the earth in his black chariot drawn by four black horses, he was seen by Cupid.

"What great good luck!" thought the mischievous god of love, as he fitted an arrow to his bow. "Here's a target I may never get a chance at again!"

Cupid took careful aim and shot his arrow straight into Pluto's heart.

Now, anyone who is hit by Cupid's arrow doesn't die but instead falls in love with the first person he sees. The first person Pluto saw was Proserpine, the lovely daughter of Ceres, goddess of the harvest. Proserpine was gathering lilies beside a gay, bubbling stream. When Pluto saw her, he was overwhelmed with love. He swept Proserpine up in his arms and carried her off in his chariot. The terrified girl screamed for help, but there was no one to hear her cries.

Pluto struck the earth with his great three-pronged spear, and the ground opened up. Into the opening, Pluto drove his plunging black horses. The earth closed again, while down, down, deep into the earth the chariot sped with Pluto and his beautiful prisoner.

Soon they arrived at Pluto's palace. The underworld king spoke words of love to Proserpine. He begged her not to be afraid. "You shall be my beloved," he said. "You shall reign as queen over all the realms of the dead."

But Proserpine only shook her head and wept. She would not look at Pluto; she would neither eat nor drink.

Far away, on the surface of the earth, Proserpine's mother, Ceres, was enveloped in despair. She searched the world over for her missing daughter, but she could not find her.

One day, weary and sad, Ceres sat down beside a river. The place she chose to rest was a fateful one. It was the very spot where Pluto had caused the earth to open so that he could pass in with Proserpine.

The nymph who lived in the nearby river had seen everything that happened. She was terribly afraid of Pluto, and dared not tell Ceres. Instead, she lifted up the sash which Proserpine had dropped and wafted it to the feet of her mother.

Ceres cried out with grief at the sight of her daughter's sash. Now she knew that Proserpine was in the earth, but she did not know what had happened. In her grief and anger, she blamed the earth itself.

"Ungrateful soil!" cried Ceres. "I have given you richness and clothed you with greenery and nourishing grain. Is this how you repay me? Now no more shall you enjoy my favors."

In her anger, Ceres sent too much rain, which killed the crops, then too much sun, which dried the fields. The leaves fell from the trees, cattle died, and ploughs broke in the furrows. The poor earth suffered terribly.

Finally, Arethusa, the nymph, interceded for the land. "Goddess," she said, "do not blame the land. Unwillingly did it open to let your daugher in. Pluto carried her off to be queen of the underworld. As my waters seeped through the earth, they saw her there. She is sad, but she is not afraid."

When Ceres heard this, she determined to get help. She quickly turned her chariot toward heaven and threw herself before the throne of Jupiter, the king of the gods. She begged him to bring Proserpine back to the earth—to force Pluto to give up her daughter.

Jupiter consented, but he was forced to make one condition. If Proserpine had not eaten anything while in the underworld she could return; otherwise, she must stay in Pluto's kingdom.

Mercury, the messenger of the gods, was then sent to Pluto with Jupiter's orders to return Proserpine to her mother.

Pluto could not refuse an order from Jupiter. But first, the clever Pluto offered Proserpine a pomegranate. No longer afraid of Pluto, Proserpine started to bite into the fruit. In alarm, Mercury stopped her—but not before she had swallowed six pomegranate seeds. Now, Pluto was able to demand that Proserpine spend six months of the year with him—one month for each seed she had swallowed.

So it was arranged. For six months each year, Proserpine must leave her mother, Ceres, and be Pluto's queen. During that time, Ceres is sad and unconcerned with the earth. Everything dies. It is winter.

At the end of six months, Proserpine comes back to her mother. She brings joy to Ceres and bright springtime to the earth.

*   *   *   *

ASK THE EXPERTS

Q: *Why can't we ever buy cashews in their shells?*

A: "Cashews aren't sold in their shells because they don't have a shell. Don't all nuts have shells? Yes. Then what gives?

"A cashew is a *seed*, not a nut. The cashew is the seed of a pear-shaped fruit, the cashew apple, which is itself edible. The cashew seed hangs at the lower end of the fruit, vulnerable and exposed. Cashews grow not on trees, but on tropical shrubs, similar to sumac plants.

"A hard leathery shell is what differentiates a nut from a seed. Kernels with thin, soft shells, such as pumpkins and sunflowers, are properly called seeds." (From *Imponderables*, by David Feldman)

Q: *Does a millipede have a million legs or a thousand legs?*

A: Neither. "Although the animal's name might suggest that it has a million legs, in fact the number of limbs on a millipede won't even total a thousand. Despite the fact that the word millipede means "thousand-legged," these many-limbed creatures actually have less than two hundred legs in all....Of course, two hundred is still a lot of legs." (From *How Do Ants Know When You're Having a Picnic?*, by Joanne Settel and Nancy Baggett)

President Calvin Coolidge liked to eat breakfast while having his head rubbed with Vaseline.

BACK ON THE CABLE

Aren't you glad you don't have a TV in your bathroom? We are, because you'd probably be sitting there for hours, watching "Dukes of Hazzard" reruns instead of reading Uncle John's Bathroom Reader. *Here's more info on cable stations.*

NICKELODEON

Background: In the 1970s, cable was still trying to find a niche as an alternative to network television. Kids' shows like *Sesame Street* and *The Electric Company* on PBS, were regarded as quality "alternative" shows—so when Nick was being launched in 1977 as "the first all-day, every day, something-for-every-kid programming package ever offered for cable TV," that's what they chose to emulate.

On the Air: Nick was the first television channel, cable or otherwise, that was devoted entirely to children's programming. It's hard to believe today, but there were no commercials—the company's budget was limited to the subscription fees paid to it by cable companies. "We don't take advertising because cable, to succeed, needs to be different from commercial broadcasting," Nickelodeon Vice President Cy Schneider explained in 1983. "It makes for a better product." It also made for enormous losses—by 1983, Nickelodeon was an estimated $20 million in debt. In 1984, it reversed course and began accepting commercials; a year later it was acquired by Viacom. By 1995, it was the most-watched basic-cable channel in the country, earning more than $100 million a year from advertising, cable subscription fees, and more than 400 licensed products.

CABLE NEWS NETWORK (CNN)

Background: By the mid-'70s, many AM radio stations had successfully moved to an all-news format. Ted Turner, owner of TBS, figured that if radio could make a 24-hour news profitable, so could TV. And he relished the idea of showing the Big 3 networks that news—which they thought of as their "crown jewel"—could be done well on cable, too. The only problem was that Turner didn't know anything about news broadcasting...and didn't even like it. But he was convinced that if he didn't follow through with the idea, some other cable entrepreneur would beat him to it. Analysts told Turner that there wasn't enough audience for an all-day news network. After a few years of waiting, he decided to do it anyway.

On the Air: Turner called Reese Schonfeld, founder of the nonprofit Independent Television News Association, and asked him: (1) if a 24-hour cable news channel was feasible; and (2) if he'd be interested in running it. Schonfeld said yes to both.

Together, Turner and Schonfeld successfully pitched CNN to cable operators at their annual convention in 1979. Turner then had to sell a TV station he owned in Charlotte, North Carolina, to raise the startup capital. CNN premiered on June 1, 1980. For years it was derided as the "Chicken Noodle Network" by the Big 3 networks and the public alike...but its respectability and clout grew steadily over time. Its crowning moment came in October 1987, when President Reagan invited "all four networks"—CBS, ABC, NBC and CNN—in for an Oval Office chat. As CNN anchor Bernard Shaw put it at the time, Reagan's invitation gave CNN "parity" with the Big-3 network news organizations for the first time.

THE FAMILY CHANNEL

Background: Pat Robertson founded the Christian Broadcasting Network (CBN) in 1960 when WYAH-TV—his little station in Portsmouth, Virginia—became the first in the country authorized by the FCC to devote more than 50% of its air time to religious programming. The network was built up with the help of donations from viewers. It started broadcasting via satellite in 1977, but continued to suffer from low ratings until 1981, when Robertson launched The Family Channel.

On the Air: The Family Channel de-emphasized religious programming in favor of reruns of wholesome shows like *Wagon Train*, *Burns and Allen*, and *I Married Joan*. "Only a masochist would want to watch religious shows all day," Robertson explained. The Family Channel also began to accept commercials. Over the years Robertson continued to shift the station's emphasis away from religious broadcasting toward more lucrative secular shows like *Newhart*. By 1991, the station was making so much money that CBN's tax exempt status was threatened. So Robertson spun it off as an independent company, naming himself as chairman. By 1995, the only preaching show left on the Family Channel was Robertson's own "700 Club." Today it is owned by media mogul Rupert Murdoch.

Country with the most elephants: Zaire, with 195,000. Country with the fewest: Vatican City.

DUMB PREDICTIONS

An enthusiastic BRI member e-mailed us this list. We print it here as a reminder that the "experts" are as clueless as the rest of us.

"Computers in the future may weigh no more than 1.5 tons."

—***Popular Mechanics*, 1949**

"I think there is a world market for maybe five computers."

—Thomas Watson, chairman of IBM, 1943

"This 'telephone' has too many shortcomings to be seriously considered as a means of communication. The device is inherently of no value to us."

—Western Union internal memo, 1876
(after Alexander Graham Bell offered to sell them the rights to the telephone)

"The wireless music box has no imaginable commercial value. Who would pay for a message sent to nobody in particular?"

—Associates of NBC president David Sarnoff
(responding to his recommendation, in the 1920s, that they invest in radio)

"We don't like their sound, and guitar music is on the way out."

—Decca Recording Company 1962
(rejecting the Beatles)

"I'm just glad it'll be Clark Gable who's falling on his face and not Gary Cooper."

—Gary Cooper *(happy he didn't take the lead role in* Gone With The Wind*)*

"A cookie store is a bad idea. Besides, the market research reports say America likes crispy cookies, not soft and chewy cookies like you make."

—Bankers' comment to Debbi Fields
(about her idea to start Mrs. Fields' Cookies)

"Heavier-than-air flying machines are impossible."

—Lord Kelvin, president, Royal Society, 1895

"If I had thought about it, I wouldn't have done the experiment. The literature was full of examples that said you can't do this."

—Spencer Silver
(*on the adhesive that led to 3-M Post-Its*)

"Professor Goddard does not know the relation between action and reaction and the need to have something better than a vacuum against which to react. He seems to lack the basic knowledge ladled out daily in high schools."

—*New York Times* editorial, 1921
(*about Robert Goddard's revolutionary rocket work*)

"You want to have consistent and uniform muscle development across all of your muscles? It can't be done. It's just a fact of life. You just have to accept inconsistent muscle development as an unalterable condition of weight training."

—Comment to Arthur Jones
(*inventor of Nautilus*)

"Stocks have reached what looks like a permanently high plateau."

—Irving Fisher, Professor of Economics, Yale University, 1929

"Everything that can be invented has been invented."

—Charles H. Duell, Commissioner, U.S. Office of Patents, 1899

"Louis Pasteur's theory of germs is ridiculous fiction."

—Pierre Pachet, Professor of Physiology at Toulouse, 1872

"640K ought to be enough for anybody"

—Bill Gates, 1981

What a way to go: Frank Sinatra's last TV appearance was on the sitcom "Who's the Boss."

PART VII: BUILDING THE EMPIRE STATE BUILDING

Here's the next-to-last section of our story on the world's tallest buildings. Part VI is on page 301.

BORROWED TIME

The Empire State Building was slated to be the world's tallest building—and it was paid for with some of the world's largest construction loans. Since the loans were going to be repaid with rent money, it was essential to finish the structure quickly and get tenants moved in. So speed was factored into every phase of design and construction. Anything that could be mass-produced was, and everything that was installed in the building was specifically designed for ease of assembly.

The architects worked at a breakneck pace, completing much of the design while construction was underway. They had to hustle to stay one step ahead of the steelworkers, who were adding 4-1/2 stories to the building every week, a record setting pace.

One architect observed: "The builders were throwing steel into the sky not just higher but faster than anybody had ever dreamed possible." And as soon as the the framework for a new floor was completed, the carpenters, glazers, masons, plumbers, and electricians would move in and finish the rest. In all, more than 4,000 workers were employed at the site when construction was at its peak.

OPEN FOR BUSINESS

Amazingly, eighteen months after the demolition of the Waldorf-Astoria began, the Empire State Building opened its doors for business. The structure's statistics were awesome: It was 1,250 feet and 86 floors high. It boasted 1.8 million square feet of office space with 6,500 windows, 7,000 radiators, and 17 million feet of telephone and telegraph wire. It was built with enough steel to build railroad tracks from New York to Baltimore and back. And the exterior

Poll results: About 25% of male employees say they take naps on the job. Only half that many women do

walls were faced with 10 million bricks, 200,000 cubic feet of stone, and 730 tons of aluminum and steel. It was billed as the Eighth Wonder of the World, and to admirers of the 1930s, it more than lived up to the title.

Hard Times

But the world around the building had changed almost as fast as the skyline. Only weeks after construction began in October 1929, the stock market crashed and ushered in the Great Depression. Nobody knew how long it would last—and besides, it was too late to stop construction. So work on the Empire State Building continued uninterrupted.

By the time the building was finished, the New York real estate market had collapsed. Practically speaking, filling it with paying customers was an impossible task.

WHITE ELEPHANT

When the Empire State Building opened in 1931, only 23% of the offices were occupied; and for the rest of the Depression, the "Empty State Building" would never be more than two-thirds full.

By 1936, there were still no tenants between the 41st and the 80th floors (although NBC had television laboratories on the 85th floor), and even the floors below the 41st floor were not fully occupied. Real estate experts predicted that if the top 45 floors were not torn down, the building would lose $3 million a year "for life." Things were so bad that the management even took to turning the lights in the empty floors on at night so that no one would know how empty the building was.

With so few rent-paying tenants, other sources of money came to count for a lot. "One of the greatest sources of income," Tauranac writes, "was the observatories. All those millions of dollar admissions contributed to the coffers of the Empire State Building, especially after King Kong (1933) had been depicted climbing to the pinnacle of the Empire State with a disheveled Fay Wray in his grasp. But even King Kong was not enough."

Hanging On

In 1936,the Empire State Building Corporation defaulted on the

Three largest Native American tribes in the U.S.: Cherokee, Navajo, Chippewa.

mortgage and became technically insolvent. The only reason it wasn't forced into bankruptcy was that Metropolitan Life, holder of the mortgage, didn't figure it could do a better job attracting tenants than the current management was. Selling the building wasn't a realistic option in the glutted real estate market, so they just left it alone, lowered the interest rate on the loan, and collected whatever money they could.

The strategy turned out to be a wise one. "By 1940," Tauranac writes, "Met Life had received $3.8 million that it would not have received had they foreclosed, and although everybody might not have been particularly happy, they were satisfied."

BOUNCING BACK

The Empire State Building began to recover in the early 1940s, thanks to the slowly improving economic situation and the buildup that accompanied America's entry into World War II. In 1942, the Office of Price Administration signed a lease for five entire floors, and 19 other federal agencies would eventually move in, too. By 1944, the building was 85% full; in 1950, *Time* magazine reported that it was "jammed to the rafters," with tenants paying $10 million worth of rent in a building that cost a little over $5 million a year to operate. In 15 years, the Empire State Building had gone from bankruptcy to one of the most profitable buildings in the world. And it would remain the tallest building in the world for more than 40 years.

Newer, taller buildings would eventually be built, but for many skyscraper buffs, there would never be anything like the Empire State Building. "It has been surpassed in height," George Douglas writes, "but it has not been displaced in the hearts of New Yorkers and of millions of visitors for whom it is *the great* skyscraper, the building that comes first to mind as the tallest of the tall. For style, grace, and dramatic thrust it is hard to find its equal anywhere in the world."

When you're ready for the exciting conclusion, flip on ahead to Part VIII on page 329.

Sweden has more telephones per capita than any country on earth.

THE WORLD'S WORST ACTOR

Some people's fame endures not because they were good at what they did—but because they were mind-bogglingly bad. The BRI's eccentric collection of history books is full of tales about people like Robert Coates. But then, he's in a category all by himself.

ROBERT "ROMEO" COATES (1772-1842)

Background: Born in Antigua, Coates had dark, exotic looks that stood out in a British crowd. But he didn't rely on nature to attract attention—he dressed in costumes covered with diamonds and feathers. In 1807, a few days before his stage debut in Bath, England, he arrived in town—in a diamond-studded carriage shaped like a seashell.

Claim to Fame: Coates became wildly popular in England for butchering Shakespeare. As Margaret Nicholas writes in *The World's Greatest Cranks and Crackpots:*

> He constantly forgot his lines, invented scenes as he went along, and turned to address the audience whenever he thought it was getting out of hand. If he enjoyed playing a scene, he would quite happily repeat it three or four times. He loved dramatic death scenes and had no qualms about "breathing his last" several times over. Exasperated playgoers would yell, "Why don't you die?"

One night during *Romeo and Juliet*, Coates dashed off stage and returned with a crowbar...which he used to try to pry open Juliet's tomb. He considered it an improvement on Shakespeare.

At another performance, someone hurled a fighting cock on stage (in "tribute" to Coates' motto, "while I live, I'll crow"). The bird pecked at Coates' feet, but the actor delivered his romantic speech without missing a beat.

Coates proved that bad acting can be very profitable.

Nicholas writes:

> His fame spread and soon he was playing to packed houses. People would travel great distances to see if he really was as bad as everyone

reported. He became such an attraction that even the Prince Regent went to see him.

When he played the part of Lothario in Rowe's *The Fair Penitent* at London's Haymarket Theater, at least a thousand people had to be turned away....

At another performance...his acting was so poor that several people laughed themselves ill and had to be helped outside into the fresh air and treated by a doctor.

Eventually, the rowdy crowds became a problem. No actress, for fear of injury, would play Juliet opposite Coates' Romeo (his favorite role). And theater owners became less willing to risk damage to their property. He often had to bribe them just to get a part in their plays.

Without the income from acting to support his lavish style Coates went bankrupt. He was killed in 1848, at age 75, when he was run down by a hansom taxi.

*　　*　　*　　*

SPEAKING OF DUMB...

"In Altoona, Pennsylvania...TV anchorman Brandon Brooks demonstrated for his viewers how to protect their homes from burglars. He used his own home to demonstrate double locks on doors, windows that will not open from the outside, burglar alarms...

"Now it appears that thieves were watching the program. They not only learned where the double locks were, but where the TV set was and the VCR and the furniture and other things.

"So nights later—while Brandon Brooks was on the air back at the studio—the thieves broke into his house and cleaned him out.

"The window that won't open from the outside: They smashed it."

—Paul Harvey's For What It's Worth

THEY WENT THAT-A-WAY

Here are a few more stories about the deaths of famous people from Malcolm Forbes' fascinating book.

MATA HARI

Claim to Fame: Nude dancer, seductress, and supposed master spy for the Germans during World War I.

Cause of Death: Firing squad.

Postmortem: Mata Hari (her real name was Margaretha Zelle) was famous before the war for dancing what she claimed was an "authentic Hindu temple ritual." It was really just an excuse for her to take her clothes off, and it gave her admirers an excuse to come and see her. "I could never dance well," she admitted. "People came to see me because I was the first who dared show myself naked to the public."

She may not have a been a spy at all—just a scapegoat. But when the French lost two hundred thousand men in the Battle of the Somme, they needed someone to blame. Mata Hari, who had antagonized authorities for years, fit the bill perfectly. She was arrested, tried for espionage, and sentenced to death. She refused to be tied to the execution pole, and reportedly also turned down a blindfold. Mata Hari was seductive to the end, smiling and winking at the firing squad as they raised their rifles in her direction.

JIMI HENDRIX

Claim to Fame: Rock musician and one of the most talented guitarists who ever lived. His hits included "Purple Haze," "Foxy Lady," and an electric guitar version of "The Star Spangled Banner."

Cause of Death: Overdosed on sleeping pills and drowned in his own vomit.

Postmortem: Was Hendrix's death purely an accident? Was it a suicide? Was it a drug-induced combination of the two? We'll never know for sure. Hendrix, who'd been sliding deeper into drug addiction in the months preceding his death, was reeling from a number of poor concert performances earlier in the year. He was booed by an audience in West Germany, and he had walked offstage in mid-song during a concert at Madison Square Garden, telling the audience, "I just can't get it together." Hendrix was also battling with his record company and having financial problems. On September 13, he had to cancel a concert performance in Rotterdam, The Netherlands, because his bass player Billy Cox had a nervous breakdown.

On September 17, 1970, Hendrix and Mick Jagger's ex-girlfriend Monika Danneman were in London. They went to a party and then to a bar, and returned home some time after 3:00 a.m. When Monika went into the bedroom, she saw Jimi with a large handful of sleeping pills. He reassured her that he was only counting them, then had a glass of wine and went to bed. Monika watched him until 7:00 a.m., when she took a sleeping pill and went to bed, too. When she awoke at 10:20 a.m., she saw that Jimi was lying still and had vomit around his nose and mouth. The sleeping pills were gone. Monika panicked and called a friend for advice, who told her to call an ambulance. It was too late—when Hendrix got to the hospital he was pronounced dead on arrival. The last recording of Hendrix's voice is a message he left on his ex-manager's answering machine at 1:30 a.m. of the morning he died. On it Hendrix says, "I need help bad, man!"

LYNYRD SKYNYRD

Claim to Fame: One of the most popular rock bands of the 1970s.

Cause of Death: Plane crash.

Postmortem: In October 1977, the band released its fourth album, *Street Survivors*. The cover showed a picture of the band, surrounded by flames, and one of the featured songs was "That Smell," which included the lyrics, "Ooh, ooh that smell. The smell of death's around you."

A week later the band's plane crashed near Gillsburg, Mississippi, while en route to a concert date at Baton Rouge, Louisiana. Two people were killed, including Ronnie Van Zant, the band's lead singer and songwriter; and twenty other people on board were injured. Immediately after the crash, the band's record producer recalled every unsold copy of *Street Survivors* and replaced the fiery album cover with one portraying the band members against a black background.

THE WORLD'S TALLEST BUILDINGS, PART VIII

With all the technological marvels taking place around us, the competition for world's tallest building may not seem as interesting or as colorful as it once did...but it continues. Here's a quick summary of the record-holders of the last 30 years.

THE WORLD TRADE CENTER

In the late 1950s, lower Manhattan was a low rent district teeming with pet shops, electronics stores, auto parts stores, and other small businesses. In 1960, David Rockefeller, chairman of the Chase Manhattan Bank, proposed building a skyscraper to help revitalize the neighborhood. In 1962, the Port Authority of New York signed on to the project, and made plans to build a single office complex that would serve the needs of the "world trade community"—importers, exporters, shippers, international bankers, and government trade agencies.

Numerous designs were considered, including building one massive 150-story building, or three or four buildings 50 or 60 stories tall. The single building idea was rejected as being too tall; the multiple buildings were nixed out of fear that they would look like a "housing project." Finally, the architects decided on two massive towers that at 1,368 and 1,362 feet tall would be scarcely more than 100 feet taller than the Empire State Building, at the time, still the tallest building in the world.

The two towers, nicknamed "David" and "Nelson" after the Rockefeller brothers, opened in 1972 and 1973...and were met with almost universal scorn. As George Douglas puts it,

> The massive towers seem entirely out of scale with the tapering tip of lower Manhattan, rising abruptly into the sky like two upended florist's boxes....They remind one of a pair of giant's legs threatening to tip the whole island on its end, perhaps sinking everything into the sea. The effect on New York's graceful skyline has mostly been annoying and mocking.

The buildings weren't just ugly, they were also money losers for years, and they failed to revitalize lower Manhattan. They dumped so much office space onto the market at once that there wasn't any incentive to build any more...and the 9-to-5 workers who overcrowded the area during the day evacuated at night, leaving the neighborhood a ghost town.

THE SEARS TOWER

In 1974, Sears & Roebuck moved into Chicago's Sears Tower, which at 1,454 feet, eclipsed the World Trade Center in New York. For the first time in nearly 75 years, the city that was the birthplace of the skyscraper was again home to the world's tallest building. Sears planned to occupy the bottom 50 floors and rent out the rest. In *The Big Store*, Donald Katz gives us the Sears' point of view:

> "Being the largest retailer in the world," former chairman Gordon Metcalf had told *Time* magazine, "we thought we should have the largest headquarters in the world." The plan was to rent out the upper floors of the Tower until Sears employees occupied all 110 floors at the end of the century....Inside the company, the Tower was named for the vainglorious executive who ordered its construction. It was called "Gordon Metcalf's erection."

Unlike the World Trade Center towers and other skyscrapers that were typical of "modernist" designs of the 1960s and early 1970s, the Sears Tower tapered gracefully as it rose skyward, with "setbacks" at the 49th, 65th, and 90th floors. It was better received than the World Trade Center, but it still had its problems—namely wind and the building's 16,000 bronze-tinted windows. As Judith Dupré writes in *Skyscrapers:*

> Tenants are subject to terrifying high winds both inside and out. An employee on the seventy-seventh floor has said, "On very windy days, the building sways noticeably...the corner columns creak and groan...and my windowpane flaps and vibrates so alarmingly that I abandon my office." The windows—shattering so frequently that the Wall Street Journal devoted a November 2, 1988 article to the subject—are fast becoming the stuff of myth: the article quotes a secretary who "heard that one man was blown out and then blown back in."

Sears had its own financial problems in the 1980s—it moved out of the Sears Tower in 1988 and sold the building a few years later.

What city has the most taxicabs in the world? Mexico City—60,000 taxis.

END OF AN ERA?

Before the computer age, housing most or all of your employees and corporate files in one building was a necessity—people could communicate easily with one another and files were within easy reach. Computers and modern telecommunications have changed this. William Mitchell writes in *Scientific American:*

> The burgeoning Digital Revolution has been reducing the need to bring office workers together, face-to-face, in expensive downtown locations. Efficient telecommunications have diminished the importance of centrality and correspondingly increased the attractiveness of less expensive suburban sites that are more convenient to the labor force....Microsoft and Netscape battle it out from Redmond, Washington, and Mountain View, California, respectively...few of their millions of customers know or care what the headquarters buildings look like.

HEADING EAST

The Sears Tower has held the record for the world's tallest building for 25 years, and there are no buildings planned in the United States that will top it. Instead, several Asian nations are constructing buildings that, when finished, will push the Sears Tower to second, third, fourth place or even further behind. The Patronas Twin Towers in Kuala Lampur, Malaysia, for example, will rise to a height of 1,476 feet, when finished in late 1998, beating out the Sears Tower by 22 feet. The Kuningan Persada Tower, under construction in Jakarta, Indonesia, will be 1480 feet tall when it is finished in 1999.

Why are so many tall buildings being built in Asia, and so few in the United States? Because for a time, the Asia of the 1990s resembled the America of the 1900s. "Buildings that grab statistics like "world's tallest" or "world's second tallest," writes *The New York Times*' Paul Goldberger, "are the product...of cultures in the first flush of excitement at moving onto the world stage. Such buildings are assertions of power, demands to be noticed, and there is a particular moment in the life cycle of a rising culture when those impulses are irresistible."

Of course, the collapse of the Asian economy in 1998 will affect the status of many "tallest" buildings. Just how remains to be seen.

28 countries fought in World War II, the most of any war in human history.

YOU AIN'T SEEN NOTHIN' YET

Will the digital revolution put a stop to the seemingly endless contest to see who can build the world's tallest building? Not likely...at least not any time soon. "In the 21st century, as in the time of Cheops, there will be undoubtedly taller and taller buildings, built at great effort and often without real economic justification," William Mitchell writes, "because the rich and powerful will still sometimes find satisfaction in traditional ways that they're on top of the heap."

* * * * *

AND NOW FOR A CHANGE OF PACE

Whew! That was a long piece—eight sections on tall buildings. Kinda makes us want to write something silly—like these kids' musical bloopers collected in the Missouri School Music Newsletter. *(They insist they're real, and, of course, we believe them.)*

- "Beethoven wrote music even though he was deaf. He was so deaf he wrote loud music. Beethoven expired in 1827 and later died from this."
- "A virtuoso is a musician with real high morals.
- "Refrain means don't do it. A refrain in music is the part you better not try to sing."
- "When electric currents go through them, guitars start making sounds. So would anybody."
- "My very best liked piece of music is the Bronze Lullaby."
- "Probably the most marvelous fugue was the one between the Hatfields and the McCoys."
- "Most authorities agree that music of antiquity was written long ago."
- "I know what a sextet is, but I had rather not say."

THE TOP 10 HITS OF THE YEAR, 1992–1995

The hits keep coming. Here's another BRI Top Ten of the Year list.

1992

(1) End Of The Road (from *Boomerang*) —*Boyz II Men*
(2) Baby Got Back —*Sir Mix A-lot*
(3) Tears In Heaven —*Eric Clapton*
(4) Save The Best For Last —*Vanessa Williams*
(5) Baby-Baby-Baby —*TLC*
(6) Jump —*Kriss Kross*
(7) My Lovin' (You're Never Gonna Get It) —*En Vogue*
(8) Under The Bridge —*Red Hot Chili Peppers*
(9) All 4 Love —*Color Me Badd*
(10) Just Another Day —*Jon Secada*

1993

(1) I Will Always Love You (from *The Bodyguard*) —*Whitney Houston*
(2) Can't Help Falling In Love (from *Sliver*) —*UB40*
(3) Whoomp! (There It Is) —*Tag Team*
(4) That's The Way Love Goes —*Janet Jackson*
(5) Weak —*SWV*
(6) Freak Me —*Silk*
(7) If I Ever Fall In Love —*Shai*
(8) Dreamlover —*Mariah Carey*
(9) Rump Shaker —*Wreckx-n-Effect*
(10) Informer —*Snow*

1994

(1) The Sign —*Ace Of Base*
(2) I Swear —*All-4-One*
(3) I'll Make Love To You —*Boyz II Men*
(4) The Power Of Love —*Celine Dion*
(5) Breathe Again —*Toni Braxton*
(6) Stay (I Missed You) (from *Reality Bites*) —*Lisa Loeb & Nine Stories*
(7) Hero —*Mariah Carey*
(8) All She Wants —Ace Of Base
(9) All For Love —*Bryan Adams / Rod Stewart / Sting*
(10) Don't Turn Around —*Ace Of Base*

1995

(1) Gangsta's Paradise (from *Dangerous Minds*) —*Coolio*, featuring L.V.
(2) Waterfalls —*TLC*
(3) Kiss From A Rose (from *Batman Forever*) —*Seal*
(4) Creep —*TLC*
(5) On Bended Knee —*Boyz II Men*
(6) Another Night —*Real McCoy*
(7) Don't Take It Personal (Just One Of Dem Days) —*Monica*
(8) Take A Bow —*Madonna*
(9) Fantasy —*Mariah Carey*
(10) This Is How We Do It —*Montell Jordan*

Originally, Jack-O-Lanterns were made from turnips.

AUNT LENNA'S PUZZLERS

She's back by popular demand! Here are two of Aunt Lenna's favorite brain twisters. See next year's Bathroom Reader *for the answers. Just kidding.* *See page 460 for the answers.*

Circle Words

The letters in the circles are in the correct order. Simply find where the words begin and in which direction the word is read.

1. T O / U P / A I

2. S N / H Y / P M

3. S U / E A / A N

Nine Dots

Using four straight lines, connect all nine dots without lifting the pen off the paper (i.e., a continuous line).

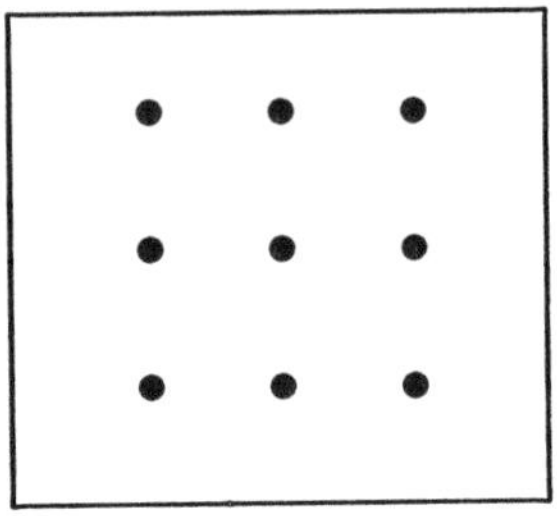

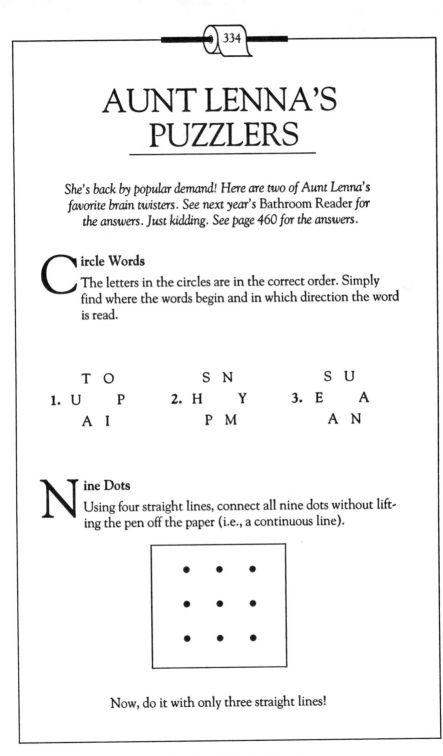

Now, do it with only three straight lines!

One in three American adults say their partner snores.

LIFE SAVERS

Longtime BRI writer Jack Mingo contributed this story of how one of the most popular candies in history was created.

MELTS IN YOUR HAND

In 1913, when air conditioning was still just a dream, candymaker Clarence Crane was having trouble with his business. He specialized in manufacturing chocolate—but it didn't travel well during hot summer months. As a result, candy stores ordered almost nothing from him between June and September.

To stay in business, the Cleveland native decided to develop a new line of hard mints—they tasted cool in the Midwestern summer, and they wouldn't melt. There was only one problem: His factory was only set up for chocolates. Luckily, he found a druggist with a pillmaking machine. Crane figured it would work for candy as well, so he commissioned the man to stamp out a batch.

HOLE LOT OF TROUBLE

As it turned out, the pill maker's machine was malfunctioning—it kept punching a hole in each mint's center. When he presented the first batch to Crane, the druggist promised he'd fix the problem for the next batch. But Crane said, "Keep it the way it is. They look like little life preservers."

That title was a little long to put on a pack, so he tried "Life Savers" and decided that he had an irresistible hook for the mints. He advertised his "Crane's Peppermint Life Savers" as a way of saving yourself from "that stormy breath" and designed a round paperboard tube with a label showing an old seaman tossing a life preserver to a woman swimmer. Still, he considered the product to be a sideline to his real business and didn't push it with any enthusiasm.

MEANWHILE, BACK IN NEW YORK...

Edward John Noble made a living selling ad space on streetcars in New York City. One day, he saw Crane's Life Savers in a candy store and bought a roll. He was so impressed that he jumped on a train to Ohio to convince Crane to buy streetcar ads. "If you spend a little money promoting these mints," Noble told Crane, "you'd make a fortune!"

A woman's sense of smell is most acute during ovulation.

Crane wasn't interested, but Noble persisted. To get rid of him, Crane sarcastically suggested that Noble buy the Life Saver brand. He'd even throw in the defective pill machine for free. Noble asked, "How much?" Caught unprepared, Crane blurted out, "$5,000."

Noble thought the price was a steal—but he didn't have that kind of money. He returned to New York and was able to raise $3,800. He went back to Cleveland and talked Crane's price down to $2,900.

PAPER-FRESH

Noble immediately ran into problems. He found that after a week on the shelves, the candy started tasting like the paperboard it came in. So he developed a tinfoil wrapper that kept the flavor fresh. But there were thousands of stale, old rolls on candy store shelves. Store owners refused to order any more unless Noble exchanged the old rolls for new ones. He made the exchanges, but the candy still didn't sell very well. Noble started giving away samples on street corners—to no avail.

COUNTER PROPOSAL

He then came up with what was, at the time, a brilliant new marketing idea: To sell his candy in other places besides candy stores.

Noble talked to owners of drug stores, barber shops, and restaurants, convincing many to carry Life Savers. He told them, "Put the mints near the cash register with a big 5¢ card. Be sure that every customer gets a nickel with his change, and see what happens."

It worked. With change in hand, some customers flipped a nickel back to the clerk and took a pack. Noble finally began making money.

SWEET SPOT

However, his success created a new problem. Other candy manufacturers quickly discovered the magic of counter displays for impulse sales. The space around cash registers started getting overcrowded.

Noble had another brilliant idea. He designed a segmented candy bin—leaving space for other candy products—but putting Life Savers in the best position...across the top. They were so successful that Life Saver counter displays are still found next to many checkout lines.

Meanwhile, the company began expanding its line from its original Pep-O-Mint flavor. Life Savers have since become the world's best-selling candy ever—with nearly 50 billion of the familiar rolls sold.

3 most landed-on Monopoly® squares: Illinois Ave., Go, and the B&O Railroad.

Q&A: ASK THE EXPERTS

More random questions, with answers from America's trivia experts.

PEEPING VINCENT

Q: *Why do the eyes in a painting or photograph follow you?*

A: "This is the result of the original sitting. If the subject was looking directly at the artist or the camera when the work was executed, they will seem to be looking directly at you, no matter where you stand. If, however, the subject was looking to one side of the artist, the eyes will never focus on the observer." (From *A Book of Curiosities*, by Roberta Kramer)

I'LL EAT JUST ONE

Q: *Why are some potato chips green?*

A: "Green potato chips are the result of something called sunscald. Potatoes are supposed to grow under the ground. Once in a while, however, part of the tuber might poke above the soil and be exposed to the sun. Being a chlorophyll-containing plant, the potato begins to turn green below the spots that were in the sun. While chlorophyll isn't bad for you, the solanine (a toxic chemical) produced may not be that great for you. There are no studies of how many green chips it would take to make you ill, but you may as well play it safe and toss them back in the bag anyway." (From *Why Does Popcorn Pop?*, by Don Voorhees)

BLINDED BY THE LIGHT

Q: *Why do moths fly into the light?*

A: "Moths aren't really attracted to light. Somehow, the brightness confuses the creature's sense of direction and it can't fly straight anymore. Scientists still don't completely understand why. They do know that, unlike human beings, the moth uses light rays from the moon or sun as a guide when it flies. The moth keeps itself moving in a straight line by constantly checking its position against the angle of the light rays striking its eyes.

"Although this complicated guidance system works fine when the light source is far away, it goes haywire when the light is close by. Stimulated by a bulb or candle, the moth's nervous system directs its body to fly so that both eyes receive the same amount of light. This locks the helpless creature onto a course toward the light and eventually causes it to blunder right into the bulb or flame." (From *How Do Ants Know When You're Having a Picnic?*, by Joanne Settel and Nancy Baggett)

LIKE A FISH UNDERWATER

Q: *Can a fish drown?*

A: Believe it or not, yes. "Fish, like people, need oxygen to live. There is oxygen both in the air and in the water. People breathe in the oxygen of the air through their lungs. When a man drowns, it's because he has used up his supply of oxygen and cannot get any from the water. So he dies. Fish breathe through gills rather than lungs. Gills can extract oxygen from water, but not from air. When a fish is pulled out of water, it soon exhausts its supply of oxygen, and 'drowns' because its gills can no longer function." (From *A Book of Curiosities*, by Roberta Kramer)

AFTER-DINNER DIP?

Q: *Should you really wait an hour after eating before swimming?*

A: "Water safety experts used to think...that stomach cramps caused by swimming on a full stomach were a leading cause of drowning. The cramps would cause you to double up in pain, you'd sink like a stone, and that would be the end of you. Later research, however, showed that stomach cramps were rare. It's still not wise to swim long distances on a full stomach because you might become dangerously tired. But splashing around in the pool is harmless." (From *Know It All*, by Ed Zotti)

MERRY XRISTOS

Q: *Why is the word* Christmas *abbreviated as* Xmas?

A: "Because the Greek letter *x* is the first letter of the Greek word for Christ, Xristos. The word *Xmas*, meaning 'Christ's Mass,' was commonly used in Europe by the 16th century. It was not an attempt to take *Christ* out of *Christmas*." (From *The Book of Answers*, by Barbara Berliner)

SERENDIPITOUS HITS

We've already done a few things with serendipity in this Bathroom Reader, *so we'll keep it going. Here are three songs that became hits...with a little help from serendipity.*

LET THE SUNSHINE IN / AGE OF AQUARIUS
—The Fifth Dimension

Background: The hit musical, *Hair*, had been on Broadway for about a year when the vocal group The Fifth Dimension arrived in New York City to perform at the Americana Hotel in 1969.

Serendipity: "Billy [Davis, of the group] lost his wallet in a cab," recalls Florence LaRue (also a group-member). "He didn't know where he'd lost it, but a gentleman called and said he'd found it and wanted to return it. Billy was grateful, but the man didn't want a reward. He just said, 'I would like you to come and see a play that I've produced.'

"Well, as it happens, he was the producer of the play *Hair*. And as we were sitting there listening to 'Aquarius,' we all looked at each other and said, 'This is a song we've got to record. It's just great.'" They took the song to their producer, who suggested that they combine it with "Let the Sunshine In." They recorded it in Las Vegas, where they were performing. "It was the quickest thing we ever recorded," says Florence. "And it was our biggest hit."

YOU AIN'T SEEN NOTHIN' YET—*Bachman-Turner Overdrive*

Background: B.T.O. was basically a family organization. Randy, who played lead guitar and sang, had been a charter member of The Guess Who. His brother Robby played drums, and his brother Tim played rhythm guitar. The bass player's name was Fred Turner (hence Bachman-Turner), but still another brother, Gary, was their first manager.

Gary had a speech impediment; whenever he got excited, he stuttered. And his brothers sometimes poked mild fun at him over it. One time, Randy brought a new song into the studio for the group's 1974 *Not Fragile* album. He started fooling around with the song, saying things like, "I'll now sing it like Frank Sinatra," and then croon away, just like Sinatra. Then he did a version in James Cagney's voice. Finally, he decided to sing it like stuttering Gary: "B-b-b-b-baby, you ain't seen nothin' yet." The brothers thought it was so funny that they decided to record it that way, intending only to send a copy of it to Gary as a gag. They planned to go back later and do a straight rendition.

Serendipity: But when they played the first takes of their album for Mercury Records, the stuttering tune was still on the tape—they'd forgotten to delete it—and Mercury wanted to include it on the record. Randy said no and tried to recut it in his regular voice, but it just didn't work. So the original rendition of "You Ain't Seen Nothin' Yet" went on the album. The next thing B.T.O. knew, Mercury wanted to release it as a single. Now Randy really objected. As the producer of the record, he could refuse to let the record company release it. And he did...for three weeks. Finally, figuring it wouldn't be a hit anyway, he relented. Within two months, it was the top record in the U.S. "It's a gold single now," he said in 1975. "I'm not so embarrassed anymore."

INCENSE AND PEPPERMINTS —*The Strawberry Alarm Clock*

Background: In 1967, a band manager brought producer Frank Slay a tape of a song that his group had recorded. "I thought it was an absolute stone smash," Slay says, "but there were no lyrics."

Slay sent the tune to a lyricist named John Carter and asked him to write "hip psychedelic" words to it. Carter wrote a song full of "meaningless nouns," which he titled "Incense and Peppermints." The group didn't like it, but they agreed to learn it.

Serendipity: Slay invited Carter to the studio for the recording session, and Carter made a major contribution. He didn't think the lead singer was right for his song, so he asked another member of the group to sing it instead. No one complained, and the group recorded "Incense and Peppermints" that day. However... the next day, the singer was gone. "Where is he?" Carter asked. "Oh, he's not even in the group," came the reply. "He's just a friend who'd dropped by for the day, to help with the harmony."

"Incense" hit at just the right time, when the "psychedelic sound" was starting to force its way into mainstream rock. It became the first psychedelic-pop hit. That anonymous singer wound up hearing himself wherever he went in 1967, on a #1 song.

VIDEO TREASURES

Here's another list of lesser-known movies available on video that the BRI recommends.

ROBIN AND MARIAN (1976) *Romance / Adventure*
Review: "Take the best director of swashbucklers, Richard Lester; add the foremost adventure film actor, Sean Connery; mix well with a fine actress with haunting presence, Audrey Hepburn; and finish off with some of the choicest character actors. You get *Robin and Marian*, a triumph for everyone involved." (*Video Movie Guide*) *Stars*: Sean Connery, Audrey Hepburn, Richard Harris, Ian Holm, Robert Shaw, Nicol Williamson. *Director*: Richard Lester.

ATLANTIC CITY (1981) *Drama*
Review: "An absolutely stunning film by Louis Malle, this English-language production is riveting from its first few shots and never lets up. It has the kind of rhythmically precise direction that bespeaks absolute artistic command, eliciting the maximum impact from the smallest of expressed emotions....Everyone involved is superlative, from Burt Lancaster and Susan Sarandon to the newcomer Robert Joy (who plays a new breed of punk kid to make your skin creep)." (*Movies On TV*) *Stars*: Burt Lancaster, Susan Sarandon, Robert Joy, Kate Reid, Hollis McLaren. *Director*: Louis Malle.

GREGORY'S GIRL (1981) *Romance / Comedy*
Review: "While American directors were churning out vile sex comedies about teenagers, Scotland's inimitable Bill Forsyth was making this charming, offbeat comedy about teenage puppy love. Gordon John Sinclair is a tall, gangly teenager who falls for the mysterious new girl in school (Dee Hepburn)—the star of the school's otherwise all-male soccer team....This sweet, extremely amusing film (which is brimming with clever sight gags) is like nothing made in the U.S." (*Guide for the Film Fanatic*) *Stars*: Gordon John Sinclair, Dee Hepburn, Chic Murray, Jake D'Arcy. *Director*: Bill Forsyth.

The U.S. has 12,383 miles of coastline; 6,640 miles of it are in Alaska.

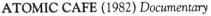

ATOMIC CAFE (1982) *Documentary*
Review: "A chilling, humorous compilation of newsreels and government films of the 1940s and 1950s that show America's preoccupation with the A-Bomb. Some sequences are in black and white. Includes the infamous training film 'Duck and Cover,' which tells us what to do in the event of an actual bombing." (*Video Hound's Golden Movie Retriever*) *Director:* Kevin Rafferty.

DARK EYES (1987) *Foreign / Drama (In Italian with subtitles)*
Review: "Mastroianni gives a tour-de-force performance as a once-young, idealistic, aspiring architect, who settled for a life of wealth and ease after marrying a banker's daughter...and proved incapable of holding on to what's important to him. A rich, beautifully detailed, multileveled film that's at once sad, funny, and haunting. Based on short stories by Anton Chekov (One of which was previously filmed as *Lady with a Dog*)." (*Leonard Maltin's 1998 Movie & Video Guide*) *Stars:* Marcello Mastroianni, Silvana Mangano, Marthe Keller, Elena Safonova, Pina Cei. *Director:* Nikita Mikhalkov.

BIG HEAT (1953) *Noir / Suspense*
Review: "This sizzling film noir directed by Fritz Lang features [Glenn] Ford (in his best performance) as an anguished cop out to smash a maddeningly effete mobster (Scourby) and break his hold on a corrupt city administration. With sensational support from [Lee] Marvin as a sadistic hood and [Gloria] Grahame as Marvin's bad / good girlfriend....Brutal, atmospheric, and exciting—highly recommended." (*Movies On TV*) *Stars:* Glenn Ford, Alexander Scourby, Lee Marvin, Gloria Grahame. *Director:* Fritz Lang.

BELIZAIRE THE CAJUN (1986) *Romance*
Review: "Belizaire the Cajun is a film that is atmospheric in the best sense of the word. The Louisiana bayou of the 1850s is richly recreated in a cadence of texture and deep, dark swamp-land colors, along with the rhythms of Cajun accents and full-bodied folk music (score by Michael Doucet). Armand Assante is Belizaire, an herbal doctor who finds himself in a mess of trouble because of his affection for his childhood sweetheart and his efforts to save a friend from persecution." (*Video Movie Guide*) *Stars:* Armand Assante, Gail Young, Michael Schoeffling, Stephen McHattie, Will Patton. *Director:* Glen Pitre.

"Nothing can be said about our politics that hasn't already been said about hemorrhoids."—Anon.

MEET MR. WHIPPLE

Finish this sentence: "Please don't squeeze..." See? It's obnoxious, but it's unforgettable. That why it's considered one of the most successful commercials of all time. Here's the story of how the great American hero of toilet paper, Charmin's Mr. Whipple, was born.

PAPER TRAIL

In 1957, Proctor & Gamble bought the Charmin toilet paper factory in Madison, Wisconsin. It was the consumer product giant's first move into the toilet paper business—and not a particularly auspicious one. At the time, Charmin was a regional brand sold in the northern, rural part of the state. It had a reputation, recalls one critic, for being a "rough-hewn, backwoods toilet tissue...a heavy-duty institutional, even *outdoorsy*-type toilet tissue." In other words, you might put it in your bomb shelter, but you wouldn't want it in your bathroom.

Proctor & Gamble improved Charmin's quality and launched an advertising campaign featuring a cartoon character called "Gentle the Dog." The new Charmin was "fluffed, buffed, and brushed," just like Gentle's fur, the ads said.

LESS IS MORE

In 1964, Proctor & Gamble researchers made a toilet paper breakthrough: they figured out how to make the paper feel softer. Instead of pressing water out of the wood pulp as it was being made into toilet paper, they dried the pulp with streams of hot air. The hot air "would actually 'fluff it up,'" one internal memo reported. "This allows for a deeper, more cushiony texture. An added benefit...is that less wood fiber per roll is required to make the same amount of this improved tissue." Less wood fiber meant the paper was cheaper to make than competing brands; the softer feel meant it could be sold for a higher price.

Throwing Ideas Around

But how would Proctor & Gamble get the word out about Charmin's new-found fluffiness? The company's ad agency, Benton & Bowles, experimented with ads showing Gentle the Dog going to court to change his name from Gentle to "Gentler." But test audiences hated the ad, so Gentle the Dog was put to sleep. What could they replace it with? A three-person creative team was assigned to come up with something. They had a roll of Charmin with them to serve as inspiration, but it didn't seem to work—no one had any viable ideas. "It was one of those Grade B movie situations," creative director Jim Haines recalls. He continues:

> We were having a think session, you know, a frustration session and we were not only kicking ideas around, we were tossing the roll around, and we started to get the giggles. John Chervokas [the junior copy writer] caught the roll and started to squeeze it and somebody said, "Don't squeeze it," and John said, "Please don't squeeze it," or "Please don't squeeze the Charmin," and it just happened. The thing just rolled off his tongue.

The team immediately sketched out a commercial that would have supermarket shoppers trying to squeeze Charmin the same way they would squeeze produce for freshness before buying it...and an angry store manager who tries to get them to stop, only to get caught squeezing it himself when he thinks no one is looking. "In an hour and a half," Chervokas recalls, "America's most universally despised advertising campaign became a reality."

FINDING MR. WHIPPLE

Proctor & Gamble, a conservative company, was reluctant to be associated with an ad that had people waving and squeezing rolls of toilet paper on TV. But they agreed to pay for three test commercials. B & B's creative team realized that the entire campaign depended on finding the right actor to play the grocer, whose name was Edgar Bartholomew.

"I was originally thinking of an Edmund Gwennish kind of character—you know, *Miracle on 34th St.* A lovable little fraud, maybe a little dumpy," Chervokas says.

What he ended up with was one of TV's biggest drunks. Until he got the Charmin part, Dick Wilson had enjoyed a long career in Vaudeville, movies and TV, playing mostly drunks. "I must have done over 350 TV shows as a drunk," Wilson recalls. "I'm the drunk on *Bewitched*. I was the drunk on *The Paul Lynde Show*. I did a lot of Disney's drunks."

Wilson still remembers the call he got from his agent about the part:

> My agent asked me, "What do you think of toilet paper?" And I told him I think everybody should use it. "No, no, no," he said, "I'm asking you how would you like to do a commercial for toilet paper, there's an audition tomorrow." I said, "How do you audition toilet paper?" and my agent said, "Please go and take a screen test." And I said a screen test would be a permanent record. But I went.

The Name Game

Wilson got the part right away, and five days later the first Charmin commercial went into production in—believe it or not—Flushing, New York. But they ran into trouble even before they started filming.

When agencies use a fictional name in an ad, it's standard procedure to find a real person with the same name and license it from them for a nominal fee—usually $1. That way, the agency can fend off anyone else who might claim their name is being used without permission. But this time, to their astonishment, the agency's lawyers couldn't find a single person named Edgar Bartholomew.

"So we looked through the Benton & Bowles employee list to see if any name there tickled our fancy," Chervokas says. "And, it just so happened that the late George Whipple, then head of Benton & Bowles' public relations department, was picked. He sold his name for a dollar." A few days later they taped the first ad, "Digby to the Rescue," in which Mr. Whipple calls on a policeman named Officer Digby to help him restore order to the toilet paper section, which is overrun with Charmin-squeezing women.

TRIAL RUN

The agency tested the first ad using what is known as a "Burke recall test"—they ran it during a television show on one TV station in the midwest, and then called viewers the next day to see if they remembered any of the commercials. Earlier advertising concepts scored as high as 27 points or as low as two points. "Officer Digby to the Rescue" scored 55 points, the highest recall score of any commercial ever tested.

The ads were just as successful when they hit the airwaves in 1964. Over the next six years Charmin shot up from zero percent of

How many times will you move in your life? If you're an average American, 11.

the toilet paper market into first place, beating out Scott Tissue for the number-one spot.

PROS AND CONS

The Mr. Whipple ads aired for 21 years, making it one of the longest-running and most successful advertising campaigns in history. And it made Dick Wilson a wealthy man. He was paid a six-figure salary, and only worked about 16 days a year.

Playing Mr. Whipple had its downside, though. As Dick Wilson the man became synonymous with Mr. Whipple, his life changed forever. "The face is so identifiable, I can't really do other work," he says. "And I've given up shopping in supermarkets. When I go through the toilet paper section I get some very strange looks.

He added, "I've guarded Whipple. I never go into blue movies or into sex shops. That wouldn't look nice, would it?"

SO LONG, MR. WHIPPLE

In 1985, Proctor & Gamble discontinued the Mr. Whipple ads in favor of something fresher. Can you remember what they replaced Mr. Whipple with? Neither can anyone else—Proctor & Gamble experimented with forgettable new campaigns for years after, and although they remained dominant in the toilet paper wars, they never found a campaign as memorable.

Likewise, Dick Wilson never had another success to match his long run as Mr. Whipple. He once did a spoof of the Mr. Whipple character in an A&W ad—he can't pick up a can of root beer without squeezing it and spilling it all over the place—but that was about it. A few years after the Whipple gig ended, Wilson retired from acting.

Not much more was heard from Wilson until 1996, when for no apparent reason, his lifetime supply of free Charmin stopped coming in the mail. The story made *USA Today* about a month later; the day after the article appeared Proctor & Gamble resumed the shipments. "He IS Mr. Whipple, and always will be Mr. Whipple," a company spokesperson told reporters, "and certainly we want to make sure nothing but Charmin goes in his bathroom."

FAMOUS FOR 15 MINUTES

Here's more proof that Andy Warhol was right when he said that "in the future, everyone will be famous for 15 minutes."

THE STAR: Jessica McClure, an 18-month-old infant in Midland Texas.

THE HEADLINE: *All's Well that Ends Well in Texas Well.*

WHAT HAPPENED: In 1987, McClure fell 22 feet down a well while playing in the backyard of her aunt's home. It was only eight inches in diameter and rescuers feared the well would collapse if they widened it. So they decided to dig another hole nearby and tunnel through solid rock to where Jessica was trapped.

After 58 hours, rescuers reached "Baby Jessica" and brought her to the surface. She had a severe cut on her forehead and gangrene on one foot that cost her her right little toe, but she was in remarkably good condition. The entire country watched the rescue unfold live on television. (At the time, it was the fourth-most-watched news story in television history.)

AFTERMATH: The McClure family was flooded with donations during and after the crisis. They used some of the money to buy a new house, then put the rest—an estimated $700,000 to $1 million—in a trust fund for Jessica to collect when she turned 25.

Baby Jessica, 12 years old in 1998, emerged from the experience unscathed (except for a few scars and the missing toe). She doesn't even remember the incident, and knows about it only from looking through her family's scrapbooks. The McClures divorced in 1990.

THE STAR: Fred Tuttle, a 79-year-old Vermont dairy farmer.

THE HEADLINE: *Man With a Plan No Flash in the Pan.*

WHAT HAPPENED: In 1996, Vermont filmmaker John O'Brien decided to make a film called "Man With a Plan," about a dairy farmer who runs for Congress because he needs the money. The farmer's campaign catches fire and he defeats the Democratic incumbent. O'Brien cast his neighbor Fred Tuttle, a retired dairy farmer, in the lead. The movie was a low-budget art house film, but it caught on in Vermont. Tuttle became one of the most recognized celebrities in the state.

AFTERMATH: When PBS made plans to air the movie nationwide in the fall of 1998, O'Brien suggested that Tuttle run against millionaire Jack McMullen for the Republican nomination for U.S. Senate as a publicity stunt to promote the film. Tuttle agreed to do it. "We thought McMullen was tremendously unqualified," O'Brien said, "but Fred's tremendously unqualified, too. So we won't hold that against McMullen."

Tuttle pledged to spend a total of $16 on his campaign. And since he was recovering from knee replacement surgery, he spent most of the campaign on his front porch, sedated with Demerol. He won the primary anyway, beating out a "carpetbagger" millionaire who'd just recently moved to Vermont. He went on to face incumbent Sen. Patrick Leahy in the general election. (He lost in a landslide.)

THE STAR: Kenneth Lakeberg, 25, father of Amy and Angela Lakeberg, conjoined or "Siamese" twins.

THE HEADLINE: *Family Faces Fears with Faith.*

WHAT HAPPENED: In 1993, Lakeberg's wife gave birth to twins who shared one heart and one liver. Their prognosis was bleak—both children were certain to die if they were not separated and one would surely die if they were. The Lakebergs decided to have the surgery. Angela was the healthiest of the twins, so she was the one doctors fought to save. The twins' plight, and the ethical issues surrounding the sacrifice of one's life to save the other, generated national attention. Thousands of dollars of donations poured in to help the financially strapped family pay for the surgery.

AFTERMATH: Within days, the story turned sour: Kenneth Lakeberg was revealed to have spent $8,000 of the contributions on a car, expensive meals, and $1,300 on a three-day cocaine binge before the surgery. "We ate at nice places," he explained. "We travelled good. I think we deserved at least that much." Later, Lakeberg spent time in and out of jail on a variety of charges, including stealing a friend's car. When Angela died in June 1994, he was in a drug rehab program, and his wife had to bail him out of jail so he could attend the

It takes twelve ears of corn to make a tablespoon of corn oil.

gram, and his wife had to bail him out of jail so he could attend the funeral.

THE STARS: Big Edie and Little Edie Beale, the aunt and cousin of Jaqueline Kennedy.

THE HEADLINE: *Filmmakers Find Two Nuts in Bouvier Family Tree*

WHAT HAPPENED: In 1961, Big Edie and Little Edie Beale, members of Jackie Bouvier Kennedy's family, travelled to Washington D.C. to attend John Kennedy's inauguration. Afterwards, they returned home to Grey Gardens, their 28-room mansion in East Hampton, New York...and never left the house again.

They were still there in 1973, living in two small rooms in an upstairs porch, along with raccoons, fleas, and dozens of cats in a "squalid" estate filled with overgrown weeds, when Jackie's sister, Lee Radziwill, approached filmmakers Albert and David Maysles about making a film portrait of her childhood with Jackie Kennedy.

The Maysles agreed and filmed various Bouvier kin...until they got to Big Edie and Little Edie. They found the pair so interesting that they abandoned Radziwill's project and made a film entirely about the Edies. In the film mother and daughter—surrounded by their cats—sing, dance, bicker, dress in bathing suits and bath towels secured with expensive broaches, and eat ice cream and boiled corn in bed. "I saw many signs of health in the Beales," Albert Maysles told the *Los Angeles Times* in 1996. "They don't have television, they don't drink, and they have a strong bond between them. I've always believed their lifestyle was their way of thumbing their noses at the aristocracy and all its snobbery."

AFTERMATH: *Grey Gardens* was released in 1976 and was an enormous critical success. It catapulted Big Edie and Little Edie into cult superstardom. "Perry Ellis was a huge fan," says Susan Fromke, who also worked on the film. "They used to have 'Grey Garden' parties with the film projected on the wall of a loft and people would wear their favorite Edie outfit."

Big Edie died about a year after the film was released. In 1979, Little Edie sold Grey Gardens to Ben Bradlee of *The Washington Post*. "Mother told me to sell it to keep it out of Jackie's hands," she explained. She moved to Miami Beach and was still living there in 1998.

10 of the tributaries flowing into the Amazon river are as big as the Mississippi river.

UNCLE JOHN'S PAGE OF LISTS

Here are a few random lists from the fabled BRI files.

5 PALINDROME SENTENCES (the same forward and backward)

1. You can cage a swallow, can't you. But you can't swallow a cage, can you?

2. Blessed are they that believe that they are blessed.

3. Parents love to have children; children have to love parents.

4. First ladies rule the state and state the rule: "Ladies first!"

THE 7 COMMANDMENTS OF ROAD RUNNER CARTOONS

1. Road Runner cannot harm coyote.

2. No outside force can harm coyote.

3. Only dialogue is "Beep-Beep!"

4. Road runner must stay on roads.

5. All locations are in the American Southwest.

6. All products must come from Acme Corp.

7. Gravity, when applicable, is Coyote's worst enemy.

—From *Chuck Amuck* (by Chuck Jones)

4 REAL-LIFE JOB INTERVIEW DISASTERS

1. A job applicant challenged the interviewer to arm wrestle.

2. A job candidate said he'd never finished high school because he was kidnapped and kept in a closet in Mexico.

3. A balding candidate excused himself and then returned wearing a full hairpiece.

4. An applicant interrupted the questioning to phone her therapist for advice.

—From *Parade*

4 WORST WARS FOR LOSS OF AMERICAN LIFE

1. Civil War: 529,332.

2. World War II: 405,399.

3. World War I: 116,516.

4. Vietnam: 54,246.

4 TERMS COINED ON "STAR TREK"

1. Warp drive

2. Mind meld

3. Phaser

4. Dilithium crystal

4 THINGS FIRST CREATED FOR THE 1960s SPACE PROGRAM

1. Freeze-dried foods

2. Cordless electric tools

3. Pocket calculators

4. Aerial photos used on TV weather reports

4 THREE STOOGES GAGS & THE SOUNDS THAT WENT WITH THEM

1. Poke in the eyes—accompanied by a violin or ukulele pluck.

2. Punch in the gut—kettle drum sound.

3. Ear twist—ratchet.

4. Curly's knees bending—a musical saw.

THE CURSE OF THE WEREWOLF, PART II

Fangs a lot for checking out Part II of our section on the werewolf legend.

ON TRIAL

Two of the best-known "werewolves" in European history are Peter Stube and Jean Grenier—famous as much for what they symbolize as for what they did. One was tortured to death; the other was confined to a mental institution. Stube lived in the 1500s; Grenier lived in the 1800s.

Peter Stube

It was big news when Stube was arrested in Cologne in 1590 and "confessed" under torture that he was a werewolf.

According to his confession, a female demon had given him a magic belt that he could use to turn into a giant wolf. For nearly 30 years, he had supposedly used this power to attack and kill villagers, livestock and even wild animals in the surrounding countryside. The townspeople accepted his confession, and he was sentenced

> to have his body laid on a wheel, and with red hot burning pincers in ten places to have the flesh pulled off from the bones, after that, his legs and arms to be broken with a wooden axe or hatchet, afterward to have his head struck from his body, then to have his carcass burned to ashes.

A pamphlet describing Stube's crimes and trial, illustrated with "gruesome" details, became a bestseller all over Europe.

Jean Grenier

By the 19th century, authorities were more enlightened about werewolves. They were skeptical when Grenier, a 13-year-old boy, "admitted" in 1849 to killing and eating "several dogs and several little girls"—all of them on Mondays, Fridays, and Sundays just before dusk, the times when he claimed to became a werewolf.

Philip Riley writes in *The Wolfman:* "The town's lawyer asked the court to set aside all thoughts of witchcraft and lycanthropy (werewolfism) and...stated that lycanthropy was a state of hallucination and the change of shape existed only in the disorganized brain of the insane, therefore, not a crime for which he should be held accountable."

Instead of sentencing Grenier to death, the judge ordered that he be confined to the monastery at Bordeaux, "where he would be instructed in his Christian and moral obligations, under penalty of death if he attempted an escape." Grenier slid even deeper into madness and died at the monastery seven years later. He was 20.

WEREWOLF DISEASES

Centuries after werewolves "roamed" Europe, scientists have found some real "curses"—diseases and physical conditions—that may have inspired the legends.

• ***Porphyria*** makes a person extremely sensitive to light...which would cause them to go out only at night. It creates huge wounds on the skin—which people used to think were caused when the afflicted person ran through the woods in the form of a wolf.

• ***Hypertrichosis*** causes excessive growth of thick hair all over the body, including the entire face. The disease is extremely rare. Scientists estimate that as few as 50 people have suffered from the disease since the Middle Ages—but it may have contributed to werewolf legends. When the sufferer shaves off the excess hair, they appear perfectly normal—which may have contributed to the idea that people were changing into wolves. Scientists believe the disease is caused by an "atavistic genetic defect," or a mutation that allows a long-suppressed gene to become active after thousands of years of dormancy. Human skin cells, the theory speculates, still have the ability to grow thick coats of fur that were normal thousands of years ago, but that evolutionary processes have "switched off."

• **The belladonna plant** was once eaten as medicine or rubbed on the skin as a salve. It also has hallucinogenic qualities when eaten in large quantities; eating too much can make people think they are flying or have turned into animals.

The real reason most of us know about werewolves today is because of the Wolfman horror films. That *story is on page 431.*

FAMILIAR PHRASES

Here are the origins of some phrases we use all the time... even when we don't know what we're saying.

COOK YOUR GOOSE

Meaning: Destroy one's chances or hopes.

Origin: "From a 16th century legend: King Eric of Sweden had come to an enemy town to attack it. The town's burghers, in a show of contempt for the king and his small band of men, hung a goose from a town tower and then sent a message to King Eric that asked, in effect, 'What do you want?' 'To cook your goose,' came the king's reply...whereupon the Swedes set fire to the town, cooking the goose in the process." (From *Eatioms*, by John D. Jacobson)

BONE UP

Meaning: Study (e.g., for an examination).

Origin: It has nothing to do with real bones. "It refers to a publishing firm named Bohn, which put out a guide (sort of like Cliff's Notes) in the early 20th century that helped the students pass Greek and Latin courses. Though the students called it 'Bohn up' at first, the term was soon changed to 'bone up' because of the obvious pun on '*bone*head.'" (From *Why Do We Say...?*, by Nigel Rees)

TO PACK A WALLOP

Meaning: Have a powerful punch or impact.

Origin: "In modern English 'to wallop' means to thrash, and in noun form, a heavy blow, but originally it...was slang for ale. The verb *pack* in this expression means 'to deliver.'" So, it was, literally, "deliver the beer." (From *Have a Nice Day—No Problem!*, by Christine Ammer)

LEAVE NO STONE UNTURNED

Meaning: Look for something in every possible place.

Origin: "Goes back to the battle between forces led by the Persian general Mardonius and the Theban general Polycrates in 477 B.C.

The Persian was supposed to have hidden a great treasure under his tent, but after he was defeated the victorious Polycrates couldn't find the valuables. He put his problem to the oracle at Delphi and was told to return and leave no stone unturned. He did—and found the treasure." (From *Dictionary of Word and Phrase Origins Vol. II*, by William and Mary Morris)

TO LOWER THE BOOM ON SOMEONE

Meaning: Attack someone unexpectedly.

Origin: "Comes from the days when pirates—or even disgruntled sailors—would rid themselves of an annoying crew member by taking advantage of the fact that he happened to be standing near the boom—a long pole which is used to extend the bottom of the sail. The sailor would quietly loosen the lines that held the boom up and quickly let it drop. The sudden drop, along with the force of wind, would cause the boom to swing violently, crashing into the unsuspecting victim, and knocking him overboard." (From *Scuttlebutt...*, by Teri Degler)

HOW NOW, BROWN COW

Meaning: What's up? What's next?

Origin: "'Brown Cow' is an old (18th century) way of referring to a barrel of beer, and it is likely that the saying was originally meant as a suggestion that everybody have another beer to prolong a pleasant interlude at the tavern. The idea of 'what's next' apparently derives from the question of whether or not to have another beer." (From *The Dictionary of Clichés*, by James Rogers)

BRING HOME THE BACON

Meaning: Win; Deliver a victory.

Origin: "In Old England any married couple who swore they hadn't quarreled for over a year, or had never wished themselves 'single again'—and could prove this to the satisfaction of a mock jury—was entitled to the famed Dunmow Flitch, a prize consisting of a side of bacon that was awarded at the Church of Dunmow in Essex County. This custom—which was initiated in 1111 and lasted until late in the eighteenth century—is how 'bacon' came to mean 'prize.'" (From *Animal Crackers*, by Robert Hendrickson)

Book with the longest English word in the title: ***The Baron Kinkvervankotsdorsprakingatchdern.***

LOST IN TRANSLATION

Have you ever thought you were communicating brilliantly, only to find out that other people thought you were speaking nonsense? That's a particularly easy mistake to make when you're speaking a foreign language. A few examples:

LAYING PIPE

When the Sumitomo Corporation in Japan developed an extremely strong steel pipe, they hired a Japanese advertising agency to market it in the United States. Big mistake: The agency named the pipe Sumitomo High Toughness, and launched a major magazine advertising campaign using the product's initials—SHT—in catchy slogans like "SHT—from Sumitomo," and "Now, Sumitomo brings SHT to the United States." Each ad ended with the assurance that SHT "was made to match its name."

PRODUCT CONFUSION

The Big Mac: Originally sold in France under the name *Gros Mec.* The expression means "big pimp" in French.

GM cars: Originally sold in Belgium using the slogan "Body by Fisher," which translated as "Corpse by Fisher."

The Jotter: A pen made by Parker. In some Latin countries, jotter is slang for "jockstrap."

Puffs tissues: In Germany, puff is slang for "whorehouse."

Cue toothpaste: Marketed in France by Colgate-Palmolive until they learned that *Cue* is also the name of a popular pornographic magazine.

Schweppes Tonic Water: The company changed the name from *Schweppes Tonic Water* to *Schweppes Tonica* when they learned that in Italian, "il water" means "the bathroom."

The Ford Caliente: Marketed in Mexico, until Ford found out "caliente" is slang for "streetwalker." Ford changed the name to S-22.

The Rolls-Royce Silver Myst: In German, *mist* means "human waste." (Clairol's Mist Stick curling iron had the same problem.)

Shortest Oscar-winning performance: Anthony Quinn's 8 minutes as Gauguin in *Lust For Life* (1956).

SERENDIPITY SELECTS A PRESIDENT

Serendipity isn't only a factor in little things, like bubble gum (see "It's Just Serendipity" on page 37). On at least one occasion, it helped pick a president of the United States. Here's the story.

TIGHT SITUATION

The presidential election of 1824 was a four-way race. Andrew Jackson got the most votes—with John Quincy Adams close behind—but didn't receive a majority. That meant the election would be decided in the House of Representatives. According to law, the candidate with the most votes in each delegation would get the state's electoral vote.

The House met to pick a president on February 9, 1825. It was close, but Adams was the favorite. Although he'd come in second in the popular vote, he had put together almost enough support to win the presidency on the first ballot.

However, if he *didn't* make it the first time around, his opponents felt sure that his support would begin slipping away. So the anti-Adams forces concentrated on keeping the election unresolved.

A CRUCIAL DECISION

As the vote approached, Adams was one state shy of victory...and there was only one state still undecided: New York. Their delegation was evenly split—half for Adams, half against. If it remained tied, New York's ballot wouldn't count...and the election would be forced into a second round. But there was a weak link in the anti-Adams camp. As Paul Boller writes in *Presidential Campaigns*:

> One of the New York votes [that anti-Adams forces] were counting on was that of General Stephen Van Rensselaer, the rich and pious Congressman from the Albany district....The old General went to the Capitol on election day firmly resolved to vote against Adams, but on his arrival he was waylaid by Daniel Webster and Henry Clay. They took him into the Speaker's Room and painted a dismal picture of what would happen to the country if Adams wasn't chosen on the first

Song with the longest title on Billboard's Top 40: "Jeremiah Peabody's Poly Unsaturated

> ballot. Van Rensselaer was deeply upset by the encounter…"The election turns on my vote," he told a cohort. "*One* vote will give Adams the majority—this is a responsibility I cannot bear. What shall I do?"

His friend urged him to vote against Adams, as planned, and Van Rensselaer agreed. Boller continues:

> But Van Rensselaer wasn't really resolved. He was still perplexed when he took his seat in the House Chamber. Profoundly religious, however, he decided to seek divine guidance while waiting to cast his [anti-Adams] ballot and bowed his head in prayer.

When he opened his eyes, the first thing he saw, lying on the floor, was a ballot with Adams' name on it. Van Rensselaer took this as a sign from God. He threw his other ballot away, picked the Adams ticket off the floor, and stuck it in the ballot box. As a result of this serendipitous moment, New York went for Adams, "and Adams was elected president on the first ballot."

* * * *

SERENDIPITY SAVES COLUMBUS

If it hadn't been for a serendipitous drink of water, Christopher Columbus might never have taken his trips across the Atlantic.

"In the 1480s," write Stefan Bechtel and Laurence Roy Stains in *The Good Luck Book*, Columbus "had been but one of many adventurers who believed it would be possible to reach the spice-rich Indies by sailing west." But he couldn't find a financial backer. For seven years he tried convincing the crowned heads of Europe to finance a voyage, and he always got "no" for an answer. "Eventually," say Bechtel and Stains, "he made his way back to the Spanish court for yet another audience with Ferdinand and Isabella. After listening to his plea, once again they turned him down."

> It was an insufferably hot day, so after leaving the court Columbus stopped at a nearby monastery to get a drink of water. He fell into conversation with one of the monks, and before long Columbus was pouring out his heart again, telling the holy man all about the voyage he hoped to make. The monk, it so happened, was also the Queen's confessor. And he was so taken with Columbus's speech that he spoke to Isabella, who granted Columbus yet another audience. And that time, at long last, Ferdinand and Isabella said yes.

Quick Dissolving Fast Acting Pleasant Tasting Green and Purple Pills," by Ray Stevens.

WHAT'S FOR BREAKFAST?

We probably take it for granted that the foods we eat for breakfast have always been around. Of course, they haven't. Here's the history of five foods we've come to expect on the table in the morning.

WAFFLES. Introduced to the United States by Thomas Jefferson, who brought the first waffle iron over from France. The name comes from the Dutch "wafel." Waffles owe much of their early popularity to street vendors, who sold them hot, covered in molasses or maple syrup. It wasn't until the twentieth century that the electric waffle iron made them an American staple.

ENGLISH MUFFINS. In 1875, Samuel Bath Thomas moved to America from England, bringing with him his mother's recipe for "tea muffins." He started out baking them in New York in 1880. In 1926, he officially named them Thomas' English Muffins.

FRENCH TOAST. Really does have its origins in France, where it's known as *ameritte* or *pain perdu* ("lost bread"), a term that has persisted in Creole and Cajun cooking. Throughout its history in America, it has been referred to as "Spanish," "German," or "nun's toast." Its first appearance in print as "French toast" was in 1871.

GRAPE JUICE. In 1869, Dr. Thomas Welch, Christian, dentist, and prohibitionist, invented "unfermented wine"—grape juice—so that fellow teetotalers would not be forced into the contradiction (as he saw it) of drinking alcohol in church. Local pastors weren't interested, so he gave up and went back to pulling teeth. His son Charles began selling it as grape juice in 1875.

PANCAKES. When the first European settlers landed in the New World, they brought pancakes with them. They met Native Americans who made their own pancakes, called *nokehic*. Even the ancient Egyptians had pancakes; in fact it's difficult to think of a culture that didn't have pancakes of one kind or another.

The first ready-made pancake mix came in 1889, when two men in St. Joseph, Missouri, introduced "Self-Rising Pancake Flour." They named it "Aunt Jemima" after a song from a minstrel show.

Wild country: 8 of the 10 largest national parks are in Alaska.

THE TOP 10 HITS OF THE YEAR, 1996–1997

Here's the last installment of BRI's Top Ten of the Year list.

1996

(1) Macarena (Bayside Boys Mix) —*Los Del Rio*
(2) One Sweet Day —*Mariah Carey & Boys II Men*
(3) Because You Loved Me (from *Up Close & Personal*) —*Celine Dion*
(4) Always Be My Baby —*Mariah Carey*
(5) Nobody Knows —*The Tony Rich Project*
(6) Give Me One Reason —*Tracy Chapman*
(7) Tha Crossroads —*Bone Thugs-n-Harmony*
(8) You're Makin' Me High / Let It Flow —*Toni Braxton*
(9) I Love You Always Forever —*Donna Lewis*
(10) Twisted —*Keith Sweat*

1997

(1) Candle In The Wind 1997 / Something About The Way You Look Tonight —*Elton John*
(2) You Were Meant For Me / Foolish Games —*Jewel*
(3) I'll Be Missing You —*Puff Daddy & Faith Evans*
(4) Un-break My Heart —*Toni Braxton*
(5) I Believe I Can Fly (from *Space Jam*) —*R. Kelly*
(6) Can't Nobody Hold Me Down —*Puff Daddy*, featuring *Mase*
(7) Don't Let Go (Love) (from *Set It Off*) —*En Vogue*
(8) Return Of The Mack —*Mark Morrison*
(9) Wannabe —*Spice Girls*
(10) How Do I Live —*Leann Rimes*

* * *

2000 Trivia

TIME FLIES. Dick Clark, America's perennial teenager, will be 70 years old in the year 2000.

HUH? According to a 1994 *Cosmopolitan* article, the "Cosmo Girl" in the year 2000 will be "an egg-freezing, libido-boosting dynamo with no glass ceiling, preparing for missions to Mars or donning the virtual-reality goggles for a shopping spree."

The U.S.S. Phoenix survived Pearl Harbor, was sold to Brazil, and sank in the Falklands war.

THE DUSTBIN OF HISTORY

Think your heroes will "go down in history" for something they've done? Don't count on it. These folks were VIP's in their time...but they're forgotten now. They've been swept into the Dustbin of History.

FORGOTTEN FIGURE: Nicholas P. Trist, Presidential envoy to Mexico, 1847-48.

CLAIM TO FAME: Trist negotiated the treaty that ended the Mexican-American war, and played a major role in opening the West. It should have been the crowning achievement of his diplomatic career. Instead, it cost him his job.

President Polk wasn't pleased with the way negotiations were going, so he ordered Trist to call them off and come home. Trist ignored Polk, stayed in Mexico and completed the negotiations. With the signing of the treaty in February 1848, he added the territories of California, Nevada, Arizona, Utah, and New Mexico to the United States, as well as parts of Colorado and Wyoming.

INTO THE DUSTBIN: Trist was fired for insubordination, and spent many years afterward working in obscurity as a railroad clerk. Finally in 1870, 20 years after Polk left office, Trist was officially recognized for achieving a major diplomatic coup.

FORGOTTEN FIGURE: Emile Coue, a pharmacist who dabbled in hypnotism.

CLAIM TO FAME: In 1920, Coue introduced a system of "healing through positive thinking" at his clinic in Nancy, France. As his reputation grew, he made appearances in London and, in 1923, the United States—where he was mobbed by throngs of admirers in packed lecture halls all over the country. He is best remembered for his famous phrase, "Every day, and in every way, I am becoming better and better." Frequent repetitions, Coue insisted, would spur the brain to cure just about anything.

Had Coue kept his claims modest, he would probably be remembered as one of the fathers of positive thinking. But he didn't; he claimed his chant could cure baldness, major illnesses, fight vice, re-

Three most common fears: spiders, people and social situations, flying.

duce crime, and even determine the gender—not to mention career—of a baby before it was born. "If a mother wants her unborn son to be a great architect," he explained, "she should visit great buildings and surround herself with pictures of architectural masterpieces and above all she should think beautiful thoughts."

INTO THE DUSTBIN: Coue returned to the U.S. for a second tour in 1924, but the crowds that greeted him this time were smaller. Reason: bald people who chanted his phrase all year were still bald, fat people were still fat, mothers gave birth to children in the wrong gender, etc. Patients began to abandon his clinic in France and Coue might have gone out of business entirely...if he hadn't dropped dead of a heart attack in 1926.

FORGOTTEN FIGURE: Cromwell Dixon, "boy" aviator

CLAIM TO FAME: The first aviator to fly over the Continental Divide. In 1911 a group of investors, which included circus owner John Ringling and the president of the Great Northern Railway, offered $10,000 to the first person who could fly over the Divide. At age 19, Dixon decided to try for the money. He left the Montana state fairgrounds in Helena on Sept 30, 1911, then headed for Blossburg, just over the Divide. His friends lit a bonfire on a high peak near the town to help him find his way. Little was known about mountain flying at the time, and a number pilots had been killed when downdrafts slammed them into the mountains. But Dixon made it, and collected both the money and considerable attention.

INTO THE DUSTBIN: Dixon was killed a few days later at Spokane, Washington when a sudden air current slammed his plane into the ground, "crushing him under the engine."

FORGOTTEN FIGURE: "Mr. Greeler," who is apparently so forgotten that nobody knows what his first name was. He was a nineteenth-century musical composer and patriot.

CLAIM TO FAME: Greeler set the entire United States Constitution to music in the 1870s. The entire composition, a six-hour opus, was performed for enthusiastic audiences in Boston in the 1870s. His recitative of the Preamble, and his fugues of the Amendments brought the house down.

INTO THE DUSTBIN: No known copies of Greeler's score survive today.

Five most commonly grown fruits on earth: Grapes, bananas, apples, coconuts, and plantains.

TARZAN AT THE MOVIES

There have been more movies about Tarzan than practically any other character. So it surprised us to find out that the first Tarzan movie was actually a flop. It took a smart press agent named Harry Reichenbach to make the "King of the Jungle" a box office success. He did it with the first film in 1917...and then he came back and did it again with the third one. By then, Tarzan was a movie franchise. Here's Reichenbach's account of what happened.

TARZAN OF THE APES

Background: In 1917, press agent Harry Reichenbach ran into a friend named Billy Parsons who'd just borrowed $250,000 to make the world's first Tarzan movie. The movie bombed at the preview and every distributor in the country turned it down. Parsons was desperate. Reichenbach watched the movie, and liked it. He agreed to publicize it if Parsons would give him a percentage of the profits.

Publicity Stunt: Reichenbach booked a theater on Broadway and filled the lobby with jungle plants, a big stuffed lion, and live monkeys in cages. And it "just happened" that on the day before the premiere, the newspapers were filled with accounts of the exploits of "Prince Charlie," an orangutan dressed in a tuxedo and top hat, who'd gotten loose inside the lobby of a fancy hotel that was filled with New York's elite. According to Reichenbach:

> Prince Charlie, timid and embarrassed, was about to introduce himself to this brilliant assemblage when he noticed a revolving door on the 42nd Street side and began to spin wildly around in it. Excited by this turn in social life, the big ape leaped into the lobby with greater confidence and cordially screeched at them to try his new sport, but they had all made a clearance in record time. The only way they could be persuaded to return was under cover of police.

When "someone" let the media know that Prince Charlie was a publicity stunt to promote *Tarzan of the Apes*, the newspapers covered the story a second time, letting the public know that the ape would be in the lobby of the theater for the opening.

What Happened: *Tarzan of the Apes* brought in more than $1.5 million at the box office, earning Reichenbach $50,000 and establishing both the Tarzan franchise on film, and Harry Reichenbach as a master press agent.

THE RETURN OF TARZAN

Background: Reichenbach was not hired to promote the second Tarzan film, *Romance of Tarzan*...and it flopped. So when Samuel Goldwyn produced the third Tarzan film, *The Return of Tarzan*, in 1920, he insisted that Reichenbach be hired again.

Publicity Stunt: A week before the film was scheduled to open, a "music professor" named Dr. T. R. Zan checked into the Belleclaire, one of New York's fanciest hotels, and had a large piano box lifted by block and tackle into his hotel room. Dr. Zan explained that he wanted to be able to play his piano in his room.

The next morning, Dr. Zan sent for room service. "I have a very delicate stomach," he told the bellhop, and he ordered two soft-boiled eggs, a piece of toast, and a glass of warm milk. "By the way," he told the bellhop, "I also want 15 lbs. of raw meat."

"With your—your delicate stomach?" The bellhop asked.

"No, it's not for me, foolish boy! That's for my pet." And with that, Dr. Zan opened the door to the adjoining room to reveal a lion sitting on the carpet. The bellhop told the management what he'd seen. They investigated and then called the police. Meanwhile, "someone" let a newspaper reporter know what was happening.

What Happened: According to Reichenbach,

> Every morning newspaper carried the story of T. R. Zan the next day. The newsreel weeklies didn't overlook it either. It was a story that caught the imagination and spread over the wires to all the papers in the country.
>
> A few days later, advertisements appeared announcing that *The Return of Tarzan* would open at the Broadway Theatre and only then did the stunt become apparent and the newspapers gave new publicity to the hoax, linking T. R. Zan of the Belleclaire Hotel with Tarzan of the pictures....The lion, Jim, appeared in person at the opening of the picture. We polled over 25,000 columns in news stories and established the film as a national hit.

THE AMAZING "SIR ORACLE"

Here's another excerpt from our book Uncle John's Indispensable Guide to the Year 2000. *At the end of the 19th century, practically every celebrity made predictions about the 20th. Most were laughably off-target...but every once in awhile someone showed an extraordinary gift at "seeing" into the future. One of these was David Goodman Croly.*

BACKGROUND In 1888, an obscure little volume with a long title—*Glimpses of the Future, Suggestions as to the Drift of Things (To Be Read Now and Judged in the Year 2000)*—appeared on bookshelves.

Ever heard of it? Its author, David Goodman Croly (who died shortly after its publication), was a newspaper columnist known as "Sir Oracle." Today, his work is considered a milestone in predictive literature. Historian I. F. Clarke calls him "one of the early American pioneers in writing about the future." To appreciate his feat, remember what life was like in 1888—the electric light had only been invented about a decade earlier; there were no cars, radios, movies, airplanes, television, etc. Here are some of his predictions....

Telecommunications: "In the year 2000, it will not be necessary to go to a meeting to hear a political orator, or to a church to be edified by a fine discourse, or to a concert hall to hear the noblest instrumental or vocal music. The telephone and the graphophone [sic] will be so perfected that we can enjoy these pleasures at our own homes."

The Green Movement: "No one should be allowed to cut down a tree without planting another in its place. Our wasteful destruction of forests is...a crime against the generations that are to follow us."

Careers for Women: "Women are largely beginning to support themselves; they are being educated with that view. Those who enter a lucrative calling do not care to be the wives of men who cannot keep up the standard of comfort they have set for themselves. Hence there are great classes of women beginning to take part in our modern life who are not dependent on the other sex."

The United Kingdom eats more cans of baked beans than the rest of the world combined.

Desktop Publishing: "It looks to me as if the journal of the future will dispense with the compositor or typesetter. The artist will be employed as well as the writer and their sketches and text will be photographs put on gelatin, or some similar menstruum, and multiplied ad infinitum. This will revolutionize the whole art of printing."

Tabloid Journalism: "It is sickening to take up a newspaper and read of murders, or of railroad and marine disasters, the abandonment of wives by their husbands and vice-versa...but it must be confessed that readers crave this kind of literary pablum."

Negative Campaigning: "The average politician wants to offend no one; this is why negative presidential candidates and 'dark horses' take the place of really able statesmen in our quadrennial contests."

No-fault Divorce: "Marriage is no longer a religious rite even in Catholic countries, but a civil contract, and the logical result would seem to be a state of public opinion which justifies a change of partners whenever the contracting couple mutually agreed to separate."

Legal Reform: "Our tedious legal forms waste the time and money of very busy people. Our Supreme Court is three years and a half behind its business. Every murderer can now have two or three trials. Thus time is wasted and costs continue to increase. By-and-by the people will not stand it, and a social convulsion may result."

Corporate Mergers: "The larger commercial movements of the age in all civilized countries are tending to mass wealth in fewer hands and to decrease the numbers and influence of the middle classes. Look at the great stores in all the capitals of the world!...These have driven out the small storekeeper, because they can give a better article for a lower price....The brain-work of the business world is destined in time to be represented by a very few great firms, who will practically be in control of the wealth of the several nations."

Air Transportation: "Aerial navigation will solve the mystery of the poles, and eventually there will be no 'dark region' on any of the continents. Of course all this seems very wild, but we live in an age of scientific marvels, and the navigation of the air, if accomplished, would be the most momentous event of all ages....If the *aerostat* should become as cheap for travelers as the sailing vessel, man may become migratory, like the birds, occupying the more mountainous regions and sea-coast in summer and more tropical climes in winter."

CROISSANT, COFFEE, AND BLOOD

This article was contributed by BRI member Jeff Cheek. It's a great example of the role serendipity plays in history (and our diet). At the very least, it should make ordering a cup of coffee and a croissant more interesting.

ON THE ROPES

From July 17 until September 12, 1683, the Austrian capital of Vienna was besieged by a Moslem army commanded by the Turkish Grand Vizier, Kara Mustafa. Historians note this as the high-water mark of Islamic influence in Europe. If the Moslems had succeeded here, it's likely they would have taken all of Europe.

After Vienna was encircled, a Polish mercenary named Kulczyski volunteered to go for help. Disguised as a Turk, he made his way through enemy lines. He was discovered, but his linguistic ability made his cover story believable. He escaped, made his way to Bavaria, and led an 80,000-man army back to Vienna.

The Viennese people had no way of knowing this—they were completely isolated as they beat back repeated Turkish assaults on their walled city. Their outer defenses were lost, but the besieged city held out.

ROLL TO VICTORY

In the early morning hours of September 12, a Viennese baker was preparing his dough for the next day's bread. He noticed that a tray of delicate breakfast rolls was vibrating. Why? They were acting as a seismograph, transmitting vibrations made by Turkish pickaxes. The Turks, it turned out, had decided to tunnel up to Vienna's walls, then launch a final assault. The baker sent his son to warn the city fathers, and the Austrians rushed to the ramparts just in time to repel the Grand Vizier's forces.

Kulczyski and the Bavarian army arrived a few hours later, sealing the Moslem defeat. After a bloody, 15-hour battle, the Turkish army fled, abandoning their tents and stores of food. The latter included thousands of sacks of hard, black beans, which the Austrians began to burn, because they believed the beans had no value.

A NEW TWIST

When the heroic baker was told to name his own reward, he asked to become chief baker in the royal palace. The request was granted. To impress his new masters, and to commemorate their narrow escape from the Moslems, he created a new breakfast roll. The star and crescent had long been a symbol of the Islamic faith, so instead of making ordinary round or oblong rolls, he rolled the dough out, then cut it into six inch triangles. He rolled these from the top corner, creating a humpbacked center with tapering horns. Just before baking, he twisted these horns down, forming a crescent.

Eighty-five years later, in 1770, a tactless Austrian princess named Marie Antoinette married Louis XVI of France. To ensure her supply of crescent rolls, she brought her own bakers from Vienna. The Royal French bakers were furious at this insult, but didn't dare protest. Instead, they fought back by creating a new and better breakfast roll. They retained the crescent shape to appease Her Majesty, but used pastry dough. Thus, the noble *croissant* was born.

BACK TO 1683

Meanwhile, back in 1683, Kulczyski was asked what reward *he* wanted for saving Vienna. His request was surprisingly modest: all he asked for was the sacks of black beans that the Austrians were destroying...and permission to open a business in Vienna.

Both were immediately granted.

It turns out that while making his way through the surrounding Moslem army, Kulczyski had been served a sweet, black beverage, which seemed to restore his energy. It was coffee—virtually unknown in Europe at that time, but a staple for the Turks.

Kulczyski collected all the Turks' unburned sacks of coffee beans and opened the first coffee house in Eastern Europe. Soon, all of Europe was drinking Viennese coffee, and Kulczyski became a wealthy and respected citizen of his adopted homeland.

There are $171 million worth of pennies, and $2.6 billion worth of dimes in circulation.

THE BIRTH OF BASEBALL CARDS

The origin of baseball cards, on page 104, is tied in with the history of cigarettes in America. The rest of the story is about kids...and money.

KIDS' STUFF

In the years following tobacco's exit from the baseball card business, cards were marketed directly to kids. They were used as promotions for candy, chewing gum, and cookies—but none were especially successful until 1928, when the Fleer Corporation invented bubblegum. As one sports historian writes, "Baseball cards had found a marketing partner to replace tobacco."

The Goudey Company was the first to combine bubblegum and cards, and they became the most popular distributor of cards in the 1930s. Other companies joined in, adding gimmicks to make cards appealing to kids. They issued sets with players' heads superimposed on cartoon bodies, included coupons for fan clubs, offered chances to win baseball gear, and so on. By the end of the 1930s, card collecting was beginning to take off as a hobby. Then World War II broke out, and resources were diverted to the war effort. Baseball cards all but disappeared.

CUTTHROAT COMPETITION

The business of baseball cards began in earnest after the war. The Bowman Company came out with the first annual sets of cards in 1948, and secured their investment by signing baseball players to contracts that gave Bowman exclusive rights to sell cards with bubblegum.

But with the introduction of color cards in 1950, baseball card collecting became the fastest growing hobby among boys in America—and competitors began lining up. The most important one was Sy Berger, an executive at Topps (the company that made Bazooka bubblegum), who genuinely liked baseball.

Berger convinced his bosses that they should start manufacturing and selling cards. He started hanging around the clubhouses of the

Five largest internal organs of the body: liver, brain, lungs, heart, and kidneys.

three New York teams, signing players to Topps contracts. To avoid infringing on Bowman's right to package cards with gum, Topps offered its cards with a piece of taffy. Bowman filed suit—but the court ruled that Bowman couldn't stop Topps from signing players to card contracts.

By 1955, Topps had outhustled its rival for player contracts. In 1956, Bowman conceded defeat and sold out to Topps. From the '50s through the '70s, Topps had a virtual stranglehold on the business. When the Fleer Corporation tried issuing cards with a cookie, Topps took them to court and won.

MONEY, MONEY, MONEY

Topps was selling 250 million cards a year, raking in millions of dollars in profits. But what did the players get? A whopping $125 for a *five-year contract*—plus a $5 "steak money" bonus. The amazing thing is, they were glad to get it; the average player salary in the 1960s was only $19,000.

Two things changed that: 1) a baseball players' union was formed and got involved in contract negotiations with Topps, and 2) in 1980, Fleer won an anti-trust suit against Topps. The judge ruled that any company was free to negotiate a card deal.

A year later, there were three companies willing to sign players to card contracts. And by 1988, there were at least a half-dozen more. Cards got fancier and more expensive...and baseball cards turned into big business.

• By 1985, baseball cards had passed stamps and coins as the most popular collecting hobby in the country.

• By 1988, card companies were selling *five billion* cards a year.

• By 1992, sports cards were nearly a $1 billion a year business. The industry leader, Upper Deck, was selling $250 million worth of cards and sports memorabilia annually. They paid former superstar Mickey Mantle—who made $100,000 a year at the peak of his career—$2.5 million to make 26 promotional appearances at memorabilia conventions.

PARADISE LOST

A baseball card glut, combined with the bad press that the 1995 baseball strike generated, slowed down the card business—and it may never hit its peak again. But there's no going back to the innocence of earlier decades. An adult attitude has settled over the hobby. As one critic puts it, "Once kids stuck the cards of their favorite players to the spokes of their bicycles. Now adults store their collections in safe-deposit boxes and fret over how much to insure their 1952 Mickey Mantles for."

MISCELLANY

- The first cards to list player stats on the back were put out by Mecca Cigarettes in 1918.
- In 1969, Topps goofed on Angel's 3rd-baseman Aurelio Rodriguez's card. They photographed the Angels' batboy, thinking he was Rodriguez, and put the *batboy*'s picture on the card.
- In 1989, a card of Baltimore Oriole Billy Ripken (brother of Cal) made headlines when it slipped past Fleer proofreaders. The card shows Ripken holding a bat over his right shoulder in a posed stance. At the bottom of the bat knob, written in black felt pen, is a "profanity." "Sometimes players play practical jokes on the photographers," said a Fleer spokesman. "We try to catch them before they go to press, but this one must have made it through."

How Baseball Cards Got Their Modern Look

Bill Hemrich owned the Upper Deck sports card and memorabilia shop, located just a short walk from the stadium where the California Angels played their home games. Around 1987, he shelled out $4000 for a stack of Don Mattingly rookie cards—which turned out to be fakes. Paul Sumner, a printing company executive, heard the story and contacted Hemrich. He sketched out an idea for a baseball card using hologram technology. The hologram design would be impossible to counterfeit, Sumner explained. Plus, it would set the cards apart from all the rest with a hip, high-tech look.

Together they formed Upper Deck Cards, got rich, and changed sports cards forever.

"I believe everyone should carry some type of religious artifact on his or her person at all times." —Bob Costas, explaining why he carried a Mickey Mantle card in his wallet.

60% of American men say they normally eat a hot dog in 5 bites or less.

THE SECRET CENSORS

We're guaranteed free speech by the Constitution. But, historically, there are lots of subtle ways the "free press" has kept that under control. Here are some amusing(?) examples from one of Uncle John's favorite books, If No News Send Rumors, *by Stephen Bates. (We highly recommend it for bathroom reading.)*

Dirty secret: "The *Los Angeles Times* bars the word 'smog' from its real-estate section. Ads may say 'cleaner skies,' but such phrases as 'no smog here' are forbidden."

Get them somewhere else: "The *Christian Science Monitor* refuses advertisements for, among other things, medicines and tombstones."

Speak no evil: "A 1985 regulatory ruling got almost no press coverage. The Occupational Safety and Health Administration (OSHA) had concluded that the oils in newspaper inks cause cancer and that ink barrels should include printed warnings."

What sweat?: "In the 50s and 60s, business considerations sometimes influenced newspapers' weather reports. Weather predictions in the *Sacramento Bee* never included the word 'hot,' which newspaper officials feared might dissuade businesses from relocating to Sacramento. Instead, even blistering weather was described as 'unseasonably warm.'"

No boycotts: "Some newspapers, at the urging of florists' trade associations, refuse to include the sentiment "Please omit flowers" in obituaries. A spokesman for one such paper, the *Pittsburgh Press*, explained that the phrase 'urges a boycott just like "Don't buy grapes," and we don't permit that.' "

Keeping people informed: "In 1966, CBS chose not to cover the Senate Foreign Relations Committee's hearings on Vietnam. Instead, it aired its regular reruns of *I Love Lucy* and *The Real McCoys*, among others....A few months later, CBS did interrupt its daytime programming for live coverage of the Pillsbury Bakeoff prize ceremony. The bake-off, unlike the Vietnam hearings, had a sponsor—Pillsbury."

BRANDO ON ACTING

Marlon Brando has long been regarded as one of America's great actors. Here are some surprising thoughts he had about his craft.

"Acting is fundamentally a childish thing to pursue. Quitting acting—that is the mark of maturity."

"I was down the tubes not long ago...you could see it when you rented a car; you could see it when you walked into a restaurant."

"If you've made a hit movie, then you get the full 32-teeth display in some places; and if you've sort of faded, they say 'Are you still making movies? I remember that picture, blah, blah, blah.' The point is, people are interested in people who are successful."

"An actor is at most a poet and at least an entertainer."

"Acting is like sustaining a twenty-five-year love affair. There are no new tricks. You just have to keep finding new ways to do it, to keep it fresh."

"If you play a pig, they think you're a pig."

"If you're successful, acting is about as soft a job as anybody could ever wish for. But if you're unsuccessful, it's worse than having a skin disease."

"If you want something from an audience, you give blood to their fantasies. It's the ultimate hustle."

"Acting is as old as mankind....Politicians are actors of the first order."

"An actor's a guy who, if you ain't talking about him, ain't listening."

"I'm convinced that the larger the gross, the worse the picture."

"Why should anybody care about what any movie star has to say? A movie star is nothing important. Freud, Gandhi, Marx—these people are important. But movie acting is just dull, boring, childish work. Movie stars are nothing as actors. I guess Garbo was the last one who had it."

Couch Potato Alert: There are 94 million TVs in the U.S....and 227 million in China.

WHATEVER HAPPENED TO FLYING CARS?

Still driving? Wouldn't you rather be doing loop-de-loops in a skycar like the Jetsons? If Paul Moller has his way, you will be, soon. Here's a piece from our book Uncle John's Indispensable Guide to the Year 2000.

UP, UP, AND AWAY

Contrary to popular belief, flying cars do exist. In fact, for three decades an inventor named Paul Moller has been hard at work developing a commercial model of his Skycar.

The Skycar is an incredible piece of machinery. It's a VTOL (vertical takeoff and landing) aircraft that rises straight up from the ground, switches to "forward-thrust," and then climbs 7,000 feet per minute. It can cruise up to 350 mph and reach a ceiling of 30,000 feet. It even goes 900 miles between refills (gas mileage is approximately 15 mpg).

MOLLER AND THE JETSONS

If it sounds like something out of *The Jetsons*, that's no coincidence. In the early 1960s, a magazine article on Moller's work caught the attention of Hanna-Barbera, the production team behind *The Jetsons*. They incorporated his design into their futuristic cartoon.

Ironically, Moller's craft is now compared to the TV series it helped inspire. "If you're thinking of the Jetsons, you have the right idea," wrote the *San Diego Union-Tribune*. "The futuristic jets driven by the cartoon family are the closest thing yet to the Skycar."

COMMUTE OF THE FUTURE?

Moller thought the Skycar would be well established by now. "It could be flying commuters to work in the millions by the year 2000," he told the *Chicago Tribune* in the late 1980s.

But he was wrong. Despite the fact that Moller has spent over $25 million developing the Skycar—and is well on his way to working out all the bugs—no major car or plane manufacturer is willing to back him financially. (Toyota and Boeing have been reportedly interested at different times.)

WHAT'S GOING ON?

One critic assesses the situation:

"Moller says that all the technical problems have been solved, and that product liability and production money are the only limiting factors left. He declares: 'If sufficient funds were available, we could...be demonstrating it in a matter of months.'

"The first units produced are estimated to cost about $800,000, and he has already 80 orders, each with a $5,000 deposit. At the production rate of several thousand units per year, each would cost about $100,000. After producing around 40,000 per year, the cost would become no more than a luxury car in comparison.

"Navigating the maze of Federal Aviation Administration approvals is still ahead...but how do you think the auto industry will react to this new airborne, commuter craft? In fact, since Moller's...designs will replace many helicopters and fixed-wing aircraft, his obstacles with powerful blocks of greedy men are only beginning."

*   *   *   *

WORD ORIGINS

LADY—Meaning: Polite term for a woman.

Origin: "In Old England a woman was proud to be known as the breadmaker, or *hlæfdige*. The word was subjected to many changes, becoming *levedi* in the thirteenth century, *levdi* and *ladi* in the fourteenth, and finally *ladie* and *lady* in the sixteenth." (From *Thereby Hangs a Tail*, by Charles Earle Funk)

JEOPARDY—Meaning: Danger.

Origin: "When a game was tied, the Romans called it *jocus partitus*, 'divided game'....The term came into French as *jeu parti*. Then it was applied also to any evenly matched opponents, so that the result was uncertain and the betting stakes (or lives) were in danger; hence, the English *jeopardy*." (From *Dictionary of Word Origins*, by Joseph T. Shipley)

DINER LINGO

Diner waitresses and short-order cooks have a language all their own—a sort of restaurant jazz, with clever variations on standard menu themes. In the second Bathroom Reader, *we listed some favorites. Here are more.*

Axle Grease: Butter

Baby: A glass of milk

Belch water: Plain soda water

A breath: A slice of onion

Burn the pup: A hot dog

Dough well done with cow to cover: Buttered toast

Mug of murk: Cup of coffee

On wheels: Take-out orders

A splash with dog biscuits: Soup and crackers

Black bottom: A chocolate sundae with chocolate ice cream

Mystery in the alley: A side order of hash

A bowl of bird seed: Cereal

Shake one in the hay: Strawberry milkshake

Pig between the sheets: Ham sandwich

All the way: Everything on it (mayonnaise, lettuce, onions)

High and dry: Plain

A crowd: Three of the same order

A team: Two of the same item

An order of down with mama: Toast with marmalade

Cream cheese with warts: Cream cheese and chopped olive sandwich

First lady: Spareribs

GAC: Grilled American cheese sandwich

Steak on the hoof: Rare steak

One on: Hamburger (on the grill)

21: Two burgers (two orders of *one*)

31: (three orders of *one*)

Keep off the grass: No lettuce

Cowboy: Western omelette

Warm a pig: Hot ham or pork sandwich

Put out the lights and cry: An order of liver and onions

A bowl of red: Chili

A cold spot: A glass of iced tea

Boiled leaves: A cup of hot tea

A brunette with a sand: Coffee with sugar only

Fish eyes: Tapioca pudding

Canned cow: Condensed milk

One on the country: Buttermilk

HANGOVER SCIENCE

If you've ever had a hangover, you've probably wondered what was going on in your body. It's surprisingly complex.

UNDER THE INFLUENCE

Here are some basic facts about drinking:

1. When you drink an alcoholic beverage, your body absorbs about 90% of the alcohol in the drink. The rest is exhaled, sweated out, or passed out in urine.

2. On average, a normal liver can process 10 grams of alcohol per hour. That's the equivalent of one glass of wine, half a pint of beer, or one shot of 80 proof spirits. (Exactly how much depends on a number of things, including your bodyweight and gender.)

3. Alcohol is a depressant, which means that it slows down the activity of your central nervous system by replacing the water around the nerve cells in your body.

4. Alcohol also changes the density of the fluid and tissue in the part of your ears that controls your sense of balance. That's why it can be difficult to walk, or even stand up, when you've had too much to drink.

WHAT CAUSES A HANGOVER?

Now we have to get a little technical:

- Your liver processes alcohol into a toxic chemical called *acetaldehyde*. Just as the alcohol made you feel good (or at least drunk), the acetaldehyde makes you feel bad. It's the accumulation of this chemical in your body, more than the alcohol itself, that causes hangover symptoms. (That's why the hangover comes *after* you've been drinking—the alcohol has been changed into acetaldehyde.) Specifically, acetaldehyde causes your blood vessels to dilate—which makes you feel warm, and can give you a headache.
- Meanwhile, the alcohol that's still in your system is raising both your pulse and blood pressure—which makes the headache even worse.

• And then there's the effect on your kidneys. When you're sober, your kidneys use a chemical called vasopressin to recycle the water in your body. But alcohol reduces the level of vasopressin in your body—which, in turn reduces your kidneys' ability to function. So instead of recycling water, you urinate it out. That makes you dehydrated...which can make your hangover worse.

• It's also possible that what you're experiencing in a hangover is a minor case of alcohol withdrawal syndrome—the same thing that chronic alcoholics experience when they stop drinking. "Your brain becomes somewhat tolerant over the course of an evening of heavy drinking," says Dr. Anne Geller, who runs the Smithers Alcoholism Treatment Center in New York City. "The next morning, as the alcohol is coming out of your system, you experience a 'rebound.' You might feel nauseous, maybe you'll have some diarrhea, maybe you'll feel a little flushed. Your tongue is dry, your head is aching and you're feeling a little bit anxious or jittery. Those are all signs of rebound, and that can be experienced as a hangover."

PREVENTATIVE MAINTENANCE

There are a few things you can do *before* you start drinking that may prevent the worst excesses of a hangover:

• Eat a substantial meal or at least have a glass of milk before you start drinking. It will help protect your stomach lining.

• Avoid champagne and dark-colored drinks, especially red wines. They contain byproducts of fermentation that may make the hangover worse.

• Drink a pint of water before you go to bed. The water will help minimize dehydration.

• The next morning, eat something sweet for breakfast, such as honey or jam. They contain fructose, which generates a chemical called nicotinamide adenine dinucleotide (NAD) that is involved in the processing of alcohol.

HANGOVER CURES

You can't cure a hangover once you've got one—it's that simple. Many "cures" only make things worse:

5 most dangerous jobs in the U.S.: logger, pilot, asbestos worker, metal worker, electrician.

• Aspirin and ibuprofin (Advil, Nuprin) can irritate your stomach lining, which is probably already upset from the alcohol. There's even some evidence that aspirin can make you feel even more drunk.

• Acetaminophen (Tylenol) can strain your liver, which already has enough on its hands processing the alcohol.

• Coffee just keeps you awake. Wouldn't you rather be asleep?

• Drinking more alcohol—the "hair of the dog that bit you"—doesn't work either; it only postpones the inevitable. The only people it helps are alcoholics, whose hangovers are compounded by symptoms of alcohol withdrawal.

Traditional Remedies

Here are some traditional hangover remedies. They don't work, either, but some are so disgusting that at least they'll take your mind off of being hungover:

• Swallow six raw owl eggs in quick succession.

• "Hangover Breakfast"—black coffee, two raw eggs, tomato juice, and an aspirin.

• Jackrabbit tea: Take some jackrabbit droppings, add hot water to make strong tea. Strain the tea; then drink. Repeat every 30 minutes until the headache goes away or you run out of droppings.

• Whip yourself until you bleed profusely. The loss of blood won't cure the hangover, but it will (1) make you groggy, and (2) serve as a distraction.

• Drink the sugary juice from a can of peaches.

• Add a teaspoon of soot to a glass of warm milk (hardwood soot is best). Drink.

• Spike some Pepto-Bismol with Coca-Cola syrup from the drugstore, or with a can of day-old Coke.

* * *

"A woman drove me to drink...and I never had the courtesy to thank her."

—**W. C. Fields**

Bob Zzzzzz, Otto Zzzzzz, and Z. Zzzzonzo are all listed in the San Francisco telephone directory.

GOING ABROAD

Here's another adventure in using foreign toilets from the book Going Abroad, *by Eva Newman.*

Have you ever been attacked by your bowel movement? Yes, actually chased? A friend experienced this event in his apartment in Moscow.

He had noticed his toilet, although outwardly appearing to be an old but normal closet-type Western-style toilet, had two internal differences. The drain hole was in the front part of the toilet bowl instead of the rear, and at the rear of the bowl was a slight spoon-shaped depression.

The surprising event occurred the first time my friend had a major movement in the toilet. He pulled the chain to flush the toilet and turned to leave. Splat! Right on the back of his legs.

Later, experimenting with his toilet, he learned the force of the water from the water tank high above the toilet propelled the excrement across the large spoon-shaped depression and over the rim of the toilet, especially when the seat was up. What a puzzling way to construct a toilet.

But why? A Russian friend helpfully explained that this toilet design was developed in the late 1800s, supposedly so that the depression could collect excrement for easy removal to the Russian fields for use as "night soil" fertilizer. The sole purpose of the water flush, the friend reported, was to rinse and clean the bowl after the excrement was manually removed.

Tall story or not, my friend in Moscow devised a way to deal manually with the spitting toilet, but how I will not reveal. I leave it to imaginative readers to ponder how they would solve my Moscow friend's toilet problem.

* * *

"Never take no for an answer from somebody who doesn't have the authority to say yes."
—*Anonymous*

Professions most likely to work nights: Police, security guard. Least likely: construction worker.

URBAN LEGENDS

Here's another batch of too-good-to-be-true stories that are floating around. Have you heard any of them?

THE STORY: Firefighters cleaning up the scene of a California forest fire are shocked to find the charred remains of a scuba diver hanging from the limbs of a burnt tree. An autopsy reveals that the cause of death was massive internal injuries sustained from a fall. An investigation reveals that he was diving off a nearby coast on the day of the fire...and was scooped up into a bucket of seawater being carried by a firefighting helicopter.

THE FACTS: The story, which sometimes involves a fisherman still clutching his fishing pole, has been around since at least 1987. It falls into one of the most popular urban legend categories of all: "What a stupid/unusual way to die!" (It's even popular in France, which has also been cited as the location of the incident.)

THE STORY: After playing a round of golf, a man with a habit of chewing his golf tee between holes complains he isn't feeling well. He checks into a hospital, and a few days later he dies. An autopsy reveals that insecticide from the golf course tainted the tee he was chewing, and poisoned him.

THE FACTS: This one is actually true. In 1982, Navy Lieutenant George M. Prior played two rounds of golf at the Army-Navy Country Club in Arlington, Virginia. By the time he finished, he was complaining of a headache; that night he checked into the hospital with nausea, fever, and a severe rash. He died ten days later. An autopsy determined that he died from an extreme allergic reaction to the pesticide used on the golf course.

THE STORY: The Red Cross conducts a volunteer blood drive at a local high school...and discovers that 20% of the student body tested positive for HIV.

THE FACTS: The rumor has been traced back to 1987, when it worked its way around the country, "attaching itself to whichever

Largest bell on earth: the Tsar Kolokol in Moscow. It weighs 222 tons and has never been rung.

high school had just hosted a blood drive." Teenage fear of the adverse consequences of sexual activity, coupled with parents' fear that their children are having sex, keeps this one alive.

Actually, between 1985 and 1996, the Red Cross tested 1.6 million samples of donated blood for HIV. Only 28 of these donors tested positive for HIV; of the 28, only one was a high school student.

THE STORY: A truck driver loses the brakes on his 18-wheeler while driving down a steep hill. He somehow manages to avoid hitting any cars and finally turns off onto an emergency exit ramp... where he runs over a picnicking family that has mistaken the emergency ramp for a rest stop.

THE FACTS: It never happened—but it's a good example of a classic urban legend theme: the tragedy is narrowly averted, only to result in a much bigger tragedy.

THE STORY: A woman buys a pair of shrink-to-fit jeans. Rather than shrink them in the washing machine, she puts them on and soaks with them in the tub, hoping they'll contour perfectly to her body. But they shrink so much that they crush her to death.

THE FACTS: It started with a TV commercial. In the mid-1980s, Levi's ran an ad for shrink-to-fit 501 jeans in which a man climbs into a tub with jeans on and soaks until they fit perfectly. The rumors started flying soon afterward.

This legend is an example of one of the most popular themes of all: the ridiculous fashion trend that kills. In the sixties, the "fatal fashion" was beehive hairdos filled with black widow spider nests; in the eighties, it was men stuffing cucumbers down the fronts of their tight pants, only to drop dead on the disco dance floor from lack of circulation.

* * * *

"Man does not live by words alone, despite the fact that sometimes he has to eat them."

—Adlai Stevenson

WORDPLAY

Another page of tidbits dug up by the erstwhile Tim Harrower while surfing the Internet.

SPECIAL WORDS

The longest word you can spell without repeating a letter: ***Uncopyrightable.***

The longest word with just one vowel: ***Strengths.***

The only English word with a triple letter: ***Goddessship.***

Longest commonly-used word with no letter appearing more than once: ***Ambidextrously.***

The word with the longest definition, in most dictionaries: ***Set.***

The longest common word without an a, e, i, o, or u: ***Rhythms.***

The shortest *-ology* (study of) word: ***oology*** (the study of eggs).

The only two common words with six consonants in a row: ***Catchphrase*** and ***latchstring.***

The longest English word with letters appearing in alphabetical order: ***Aegilops*** (an ulcer in the eye—we've never heard of it, either).

UGLY WORDS

According to a poll by the National Association of Teachers of Speech, the ten worst-sounding words in the English language are: *Cacophony, Crunch, Flatulent, Gripe, Jazz Phlegmatic, Plump, Plutocrat Sap, Treachery.*

MULTI-PURPOSE SYLLABLE

You can pronounce ***-ough*** eight different ways in the following sentence: *A rough-coated, dough-faced, thoughtful ploughman strode the streets of Scarborough; after falling into a slough, he coughed and hiccoughed!*

LEARN A FOREIGN LANGUAGE

Taxi is spelled the same way in nine languages: *English, French, Danish, Dutch, German, Swedish, Spanish, Norwegian, and Portuguese.*

EXCEPTIONAL WORD

Of is the only word in which an "*f*" is pronounced like a "*v*".

3 most popular dogs in the U.S.: Labrador Retrievers, Rottweilers, and Cocker Spaniels.

DOWN-HOME TYCOON

Some observations from one of America's richest men—Warren Buffet.

"That which is not worth doing is not worth doing well."

"If at first you succeed, quit trying."

"In the end, I always believe my eyes rather than anything else."

"It takes 20 years to build a reputation and five minutes to ruin it. If you think about that, you'll do things differently."

"Chains of habit are too light to be felt until they are too heavy to be broken."

"The only way to slow down is to stop."

"Someone's sitting in the shade today because someone planted a tree a long time ago."

"If principles can become dated, they're not principles."

"I keep an *internal* scoreboard. If I do something that others don't like but I feel good about, I'm happy. If others praise something I've done, but I'm not satisfied, I feel unhappy."

"I remember asking that question [How does he define friendship?] of a woman who had survived Auschwitz. She said her test was, 'Would they hide me?'"

"With enough insider information and a million dollars, you can go broke in a year."

"What I am is a *realist*. I always knew I'd like what I'm doing. Oh, perhaps it would have been nice to be a major league baseball player, but that's where the realism comes in."

"Wall Street is the only place that people ride to work in a Rolls Royce to get advice from those who take the subway."

"I want to explain my mistakes. This means I do only the things I completely understand."

The Arabic word for "forbidden" is "Harem."

A COMIC STRIP IS BORN

Here are more stories behind the creation of some of the world's most popular comic strips.

BLONDIE

Background: Blondie is the most popular "family" comic strip in the world, appearing in 55 countries and 2,200 newspapers. But it started out in 1930 with a very different story line. The stars were Blondie Boopadoop, a gold digger looking for a rich husband, and Dagwood Bumstead—who was, believe it or not, "a playboy, party animal, and polo player," and heir to the Bumstead railroad fortune. Dagwood spent most of his time partying and chasing Blondie.

A Strip Is Born: As the Depression got more severe, the company that distributed "Blondie" to newspapers worried that rich airheads wouldn't amuse people anymore. They told the strip's creator, Chic Young, to "go back to the drawing board and start over" with something readers could relate to. He did. In 1933, Dagwood and Blondie surprised everyone by falling in love. Dagwood's parents objected to their marriage...and disinherited him. Result: He had to get a job, which made the Bumsteads "common folk." From then on, the jokes could be about the problems of ordinary life—getting up for work, missing the bus, pleasing the boss, making ends meet, etc.

CATHY

Background: In 1976, at age 26, Cathy Guisewite was already a VP at an ad agency...but she was 50 pounds overweight and not terribly happy. One night, as she waited for a boyfriend to call, she realized "how pathetic" she'd become. She drew a few humorous pictures of herself eating junk food, waiting at the phone, and sent them to her mother.

Soon, she was sending these "illustrated versions of my anxieties" to her parents regularly. "Instead of writing in my diary," she says, "I sort of started summing up my life—my pathetic moments in pictures—and sending them home."

A Strip Is Born: Her parents saved the drawings and eventually suggested she try to sell them as a comic strip. "My mother had always taught me to write about things instead of talking to anyone," Guisewite says. "'If you're angry,' she'd say, 'don't scream at the person. Write about it. If you're hurt or jealous, don't go gossiping to girlfriends. Write about it. If you're lonely or sad or depressed, write about it.' Try to imagine my horror when—after a lifetime of teaching me to keep my feelings private—she insisted my drawings were the makings of a comic strip for millions of people to read."

Her timing couldn't have been better. Universal Press Syndicate had been looking for a strip dealing with women's issues, and this one, they said, was the first that had "some feeling, some soul." They bought the strip and named the main character after its author. Today, Guisewite says, "If I had ever had any idea how many people would one day be reading it, I would never have agreed to name her Cathy."

GARFIELD

Background: Jim Davis was too sickly to work on the family farm in Indiana, so his mother kept him supplied with pencils and paper and encouraged him to draw. When he graduated from college, he got a job as assistant to Tom Ryan, creator of the syndicated comic strip "Tumbleweeds."

A Strip Is Born: A few years later, Davis went to New York to sell his own strip—"Gnorm Gnat," about an insect. It was turned down. "They told me nobody could identify with a bug," Davis says. He looked for a subject people *could* identify with and noticed there were lots of dogs in successful comic strips—Snoopy, Marmaduke, Belvedere—but almost no cats.

So he decided to fashion a cat character after his "big, opinionated, stubborn" grandfather, James Garfield Davis, and sold it to United Features. The strip debuted on June 19, 1978, in 41 newspapers. During the 1980s, Garfield merchandising became a billion-dollar-a-year industry. For example, between 1987 and 1989, 225 million of those suction-cupped Garfield dolls sold.

Average number of bathing suits sold in America every second: 4.

STARWATCH 101

BRI member Jessica Vineyard contributed this illuminating piece on some astronomical basics. Perfect for reading by flashlight when you're out at night stargazing.

WHY DO STARS TWINKLE?

Have you ever tried to figure out whether something is a star or a planet by looking at the light shining from them? The easiest way to tell the difference is that stars twinkle, planets do not.

Why is this true? It's fairly simple, actually. Stars are so far away that the light from a single star—even the nearest ones (besides the Sun)—takes years to get to your eye. By that time, the beam of starlight that enters your eye is actually a delicate filament of light, easily affected by the ripples in the atmosphere. The rippling effect of the air around us is what makes the star appear to twinkle.

Planets, on the other hand, are much closer to us. In binoculars, or even with the unaided eye, you can actually *see* the round discs of planets. This light is from such a large, nearby source that it's not as easily affected by the turbulence in our atmosphere. Planets appear to have a strong, steady beam of light.

If you're not sure whether you're looking at a planet or a star, compare your target object with another source of light nearby. See if either of them twinkle.

WHY ARE STARS MEASURED IN LIGHT-YEARS?

A *light year* is the distance light travels in a year. How far is that? Well, light moves at 186,000 miles a second (it's the fastest thing in the universe), and there are 31,536,000 seconds in a year. So the equation is:

186,000 (miles) x 31,560,000 (seconds)

That comes out to about 6 trillion miles. Stars are incredibly far away. Our galaxy, for example, is more than 100,000 *light years* across. It's a heck of a lot easier to refer to their distances in terms of light years than any smaller measurement.

WHY ARE STARS DIFFERENT COLORS?

A star's color usually indicates its temperature. Generally speaking, blue stars are the hottest. The coolest are often red...and very large (called "red giants" because at the end of their lives, stars simultaneously cool off and swell up to 100 times their normal size). In between blue and red, in decreasing order, are white, yellow, and orange.

WHAT ARE "SHOOTING STARS?"

Meteors.

Okay, then—what are meteors?

Meteors are often the byproduct of comets, especially when they're in "meteor showers."

Explanation: When a comet passes near the sun, it leaves particles of rock and dust in its wake, called *meteoroids*. If the Earth passes near or through this trail of comet debris, some meteoroids are pulled toward us by gravity. They may get so close that they pass into our atmosphere—which quickly slows them down. (A lot like throwing a small rock into a pond of water.) We see a streak of light in the night sky, caused by vaporization of the meteoroid's particles. And that's when the meteoroid becomes a *meteor*, or shooting star.

How big are they? Most meteors are no larger than the toenail on your little toe. Many are just the size of a grain of sand. (Really!) But some can be the size of your fist and, in rare cases, the size of a large dog or even a car. Most burn out before reaching the ground, but when a large meteor enters the Earth's atmosphere, it can survive its fall and land somewhere on the planet.

Many meteors disappear into the water, never to be seen again. But some are found on land—especially on the Antarctic icefields. (If a rock is found on an icefield, it can only be from a meteor, since there are no other rocks around.)

When a meteor lands on the solid surface of the Earth, it becomes a *meteorite*. They're hard to find because, to the untrained eye, they look just like any other rocks. Good luck.

THE ANIMALS AT THE ZOO, Part 4

Here's more research from Uncle John's trip to zoo. For more, we recommend the book Beastly Behaviors by Janine Benyus.

WATCHING ZEBRAS

Behavior: Rubbing.

What It Means: They have an itch to scratch. Zebras rub up against trees, termite mounds or rubbing posts to scratch places they can't reach by themselves. They also rub to remove insects, loose hair...or dandruff

Behavior: Sniffing / Rubbing noses.

What It Means: Hello. Stallions from different groups will sniff each other's noses as part of a greeting ceremony. This defuses any potential tension or aggression.

Behavior: Circling.

What It Means: They're fighting. Zebras circling one another will try to bite each other while trying to avoid being bitten. They'll continue around and around, crouching to protect their hind legs until they're practically pivoting on their haunches.

Behavior: Neck wrestling.

What It Means: Fighting. After circling for some time, zebras often begin neck wrestling (similar to humans thumb wrestling). While one places his neck on top of the other's and pushes down, the zebra underneath is pushing up. Often, the zebra on the bottom will suddenly drop down and pull his head out, trying to get his neck across his opponent's.

Behavior: Lip curling.

What It Means: Courtship. After sniffing a female's rear and urine, a zebra stallion will raise his head with a lip curl gesture—nose in the sky and lips curled back. This seals his nostrils, helping the odor to travel quickly to his scent receptors.

5 most popular dog tricks in the U.S.: Sit, shake paw, roll over, speak, and lie down.

Behavior: Nibbling.

What It Means: Grooming. Zebras nibble by scratching their upper incisors against the other's coat, getting rid of loose hair and cleaning the skin. They begin by nibbling one side of each other's necks and backs. They continue on to their tails, then turn around and start working on the other side.

WATCHING PENGUINS

Behavior: "Slender walking"—walking with the beak pointed up, feathers sleeked back, and flippers held to the sides.

What It Means: "I mean no harm." Since penguins live in crowded colonies, they often have to walk by many other penguins just to get a drink of water. By putting its bill in the air, the bird is "symbolically taking its weapon out of commission." The slender walk is a penguin's way of saying "Don't mind me. I'm not going to bother you."

Behavior: Panting.

What It Means: Penguins pant to cool themselves down. Their bodies are designed to keep heat in; when temperatures reach 32°F, they need to cool off. They pant with their beaks open to take advantage of the cooling effects of evaporation.

Behavior: Pecking at another penguin.

What It Means: They're fighting. Penguins spar bill to bill. They'll peck and pull at each other trying to grab hold of the other's body. When they do get a grip, they often strike each other with their flippers.

Behavior: Mutual bowing.

What It Means: Courtship. Though a pair of penguins may be attracted to each other, both need to overcome their aggressive tendencies. Bowing helps them become more comfortable with one another.

Behavior: "Ecstatic displaying."

What It Means: This is a way for male penguins to announce ownership of nest sites and to attract females. An ecstatic displaying penguin will rear his head back, point his bill at the sky, fluff his crest feathers, roll his eyes back, wave his flippers, and give a loud *gaa aah aah aah* call.

The deepest trench in the Pacific Ocean is 28 times as deep as the Empire State Building is tall.

NOSTRADAMUS TODAY

Here's more on Nostradamus, from our book Uncle John's Indispensable Guide to the Year 2000. *For "The Secrets of Nostradamus," turn back to page 169.*

A BIG INFLUENCE

Even if you think Nostradamus and his prophecies are nonsense, you can't dismiss him as a cultural force. More than 400 years after his death, he still has an impact on people's lives.

For example:

- In 1980, a book by Jean Charles de Fontbrune, *Nostradamus: Historien et Prophète*, created a sensation in France with the claim that Nostradamus predicted an Arab attack on Europe that would soon trigger World War III. A poll conducted by *Paris Match* revealed that 75% of French citizens had heard of the book and 25% (17 million people) believed it.
- In 1988, a "mini-crisis" occurred in California when *The Man Who Saw Tomorrow*—a documentary about Nostradamus hosted by Orson Welles—predicted that a terrible earthquake would imminently destroy Los Angeles. Gossip columnists reported that so many celebrities had left town, it was easy to get good tables at Hollywood restaurants.
- In 1991, Japanese author Ben Goto reached the top of his country's bestseller list with *Predictions of Nostradamus: Middle East Chapter*, which purported to show how Nostradamus had predicted events leading to the Gulf War.

There are new Nostradamus books every year, adding to the thousands already in print. A bewildered publishing executive once told Uncle John: "It's amazing, but it seems that we just can't lose money doing books about Nostradamus." And in recent years, tabloids have cashed in on our fascination with Nostradamus. A typical headline in the *Weekly World News*: "New! Secret Predictions of Nostradamus! The Date Jesus Will Return to Earth...and Bring Peace to the Planet!"

The Battle of Bunker Hill was fought on Breed's Hill. Bunker Hill was nearby, though.

NOSTRADAMUS AND THE MILLENNIUM

As the millennium approaches, Nostradamus is becoming even more visible than ever. One reason is that he's in the public domain—no one owns the rights to his name or image, so companies can use it on products for free. For example, starting in 1998, people could call Nostradamus's 900 number for "psychic advice"...or buy a Nostradamus Watch to count down to the year 2000.

But a bigger reason is that Nostradamus is the father of apocalyptic prophecy for the millennium. He even gave us a specific date to fear—the seventh month of 1999.

DOOMSDAY 2000

In what is possibly his most famous passage—Quatrain 72 of *Centuries 10*—he predicts a millennial catastrophe.

> The year 1999, seventh month,
> A great king of terror will descend from the skies,
> To resuscitate the great king of Angolmois,
> Around this time Mars will reign for the good cause.

There are plenty of "expert" interpretations of this quatrain...and as you might guess, none of them are particularly cheery. For example:

- In *The Prophecies of Nostradamus*, Erika Cheetha concludes: "Nostradamus seems to foresee the end of the world at the Millennium, the year 2000....[But] first we must suffer the Asian antichrist, 'the King of the Mongols'."
- In *The Complete Prophecies of Nostradamus*, Henry C. Roberts says that "a tremendous world revolution is foretold to take place in the year 1999, with a complete upheaval of existing social orders, preceded by world-wide wars."
- In *Doomsday: 1999 A.D.*, Charles Berlitz warns of "the possibility of the earth being struck by a gigantic heavenly body" which he believes could refer to a comet, planetoid, or giant meteor.

No one knows exactly what he meant—if anything. But if you're reading this before July 1999, keep watching the skies. And if you're reading this after...well, not even Nostradamus could get *everything* right.

PARLEZ-VOUS BUREAUCRAT-ESE?

The phrases in the left column are terms you might hear dedicated bureaucrats use. The words in the right column are plain English. If you can match them, you may have a future in the government.

Doublespeak

1. "Decommissioned aggressor quantum"

2. "Negative gain in test scores"

3. "Retroactive definition"

4. "Wage-based premium"

5. "Wet deposition"

6. "Pre-dawn vertical insertion"

7. "Terminological inexactitude"

8. "Air curtain incinerator"

9. "Preventative detention"

10. "Consenual encounter"

11. "Ethnic cleansing"

12. "Neutralized"

13. "Gifts"

14. "Inhalation hazard"

15. "Inappropriate relations"

Real English

A. A lie

B. Police questioning

C. Jail

D. Um...well...never mind.

E. Dead enemy soldiers

F. Invasion

G. Open pit for burning trash

H. Killed

I. Drop in test scores

J. Money

K. This is what I really meant, though I said something else.

L. Tax

M. Acid rain

N. Genocide

O. Poison gas

Answers

1.E; 2.I; 3.K; 4.L; 5.M; 6.F; 7.A; 8.G; 9.C;
10.B; 11.N; 12.H; 13.J; 14.O; 15.D

5 countries with the highest divorce rates: Maldives, Liechtenstein, Peru, the U.S., Ukraine.

CLARKE'S COMMENTS

Here are a few thoughts from the eminent science fiction writer Arthur C. Clarke, author of 2001: A Space Odyssey.

"Politicians should read science fiction, not westerns and detective stories."

"Any sufficiently advanced technology is indistinguishable from magic."

"A faith that cannot survive collision with the truth is not worth many regrets."

"It may be that our role on this planet is not to worship God but to create him."

"This is the first age that's paid much attention to the future, which is a little ironic since we may not have one."

"How can extreme forms of nationalism survive when men have seen the Earth in its true perspective—as a single, small globe against the stars?"

"Sometimes I think we're alone in the universe, and sometimes I think we're not. In either case the idea is quite staggering."

"If an elderly but distinguished scientist says that something is possible, he is almost certainly right. But if he says that it is *im*possible, he is probably wrong."

"The realization that our small planet is only one of many worlds gives mankind the perspective it needs to realize that our own world belongs to all of its creatures."

"I don't believe in God but I'm very interested in her."

"The production of natural meat is so inefficient a process that it may even be prohibited by the twenty-first century. (But) the biochemists are making great progress; our grandchildren will love grass, and won't even know that they're eating it."

"The only way to discover the limits of the possible is to go beyond them into the impossible."

Number-one reason Americans give for visiting the doctor: "upper respiratory tract infection."

THE "EXTENDED SITTING" SECTION

A Special Section of Longer Pieces

Over the years, we've gotten numerous requests from BRI members to include a batch of long articles—for those times when you know you're going to be sitting for a while. Well, the BRI aims to please... So here's another great way to pass the...uh-h...time.

LIFE IN THE WHITE HOUSE

Just about everyone has wondered what it would be like to live at 1600 Pennsylvania Ave...but most of us will never know. Judging from the experiences of people who have *lived there, maybe that's not such a terrible thing...*

JAMES MADISON (1809-1817)

The first and so far the only president to be burned out of (white) house and home, was James Madison, president during the War of 1812. On August 24, 1814, four thousand British troops marched on Washington, D.C., setting fire to the Capitol building, the White House, and just about everything else they could torch. Madison wasn't home at the time—he was either out directing troops, or running away. But his wife, Dolly Madison, hung in there and managed to remove the Gilbert Stuart portrait of George Washington before the British arrived and gutted the building.

Washington, D.C. suffered so much damage that there was serious talk of moving the capital to some other city. It stayed put, of course, and the White House was rebuilt. But not before Madison left office. For about a year, he ran the country from Octagon House, the residence of the French Minister; and later from a house at 19th St. and Pennsylvania Avenue. Madison's successor, James Monroe moved back into the White House in 1817.

MARTIN VAN BUREN (1837-1841)

President Van Buren had the misfortune of being the person who moved into the White House right after it was vacated by President Andrew Jackson—probably the most raucous president ever to live there.

He inherited a White House "in a pretty sorry state of repair," Ethel Lewis writes in *The White House*. "The walls were all grimy with smoke, the floor coverings had had more than their share of tobacco juice, and most of the china and silver and glass had been broken."

The snow scenes in "It's A Wonderful Life" were shot during a record heat wave in Southern California.

Van Buren spent $60,000 on cleaning, whitewashing, and furniture repairs for the White House...only to have Congressman Charles Ogle from Jackson's own Whig party attack the newfound "regal splendor of the Presidential Palace," citing such wretched excesses as bracket lights, "ice cream vases," and the president's private bathtub. Van Buren spent less on the White House than Jackson had, but Ogle's attacks contributed to his losing the 1840 presidential election to William Henry Harrison.

JAMES BUCHANAN (1857–1861)

By the middle of the 19th century, Washington, D.C. had grown into a city with 50 thousand people. But it had no sewage treatment facilities, which resulted in serious sanitation problems for the city. The problem was so bad near the White House, Ethel Lewis writes, that:

> There was serious consideration of removing the President's house to a more salutary place and using the present building for offices only. Up to 1850, sewers from public buildings emptied onto the open ground south of the White House. There the water stagnated and made a marsh. Immediately following Buchanan's Inauguration, several residents of the National Hotel and its neighborhood died as the result of poison gases from obstructed, inadequate sewers.

CHESTER A. ARTHUR (1881–1885)

President James A. Garfield lived long enough to install the White House's first elevator for his mother, Grandma Garfield, but that was about it: he was assassinated four months into his term and Vice President Chester A. Arthur became president.

Unlike his plain predecessor, Arthur was a dandy who kept up with the latest fashions. He was so appalled at the condition of the White House that he refused to move in—even in time of crisis (Garfield's death)—until the White House was redecorated to his taste. On April 15, 1881, 24 wagonloads of White House furnishings were carted away and sold at auction to the highest bidder. Items sold included cuspidors, hair mattresses, marble mantles, a globe that had belonged to President Grant's daughter, and a pair of Lincoln's pants. Arthur then hired New York artist and decorator Louis Comfort Tiffany to redecorate from floor to ceiling. "Tiffany transformed the old mansion into an *art nouveau* palace," Kenneth Leish writes. "Throughout the house, everything that could be sprayed with

Rolls Royces being sent to Saudi Arabia are shipped without the

gold, was; everything that could be overstuffed, was; and every space that could hold a potted plant, held two." Arthur finally took up residence in the White House in December 1881.

BENJAMIN HARRISON (1889-1892)

Living in the White House must have been particularly difficult for Harrison, who shared the five-bedroom residence with his wife, her 90-year-old father, her sister, a niece, the Harrison's two daughters and son, the son's wife and daughter, and two other infants. There were five bedrooms in the residence at the time; so it's not surprising that First Lady Caroline Harrison was a strong proponent of enlarging the White House.

In 1891, Mrs. Harrison had an architect draw up plans adding an enormous wing to each end of the White House. The ends of the two wings would be connected by a long conservatory, creating an enclosed courtyard in back of the White House. Inside the courtyard, Mrs. Harrison proposed, would be a fountain commemorating both Columbus' discovery of the New World, and the laying of the White House cornerstone 300 years later. And the best part of all, at least as far as Mrs. Harrison was concerned, was that there would be plenty of room on the upper floors of the new wings for additional bedrooms and office space.

Mrs. Harrison's plans might well have succeeded if President Harrison hadn't offended Speaker of the House Thomas Reed, the "Czar" of Capitol Hill, by refusing to appoint one of Reed's cronies to a government job. Reed was so angry that he prevented the White House bill from ever coming to a vote. The Harrisons, all twelve of them, stayed put for four years.

THEODORE ROOSEVELT (1901-1908)

Roosevelt, who became president when McKinley was assassinated, was determined to enlarge the White House to suit the needs of both the growing country and his growing family—which numbered six children. Roosevelt added the West Wing, which houses the Oval Office, the Cabinet Room, the White House press office, and other Executive offices. Because the West Wing was built only one story high and was separated from the rest of the mansion by a long corridor, the appearance of the White House changed very little. Roose-

hood ornament depicting a woman reaching upward.

velt's distant cousin, Franklin Roosevelt, added the East Wing during World War II. It contained three stories of office space, including new offices for the First Lady, and the White House's first bomb shelter.

HARRY TRUMAN (1944–1952)

In 1948, Harry Truman authorized an expenditure of $10,000 to have a balcony installed on the south side of the second floor of the White House. He'd barely gotten around to enjoying it when he became the first president since James Madison to evacuate the White House out of fear for his life. "Found the White House 'falling down,'" he wrote in his diary. "My daughter's sitting room floor had broken down into the family dining room."

Truman had lived in the White House long enough to know that it wasn't in the best of shape—the floor in the upstairs study swayed and creaked when he walked across it, and the chandelier in the Blue Room swung back and forth for no reason. But he was astonished at what structural engineers told him: The beams that held the building up had been cut into so many times, and were carrying so much more weight than they had been designed to carry, that they had begun to split under the strain. The entire building was on the verge of collapse. The family quarters on the second floor were in particularly bad shape—they were being held up "purely by habit," the engineers told Truman.

Truman had three choices: (1) move away and have the White House designated a museum; (2) tear the White House down and build a replica in its place; and (3) save the exterior walls, tear down everything else, and replace it with an exact replica of the original interior. Truman chose the third option, and moved across the street to Blair House, normally the government's guest house for visiting heads of state. According to Kenneth Leish:

> Mantelpieces, wall paneling, fixtures, moldings—all were taken apart and stored away for later reinstallation. Then the whole interior was demolished....Steel beams were erected to support the new interior. The entire structure was fireproofed and air-conditioned. And the...outer walls were shored up....It took four years and more than $5 million, but when Truman moved back, in 1952, the presidential mansion was, as Abigail Adams had said too optimistically 150 years earlier, "built for ages to come."

You don't have to go to a Chinese restaurant for MSG. It occurs naturally in wheat.

OY VEY! *THIS* IS SESAME STREET?

Uncle John spotted this article in the Wall Street Journal *one day while he was doing "research." (You know where.) It's by Amy Dockser Marcus.*

PEACEFUL COEXISTENCE

Can you tell me how to get, how to get to Sesame Street? In the Middle East, the directions are downright confusing.

If you want the Israeli Sesame Street, look for a boardwalk with an ice-cream parlor and a view of the Mediterranean. For the Palestinian version in the same episode, head for street with a water well and a shop selling Arab sweets and a backdrop of West Bank-style hills and olive trees.

And if you want Muppets from both streets to get together, call in the American mediators.

In fact, Americans have been involved in this peace process from the beginning. A few years ago, producers at Children's Television Workshop, creators of the original "Sesame Street," came up with the idea of a joint Israeli-Palestinian version of the popular childrens' show. If former enemies like Yitzak Rabin and Yasser Arafat could shake hands, they figured, then why not Israeli and Palestinian Muppets?

NICE TRY

Both sides loved the idea, but with changes. After so many years of conflict, the Israelis and Palestinians didn't want to live together, even on Sesame Street. "They each insisted on having their own street," says Lewis J. Bernstein, the show's executive producer.

This isn't the first time the program has been tailored for a foreign audience. Seventeen foreign versions of *Sesame Street* are broadcast around the globe, and each has its own idiosyncrasies. The Russians came up with plot lines more appropriate for a Tolstoy novel, arguing that their children aren't used to more lighthearted fare. The French, Mr Bernstein says, insisted on giving Big Bird a face lift so he has a profile akin to Charles DeGaulle's. But the Israeli-Palestinian show is unique, the only one made by former enemies. In uncanny ways, the production mirrors the difficulties of the peace process itself.

"At one point I thought to myself, 'If it's like this between puppets, just imagine resolving all the difficulties between people,'" says Dolly Wolbrum, the Israeli producer.

BUMPY ROAD

From the start, there have been conflicts, large and small. The Israeli and Palestinian television studios signed separate contracts with the New York-based production company, rather than with each other. Each side has its own production crew, writes its own scripts and looks at (but can't veto) the other's story lines. The two sides' skits appear together on each episode, and both make concessions on dialogue and characters—often after endless discussions.

The Palestinians, for example, wanted one of their characters to say he learned Hebrew while serving time in an Israeli jail. The Israelis said that wasn't the right message. In the end, the Palestinians agreed the character could say he learned Hebrew while "working" in Israel.

The Palestinians insisted that the Israeli Muppets come to the Palestinian side only if they were invited, in contrast to the real-life period when, under Israeli military occupation, soldiers could enter homes at any time. The Israelis wanted to be more informal but conceded to the Palestinian request. As a compromise, two of the characters were made cousins to facilitate visits.

"STILL A TENSION"

Even so, the Palestinians insisted that the Muppets not be portrayed as being too friendly to each other. "The Israeli wanted 'full normalization,'" says Daoud Kuttab, the Palestinian producer, echoing the term Israelis use in peace talks with their Arab neighbors. "They wanted the Muppets to start dancing right away. We said no kissing, no hugging. There is still a tension between our two peoples. If the characters are too happy, the show won't succeed."

In many ways, this "Sesame Street" (which will appear on the same screen as "Rehov Sumsum" in Hebrew and "Shariyee Sumsum" in Arabic) is similar to the American original. The 60 half-hour shows, in production now and set for broadcast this winter in Israel,

Most common surnames in the U.S.: Smith, Johnson, Williams/Williamson, Brown, & Jones.

the West Bank and Gaza, teach children letters, numbers, colors and shapes. The program promotes awareness of the environment, health and safety and tolerance.

A big issue has been language. In some scenes, Ernie will ask a question in Hebrew, and Bert will answer in Arabic. Producers try to use a core of 3,000 words that are similar in both Semitic languages. Subtitles are out, for reasons practical (most viewers can't read yet) and cultural: "We insisted that there should be no Hebrew subtitles when our characters speak Arabic," Mr. Kuttab says. "We wanted Israeli children to accept us as we are. And Arabic is part of who we are."

ETHNICALLY CORRECT

The program has a Middle Eastern flavor. The Israelis created their own Oscar the Grouch named Moses; he lives in a broken-down car and often says "oof," a favorite expression of disdain among Israeli children. The Palestinians decided to pass on Oscar. "One Israeli grouch is enough," Mr. Kuttab says with a smile.

Each side was eager to create its own version of a Big Bird-type character—a lovable creature who would be central in the show. The Palestinians came up with Karim, a rooster typical of their villages and a symbol of national pride. The Israelis revived Kippy, a giant purple porcupine who had starred on a Hebrew version of "Sesame Street" produced in the 1980s. At that time, the Israelis even considered putting "an eye patch on Big Bird to make him look like Moshe Dayan," the famous one-eyed Israeli war hero, says Mr. Bernstein, who also worked on the earlier production. "He's practically a national figure," Mr. Bernstein says.

AVOIDING POLITICS

On the set at Israeli Educational Television's Tel Aviv studio, actors say that politics doesn't usually intrude. During a break in the filming, one Israeli crew member discovers that Husam Abu Eshee, a Palestinian actor who plays a music teacher on the show, learned to speak Hebrew in an Israeli jail while serving a four-year sentence on security charges. An Israeli crew member shrugs off Mr. Abu Eshee's past, saying she prefers to look forward.

The Palestinian actors didn't know that Guy Friedman, who plays

1st city in the world with a population greater than 1 million: Rome. 2nd: Ankor, Cambodia.

Kippy, served as an Israeli medic in the Gaza Strip during the Palestinian *intifada*, or uprising. That isn't a problem. Mr. Abu Eshee seems more interested in learning that this isn't Mr. Freidman's first time playing an animal; his last gig was as a cat in a production of "Alice in Wonderland."

Still, politics is always in the backdrop. When Palestinians brought their set to the Israeli studio, a security squad checked it for bombs. One of the "crossover" scenes, when Palestinian and Israeli Muppets visit each other's streets, was filmed a few days after a Palestinian blew up a Tel Aviv café, killing himself and four women. "We often ended up apologizing or explaining ourselves to each other," says Mr. Kuttab.

NO NEUTRAL GROUND

The American producers often find themselves serving as mediators.

After the Israelis and Palestinians nixed the idea of living on one Sesame Street, the Americans suggested building a third set, a park where residents of both streets would meet and play. The Israelis say they were willing to consider the proposal. But the Palestinians wanted to know who owned the park. "There is no neutral ground in this conflict," Mr. Kuttab says. "We felt strongly that there should at least be a sign in the park marking the border between Israel and Palestine."

Sitting in the studio waiting for Kippy and Karim to begin a scene together, Ms. Wolbrum, the Israeli producer, becomes agitated recalling the dispute over the park. "I kept arguing that no child would ask who the park belongs to. That's an adult perspective. The Palestinians kept saying that isn't how things are in real life. That's true, but is there an Israeli street with a purple porcupine walking around it in real life?" Ms. Wolbrum says.

The Palestinians wouldn't budge, and the idea was dropped.

Another American compromise, to have a joint water fountain located between the two streets, was nixed by the Israelis. The Americans liked the idea since the word for a spring is the same in Hebrew and Arabic, but the Israelis argued that the their children would confuse it with a similar-sounding Hebrew word that means "none." As a result, there is still no place on the show that Palestinians and Israelis share.

Bet on it: All 10 of the 10 largest hotels in the U.S. are in Las Vegas, Nevada.

There have been victories in how the two sides present each other. In one skit, Haneen, a Palestinian Muppet, comes to buy a book at a store on the Israeli Sesame Street. In another scene, an Israeli boy riding his bicycle takes a wrong turn and ends up on the Palestinian street. The Palestinian Muppets help him fix a flat tire.

Kippy learns that the Arabic and Hebrew words for body parts sound the same, and that Israelis and Palestinians like to eat falafel and hummus. After years of viewing each other as terrorists or occupiers, these images of normal daily life represent a sea change, some cautious stirrings of hope amid a peace process that has all but broken down.

The Israelis and Palestinians are now working on separate theme songs, and Mr. Bernstein is already worried about weaving the two tunes together. "I know we'll get there in the end," he says, "but there are times when I want to stand up and shout, 'Hey, you guys, enough already, we're talking about Sesame Street.'"

* * *

Dumb Riddles

1. A man builds a house with all four sides facing south. A bear walks past the house. What color is the bear?

2. Before the days of motor cars, a man rode into town on his horse. He arrived on Friday, spent three days in town and left on Friday. How is that possible?

3. Can a man legally marry his widow's sister in the state of California?

4. How much dirt is in a hole four feet deep and two feet wide?

Answers

1. White: the house is built directly on the North Pole. **2.** The horse's name was Friday. **3.** No—he's dead. **4.** There's no dirt in a hole.

"Booby prize" comes from the German *bubenpreis,* which means "boy's prize."

A BRIEF HISTORY OF THE JUKEBOX

Most of us think of jukeboxes as frivolous (or nostalgic) entertainment, but once they were considered mechanical marvels. They played a critical role in developing popular music; in the early 20th century, they were the first phonographs most people saw, and the only ones people could afford. Without them, there would have been no market for blues, jazz, or "hillbilly" music, and the record industry might not have survived. Hard to believe? Read on.

THAT'S AN EARFUL

When Thomas Edison invented the "Edison Speaking Phonograph" in 1877, it was an accident—he was actually trying to create a telephone answering machine. When that didn't work, he suggested a new use for it: a dictation machine for business executives.

The one thing Edison did *not* want his proud machine used for was entertainment. But that's precisely what happened.

THE MUSIC MACHINE

On November 23, 1889, a man named Louis Glass bought an Edison machine, installed a coin slot, and set it up inside the Palais Royale Saloon in San Francisco. Glass's phonograph didn't have much in common with 20th century jukeboxes: it played a wax cylinder; it had no electric amplifiers—just four listening tubes, so only four people could use it at a time—and it could only play a single song over and over.

But most people had never even *seen* a record player...so it was quite a novelty. The machine—which cost a nickel for a two-minute song—reportedly brought in more than $15 a week, big money in 1889. Glass set up a dozen more around San Francisco, and raked in the profits.

A NEW BUSINESSS

Word of the money-making machine quickly spread. Dozens of

saloons around the country copied the idea, and within a year a whole new industry had sprung up to capitalize on the fad.

THE AMERICAN ENTERTAINER

Seventeen years later, the first true "juke box" was introduced. It was called the "Automatic Entertainer"—a slightly misleading name, since it had to be cranked by hand. But it did play the new 10-inch discs instead of wax-and-cardboard cylinder recordings. It also offered more than one selection; it had a huge 40-inch horn instead of listening tubes (though you still couldn't hear it unless you were standing nearby); and it could even tell the difference between "slugs" and real coins.

Its most impressive feature, however, was its record-changing mechanism. This was mounted inside a glass cabinet at the top of the machine, and customers could actually watch the machine pick their record and play it. For most people, that was worth a nickel by itself. They would stand and gawk as the machine performed for them. Thereafter, the jukebox was as much of an attraction as the music it played.

AN ELECTRIFYING DEVELOPMENT

The Automatic Entertainer and its descendants dominated the industry for the next 20 years. But they were still missing something: volume.

In 1927—at about the same time that the electric guitar was being developed—the Automatic Music Instrument Company (AMI) changed that. They introduced the world's first electrically amplified music-playing machine.

"Electrical amplification was the single most important technical improvement in the history of the machine," Vincent Lynch writes in *Jukebox: The Golden Age*. "Suddenly the jukebox was capable of competing with loud orchestras. It could entertain large groups of people in large halls, all at once, for a nickel."

MUSIC NOT PROHIBITED

The timing couldn't have been better. In the late 1920s and early 1930s, radio was the hot new medium. It threatened to make both jukeboxes *and* phonographs obsolete.

If you're average, you'll look around a store for about 15 minutes before you buy anything.

But as soon as jukeboxes could be heard in crowds, they found a profitable new home: speakeasies. Alcohol had become illegal in 1920, and rather than stop drinking, millions of Americans started frequenting these illegal bars. They needed entertainment. "Automatic phonographs" were the perfect solution: they were cheaper and less risky than big bands, and more entertaining than a piano player.

In small, low-rent speakeasies, they were also the only way to get around the prejudice and elitism of radio. Network radio—as powerful an influence on music trends in the 1930s as MTV is on rock today—shunned most "race" music such as jazz, rhythm and blues in favor of classical and mainstream pop hits.

Because of this, black speakeasies—known as *juke joints* (originally slang for prostitution houses, *juke* came to mean "dance")—preferred to get their music from automatic phonographs. "For all practical purposes," says one music critic, "there was no place a black musician could have his records heard on a large scale but the jukebox." In time, the machines became so closely associated with juke joints that they became known as *jukeboxes*.

Well... To be fair, it wasn't just booze that saved the jukebox. Because of the Great Depression in the 1930s, most families couldn't afford their own Victrola phonographs and records. But they *could* afford to pop an occasional nickel into a jukebox.

THE GOLDEN AGE

Jukeboxes were a thriving industry in the late 1930s; their impact on the recording industry is hard to imagine today. In 1939, jukeboxes used 30 million records. In 1942, that number was up to about 60 million—half of all records produced that year.

But competition from network radio, home phonographs, and other sources grew increasingly fierce. One way jukebox manufacturers distinguished themselves was by making their machines as pleasing to the eye as they were to the ear. As late as 1937, jukeboxes had been virtually indistinguishable from the large wooden radios of the day. "But from then on," says Charles McGovern of the Smithsonian Institution, "the jukebox was more than a source of music. It was a showpiece, a spectacle with lights, color, and observable mechanical motion."

Manufacturers experimented with new designs involving glass, chrome, ornate metals, bubble lights, mirrors, special lighting, and plastics—which had just been invented—to give their machines beautiful new art deco designs that would stand out in any environment. Even the names of the machines were flashy: some popular models included Singing Towers, the Throne of Music, the Mother of Plastic, and the Luxury Light-Up.

The Wurlitzer 1015

But the most famous design of all was the Wurlitzer 1015, better known as "The Bubbler," thanks to its famous bubble tubes, which was introduced in 1946. In the next two years the company manufactured and sold more than 60,000 of them, making it the most popular jukebox in history and establishing Wurlitzer as the industry giant. "In most peoples' minds," says McGovern, "the 1015 is *the* Jukebox."

THE END OF AN ERA

Post-war sales of all jukeboxes were enormous: by the late 1940s there were more than 700,000 of them in the U.S., filling nearly every bar, bowling alley, malt shop—even gas stations and schools—with music. But mechanically they weren't all that different than the ones that had been around in the 1930s. Most jukeboxes contained about 20 records and played between 20 and 40 songs (depending on whether they could play the "B" sides).

The Seeburg

That changed in December 1948, when the Seeburg company introduced the Model M100-A, a jukebox that wasn't nearly as nice looking as the competition, but had a whopping 100 selections. Because it offered so many musical choices, it had the potential to make a lot more money than any other jukebox on the market. The golden age of jukeboxes was over—beauty would never again count as much as performance and profitability.

THE JUKEBOX BUST

The market for jukeboxes grew through the 1960s, but by the 1970s, it started to decline. There were lots of reasons: alternative rock, FM radio, cassette tapes, the rising cost of records (which

How about you? In 1997, the average American ate 131 restauarant meals.

forced operators to charge more for each play), and even drunk-driving laws. "That was a 'problem' I heard about from Virginia to Mississippi," says a veteran jukebox distributor. "The fact that the drunk driving laws were being enforced, that they got a little stricter, meant that bars started closing down. Took away a big market."

By 1992, there were fewer than 180,000 jukeboxes in America. Recently, compact-disc technology has created a new market for them—and there's talk of developing "digital" jukeboxes....But none of them is likely to be as exciting or important as the originals. To most of us, the machines that shaped pop music in America are just collector's items or curiosities.

*   *   *   *

OFF THE WALL

In 1937, the Seeburg Jukebox Co. introduced a machine that *didn't* have a record-changing mechanism exposed—so people couldn't watch the machine play their selection. Watching was such a big part of the jukebox experience that Seeburg, fearing customers would turn away, invented the "Wall-o-Matic" for diners and restaurants to install at every table, so customers didn't have to leave their seats to play music. They were a huge success. Other companies attempted variations, as Jack Mingo writes in *The Whole Pop Catalog:*

> Until 1941, Wurlitzer made an oversized counter-top jukebox that housed an entire phonograph. Another company put wheels on large wireless units, enabling waitresses to roll jukebox selectors up to their patrons. Neither overtook the Wall-O-Matic, which remains an integral part of diner decor today.

How did those wall units work? Nothing complicated—they were basically just speakers plugged into ordinary A/C outlets. When you choose your song, the box sends electrical impulses through the electrical wiring to the main jukebox—which registers the musical selection and returns it to the speaker the same way.

First National Historic Site in the U.S.: Ford's Theater, where Abraham Lincoln was shot.

GREASE IS THE WORD

More than $400 million and counting—that's what the movie Grease *has grossed worldwide. Not bad for a film that reviewers dismissed as "a thin joke" when it was released in 1978. Here's the story behind one of the most successful musicals of all time.*

DOO-WOP

In 1970, a Chicago advertising copywriter named Jim Jacobs threw a party for the cast of an amateur theater group he worked with.

"I [went] into my closet and dragged out all my old 45 records from the 1950s—Little Richard, Dion and the Belmonts, The Flamingos," he told Didi Conn in her book, *Frenchy's Grease Scrapbook*. "I started playing them in the midst of all the acid rock and psychedelic. Everyone at the party was going, 'What's this stuff?' And I said, 'Doo-wop. Don't you just love to doo-wop?'"

At some point during the party, Jacobs remarked to his friend, Warren Casey, that he thought it would be fun to write a 1950s musical about the kinds of kids he knew in high school...and score it with doo-wop. He even had a title—"Grease"—because in the 1950s "everything was greasy," he says. "The hair, the food, the cars, you know, everything."

THE MORNING AFTER

It was just a passing thought; Jacobs immediately forgot about it. But Casey didn't. He'd just been laid off from his job and had always envied the freedom Jacobs seemed to have as a writer. So he bought a typewriter and started pounding away. Two weeks later, he showed up at Jacobs's apartment with a scene he'd written for their musical. Jacobs was dumbfounded. "What musical?" he asked.

Then Jacobs read what his friend had written (it was the pajama party scene) and liked it so much that he agreed to collaborate on the play.

THE REAL THING

Grease debuted on February 5, 1971, in an old Chicago trolley barn

Second National Historic Site in the U.S.: the Abraham Lincoln Birthplace, in Kentucky.

that had been converted into a theater. (There's a story that it was originally five hours long—which we printed in our *Ultimate Bathroom Reader*. But Jacobs says that's not true—it was two hours long.) Their timing was perfect—a wave of '50s nostalgia was about to sweep America.

One night not long after it opened, two New York producers happened to catch the play. They realized how on-target it was and bought the rights. Then they helped rewrite it and took it to New York. *Grease* opened off-Broadway in early 1972...and was so successful that it moved to Broadway by June. It ran there for 3,388 performances. When it closed on April 13, 1980, it was the longest-running musical in Broadway history (*A Chorus Line* broke its record shortly after).

GOING TO THE BIG SCREEN

In the summer of 1974, a film producer named Allan Carr saw *Grease* on Broadway. He was so impressed that he called the next day to see if the film rights were still available. They weren't—someone was already planning to turn *Grease* into a feature-length cartoon.

Two years later, Carr went to the New York opening of Bette Midler's *Clams on the Halfshell*. "I'll never forget it," he says. "I was on the escalator going down to the lower lobby and realized that right in front of me were Ken Waissman and Maxine Fox, the producers of *Grease*. I tapped them on the shoulder and said, 'By the way, what ever happened with the film rights to *Grease*?'"

"'Funny you should ask,' Ken said. 'The rights lapsed today and the owners didn't pick up their option, so the film rights are available again.'"

Ugly Duckling

Grease was a legitimate Broadway hit by 1976, but newer, more serious plays like *Man of La Mancha* and *Company* were getting all the respect. *Grease* was considered the "bastard child of Broadway," Carr says, kind of like *The Beverly Hillbillies* on stage. That may have helped keep the film rights affordable—Carr got them for a paltry $200,000.

There was only one problem: Carr didn't have $200,000. As he tells Conn:

Only player ever to play for all 4 N. Y. baseball teams (Mets, Dodgers, Giants, Yankees): Darryl Strawb

> I asked if I could pay it on an installment plan, like I was buying a used car, and surprisingly, and happily for me, they agreed. And even more important, they also agreed that if some of the music from the stage musical wasn't quite right for the movie, we had the right to add additional songs to the picture. Without that interpolation clause, something that composers for the legitimate theater never agree to, "You're the One That I Want," "Grease," "Sandy," and "Hopelessly Devoted" could never have been in the movie.

Carr was a big believer in the film, but Paramount Pictures wasn't convinced. "Hollywood had stopped making musicals at that point," he says, "and they didn't think audiences wanted to see them. Paramount agreed to do it, but at a very modest budget." The studio coughed up $6 million, about half the usual budget for a feature film in the late 1970s.

CASTING ABOUT

Here's who would've been in the movie if Carr had landed his first choices.

• **Henry Winkler as Danny Zuko.** The Fonz from *Happy Days* was the logical choice for the part. And, as far as Winkler was concerned, that was exactly the problem. "I play this every week on TV," he told Carr. "Why would I do this as a movie?"

• **Susan Dey as Sandy.** The *Partridge Family* regular (later star of *L.A. Law*) turned it down. She was tired of playing a teen.

• **Stephen Ford (President Gerald Ford's son) as Tom,** Sandy's jock boyfriend. The aspiring actor made everyone jittery, including himself, when he showed up on the set with enough bodyguards to take on the Rydell High basketball team. A bad case of nerves wouldn't allow him to step in front of the camera.

• **Dick Clark as Vince Fontaine,** host of *National Bandstand.* Clark's price was too high. "He wanted more money than Travolta was getting," recalled Carr.

• **Cheryl Ladd as cheerleader Patty Simcox.** Not yet famous, Ladd was the wife of one of Carr's friends. She didn't mind being asked to be in the movie, but she'd already committed to replacing Farrah Fawcett on *Charlie's Angels.*

• **Lucie Arnaz as Rizzo.** Lucie's mom, Lucille Ball, was insulted when Carr requested a screen test. "I'm not letting my daughter do a screen test," she fumed. And that was that. Three days later, Stockard Channing was hired.

• **Andy Warhol as Rydell High art teacher.** Carr's "one and only regret" was that a studio executive shot down this idea. "I will not have that man in my movie," said the bigwig.

ENTER TRAVOLTA

After Winkler turned him down, Carr started looking for the right Danny again. He found his man by accident. Years earlier, a casting director had sent him a photo of an attractive young actor who was also an excellent singer and dancer. Carr didn't have any roles for the young man at the time, so he shoved the photo in a drawer. He found the photo—of John Travolta (then playing Vinnie Barbarino on *Welcome Back Kotter*)—and auditioned him.

Travolta had played Doody in the touring company of *Grease*. When he got the part as Danny, Carr arranged for Paramount to sign him to *Grease* as part of a three-picture deal; *Saturday Night Fever* was one of them.

Travolta was supposed to film *Grease* before he filmed *Saturday Night Fever*. But there was a clause in the contract that said *Grease* couldn't begin filming until the play ended on Broadway. "Well, the play went on for nine years," Carr says. "So we had to buy that part of the contract out. In the meantime, *Saturday Night Fever* came along....We finished in September, and *Saturday Night Fever* came out in late December, so by the time *Grease* was released, we did have a superstar." Travolta's celebrity helped turn *Grease* into the most profitable movie musical in Hollywood history.

ENTER NEWTON-JOHN

Meanwhile, Allan Carr set about finding another actress to play Sandy. He couldn't find anyone...until one evening when singer Helen Reddy invited him over for dinner. Pop singer Olivia Newton-John was the other invited guest. Carr was impressed by her innocent beauty, and he offered her the part. Newton-John agreed to have a look at the script, and by the time she got it, Sandy Dumbrowski from Chicago had been rewritten into Sandy Olsen from Australia. (Carr figured changing the script would be easier than changing Newton-John's accent.)

Newton-John was still smarting from her first film role, in a movie called *Tomorrow*. She hated the film and didn't want to be trapped in another film she didn't like. So she insisted on filming a screen test for *Grease*, and she reserved the right to turn down the part if she didn't like herself in the test. The test went fine, and she took the part.

CHECK THEIR I.D.'S

Dinah Manoff (Marty) was the only real teenager among the cast. She was 19. Travolta was 24, Newton-John 29, Jeff Conaway (Kenicke) 27, Didi Conn (Frenchy) 26, Barry Pearl (Doody) 27, Michael Tucci (Sonny) 28. Stockard Channing (Rizzo) was the oldest. She was 34.

BOOM AND BUST

Film critics hated *Grease* as much as the fans loved it. The *New Yorker*, for example, called it "a bogus, clumsily jointed pastiche of late 1950s high school musicals." Yet it was the #1 moneymaking film of the year and has since become the highest-grossing musical flick ever ($400 million worldwide).

In 1998, the critics greeted the 20th anniversary reissue of the film with their usual chorus of boos. "No revival, however joyously promoted, can conceal the fact that this is an average musical, pleasant, upbeat, and plastic," said one. "Because she looks genetically engineered," snapped another, "Newton-John didn't bring much life to the party."

Yet Grease keeps rolling on.

- The play has been staged an estimated 90,000 times by amateur and stock companies.
- The video of the movie has sold more than 11 million copies since its release in 1983, making it one of Paramount's top ten best-selling videos of all time.
- The soundtrack—with its three former Top Ten hits—still sells about 9,000 copies per week in this country. Total copies sold around the world: 20 million.

J. EDGAR HOOVER'S BIGGEST BLUNDER

Ever since the Japanese attacked Pearl Harbor in 1941, people have wondered if the U.S. could have prevented it. In our 7th Bathroom Reader, *we reprinted an article that speculated on whether President Roosevelt knew it was coming, and let it happen anyway, to draw America into World War II. (Answer: probably not.) In another volume, we told the story of how radar operators mistook Japanese planes on their screen for a mechanical malfunction. Now we have the ultimate story—the tale of how FBI Director J. Edgar Hoover had advance information about Pearl Harbor...and ignored it.*

POPOV...DUSKO POPOV

In 1940, agents for the Abwehr, Nazi Germany's military intelligence service, approached a 30-year-old Yugoslavian playboy named Dusko Popov, and asked if he'd like to become a spy for Hitler's war machine.

Popov detested the Nazis. But he accepted their offer...and then turned himself in to MI-6, the British counterintelligence agency. "Following intensive training by both the Germans and the British," Curt Gentry writes in *J. Edgar Hoover: The Man and the Secrets*, "Popov became one of Britain's most successful double agents, the misleading information he fed the Nazis resulted in a number of major intelligence victories."

Helping Out

Popov betrayed every German agent with whom he came into contact. As Ernest Volkman writes in *Spies: The Secret Agents Who Changed History*, because of Popov's work, the British "were able to identify every single agent or asset dispatched from Germany. Those sent to British territory were rounded up and evaluated as possible double [agent]s; those who either refused or did not seem suitable for the task were executed."

And because the British had cracked the Abwehr's secret codes, they could even monitor how well Popov's steady stream of misinformation was influencing decision-making in Berlin.

Most frequent "strange" customer request, according to supermarket managers:

...On Second Thought, Let's Not Invade

Popov's efforts may have even altered the course of the war by saving Great Britain from invasion and defeat at the hands of the Nazis. According to Volkman, Popov's greatest achievement was to convince the Germans, via cooked documents, that the British were militarily much stronger than the Germans assumed (although, in fact, Britain had no real power to halt a German attack in 1940). The deception played no small role in Hitler's eventual decision to abandon Operation Sea Lion, the planned invasion of the British Isles.

COMING TO AMERICA

The Abwehr was so completely fooled by Popov's deception, and so impressed with his work, that it gave him one of the most important intelligence assignments of the war. Suspecting that the United States would soon enter the war on the side of the British, the Abwehr ordered Popov to travel to New York and set up a spy ring that would study and report back on the size and strength of the U.S. military.

The assignment represented an incredible opportunity—not for the Nazis, but for the U.S. and Britain: With Popov's help, the U.S. government, acting through the FBI, might be able to monitor, mislead, and ultimately destroy all Nazi espionage efforts in the United States for the remainder of the war.

Meeting with the FBI

There was more: When Popov met with agents in the FBI's New York field office, he took with him two items of interest to the bureau.

The first was samples of the Abwehr's new "microdot" technology, which was capable of shrinking an entire page of text to a tiny dot the size of the period at the end of this sentence. The microdot could then be glued on top of a comma or a period in an ordinary typed letter and sent back to Germany through the regular mail. Even if the letter were intercepted and read, it was unlikely the microdot would be discovered because Great Britain and the United States had never seen anything like it.

The second item of interest was a 97-line questionnaire listing the information that Germany's ally, Japan, hoped to obtain with the help of Popov's spy ring. Most of the questions were general in nature, but four addressed military installations on the Hawaiian Islands, and five additional questions, the most specific of the list, asked about a naval base called Pearl Harbor. Here's the questionnaire that the FBI was handed:

Hawaii—Ammunition dumps and mine depots.

1. Details about naval ammunition and mine depot on the Isle of Kushua [sic] (Pearl Harbor). If possible, sketch.
2. Naval ammunition depot Lualuelei. Exact position? Is there a railway line (junction)?
3. The total ammunition reserve of the army is supposed to be in the rock of the Crater Aliamanu. Position?
4. Is the Crater Punchbowl (Honolulu) being used as ammunition dump? If not, are there other military works?

Naval Strong Point Pearl Harbor.

1. Exact details and sketch about the situation of the state wharf, of the pier installations, workshops, petrol installations, situations of dry dock No. 1 and of the new dry dock which is being built.
2. Details about the submarine station (plan of situation). What land installations are in existence?
3. Where is the station for mine search formations? How far has the dredger work progressed at the entrance and in the east and southeast lock? Depths of water?
4. Number of anchorages?
5. Is there a floating dock in Pearl Harbor or is the transfer of such a dock to this place intended?

BOMBS AWAY!

Popov had learned from a friend named Johann Jebsen, also a double agent, that the Japanese foreign minister and several top naval officials had taken an unusual interest in a stunningly effective attack by the British navy on the Italian port of Taranto. Using only 19 bombers launched from a single aircraft carrier more than 170 miles out to sea, the British navy had knocked nearly half the entire Italian fleet out of commission.

Jebsen himself had escorted the Japanese officials to Taranto, and he noted that they were particularly interested in the success of the British technique of dive-bombing the naval targets. When he learned of the questionnaire that the Abwehr had given Popov, he was convinced that the two were connected. "If my calculated opinion interests you," Jebsen told Popov, "the Japanese will attack the United States." Most likely at Pearl Harbor, most likely using dive-bombers.

STUCK IN NEW YORK

Popov told the FBI everything he knew. His information was good...perhaps too good. Percy "Sam" Foxworth, the FBI's Agent in Charge of the New York office, was skeptical from the start. "It all looks too precise, too complete, to be believed," he told Popov. "The questionnaire plus the other information spell out in detail exactly where, when, how, and by whom we are to be attacked. If anything, it sounds like a trap."

Popov was under orders from the Abwehr to go immediately to Hawaii, but the FBI vetoed the trip and ordered him to remain in New York until Director J. Edgar Hoover decided whether to approve the Nazi spy ring. So Popov took up residence in an exclusive Park Avenue penthouse, where he resumed his passions for women (his British code name was "Tricycle," reportedly because of his penchant for taking two women—preferably twins—to bed at the same time), alcohol, and the good life while waiting for Hoover to make up his mind.

Keeping an Eye on Things

Unfortunately for Popov and the Allied war effort, Hoover ordered Popov's penthouse placed under surveillance. Heavy surveillance. "If I bend over to smell a bowl of flowers," Popov later complained, "I scratch my nose on a microphone."

When word of Popov's lavish accommodations and lurid lifestyle found its way to Hoover's desk, the director was furious. Any link with Popov, if exposed, could sully the FBI's carefully constructed, squeaky-clean public image. What would happen to the Bureau's reputation if the public learned that it couldn't catch Nazi spies on its own without the help of a womanizing foreigner who wore too much cologne and smoked cigarettes out of an ivory holder?

MEETING MR. HOOVER

Popov spent more than five weeks in New York before J. Edgar Hoover finally agreed to meet with him.

The meeting did not go well. "There was Hoover," Popov wrote in his autobiography, "looking like a sledgehammer in search of an anvil."

> "I can catch spies without your or anybody else's help," Hoover barked. "What have you done since you came here?"
>
> "Nothing but wait for instructions, which never came," I answered. Hoover breathed in deeply and noisily. It seemed to calm him. "What kind of a bogus spy are you?" he said accusingly...."You're like all double agents....You're begging for information to sell to your German friends so you can make a lot of money and be a playboy...." He turned to [an assistant] and said, "That man is trying to teach me my job."
>
> ....I recognized the futility of it all. "I don't think anyone could teach you anything," I told the FBI chief, and walked toward the door.
>
> "Good riddance," he screamed after me.

Hoover vetoed the German spy ring. That was just the beginning. He also confiscated the funds Popov received from Germany and nearly arrested his Abwehr handler, which would have exposed him as a double agent and made him useless to the British; and then he forced the British to withdraw Popov from the U.S. Not that Popov minded—as Curt Gentry writes, Popov wasn't unhappy about leaving. The trip had, he felt, been a waste of time—with one extraordinarily important exception. When the Japanese launched their "surprise" attack on Pearl Harbor, Popov knew, the United States would be ready and waiting.

MISSED OPPORTUNITY

Did Hoover's insecurities cost the United States the most important intelligence coup of the war? Popov wasn't alone in thinking so. In 1945, Rear Admiral Edwin Layton, the Fleet Intelligence Officer at Honolulu during the bombing of Pearl Harbor, published a report on the attack. He found that where Popov's warning was concerned, Hoover "dropped the ball completely....His failure," Layton concluded, "represented another American fumble on the road to Pearl Harbor."

NAZIS INVADE AMERICA!...A TRUE STORY

In June 1942, J. Edgar Hoover claimed credit for the FBI's capture of eight Nazi saboteurs who were deposited by submarine along the New York and Florida shores. Here's what really happened....

ALONG THE WATERFRONT

Not long after midnight on June 13, 1942, a Coast Guardsman named John Cullen saw four men struggling with an inflatable raft in the heavy surf off the town of Amagansett, on the eastern coast of Long Island.

Cullen stopped to investigate. The men told him they were fishermen, and Cullen might have believed them...except that the men were armed (fishermen at sea usually aren't), and they offered him $260 to forget he'd ever seen them. Why would fishermen do a thing like that?

Plus, when Cullen looked out to sea, he thought he saw a long, flat shape about 150 feet offshore, kind of like a submarine.

Getting Help

Cullen was alone and unarmed. He suspected the men were foreign agents (this was World War II, after all), but there wasn't much he could do about it by himself, and he feared that more foreign agents might be on the way. So he pretended to accept the bribe and then ran back to base to get help.

Cullen's superiors were skeptical, not to mention afraid of what would happen if they sounded a false alarm. So they did nothing...until just before dawn, when they sent Cullen and several other armed men to investigate. The "fishermen" were gone and so was the submarine (it was beached on a sandbar when Cullen first saw it, but had since freed itself). But the men left behind several hastily and poorly concealed caches containing explosives, timers, blasting caps, incendiary devices, cigarettes, brandy...and German uniforms.

The Nazis had landed on U.S. soil and nobody knew where they were.

SOUNDING THE ALARM

The FBI didn't learn of the incident until noon and didn't arrive at the scene until a couple of hours later; by then the saboteurs had already slipped into New York City and checked into a hotel.

J. Edgar Hoover was immediately informed of the landing. "All of Hoover's imaginative and restless energy was stirred into prompt and effective action," Attorney General Francis Biddle recalled years later. "His eyes were bright, his jaw set, excitement flickering around the edge of his nostrils....He was determined to catch them all before any sabotage took place."

After alerting President Roosevelt to the crisis, Hoover put the Bureau on full alert and launched the largest manhunt in FBI history. He also ordered a news blackout, for three reasons: (1) he didn't want the saboteurs to learn that they had been discovered; (2) he wanted to avoid a public panic; and (3) he wanted to avoid public embarrassment in the event that the FBI could not catch the German agents.

Secret Heroes

Nobody knew it at the time, but Hoover had nothing to worry about. Colonel George John Dasch, the leader of the Nazi saboteurs, had lived in the U.S. for twenty years before the war and secretly hated the Nazis. The only thing he wanted to sabotage was his own mission, and he had talked one of his compatriots, a naturalized U.S. citizen named Ernst Peter Burger, into joining him. Their plan: Surrender to the FBI.

CRAZY

The two men telephoned the FBI's New York City Field Office (NYFO) and tried to turn themselves in. It didn't work, as Curt Gentry relates in *J. Edgar Hoover: the Man and the Secrets:*

> In most of the large bureau field offices there is what the agents themselves refer to as the "nut desk." The special agent who had the unwelcome task of manning it that day at NYFO listened skeptically to Dasch's tale and observed, "Yesterday Napoleon called," and hung up. Although the whole bureau was on alert, nobody had informed him. He thought the call so ridiculous he didn't even bother to log it.

With no luck on the phone, Dasch decided to take a train to Washington, D.C., and turn himself in to J. Edgar Hoover at FBI headquarters. He brought with him a suitcase containing $84,000 in U.S. currency, the money his team was supposed to use to fund their sabotage efforts. Burger stayed behind in New York.

HOOVER'S HELPERS

The trip to FBI headquarters didn't work, either: Nobody believed Dasch's story, and he was passed from one bureau official to another like a hot potato. No one he talked to would let him speak with Hoover.

Finally, Dasch landed at the desk of D. M. "Mickey" Ladd, head of the bureau's Domestic Intelligence Division and the man leading the hunt for the Nazi saboteurs. Ladd didn't believe Dasch either—he figured the strange man with the German accent was some kind of kook who'd somehow learned of the landing at Amagansett and wanted to hone in on the excitement. He listened to Dasch for about five minutes and then showed him the door. After all, Ladd had Nazis to catch.

Surprise!

Dasch lost his patience. As he later wrote in his memoirs: "I seized the suitcase that had been lying on the floor, tore its snaps, and dumped the contents on the desk. The three feet of polished wood were too narrow to hold the eighty-four thousand dollars in cash. Packets of bills cascaded over the sides to create the illusion of a miniature waterfall."

"Is this stuff real?" Ladd asked.

SPILLING HIS GUTS

Once Ladd confirmed the money was real, the FBI sprang into action. It arrested Dasch and interrogated him for eight days. He told them how he'd been trained, who his contacts were in the U.S., and what his targets were (they included the New York City water supply and the hydroelectric plant at Niagara Falls). He told the FBI where to find Burger and the two other men on his sabotage team.

The landings, Dasch explained, were the first of several scheduled to land every six weeks. The sabotage campaign had two goals: the disruption of vital war industries, and the launching of a wave of ter-

Most dangerous animal in the zoo, according to zookeepers: the panda. The elephant is second.

ror by leaving time bombs at railway stations, department stores, and other public places.

Acting on Dasch's information, the FBI picked up Burger and arrested the remaining saboteurs. Burger, like Dasch, cooperated immediately. He volunteered that a second team of saboteurs had landed along the coast of Florida, and FBI agents in Florida began their own roundup. They captured their last man on June 27, two weeks to the day after the landing at Amagansett. Neither sabotage team had been able to attack a single target.

SHHHH!

Hoover decided to keep the details of the arrests under wraps. The official explanation given was that if Dasch's and Burger's defection were kept secret, Hitler might think that the East Coast was so heavily guarded that further landings would be futile, not to mention a waste of valuable agents.

Fooling FDR

"This explanation makes of the FBI's decision an ingenious disinformation ploy," Gentry writes in *J. Edgar Hoover: The Man and the Secrets*. "It fails to account, however, for why Hoover also felt it necessary to deceive the president of the United States."

In the two weeks between the Amagansett landing and the capture of the last saboteur, Hoover sent FDR three different "personal and confidential memos" keeping the president updated on the progress of the manhunt. None of the memos mentioned the fact that Dasch had turned himself in or that he and Burger were cooperating fully, nor did they admit that the arrests of the Florida saboteurs were possible only because of the information Burger had volunteered to the FBI.

Instead, in the memos Hoover moved the date of Dasch's "arrest" to two days after that of his compatriots to make it look like their capture had led to his, and not vice versa. The director gave all of the credit to the FBI, which had nearly blown the case.

GOING PUBLIC...SORT OF

Hoover announced the arrests—his version, anyway—in a public press conference on June 27. The story made headlines across the country:

FBI CAPTURES 8
GERMAN AGENTS
LANDED BY SUBS

As the *New York Times* reported at the time, Hoover "gave no details of how the FBI 'broke' the case. That will have to wait, FBI officials insist, until after the war." The press had little choice but to speculate on how the arrests had been made, and much of the speculation erred on the side of the FBI, according to then-Attorney General Francis Biddle:

> It was generally concluded that a particularly brilliant FBI agent, probably attending the school in sabotage where the eight had been trained, had been able to get on the inside, and make regular reports to America. Mr. Hoover, as the United Press put it, declined to comment on whether the FBI agents had infiltrated not only the Gestapo but also the High Command, or whether he watched the saboteurs land.

THANKS, GUYS

What did Dasch and Burger get for: (1) singlehandedly destroying Hitler's entire North American sabotage program; and (2) handing Hoover his biggest intelligence coup of the war? (Dasch was hoping for a Congressional Medal of Honor.)

Not much. Like the other six saboteurs, they were hauled before a military tribunal, tried, found guilty, and sentenced to death. Acting on the recommendation of military commission, however, President Roosevelt commuted Dasch's sentence to 30 years of hard labor and Burger's to life at hard labor. Everyone else was executed within a month.

Dasch and Burger languished in prison until 1948, when President Truman pardoned both men and ordered them deported to Germany. There, according to Gentry, "they were treated as traitors who not only had betrayed the fatherland, but also were responsible for the deaths of six of their comrades."

Last inhabited place on earth "discovered" by European explorers: Papua New Guinea, in 1904.

THE KING OF THE FERRET-LEGGERS

This article by Donald Katz first appeared in Outside *magazine in 1987. We've had it in our files for awhile, waiting for the opportunity to use it. Now that we've created our "Extended Sitting Section," this is perfect. So sit back, relax, and enjoy this bizarre story.*

BACKGROUND

Some 11 years ago I first heard of the strange pastime called ferret-legging, and for a decade since then I have sought a publication possessed of sufficient intelligence and vision to allow me to travel to northern England in search of the fabled players of the game.

Basically the contest involves the tying of a competitor's trousers at the ankles and the subsequent insertion into those trousers of a couple of peculiarly vicious fur-coated, foot-long carnivores called ferrets. The brave contestant's belt is then pulled tight, and he proceeds to stand there in front of the judges as long as he can while animals with claws like hypodermic needles and teeth like number 16 carpet tacks try their damndest to get out.

From a dark and obscure past, the sport has made an astonishing comeback in the past 15 years. When I first heard about ferret-legging, the world record stood at 40 painful seconds of "keepin' 'em down," as they say in ferret-legging circles. A few years later, the dreaded one-minute mark was finally surpassed.

The current record—implausible as it may seem—now stands at an awesome 5 hours and 26 minutes, a mark reached last year by the gaudily tattooed 72-year-old little Yorkshireman with a waxed military mustache who now stood two feet away from me in the middle of the room, apparently undoing his trousers.

"The ferrets must have a full mouth o' teeth; no clipping. No dope for you or for the ferrets. You must be sober, and the ferrets must be hungry—though any ferret'll eat yer eyes out even if he isn't hungry."

LONG LIVE THE KING

Reg Mellor lives several hours north of London atop the thick central seam of British coal that once fueled the most powerful surge into modernity in the world's history. He lives in the city of Barnsley, home to a quarter-million downtrodden souls, and the brunt of many derisive jokes in Great Britain. Barnsley was the subject of much national mirth recently when "the most grievously mocked town in Yorkshire"—a place people drive miles out of their way to circumvent—opened a tourist information center. Everyone thought that was a good one.

When I stopped at the tourist office and asked the astonished woman for a map, she said, "Ooooh, a mup ees it, luv? No mups 'ere. Noooo." She did, however, know the way to Reg Mellor's house. Reg is, after all, Barnsley's only reigning king.

Mr. Reg Mellor, the "king of the ferret-legging," paced across his tiny Yorkshire miner's cottage as he explained the rules of the English sport that he has come to dominate rather late in life.

"Ay lad," said the 72-year-old champion, "no jockstraps allowed. No underpants—nothin' whatever. And it's no good with tight trousers, mind ye. Little bah-stards have to be able to move around inside there from ankle to ankle."

THE KING AND I

Finally, then, after 11 long years, I sat in front of a real ferret-legger, a man among men. He stood now next to a glowing fire of Yorksire coal as I tried to interpret the primitive record of his long life, which is etched in tattoos up and down his thick arms. Reg finally finished explaining the technicalities of this burgeoning sport.

"So then, lad. Any more questions for I poot a few down for ye?"

"Yes, Reg."

"Ay, whoot then?"

"Well Reg," I said. "I think people in America will want to know. Well...since you don't wear any protection...and, well, I've heard a ferret can bite your thumb off. Do they ever—you know?"

Reg's stiff mustache arched toward the ceiling under a sly grin.

Tallest pyramid on Earth: the Transamerica Pyramid, in San Francisco.

"You really want to know what they get up to down there, eh?" Reg said, looking for all the world like some working man's Long John Silver.

"Well, take a good look."

Then Reg Mellor let his trousers fall around his ankles.

FUR-COATED EVIL

A word is in order concerning ferrets, a weasel-like animal well known to Europeans but, because of the near extinction of the black-footed variety in the American West, not widely known in the United States.

Alternatively referred to by professional ferret-handlers as "shark-of-the-land," a "piranha with feet," "fur-coated evil," and "the only four-legged creature in existence that kills just for kicks," the common domesticated ferret—*Mustela putorius*—has the spinal flexibility of a snake and the jaw musculature of a pit bull. Rabbits, rats, and even frogs run screaming from hiding places when confronted with a ferret. Ferreters—those who hunt with ferrets, as opposed to putting them in their pants—sit around and tell tales of rabbits running toward hunters to surrender after gazing into the torch-red eyes of an oncoming ferret.

Before they were outlawed in New York State in the early part of the century, ferrets were used to exterminate rats. A ferret with a string on its leg, it was said, could knock off more than a hundred street-wise New York City rats twice its size in an evening.

In England the amazing risk of ferret-legging pales before the new popularity of keeping ferrets as pets, a trend replete with numerous tragic consequences. A baby was killed and eaten in 1978, and several children have been mauled by ferrets every year since then.

BITE OFF THE HAND THAT FEEDS

Loyal to nothing that lives, the ferret has only one characteristic that might be deemed positive—a tenacious, single-minded belief in finishing whatever it starts. That usually entails biting *off* whatever it bites. The rules of ferret-legging *do* allow the leggers to try to knock the ferret off a spot it's biting (from outside the trousers only), but that is no small matter, as ferrets never let go. No less a source than The *Encyclopaedia Britannica* suggests that you can get a ferret to let go by pressing a certain spot over its eye, but Reg Mellor and the other ferret specialists I talked to all say that is absurd. Reg favors a large screwdriver to get a ferret off his finger. Another ferret-legger told me that a ferret that had almost dislodged his left thumb let go only after the ferret and the man's thumb were held under scalding tap water—for ten minutes.

Mr. Graham Wellstead, the head of the British Ferret and Ferreting Society, says that little is known of the diseases carried by the ferret because veterinarians are afraid to touch them.

MUSKRAT LOVE?

Reg Mellor, a man who has been more intimate with ferrets than many men have been with their wives, calls ferrets "cannibals, things that live only to kill, that'll eat your eyes out to get at your brain" at the worst, and "untrustworthy" at their very best.

Reg says he observed with wonder the growing popularity of ferret-legging througout the seventies. He had been hunting with ferrets in the verdant moors and dales outside of Barnsley for much of a century. Since a cold and wet ferret exterminates with a little less enthusiasm than a dry one, Reg used to keep his ferrets in his pants for hours when he hunted in the rain—and it always rained where he hunted.

"The world record was 60 seconds. Sixty seconds! I can stick a ferret up me ass longer than that."

So at 69, Reg Mellor found his game. As he stood in front of me now, naked from waist down, Reg looked every bit a champion.

ENQUIRING MINDS...

"So look close," he said again.

I did look, at an incredible tattoo of a *zaftig* woman on Reg's thigh. His legs appeared crosshatched with scars. But I refused to "look close," saying something about not being paid enough for that.

"Come on, Reg," I said. "Do they bite your—you know?"

"Do they!" he thundered with irritation as he pulled up his pants.

"Why, I had 'em hangin' off me—"

Reg stopped short because a woman who was with me, a London television reporter, had entered the cottage. I suddenly feared that I would never know from what the raging ferrets dangle. Reg offered my friend a chair with the considerable gallantry of a man who had served in the Queen's army for more than 20 years. Then he said to her, "Are ye cheeky, luv?"

My friend looked confused.

"Say yes," I hissed.

"Yes."

"Why," Reg roared again, "I had 'em hangin' from me tool for hours an' hours an' hours! Two at a time—one on each side. I been swelled up big as that!" Reg pointed to a five-pound can of instant coffee.

I then made the mistake of asking Reg Mellor if his age allowed him the impunity to be the most daring ferret-legger in the world.

"And what do ye mean by that?" he said.

"Well, I just thought since you probably aren't going to have any more children. . . ."

"Are you sayin' I ain't pokin' 'em no more?" Reg growled with menace. "Is that your meaning? 'Cause I am pokin' 'em for sure."

FREE SHOW

A small red hut sits in an overgrown yard outside Reg Mellor's door.

"Come outta there, ye bah-stards," Reg yelled as he flailed around the inside of the hut looking for some ferrets that had just arrived a few hours earlier. He emerged with two dirty white animals, which he held quite firmly by their necks. They both had fearsome unblinking eyes as hard and red as rubies.

Reg thrust one of them at me, and I suddenly thought that he intended the ferret to avenge my *faux pas* concerning his virility; so I began to run for a fence behind which my television friend was already standing because she refused to watch. Reg finally got me to take one of the ferrets by its steel cable of a neck while he tied his pants at the ankle and prepared to "put em down."

A young man named Malcolm with a punk haircut came into the yard on a motorbike. "You puttin' 'em down again, Reg?" Malcolm asked.

Reg took the ferret from my bloodless hand and stuck the beast's head deep into his mouth.

"Oh yuk, Reg," said Malcolm.

Reg pulled the now quite embittered-looking ferret out of his mouth and stuffed it and another ferret into his pants. He cinched his belt tight, clenched his fists at his sides, and gazed up into the gray Yorkshire firmament in what I guessed could only be a gesture of prayer. Claws and teeth now protruded all over Reg's hyperactive trousers. The two bulges circled round and round one leg, getting higher and higher, and finally...they went up and over one to the other leg.

"Thank God," I said.

"Yuk, Reg," said Malcolm.

"The claws," I managed, "Aren't they sharp, Reg?"

"Ay," said Reg laconically. "Ay."

RETIRED "FER-LANTHROPIST"

Reg Mellor gives all the money he makes from ferret-legging to the local children's home. As with all great champions, he has also tried to bring more visibility to the sport that has made him famous. One Mellor innovation is the introduction of white trousers at major competitions ("shows the blood better").

Mellor is a proud man. Last year he retired from professional ferret-legging in disgust after attempting to break a magic six-hour mark—the four-minute-mile of ferret-legging. After five hours of having them down, Mellor found that almost all of the 2,500 spectators had gone home. Then workmen came and began to dismantle the stage, despite his protestations that he was on his way to a new record. "I'm not packing it in because I am too old or because I can't take the bites anymore," Reg told reporters after the event, "I am just too disillusioned."

First movie made in Hollyood: *The Law and the Range*, 1912.

FERRET DIPLOMACY

One of the ferrets in Reg's pants finally poked its nose into daylight before any major damage was done, and Reg pulled the other ferret out. We all went across the road to the local pub, where everyone but Reg had a drink to calm the nerves. Reg doesn't drink. Bad for his health, he says.

Reg said he had been coaxed out of retirement recently and intends to break six—"maybe even eight"—hours within the year.

Some very big Yorkshiremen stood around us in the pub. Some of them claimed they had bitten the head off sparrows, shrews, and even rats, but none of them would compete with Reg Mellor. One can only wonder what suffering might have been avoided if the Argentine junta had been informed that sportsmen in England put down their pants animals that are known only for their astonishingly powerful bites and their penchant for insinuating themselves into small dark holes. Perhaps the generals would have reconsidered their actions on the Falklands.

But Reg Mellor refuses to acknowledge that his talent is made of the stuff of heroes, of a mixture of indomitable pride, courage, concentration, and artless grace. "Naw noon o' that," said the king. "You just got to be able ta have your tool bitten and not care."

*   *   *   *

RANDOM "THOUGHTS"

"We're going to turn this team around 360 degrees."

—Jason Kidd, on being drafted by the Dallas Mavericks

"It's like an Alcatraz around my neck."

—Boston Mayor Menino, on the shortage of city parking spaces

"It is bad luck to be superstitious."

—Andrew Mathis

THE WOLFMAN AT THE MOVIES

The werewolf is one of the most recognized movie monsters in history, thanks in large part to the 1941 film The Wolf Man, *starring Lon Chaney Jr. Here's a behind-the-scenes look at the making of that classic film.*

FRIGHT FACTORY

The early 1930s was the golden age of movie monsters. In 1930, Universal released the classic *Dracula*, starring Bela Lugosi; a year later it had another huge hit with Boris Karloff's *Frankenstein*. Inspired by their success, Universal decided to make a movie about a werewolf. In 1931, they handed writer/director Robert Florey a title—*The Wolf Man*—and told him to come up with an outline.

A few months later, Florey submitted notes for a story about a Frenchman who has suffered for 400 years under a witch's curse that turns him into a werewolf during every full moon...unless he wears a garland of wolf-bane around his neck.

The studio approved the idea and scheduled the movie as a Boris Karloff vehicle for 1933. A shooting script was written...and rewritten...and rewritten several more times. By the time it was finished, the script was about an English doctor who is bitten by a werewolf in Tibet, then turns into one himself on his return to London. Universal renamed the picture *Werewolf of London*.

BAT MAN

By now, however, Boris Karloff was too busy to take the part....So it went to a Broadway actor named Henry Hull. *Werewolf of London* hit theatres in 1935.

The movie wasn't very good: One critic has called it "full of fog, atmosphere, and laboratory shots, but short on chills and horror." That was largely because Hull didn't *look* scary. He refused to cover his face with werewolf hair, complaining that it obscured his features. Makeup man Jack Pierce—already a legend for creating Bela

The dome in the Kentucky state capitol is modeled after Napoleon's tomb.

Lugosi's *Dracula* and Boris Karloff's *Frankenstein*—had no choice but to remove most of the facial hair, leaving Hull looking like a demonic forest elf. *Werewolf of London* was a box office disappointment. It was also Hull's last werewolf film.

SECOND TRY

In the early 1940s, Universal launched a second wave of horror films featuring Dracula, Frankenstein, and other classic monsters. They decided to give the werewolf another try, too.

This second werewolf film started the same way the first one did: with the title *The Wolf Man*. This time the scriptwriter was Curt Siodmak. He started from scratch, researched werewolf legends himself, and used what he learned to write the script. The story he concocted was about an American named Lawrence Talbot who travels to his ancestral home in Wales and is bitten while rescuing a young woman from a werewolf attack.

Once again, the studio wanted to cast Karloff in the lead...and once again, he was too busy to take it. They considerd Bela Lugosi, but he was too old for the part. So they gave it to newcomer Lon Chaney, Jr., son and namesake of the greatest horror star of the silent movie era. Chaney, Sr. was known all over the world as "the Man of 1000 Faces," for his roles in *The Phantom of the Opera* and *The Hunchback of Notre Dame*. Chaney, Jr. had recently starred in *Man Made Monster*, and Universal thought he had potential in horror films.

THE MAKEUP

Jack Pierce was still the makeup artist at Universal, and he welcomed the chance to use his original design: a hairy face complete with fangs and a wolfish nose, plus hairy hands and feet. The makeup took a total of four hours to apply, most of which was spent applying tufts of fur—authentic yak hair imported from Asia—one by one, and then singeing them to create a wild look.

Chaney's wolfman didn't talk—all it did was grunt, growl, and howl—and that was no accident: when Chaney was fully made up, he couldn't talk and could only eat through a straw. As he recounted years later, the only thing worse than wearing the makeup was taking it off:

> What gets me is when it's after work and I'm all hot and itchy and tired, and I've got to sit in that chair for forty-five minutes more while Pierce just about kills me ripping off the stuff he put on in the morning! Sometimes we take an hour and leave some of the skin on my face!

THANKS, DAD

Most actors would probably have refused to wear such difficult makeup, but Chaney (whose real first name was Creighton) had no choice: he was desperate to make it in the film business.

While he was alive, Lon Chaney, Sr. had fought Creighton's attempts to become an actor. He even forced his son out of Hollywood High and into a plumbing school when he asked to take acting lessons. As Chaney, Sr.'s career soared to its heights in the late 1920s, Chaney, Jr. was working as a boilermaker.

The elder Chaney died of throat cancer in 1930; Creighton Chaney signed with RKO studios two years later. After moving from bit part to bit part for more than two years, he reluctantly changed his name to Lon Chaney, Jr. to cash in on his father's fame. "They had to starve me to make me take his name," he groused years later.

Finally, in 1939—only days after his car and furniture were reposessed by a furniture company—Chaney scored a hit in a stage version of *Of Mice and Men*. That led to a starring role in the movie version, and in 1940, a contract with Universal.

ALL THIS AND WORLD WAR II

The studio had modest hopes for *The Wolf Man*. They scheduled its release for December 11, 1941, right before Christmas. But on December 7, Japan bombed Pearl Harbor and the United States entered World War II. Universal was sure the movie would become a box office disaster. After all, who was going to take time out for the movies when they were going to war?

Good vs. Evil

To their surprise, it was a hit. The film played to packed movie houses all over the country, and was the studio's biggest moneymaker of the season. It established the Wolf Man as an important movie monster, along with Dracula and Frankenstein. It almost singlehandedly made werewolves a part of the popular culture, and it turned Lon Chaney Jr. into one of the best known actors in the country.

World War II probably had more to do with making *The Wolf Man* a hit than any other factor. What Universal had failed to realize was that the war fueled a need for the kind of escape that horror films provided. Inside a darkened theater, moviegoers could forget their troubles, at least for a while, as they watched ordinary mortals triumph over seemingly insurmountable evil. As David Skal writes in *The Monster Show: A Cultural History of Horror*,

> Talbot's four-film quest to put to rest his wolf-self is, in a strange way, an unconscious parable of the war effort. The Wolf Man's crusade for eternal peace and his frustrated attempts to control irrational, violent, European forces.... The Wolf Man's saga was the most consistent and sustained monster myth of the war, beginning with the first year of America's direct involvement in the war, and finishing up just in time for Hiroshima.

WOLF MAN FACTS

• The hardest scene to shoot was the final "metamorphosis" scene, in which Chaney turns from a werewolf to a human as he dies. Chaney describes the process:

> The way we did the transformation was that I came in at *2:00 a.m.* When I hit the position, they would take little nails and drive them through the skin at the edge of my fingers, on both hands, so that I wouldn't move them anymore.
>
> While I was in this position, they would take the camera and weigh it down with one ton, so that it wouldn't move when people walked. They had targets for my eyes.
>
> Then, they would shoot five or ten frames of film in the camera. They'd take the film out and send it to the lab. While it was there, the make-up man would come and take the whole thing off my face and put on a new one. I'm still immobile. When the film came back from the lab, they'd put it back in the camera and then they'd check me.
>
> They'd say, "Your eyes have moved a little bit, move them to the right...." Then they'd roll it again and shoot another 10 frames. Well, we did 21 changes of make-up and it took twenty two hours. I won't discuss about the bathroom...

• For the rest of the cast and crew, the worst part of filming *The Wolf Man* was breathing the special effects fog that was used in the outdoor scenes. "The kind of fog they used in those days was nothing like the kind we have today," cameraman Phil Lathrop remembers. "It was greasy stuff made with mineral oil. We worked in it for weeks and the entire cast and crew had sore eyes and intestinal trouble the entire time. Besides that, we were all shivering with cold because it was necessary to keep the temperature below 50 degrees when using the fog." Female lead Evelyn Ankers fainted on the set after inhaling too much fog during a chase sequence.

• *The Wolf Man* made a lot of money for Universal, but not much of it filtered down to the writers and actors who actually brought it to life. "My salary was $400 a week," scriptwriter Curt Siodmak recalls. "When the picture made its first million, the producer got a $10,000 bonus, the director got a diamond ring for his wife, and I got fired, since I wanted $25 more for my next job."

LON CHANEY'S WOLFMAN SEQUELS

Chaney made four wolfman movies for Universal during the war years...more than Universal made of Dracula or Frankenstein. The others were:

• ***Frankenstein Meets the Wolfman* (1943).** Chaney travels to Castle Frankenstein to see if he can find a cure for his wolfman condition in Dr. Frankenstein's notes. All he finds is the Frankenstein monster, played by Bela Lugosi, who had turned down the original *Frankenstein* in 1931 because there wasn't any dialogue.
Movie Note: Lugosi played a particularly stiff Frankenstein, not just because he was growing old, but also because in the original version of the film, Frankenstein is left blind and mute after a botched brain transplant. In the version released to theaters, all references to blindness, muteness and the brain transplant were removed, so he just looks old.

• ***House of Frankenstein* (1944).** Mad scientist Dr. Gustav Niemann (Boris Karloff) escapes from an insane asylum with the help of his hunchback assistant Daniel (J. Carrol Naish) and flees to Castle Frankenstein. There he teams up with Dracula (John Carradine), Frankenstein (Glenn Strange), and the Wolfman

(Chaney) to terrorize the countryside until they are finally killed by villagers.

• ***House of Dracula* (1945).** Dr. Franz Edelman (Onslow Stevens) finds a way to cure Dracula (John Carradine) of his vampirism, but Dracula refuses to submit. Instead, he bites Dr. Edelman and turns him into a vampire; then Edelman raises Frankenstein from the dead, just as the Wolfman arrives on the scene.
Movie Note: Originally titled *The Wolfman vs. Dracula,* the movie had to be renamed because the Wolfman and Dracula do not actually meet in the film.

• ***Abbot and Costello Meet Frankenstein* (1948).** Bud Abbott and Lou Costello team up with the Wolfman to prevent Dracula (Lugosi) and a mad female scientist (Lenore Aubert) from transplanting Costello's brain into the Frankenstein monster. Critics say the film is symbolic of the decline of Universal's horror classics in the late 1940s—fans say it is one of the best films Abbot and Costello ever made.

THE END

Chaney would reprise the wolfman role in movies and in television for the rest of his life, including appearances on *The Pat Boone Show*, and *Route* 66. He also played the Frankenstein monster in *The Ghost of Frankenstein* (1942), Count Dracula in *Son of Dracula* (1943), and the Mummy in three Mummy movies.

A heavy drinker, by the 1960s he was reduced to appearing in low-budget schlock like *Face of the Screaming Werewolf* (1965); *Hillbillies in a Haunted House* (1967); and *Dracula vs. Frankenstein* (1970). He died of a heart attack in 1973. But the wolfman lives on.

The Legend Lives On. Like all classic Hollywood monsters, the werewolf was spun off into dozens of movies, many of them low-budget, some just plain unusual. Take these, for example:

• ***I Was A Teenage Werewolf* (1957)**

The original "teenage" horror film, *I Was a Teenage Werewolf,* was filmed in seven days at a cost of $125,000…and made $2,000,000. It launched an entire genre of low-budget, B-movie films, includ-

Most common reason for requesting emergency roadside service: "automobile won't start."

ing *I Was a Teenage Frankenstein, I Was a Teenage Zombie*, and *I Was a Teenage TV Terrorist*.

The movie stars a young Michael Landon (of *Bonanza* and *Little House on the Prairie* fame) in his first feature film role. He plays an emotionally disturbed teenager seeking treatment for his problems. A mad scientist hypnotizes him and he "regresses" so far back in time that he becomes a prehistoric werewolf. Landon's girlfriend is not amused, and neither are the police. They gun him down at the end of the film.

• *The Mad Monster* (1942)

Dr. Cameron, a mad scientist, injects a handyman with the blood of a wolf, "turning him into the prototype for an army of wolfmen to battle the Nazis." In the end, however, Dr. Cameron succumbs to pettiness and uses the werewolf "to kill the men he believes responsible for destroying his reputation." The film, banned in the UK until 1952, was finally released with an X rating and a medical disclaimer touting the safety of blood transfusions.

• *Werewolf In A Girl's Dormitory* (1961)

When a series of ghastly murders take place at a correctional school for wayward girls, investigators discover that Mr. Swift, the school's superintendent, is a werewolf.

• *Werewolves On Wheels* (1971)

"With surfing music blaring on the soundtrack, motorcycle gang members curse, attend impromptu orgies, drink barrels of beer and rough up some monks. In retaliation, cyclists are cursed with lycanthropy [they're turned into werewolves]. What follows is some very unintentional comedy and some very unnecessary nudity."

—***The Creature Feature's Movie Guide***

• *Leena Meets Frankenstein* (1993)

"A hardcore remake of *Abbot and Costello Meet Frankenstein* (1948), which changes from black and white to color for the sex scenes. When their car breaks down, two street-wise babes are stranded at a time-share condo with the classic monsters—the

Wolfman, Dracula, his vampire wives, and the Frankenstein monster."

—*The Illustrated Werewolf Movie Guide*

• ***The Rats Are Coming! The Werewolves Are Here!* (1972)**

"When a newly married man discovers that his inlaws are incestuous werewolves, he and his wife set out to break the family curse. The characters include a 108-year-old family patriarch and the wife's brother Malcolm, who is kept in shackles in a locked room, where he commits unspeakable crimes against chickens and mice. "To pad its short running time, producer Andy Milligan filmed a subplot of man-eating rats in Milligan's hometown of Staten Island. Ads offered: 'Win a live rat for your mother-in-law.'"

—*Cult Flicks and Trash Pics*

• ***Night Stalkers* (1995)**

A private detective stumbles onto a society of werewolves while investigating the murder of someone who was skinned alive. Probably the world's first all-deaf werewolf film, directed by a deaf director and "shot on video in London and Liverpool with an all-deaf cast for an incredible $600, utilizing sign language, subtitles, and voice-over for the hearing impaired."

—*The Illustrated Werewolf Movie Guide*

• ***Werewolf Of Woodstock* (1975)**

A few days after the Woodstock festival, a beer-drinking, hippie-hating farmer (Tige Andrews from TV's *The Mod Squad*) who lives next to the farm, is struck by lightning and turns into a beer-drinking, hippie-hating werewolf who preys on slow-to-leave concert-goers. *The Creature Features Movie Guide* describes it as "undoubtedly one of the dumbest lycanthropy [werewolf] movies ever produced."

• ***Curse Of The Queerwolf* (1987)**

"A straight man is bitten on the butt by a gay werewolf(!) and transforms into the title character. When the moon is full, he finds himself turning into a werewolf—and gay! [Director Michael] Pirro takes advantage of the outrageously funny idea of turning homophobia into a horror movie."

—Cult Flicks and Trash Pics

• ***The Werewolf And The Yeti* (1975)**

A man on a Tibetan expedition in search of the Yeti is bitten by two cannibalistic sisters he finds in a cave. He becomes a werewolf during the next full moon, and battles the abominable snowman.

• ***Full Moon High* (1981)**

A 1950s high school student (Adam Arkin of TV's *Chicago Hope*) is bitten by a werewolf while on a trip to Armenia with his CIA agent father. Forever young, he returns to Full Moon High twenty years later disguised as his own son.

• ***Blood!* (1974)**

Dracula's daughter Regina meets the son of Laurence Talbot (the Wolfman) and falls in love. "They get married, move to America, and attempt to raise flesh-eating plants to cure their respective curses."

—The Illustrated Werewolf Movie Guide

* * * *

ASK THE EXPERTS

Q: *Why is it considered bad luck for a black cat to cross one's path?*
A: "[This superstition] is probably a survival of the medieval belief that Satan often assumed the form of a black tom-cat when he sallied out upon an excursion for mischief. The ancient Egyptians regarded the cat as sacred, but during the Middle Ages this animal fell into bad repute among Europeans, who associated black specimens especially with the devil and darkness. In some countries it was believed that all black cats were transformed into evil spirits at the end of seven years. Up until a few hundred years ago all witches were supposed to have black cats as familiars, and in popular representations at Halloween time witches are still shown accompanied by black cats while on their nocturnal journeys. Strangely enough, the appearance of a stray cat of any color into a home has always been regarded as a sign of good luck, especially if it remains." (From *Why Do Some Shoes Squeak?*, by George W. Stimpson)

It isn't blood that attracts mosquitoes, it's the scent of bacteria growing in your skin.

NASTY SECRETS OF ADVERTISING

Professor William Lutz is the author of Doublespeak *and* The New Doublespeak*—two books that detail the way people in our culture manipulate language to hide the truth. Both are fascinating—and it was hard to pick just one subject from the books to reprint. We chose a part of his section on advertising doublespeak, which he calls "weasel words."*

THE RULE OF PARITY

The first rule of advertising is that nothing is what it seems...which brings us to the Rule of Parity.

Products such as gasoline, toothpaste, soap, aspirin, and cold remedies (plus a long list of others) are called *parity products.*

This simply means that most of the brands in their category are pretty much the same. Most toothpastes, for example, are made the same way, with pretty much the same formula. There is no essential difference—so as far as the law is concerned, all toothpastes are equal.

Now comes the interesting part.

- Since all toothpastes are equal, no one brand is superior to any of the others.
- Therefore, not only are all parity products "good" products, they are all the "best" products.
- Thus, you can legally advertise your toothpaste, gasoline, deodorant, or other parity product as the "best" and not have to prove it.
- However, if you claim your parity product is "better" than another parity product, you have to prove your claim because "better" is comparative and a claim of superiority, and only one product can be "better" than the others in a parity class.

Get that? In the world of advertising doublespeak, "better" means "best," but "best" means only "equal to."

The next time you see an ad for the gasoline that claims to be "the best for your car," the razor that gives you the "best shave going," or the toothpaste that is "best for your teeth," remember that these

Most frequent outrageous customer behavior at grocery stores: fist fights with cashiers.

claims simply mean that each of these brands is as good as any other brand. As Humpty Dumpty said to Alice, "When I use a word, it means just what I choose it to mean—neither more nor less."

THE WEASEL WORDS

Advertisers can get just so much mileage out of parity claims. If that was all they used in their ads, the ads would get pretty boring—and *that* is one thing advertisers want to avoid at all costs. So they need other ways to convince you their product is different from others.

They can't just say anything they want—their claims are subject to some (though not many) laws designed to prevent fraudulent or untruthful claims in advertising. So instead of making outright false claims, they use *weasel words*.

Weasel words get their name from the way weasels eat eggs from other animals' nests. They make a small hole in the egg, suck out the insides, then put the egg back in the nest. You can only tell the egg is hollow if you examine it closely.

That's the way it is with weasel words in advertising: Examine them closely and you'll find they're as hollow as any egg sucked by a weasel. They appear to say one thing when in fact they say the opposite, or nothing at all.

"HELP"

The biggest weasel word used in advertising is "help." It only means "to aid or assist," but once an ad says "help," it can say just about anything *after* that—because "help" qualifies everything following it.

The trick is that the claim that comes after "help" is usually so strong and dramatic that you forget the weasel word and concentrate only on the dramatic claim. You read into the ad a message that the ad does not contain. More importantly, the advertiser is not responsible for the the claim that you read into the ad, even though the advertiser wrote the ad so you would read that claim into it.

A toothpaste ad may say, "Helps prevent cavities," but it doesn't say it will *actually prevent cavities*. A liquid cleaner ad says, "Helps keep your home germ free," but it doesn't say it *actually kills germs*, nor does it even specify which germs it might kill.

Look at the ads in magazines and newspapers, listen to ads on radio and television, and you'll find the word "help" in ads for all kinds of products, combined with action words to make such convincing-sounding phrases as "helps stop...," "helps overcome...," "helps eliminate...," "helps you feel...," or "helps you look...." If you start looking for the weasel word in advertising, you'll be amazed at how often it occurs. Analyze the claims in the ads using "help," and you'll discover that these ads are really saying nothing.

VIRTUALLY SPOTLESS

One of the most powerful weasel words is "virtually," a word so innocent that most people don't pay any attention to it when it is used in an advertising claim. But watch out. "Virtually" is used in advertising claims that appear to make specific, definite promises when there is no promise.

In 1971, a federal court rendered its decision on a case brought by a woman who became pregnant while taking birth control pills. She sued the manufacturer, Eli Lilly and Company, for breach of warranty. The woman lost her case. Basing its ruling on a statement in the pamphlet accompanying the pills, which stated that, "When taken as directed, the tablets offer virtually 100% protection," the court ruled that there was no warranty, expressed or implied, that the pills were absolutely effective. In its ruling, the court pointed out that, according to *Webster's Third New International Dictionary*, "virtually" means "almost entirely" and clearly does not mean "absolute" (*Whittington v. Eli Lilly and Company*, 333 F. Supp. 98). In other words, the Eli Lilly company was really saying that its birth control pill, even when taken as directed, *did not in fact* provide 100% protection against pregnancy. But Eli Lilly didn't want to put it that way because then many women might not have bought Lilly's birth control pills.

The next time you see the ad that says that this dishwasher detergent "leaves dishes virtually spotless," just remember: You can have lots of spots on your dishes after using this detergent and the ad claim will still be true, because this claim really means the detergent does not *in fact* leave your dishes spotless.

The television set that is "virtually trouble free" becomes the television set that is not in fact trouble free, the "virtually foolproof operation" of any appliance becomes an operation that is in fact not foolproof.

When you use a cell phone in the car, the risk of an accident goes up 34%.

NEW AND IMPROVED

Some products have been around for a long time, yet every once in a while you discover that they are being advertised as "new." Why? Because an advertiser can call a product new if there has been "a material functional change" in the product.

The change doesn't have to be an improvement. One manufacturer added an artificial lemon scent to a cleaning product and called it "new and improved," even though the product didn't clean any better. The manufacturer defended the use of the word "new" on the grounds that the artificial scent changed the chemical formula of the product and therefore constituted "a material functional change."

Which brings up the word "improved." When used in advertising, "improved" does not mean "made better." It only means "changed" or "different from before." So, if the detergent maker puts a plastic pour spout on the box of detergent, the product has been "improved." Now you know why manufacturers are constantly making little changes in their products. Whole new advertising campaigns, designed to convince you that the product has been changed for the better, are based on small, superficial changes.

ALMOST NEW

The use of the word "new" is restricted by regulations, so an advertiser can't just use it without meeting certain requirements. But "new" is too useful and powerful a concept in advertising to give it up easily. So advertisers use weasel words that say "new" without *really* saying it. One of their favorites is "introducing," as in "Introducing improved Tide," or "Introducing the stain remover." The first is simply saying, here's our improved soap; the second, here's our new advertising campaign for our detergent.

Another favorite is "now," as in, "Now there's Sinex," which simply means that Sinex is available. Then there are phrases like "Today's Chevrolet," "Presenting Dristan," and "A fresh way to start the day." The list is really endless because advertisers are always finding new ways to say "new" without really saying it.

ACTS FAST

"Acts" and "works" are two popular weasel words in advertising because they bring action to the product and to the advertising claim.

When you see the ad for the cough syrup that "Acts on the cough control center," ask yourself what this cough syrup is claiming to do. The just claims the cough syrup will "act,"—i.e., do something. By the way, what and where is your "cough control center?" I don't remember learning about that part of the body in human biology class.

Ads that use such phrases as "acts fast," "acts against," "acts to prevent," and the like are saying essentially nothing, because "act" is a word empty of any specific meaning. The ads are always careful not to specify exactly what "act" the product performs.

WORKS LIKE ANYTHING ELSE

If you don't find the word "acts" in an ad, you will probably find the weasel word "works." In fact, the two words are almost interchangeable in advertising. Watch out for ads that say a product "works against," "works like," "works for," or "works longer." "Works" is a meaningless verb used to make you think a product really does something.

LIKE MAGIC

Whenever advertisers want you to stop thinking about the product and start thinking about something bigger, better, or more attractive, they use that very popular weasel word, "like."

"Like" gets you to ignore the product and concentrate on the claim an advertiser is making about it. "For skin like peaches and cream" claims the ad for a skin cream. What is this ad really claiming? It doesn't say this cream will give you peaches-and-cream skin. There is no verb in this claim, so it doesn't even mention using the product. How is skin ever like "peaches and cream?" Remember, ads must be read literally and exactly, according to the dictionary definition of words. The ad is making absolutely no promise or claim whatsoever for this skin cream. If you think this cream will give you soft, smooth, youthful-looking skin, you are the one who has read that meaning into the ad.

The wine that claims "It's like taking a trip to France" wants you to think about a romantic evening in Paris as you walk along the boulevard after a wonderful meal in an intimate little bistro. Of course, you don't really believe that a wine can take you to France, but the goal of the ad is to get you to think about pleasant, romantic

When a yellow jacket is agitated, it gives off a sound that tells other yellow jackets to attack.

thoughts about France and not about how the wine tastes or how expensive it may be. That little word "like" has taken you away from crushed grapes into a world of your own imaginative making.

UNFINISHED WORDS

The claim that a battery lasts "up to twice as long" usually doesn't finish the comparison—twice as long as what? A birthday candle? A tank of gas? A cheap battery made in a country not noted for its technological achievements? The implication is that the battery lasts twice as long as batteries made by other battery makers, or twice as long as earlier model batteries made by the advertiser, but the ad doesn't really make these claims. You read these claims into the ad, aided by the visual images the advertiser so carefully provides.

Some years ago, Ford's advertisements proclaimed "Ford LTD—700% quieter." Now, what do you think Ford was claiming with these unfinished words? What was the Ford LTD quieter than?...A Cadillac?...A Mercedes Benz?...A BMW? Well, when the FTC asked Ford to substantiate this unfinished claim, Ford replied that it meant that the inside of the LTD was 700% quieter than the outside. How did you finish those unfinished words when you first read them? Did you even come close to Ford's meaning?

READ THE LABEL, OR THE BROCHURE

Weasel words aren't just found on television, on the radio, or in newspaper and magazine ads. Just about any language associated with a product will contain the doublespeak of advertising.

The variations, combinations, and permutations of doublespeak used in advertising go on and on, running from the use of rhetorical questions ("Wouldn't you really rather have a Buick?" "If you can't trust Prestone, who can you trust?") to flattering you with compliments ("The lady has taste." "We think a cigar smoker is someone special." "You've come a long way baby.").

You know, of course, how you're *supposed* to answer those questions and you know that those compliments are just leading up to the sales pitches for the products.

But before you dismiss such tricks of the trade as obvious, just remember: all of these statements and questions were part of very successful advertising campaigns. And after all, isn't that the point in the first place?

Each year, 16,000 cheerleaders seek emergency room treatment for cheerleader-related injuries.

THE WARREN COMMISSION

Everyone has heard of the Warren Commission—but do you know anything about it? Do you even know who was on it? This piece from It's a Conspiracy, *by the National Insecurity Council, is a conspiracy-minded introduction to the group.*

When Lee Harvey Oswald was murdered in police custody, many Americans began to suspect a conspiracy. Authorities in Dallas and Washington, D.C. immediately investigated the murder and concluded that neither Oswald nor Jack Ruby were involved in any conspiracy. They made their findings and much of their evidence public, but most Americans still had their doubts: a Gallup poll taken early in December 1963 found that 52% of Americans "believed that Oswald had not acted alone." (*Crossfire*)

There were calls for an independent congressional investigation. To forestall them, President Lyndon Johnson announced on November 29, 1963—just one week after JFK's death—that he had created a federal panel to "uncover all the facts concerning the assassination of President Kennedy and to determine if it was in any way directed or encouraged by unknown persons at home or abroad." The bipartisan panel was to be chaired by the Chief Justice of the U.S. Supreme Court, Earl Warren, and comprised of seven men "of unimpeachable integrity."

COMMISSION MEMBERS

- Earl Warren, Chief Justice, U.S. Supreme Court
- Hale Boggs, Democratic representative from Louisiana
- John Sherman Cooper, Republican senator from Kentucky
- Gerald Ford, Republican representative from Michigan
- Richard Russell, Democratic senator from Georgia
- Allen Dulles, Wall Street lawyer, former director of the CIA
- John J. McCloy, post-WWII High Commissioner of Germany, former president of the World Bank

THE FINDINGS

In September 1964, the Warren Commission presented a 26-volume report. Its findings included:

• "The shots which killed President Kennedy and wounded Governor Connally were fired from the sixth floor window of the Depository Building....There were three shots fired."

• "There is persuasive evidence from the experts to indicate that the same bullet which pierced the President's throat also caused Governor Connally's wounds."

• "The shots which killed President Kennedy...were fired by Lee Harvey Oswald."

• "The Commission has found no evidence that either Lee Harvey Oswald or Jack Ruby was part of any conspiracy, domestic or foreign, to assassinate President Kennedy."

THE CONSPIRACY THEORY

• The FBI and the CIA prejudged the case, assumed Oswald to be the lone assassin, suppressed evidence to the contrary, and deliberately lied to the Warren Commission. The commissioners knew they weren't getting all the facts, but they went along.

• Senator Richard Schweiker, a member of the Senate Intelligence Committee's subcommittee that investigated the FBI's and CIA's role, said in 1976: "I believe the Warren Commission was set up at the time to feed pablum to the American people for reasons not yet known, and that one of the biggest coverups in the history of our country occurred at that time."

SUSPICIOUS FACTS

• "Almost immediately after the assassination," said a 1976 Senate Intelligence Committee report, Lyndon Johnson rushed to wrap up the case; his aides pressed the FBI "to issue a factual report supporting the conclusion that Oswald was the lone assassin." At first, Johnson had wanted *no* investigation.

• In this, LBJ had the full support of J. Edgar Hoover. On November 24, 1963, Hoover said to Johnson's aide Walter Jenkins, "The thing I am concerned about...is having something issued so we can convince the public that Oswald is the real assassin."

In 19th-century England, "pants" was considered an obscene word .

• Once he realized that the public demanded a federal inquiry, LBJ hand-picked a panel. Chief Justice Warren wanted no part of it: he at first refused, saying that one branch of the government should not investigate another. But Johnson pressured him. Following the closed meeting in which LBJ convinced him to head the Commission, Warren emerged "with tears in his eyes."

A Stacked Deck

• The CIA and the FBI, both potential suspects in the inquiry, were well represented on the Warren Commission. John J. McCloy had helped to establish the CIA. *Newsweek* called Gerald Ford "the CIA's best friend in Congress." Allen Dulles had been the director of the CIA for eight years before being fired by John Kennedy.

• According to *Crossfire*, "Dulles withheld CIA information from the Warren Commission, particularly concerning assassination plots between the Agency and organized crime." Had other Commission members known of the CIA's ties to the Mafia, mafioso Jack Ruby might have looked more like a "silencer" and less like a patriot distraught about the president's murder.

• Moreover, when he was asked in executive session about rumors tying Oswald to the agency, Dulles admitted that he and his agents "would lie about whether or not Oswald worked for the CIA." (*Coup d'Etat in America*)

• But the FBI's top "informant" may have been Gerald Ford, who, while supposedly conducting an impartial investigation, allegedly passed along information to the FBI. A memo from Cartha DeLoach, a close Hoover aide, said, "Ford indicated he would keep me thoroughly advised as to the activities of the Commission. He stated this would have to be on a confidential basis."

Roads Not Taken

• Until commissioner John J. McCloy pointed out that the Secret Service and the FBI might be culpable and thus could not be counted on to provide an impartial investigation, Chairman Warren was not inclined to ask for subpoena powers or to hire independent investigators.

• Congress eventually did authorize the Warren Commission "to compel testimony by providing immunity from prosecution," but the Commission never once used this power.

• One striking failure: Although Commission members could have demanded to see the actual autopsy photos of the president's wounds, they settled for artists' drawings. Nor did they ask the Dallas doctors who'd attended the dying president if the drawings of his wounds were accurate.

• The Commission's interviews with Jack Ruby were superficial. Ruby, fearing for his life in Dallas, said he'd tell all if only the commissioners would take him to Washington. They refused.

Ignored Witnesses

The Warren Commission questioned only 126 of the 266 witnesses to the killing, by testimony or affidavits. Among those it never called:

√ James Chaney, the motorcycle policeman who had been nearest Kennedy and saw the shot that killed him.

√ Senator Ralph Yarborough, part of the motorcade, who smelled gunpowder as he and LBJ drove past the infamous grassy knoll.

√ Bill and Gayle Newman, among the closest bystanders to JFK when he was hit, who insisted that the shot came from behind them on the grassy knoll.

√ Railroad employees Richard Dodd and James Simmons, who claimed that shots came from the picket fence behind the grassy knoll.

√ John Stringer and William Pitzer, medical technicians who photographed and X-rayed Kennedy's body.

√ Admiral George Burkley, Kennedy's personal physician, who attended the autopsy and allegedly passed on the medical evidence to the National Archives.

Badgered Witnesses

• Several witnesses who offered views that contradicted the lone-assassin theory were badgered to change their accounts. Witness Jean Hill, who said she saw a rifleman on the grassy knoll, was interviewed by Warren Commission junior counsel Arlen Specter (later a U.S. senator from Pennsylvania). She also said she heard four to six shots.

• When she refused to change her story, she said Specter got "angrier and angrier and finally told me, 'Look, we can make you look as crazy as Marguerite Oswald [Lee's mother] and everyone knows how crazy she is. We could have you put in a mental institution if you don't cooperate with us.' " Specter promised Hill that he would not publish the interview until she had approved it. But according to Hill, she never got the chance: "When I finally read my testimony as published by the Warren Commission, I knew it was a fabrication from start to finish." (*Crossfire*)

Dissenting Voices

• Although all seven members eventually endorsed the Warren Report in 1964, the Commission had its doubters. As author Anthony Summers points out in his book *Conspiracy*: "Three of the seven members of the Warren Commission did not fully believe the theory of the magic bullet, even though it appeared in their report. The commissioners wrangled about it up to the moment their findings went to press. Congressman Hale Boggs had 'strong doubts.' Senator Sherman Cooper was, as he told me in 1978, 'unconvinced.' Senator Richard Russell did not want to sign a report which said definitely that both men were hit by the same bullet and wanted a footnote added indicating his dissent. Warren declined to put one in."

• In 1970, Russell became the first to question the Commission's findings publicly. He told the *Washington Post* that he had come to believe Kennedy's death was caused by a conspiracy. He also called the report "a sorrily incompetent document." He died shortly after, of natural causes.

• Within a year, Representative Hale Boggs, the majority leader of the House, also expressed doubts about the Commission's findings, especially the "magic bullet" theory. He followed that on April 1, 1971, with a stinging attack on J. Edgar Hoover, whom he accused of Gestapo tactics. Because Boggs was likely to become Speaker of the House, rumors flew that he was going to reopen the JFK assassination investigation. But it never happened: On October 16, 1972, while on a junket to Alaska, Boggs's plane disappeared and was never found, despite a massive search.

WHO WAS JACK RUBY?

As we mentioned elsewhere in the book, Jack Ruby was the first person to kill someone live on TV. And not just anybody—he killed the man accused of assassinating JFK. Ruby is more than a footnote to history ...yet once again, we know very little about him. This piece from It's a Conspiracy *might start you thinking: Was Jack Ruby just another "lone nut" killer, or one of the key players in the Kennedy assassination?*

Jack Ruby was a 52-year-old nightclub owner well-known to the Dallas underworld and the police. On Sunday, November 24—two days after Kennedy was killed—Ruby became known to the whole world. As the Warren Report tells it:

> At approximately 11:20 a.m. Oswald emerged from the basement jail office flanked by detectives on either side...a man suddenly darted out from an area on the right of the cameras where newsmen had been assembled. The man was carrying a Colt .38 revolver in his right hand and, while millions watched on television, he moved quickly to within a few feet of Oswald and fired one shot into Oswald's abdomen. Oswald groaned with pain as he fell to the floor and quickly lost consciousness...he was pronounced dead at 1:07 p.m.
>
> The man who killed Oswald was Jack Ruby. He was instantly arrested and, minutes later, confined in a cell on the fifth floor of the Dallas police jail. Under interrogation, he denied that the killing of Oswald was in any way connected with a conspiracy involving the assassination of President Kennedy. He maintained that he had killed Oswald in a temporary fit of depression and rage over the President's death.

On March 14, 1964, Ruby was found guilty of killing Oswald and was sentenced to death. Following an appeal, however, Ruby's conviction was overturned in October 1966—which meant he could have gone free on bail within months. But it never happened. Two months later, on December 9, Ruby was diagnosed as having inoperable cancer. On January 3, 1967, he died.

WAS IT A CONSPIRACY?

Was Jack Ruby just a distraught admirer of John F. Kennedy, acting on his own—or did the Mafia order him to silence Lee Harvey Oswald?

Anguished American?

• In an interview with the FBI, Ruby said he'd shot Oswald because he "had cried a great deal," and his anguish about the president's death finally "reached the point of insanity." The national media duly reported Ruby's grief and love of the Kennedy family as fact. Yet on Saturday, the day after Kennedy was slain, Ruby was seen at the Dallas police station joking with reporters and passing out cards to his strip joint.

• Later that same day, he visited a newspaper production room to display a "twistboard" exercising device that he was trying to sell. "Considerable merriment developed when one of the women employees of the *Times-Herald* demonstrated the board, and Ruby himself put on a demonstration." (Warren Report)

• At a polygraph hearing in 1964, Ruby himself dismissed the story he had told the FBI: "If I loved the President so much, why wasn't I at the parade [motorcade]?...It's strange that perhaps I didn't vote for Kennedy, or didn't vote at all, that I should build up such a great affection for him."

Ruby and the Mob

• Jack Ruby's connections to the Mafia and Teamster President Jimmy Hoffa—which went back thirty years—were well-known to the Dallas police and the FBI. Yet, strangely, the news media largely ignored those ties.

• After being declared an "incorrigible youth" and put into a foster home, Ruby (known then as Jack Rubenstein) gravitated to crime. Boxer Barney Ross, a close friend of Ruby, told the FBI that he "might have run innocuous errands for Capone."

• Ruby may have been a Mob hit man. A December 9, 1939, story in the *Chicago Tribune* describes Jack Rubenstein as the prime suspect in the killing of Leon Cooke, the honest president of a local Teamster's Union, No. 20467. Because police records on the case disappeared, it's unclear how the case was resolved, but Local 20467 was soon taken over by the Mafia.

• According to David Scheim in his book, *Contract on America*,

Rubenstein moved from Chicago to Dallas in 1947, as part of a Mafia takeover of Dallas crime. There he changed his name to Ruby and bought the first of several bars. Scheim says that Ruby was a Mob "lieutenant" who made sure Chicago bosses got their cut from Dallas gambling, prostitution, and narcotics. In time, Ruby became the Mob's "pay-off man for the Dallas Police" and used those contacts to get into the police station to kill Oswald.

• According to FBI and U.S. Army Intelligence reports quoted in *Contract on America*, Ruby "was active in arranging illegal flights of weapons from Miami to the Castro organization in Cuba" in the 1950s. When Castro double-crossed the Mob and threw it out of Cuba, Ruby then began supplying weapons to anti-Castro Cubans being trained by the CIA, according to several sources.

A Mafia-Ruby-CIA Hypothesis

• According to *Double Cross*, an account of the life of Mafia boss Sam Giancana, Ruby did more than kill Oswald. The book alleges that a CIA-Mafia plot resulted in Kennedy's death and asserts that Giancana "put Ruby in charge of overseeing the Outfit's [Mafia's] role in the assassination, collaborating in Dallas with the [CIA] government agents."

• *Double Cross* also claims that Oswald—whose uncle worked for New Orleans mobster Carlos Marcello—was in on the plot and was killed so he wouldn't talk. So, because Ruby was "the person representing the Outfit in Dallas, the task had quite naturally fallen to Ruby to silence Oswald when he was unexpectedly captured alive."

• At least one part of *Double Cross*'s theory has been corroborated. In the mid-1970s, mobster John "Handsome Johnny" Roselli, who had close ties to Ruby, "began to describe Ruby as 'one of our boys' and speak of Ruby's having been ordered to eliminate Oswald to silence him." Roselli repeated that claim to columnist Jack Anderson, Senate investigators, and others before his dismembered body was found in an oil drum in Miami's Biscayne Bay. (*Contract on America*)

FBI Ties

• Author Jim Marrs corroborates Ruby's Mafia-CIA ties and implicates one more U.S. agency in his book *Crossfire*: "In early 1959, at

In Japan there are vending machines that dispense fresh-cooked spaghetti.

a time when Jack Ruby may have been involved in smuggling activities with Cubans, he contacted the FBI and said he wanted to provide the Bureau with information....The relationship between Ruby and the Bureau was mentioned in a letter from Hoover to the Warren Commission dated June 9, 1964." The letter remained classified until 1975.

• In the letter, Hoover claimed that Ruby "furnished no information whatsoever and further contacts with him were discontinued." However, Bureau records show that FBI agents met eight times with Ruby between April and October of 1959—which makes Hoover's assertion extremely suspect. (*Crossfire*)

The Songbird

• When Earl Warren, Gerald Ford, and lawyers from the Warren Commission interviewed Ruby in Dallas on June 7, 1964, he begged them eight times to take him back to Washington, because he feared for his life if he told the truth in Dallas. The commissioners refused.

• When it became obvious that the commissioners were leaving without really probing for what he knew, Ruby persisted, "You can get more out of me, let's not break up too soon." Finally, despairing, he said, "Well, you won't ever see me again. I tell you that.... A whole new form of government is going to take over the country, and I know I won't live to see you another time." (Warren Report)

• Not long before his death, Ruby told psychiatrist Werner Teuter that Kennedy's assassination was "an act of overthrowing the government," that he knew "who had Kennedy killed," that he had been part of that plot, and that he "was framed to kill Oswald."

Ruby's Death

• On October 5, 1966, the Texas Court of Criminal Appeals overturned Ruby's conviction and ordered a new trial. It seemed likely that Ruby would be released in a matter of months; authorities anticipated that he would receive a short prison sentence, and that his time served would count against it. (*Crossfire*)

• "On December 9, 1966...Ruby was moved from the Dallas County Jail to Parkland Hospital after complaining of persistent coughing and nausea. Doctors initially diagnosed his problem as 'pneumonia.' The next day, however, the diagnosis was changed to cancer and shortly after, it was announced that Ruby's lung cancer was too far advanced to be treated by surgery or radiation." At 9 a.m. on January 3, 1967, "he suffered a spasm and, despite emergency procedures, he was pronounced dead at 10:30 a.m." (ibid.)

• Ruby believed that he had been injected with a carcinogen. One of Ruby's Dallas County jailers, Deputy Sheriff Al Maddox, told researchers in 1982 that "a phony doctor came in from Chicago" who, though supposed to care for all the inmates, "spent half his time up there talking with Ruby." One day, said Maddox, Ruby told him that that doctor, while pretending to treat him for a cold, had injected him with cancer cells. When Maddox said, "You don't believe that shit," Ruby replied, "I damn sure do!" (ibid.)

• Could Ruby's claim be credible? Perhaps. Such carcinogens were known at the time. A 1952 CIA memo, for example, reported on the cancer-causing effects of beryllium: "This is certainly the most toxic inorganic element and it produces a peculiar fibrotic tumor at the site of local application. The amount necessary to produce these tumors is a few micrograms." (ibid.)

FOOTNOTE

Did Ruby Know Oswald?

A number of witnesses claimed they saw Jack Ruby and Lee Harvey Oswald together *before* the assassination of JFK. But the Warren Report says: "All assertions that Oswald was seen in the company of Ruby or anyone else...have been investigated. None of them merits any credence."

• Karen Carlin, a stripper at Ruby's Carousel Club, talked with the Secret Service on the evening of Oswald's death. She told them that Oswald and Ruby had been involved together in a plot to assassinate President Kennedy. Terrified, she asked that any information that she gave "be kept confidential to prevent retaliation." Months later she was found shot to death in a Houston hotel. The Warren Report says: "Mrs. Carlin was...not certain that the man was Oswald nor was she sure where she had seen him."

• The Associated Press reported that William Crowe, an entertain-

It takes four to five months to re-grow an entire fingernail.

er who specialized in memory tricks, said he was "positive" he had seen and interacted with Oswald at the Carousel Club. Crowe later told the *Dallas Morning News* that after the AP story appeared, the FBI advised him to go into hiding for a while. The Warren Report quoted Crowe as telling the Commission: "I never stated definitely, positively, and they said that I did, and all in all, what they had in the paper was hardly even close to what I told them." The report added: "When asked how certain he was that the man he saw was Oswald, Crowe testified: 'The face seemed familiar as some faces do, and I had associated it with a patron that I had seen in the club a week before. That was about it.' "

• While seated in the Carousel Club, Dallas attorney Carroll Jarnagin "overheard Jack Ruby—whom he knew well—talking with another man. Jarnagin heard the man tell Ruby, 'Don't use my real name. I'm going by the name O. H. Lee.' " According to Jarnagan, they discussed killing Governor John Connally and Robert Kennedy. Jarnagin gave the Texas Department of Public Safety this information—before JFK's assassination—but nothing came of the warning. (*Crossfire*)

RECOMMENDED READING

• *Crossfire: The Plot to Kill Kennedy*, by Jim Marrs (Carroll & Graf, 1989)

• *Contract on America: The Mafia Murders of JFK*, by David Scheim (Zebra, 1991)

• *Double Cross*, by Sam & Chuck Giancana (Warner Books, 1992)

* * *

TALES OF THE CIA

Quiz: What motto is inscribed on the wall of the CIA headquarters in Langley, Virginia?

A) "Keep the Faith" **B)** "And Ye Shall Know the Truth and the Truth Shall Make You Free" **C)** "A Secret Kept Is a Secret Saved"

Answer: B

HITS OF THE 70s QUIZ — Answers (from page 43)

1 — a

In 1978, Gary Guthrie, a disc jockey for WAKY AM in Louisville, Kentucky, was in the process of breaking up with his wife. One night, a friend played them the new Neil Diamond album. Guthrie recalls: "When it got to 'You Don't Bring Me Flowers,' my wife started crying and this other lady started crying. I knew it was special, but I couldn't help feeling there was something missing. I just couldn't figure out what. A few days later, the new Barbra Streisand LP came into the radio station, and she was doing the song too. It set off this image in my mind, in *The Sound of Music*, when Christopher Plummer and Julie Andrews were onstage singing 'Edelweiss' at the Austrian Music Festival . . . and a lightbulb! It needed *two* people singing it to each other."

The Diamond and Streisand versions happened to be in the same key. Guthrie had a brainstorm. "I went into the studio, and after sixteen hours and five days of putting things together, I came out with my finished product of 'You Don't Bring Me Flowers.'" Guthrie had spliced the songs together to create a duet.

"I put it on the radio as a going away present for my wife," he continues. "I called her up and played it for her, and the phones started going crazy: 'What is that song?'" So many people asked for it at local record stores that the stores finally demanded the station stop playing it.

When Columbia Records got wind of the uproar in Louisville, they got the two stars together to duplicate Guthrie's recording. The "official" duet version reached #1 in five weeks. Guthrie ended up without a wife...or a song. Claiming he'd been wronged by the company after selling them the idea for the duet, he filed a $5 million breach of contract lawsuit against CBS.

2 — a

The session in which Led Zepplin recorded "Stairway to Heaven" was pretty spontaneous. Drummer John Bonham worked out his part on the spot...and singer Robert Plant made up the lyrics as he was getting set to record them. Although he later cited a book called *Magic Arts in Celtic Britain* by Lewis Spence as the inspiration for the words, Plant also admitted that he didn't really know what they meant. They were just words he put together in a hurry. "Really," he

Eighty-Eight, Kentucky was named by a guy who had 88¢ in his pocket on the day he named it.

said, "I have no idea why 'Stairway to Heaven' is so popular. No idea at all. Maybe it's because of its abstraction. Depending on what day it is, I still interpret [the song] a different way—and I wrote those lyrics."

How do people turn that into devil-worship? Simple—"automatic writing." The reason, some people say, that Plant doesn't know the meaning of his own song is that Satan guided his hand when he was writing it, and if you play it backwards (who'd want to play a record *backwards?*), you can hear evil messages.

For the Record: It wasn't released as a single—a decision which boosted the sales of the album by an estimated 500,000 copies.

3 — c

The group, four Americans from Rockford, Illinois, had been trying to get some recognition in the U.S. for several years. They'd released three albums, all of which bombed. They couldn't make it in Europe, either. In fact, the only place they were popular was Japan.

There, they were heroes with hit singles and tremendously successful tours. When the group's third album flopped in the States, they headed for Japan to tour again. Their record company, Epic, decided to tape their performances in Osaka and Tokyo and come out with a quickie "live" album exclusively for the Japanese market. "Some of the songs," their lead singer said, "were single takes." But for some reason, *Live at Buddokan*—which wasn't released anywhere except Japan—caught on in America, and the live version of "I Want You To Want Me," complete with screaming, became Cheap Trick's first hit. It was a twist on a classic rock 'n' roll story. Jimi Hendrix and the Stray Cats had to go to England to become popular in America; Cheap Trick went to Japan.

4 — a

It seemed so tailored to The Captain and Tennille that no one thought to ask what it was really about. Actually, it had a very different origin. For over twenty years, Neil Sedaka had co-written songs with his high school buddy, Howard Greenfield. Their hits included "Calendar Girl" and "Breaking Up Is Hard to Do." But by 1973, their Midas touch had worn off and they decided to break up the team. "Our last song together was called 'Love Will Keep Us Together.' says Sedaka. It was actually written about us and our collaborating."

According to language experts, virtually every language on earth has a word for "yes-man."

5 — b

"Brand New Key" was banned from some radio stations for being "too suggestive." It was interpreted as promoting drug use (a "key" being a kilo of marijuana) or sexual freedom (a wife-swapping club in L. A. used it as a theme song). Actually, the inspiration was an impulsive visit to McDonald's.

Melanie's search for enlightenment and purification had inspired her to go on a twenty-seven day fast in which she drank nothing but distilled water. Coming off the fast, she was eating transitional food—grated raw carrots, a sip of orange juice—when suddenly she felt an incredible urge, like an "inner voice," telling her to go out and get a McDonald's hamburger and french fries. After three years of following a strict vegetarian diet and a month spent cleansing her body, she gave in to what she "assumed to be the voice of spiritual awareness." "I ran down," she says, "and got the whole meal. And then on the way home, in the car, I started to write 'Brand New Key.' So if you are what you eat. . . (laughs). . . I totally connect the McDonald's meal and the song.

6 — a

The Bee Gees had a #1 record in 1972. But by 1974, they had released two stiff albums in a row and two years passed without a single in the Top 40. They had fallen so low that they were relegated to the oldies circuit when they toured.

Arif Mardin, Atlantic's superstar producer, had produced their "Mr. Natural" album. It flopped (peak: #178 on the charts), but the band developed a good rapport with him and requested that he produce their next album as well. Mardin accepted. His first advice to the band this time was to listen to the radio and get back in touch with what was happening in pop music. Open their ears. Then he said, "I'm going away for a week. I want you to write while I'm away." It was a "do or die" situation.

Luckily, Barry Gibb's wife, Linda, took Mardin's advice and kept her "ears open." "We used to go over this bridge every night on the way to the studio," she told a critic later. "I used to hear this 'chunka-chunka-chunka' just as we went over the railroad tracks. So I said to Barry, 'Do you ever listen to that rhythm when we go across the bridge at night?' He just looked at me." That night, as they crossed the Sunny Isles Bridge headed for Miami's Criterion Studio, Linda brought it up again.

Chinese gooseberries didn't sell well in the U.S. until grocers renamed them kiwis.

"I said, 'Listen,' and he said, 'Oh, yeah.' It was the chunka-chunka. Barry started singing something and the brothers joined in." It became "Drive Talking," which became "Jive Talkin'," which became a #1 record and the first step in the Bee Gees' astounding comeback.

7 — a

The song was originally written as "Le Moribund" (literal translation: "The Dying Man") by Jacques Brel in 1961, and adapted to English by Rod McKuen in 1964. Jacks heard it on a Kingston Trio record, and in 1972, he took it to a Beach Boys' session he was involved with. The Beach Boys recorded it but didn't release it, so Jacks, who was distraught over a friend's death, decided to do his own version of it. He rewrote the last verse.

One day a year later, he was playing his recording of it when the boy who delivered his newspapers overheard it; the boy liked it so much that he brought some friends over to Jacks' house to listen to it, and their enthusiastic response inspired him to release it on his own Goldfish label.

AUNT LENNA'S PUZZLERS—Answers (from page 334)

1. Utopia
2. Nymphs
3. Nausea

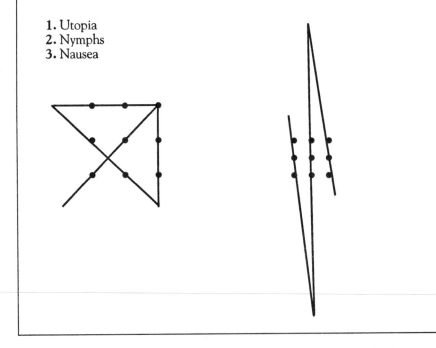

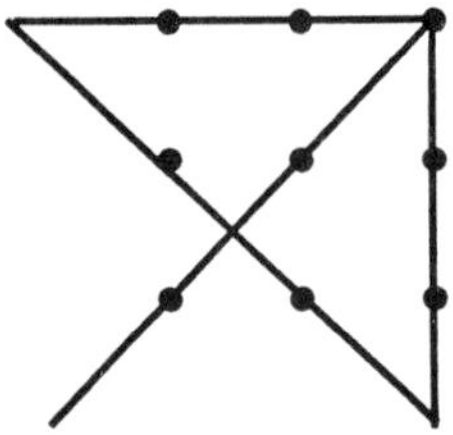

Which recreational activity causes more bone fractures than any other? Aerobic dancing.

BRAIN TEASERS—Answers (from page 172)

1. They were at a drive-in movie.

2. The poison was in the ice cubes. When the man drank the punch, the ice was fully frozen, but as it melted, it poisoned the punch.

3. The twins were born while their mother was on an ocean cruise. The older twin, Terry, was born first—on March 1. The ship, traveling west, then crossed a time zone and Kerry, the younger twin was born on February 28. In a leap year, the younger twin celebrates her birthday two days before her older brother.

4. Not a single word in this paragraph uses the most common letter in the alphabet: "e."

5. It's the bottom of the ninth. The score is tied; a runner is on third—and the batter hits a foul ball. If the right fielder catches it, the runner will tag up, score and win the game.

6. John.

7. The math does add up—the question is just worded in a misleading way. Look at it like this: The $27 spent by the men *includes* the $2 kept by the bellhop. Thus, the men paid $27 (the bellboy kept $2, and $25 went to the desk clerk).

8. The women paid $28 (the bellboy kept $3, and $25 went to the desk clerk). You *subtract* the bellhop's tip from what the guests paid; you don't add it.

9. The "bicycles" are Bicycle playing cards. The guy was cheating; when the extra card was found, he was killed by the other players.

10. Alice is a gold fish; Ted is a cat.

11. The blind man says, "I'd like to buy a pair of scissors."

POLITICALLY CORRECT QUIZ—Answers (from page 295)

1 — c) "The real-life sexual harassment problems the Army was having kind of spilled over onto us," Walker told reporters. "Some editors felt that although we weren't condoning it, we were on the edge. So Halftrack went off to a training course. When he returned, he apologized to the women in his office: "Y'know, I never meant to offend you with sexist remarks....I like and respect both of you."

2 — a) The ACLU and NOW each informed the school board that the move was illegal and would probably threaten their federal funding. The board decided to deal with it on a case-by-case basis. What we at BRI are curious about is this: if 25% of your cheerleaders are pregnant, doesn't that suggest some lack of sex education?

3 — c) In 1998, a group of meat shop owners in France announced they were "hurt by reporters who routinely refer to vicious murderers as butchers." The group insists that butchers are "gentle, peace-loving artisans."

4 — b) It's not an issue anymore, because Sears is out of the catalog business. But because of the letter, all the maternity models wore rings the following year.

5 — b) In February, 1996, a guy named John Howard opened an apparel store called The Redneck Shop, in Laurens, South Carolina. The problem was that he sold Ku Klux Klan apparel. Also in the store: a Klan museum. When a reporter asked how people in town had responded, he said: "The only people I've had a problem with, who took it as an insult and a racial situation, have been blacks. I didn't know blacks here were so prejudiced." It didn't last long. Someone rammed the store with a pickup truck and closed it down.

6 — b) Apparently it made sense to the women to discriminate in the name of anti-discrimination. The director of the University of Pennsylvania Women's Center, which co-sponsored the event, told reporters: "[Racism] is a white problem and we have a responsibility as white women in particular to do what we can to eradicate [it]."

7 — b) What can we say?

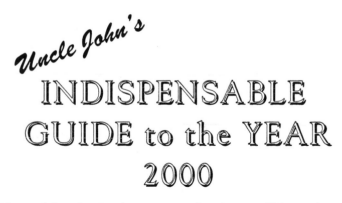

THE LAST PAGE

FELLOW BATHROOM READERS:

The fight for good bathroom reading should never be taken loosely—we must sit firmly for what we believe in, even while the rest of the world is taking pot shots at us.

Once we prove we're not simply a flush-in-the-pan, writers and publishers will find their resistance unrolling.

So we invite you to take the plunge: Sit Down and Be Counted! by joining The Bathroom Readers' Institute. Send a self-addressed, stamped envelope to: BRI, PO Box 1117, Ashland, Oregon 97520. or contact us through our Website at: *www.bathroomreader.com*. You'll receive your attractive free membership card, and a copy of the BRI newsletter (if we ever get around to publishing one), and earn a permanent spot on the BRI honor roll!

UNCLE JOHN'S NEXT BATHROOM READER IS IN THE WORKS!

Don't fret—there's more good reading on its way. In fact, there are a few ways *you* can contribute to the next volume:

1. Is there a subject you'd like to see us cover? Write to us or contact us through our Website (*www.bathroomreader.com*) and let us know. We aim to please.

2. Got a neat idea for a couple of pages in the new *Reader*? If you're the first to suggest it, and we use it, we'll send you a free book.

3. Have you seen or read an article you'd recommend as quintessential bathroom reading? Or is there a passage in a book or other websites that you want to share with us and other BRI members? Tell us how to find it. If you're the first to suggest it and we publish it in the next volume, there's a free book in it for you.

Well, we're out of space, and when you've gotta go, you've gotta go. Hope to hear from you soon. Meanwhile, remember:

Go with the flow.